The Gender In

This collection of essays by feminist scholar-activists addresses the crucial problem of human security in a world of heavily armed, militarized states. It describes the gendered aspects of human security excluded from the realist militarism that dominates current security policy in most nation states. The book deepens and broadens current security discourses, encouraging serious consideration of alternatives to the present global security system that functions to advantage state security over human security, a system the contributors perceive to be rooted in the patriarchal nature of the nation state.

This second edition will be of interest to academics and students of gender studies, women's studies, international studies, development studies, human rights, security studies, peace studies and peace education.

Betty A. Reardon is Founding Director Emeritus of the International Institute on Peace Education (IIPE), a global consortium for continuing education on issues of peace, and a feminist peace educator. Her work with IIPE and as a theorist and designer of pedagogic materials and processes in peace education was recognized by the special Honourable Mention Award from UNESCO at the Peace Education Prize Ceremonies of 2001. She was the initiator and the first academic coordinator of The Hague Appeal for Peace Global Campaign for Peace Education launched in 1999. She is the recipient of the 2009 Sean MacBride Peace Prize awarded by the International Peace Bureau. Her published and unpublished professional papers are archived in the Ward M. Canaday Special Collections at the University of Toledo Library in Ohio.

Asha Hans is Founder Director of the School of Women's Studies, Utkal University, Bhubaneswar, Odisha, India, and heads the gender research institute Sansristi. A peace activist, she has written extensively on issues of peace and security, including Kashmiri women, refugee women and disability issues. Her recent work is on UN Security Council Resolution 1325. She is currently Co-Chair for the Pakistan India People's Forum for Peace and Democracy and serves on the editorial board of the *Journal of Peace Education*.

'Betty A. Reardon and Asha Hans have provided an essential gift for anyone fed up with and tired of war. This book, on why we need to figure out and implement alternatives to war, and why gender and war are totally related, belongs in every women's and gender studies classroom, every peace studies and peace education course, on the reading lists for peace organizations and on the night tables of government officials and generals who take our money and send our youth to kill and be killed. The time for war to go has come. It steals resources from desperately needed health and education budgets, among other needed domestic programmes; it destroys people and other living things. We have advanced in science, technology, art and music. Why can't we settle our differences without killing one another and destroying our homes, polluting water supplies and torturing the enemy?

"It's time to abolish war", declared 10,000 people at the end-of-the-century Hague Appeal for Peace Conference in 1999. That call for institutional change could be traced to the 50-year-old motto of Women Strike for Peace – 'War is not healthy for children or other living things'. And, as UN Security Council Resolution 1325 on women, peace and security and 1820 on sexual abuse of women make clear, war is not healthy for women. The men at the table who unanimously adopted these resolutions understood that neither oppression of women nor war would cease without women's full participation in the politics of security. Gender equality is essential to the reduction and elimination of armed conflict. The Hague Agenda for Peace and Justice for the 21st Century, now a UN document (A/54/98), has 50 points for getting from a culture of war to a culture of peace, including assurances of gender equality and the demilitarization of security. It also proposes the institutional changes needed to eliminate war. A decade after the publication of The Hague Agenda and the adoption of Resolution 1325, the editors and contributors to *The Gender Imperative: Human Security vs State Security* call for applying ourselves to the same goal through serious public discussion of alternatives to war. We can't wait for another war. It's must reading now.'

Cora Weiss, a leader of Women Strike for Peace;
President of The Hague Appeal for Peace; Former
President of the International Peace Bureau; and
among the civil society initiators of UN Security
Council Resolution 1325

'Betty A. Reardon and Asha Hans have brought together in this volume a collection of powerful statements on the human cost of militarism and set before us a line of serious inquiry into possibilities for alternatives. The contributors paint vivid pictures of the interplay between the gendered inequality integral to militarism and the consequent frustration of human security. We Afghan women know well the price of war and understand that our human security depends upon peace. As one who has so long worked to provide the education necessary for women's full participation in their own and world society, I welcome this book as an important contribution to the global movement for gender equality, peace and human security.'

Sakena Yacoobi, Founder and Director,
Afghan Institute for Learning; recipient of multiple
awards for contribution to the education
of Afghan women

'This volume commits to the daring task of reclaiming the notion of Utopia. Against the grain of dismissive real politique, its scholar-activist authors study the practicalities of demilitarizing national security systems in a crucial expansion of the body of feminist analyses and knowledge of the essentially patriarchal worldwide war system. A concrete exploration of security for and of the living individual human beings who make up states, this project is sorely needed and inspiring, a rare resource for scholars, activists and scholar-activists alike.'

Rela Mazali, author and contributor to *Sexed Pistols:
The Gendered Impacts of Small Arms and Light
Weapons* (2009), a founder of Gun Free Kitchen
Tables and member of New Profile, a women's peace
organization working for the demilitarization
of Israeli and world society

'The book is an excellent contribution to the discourse on human security and to the vision of a truly secure humanity and planet Earth. Skeptics may say that the authors' vision is utopian, but this attitude is in itself a characteristic of patriarchal thinking, dismissing alternative thinking and proposals as unrealistic and impossible.'

Loreta Navarro-Castro, Global Campaign
for Peace Education, January 2011

The Gender Imperative
Human Security vs State Security

Second Edition

Edited by Betty A. Reardon
and Asha Hans

LONDON AND NEW YORK

Second edition published 2019
by Routledge
2 Park Square, Milton Park, Abingdon, Oxon OX14 4RN

and by Routledge
711 Third Avenue, New York, NY 10017

Routledge is an imprint of the Taylor & Francis Group, an informa business

© 2019 selection and editorial matter, Betty A. Reardon and Aṣha Hans; individual chapters, the contributors

The right of Betty A. Reardon and Asha Hans to be identified as the authors of the editorial material, and of the authors for their individual chapters, has been asserted in accordance with sections 77 and 78 of the Copyright, Designs and Patents Act 1988.

All rights reserved. No part of this book may be reprinted or reproduced or utilized in any form or by any electronic, mechanical, or other means, now known or hereafter invented, including photocopying and recording, or in any information storage or retrieval system, without permission in writing from the publishers.

Trademark notice: Product or corporate names may be trademarks or registered trademarks, and are used only for identification and explanation without intent to infringe.

First edition published by Routledge 2010

British Library Cataloguing-in-Publication Data
A catalogue record for this book is available from the British Library

Library of Congress Cataloging-in-Publication Data
A catalog record for this book has been requested

ISBN: 978-1-138-32090-1 (hbk)
ISBN: 978-1-138-32094-9 (pbk)
ISBN: 978-0-429-45213-0 (ebk)

Typeset in Sabon
by Apex CoVantage, LLC

Contents

Notes on contributors   x
Foreword   xv

Introduction: challenging patriarchal violence   1

PART I
Confronting the militarized state security paradigm: human security from a feminist perspective   5

1 Women and human security: a feminist framework and critique of the prevailing patriarchal security system   7
BETTY A. REARDON

2 Gendered insecurity under long-term military presence: the case of Okinawa   37
KOZUE AKIBAYASHI AND SUZUYO TAKAZATO

3 Human security and intersectional oppressions: women in South Africa   59
BERNEDETTE MUTHIEN

PART II
Patriarchal conditioning to violence and human insecurity   83

4 Challenging the patriarchal national security paradigm: the role of Ethiopian women in peace and security   85
MESFIN G. AYELE

5 War and armed conflict: threat to African women's human security 108
FATUMA AHMED ALI

6 Sexual violence and genocide, the greatest violation of human security: responses to the case of Darfur 134
LISA S. PRICE

7 Security discourses: a gender perspective 167
MICHELE W. MILNER

PART III
Militarization/demilitarization: eroding and promoting human security 189

8 Seeking human security in a militarized Pacific: struggles for peace and security by Pacific Island women 191
RONNI ALEXANDER

9 Education, violence and schools: the human security of girls in Afghanistan 222
CHLOE BREYER

10 The Soldiers' Mothers, human security and the Russian-Chechen Wars 246
VALERIE ZAWILSKI

PART IV
Alternative and transitional approaches to human security 275

11 Security Council Resolution 1325: toward gender equality in peace and security policymaking 277
SOUMITA BASU

12 Jordanian women define security: a feminist approach to an age-old problem 303
NORMA NEMEH

13 Public health and patriarchy: militarism and gender as determinants of health insecurity 335
ALBIE SHARPE

14 Human security: the militarized perception and space for gender 366
ASHA HANS

15 Patriarchy and the bomb: banning nuclear weapons against the opposition of militarist masculinities 392
RAY ACHESON

Conclusion: framing a gender and human security discourse: initiating the inquiry 410

Annexure: Security Council Resolutions 1325 and 1820 427
Index 438

Contributors

Ray Acheson is Director of Reaching Critical Will, the disarmament programme of the Women's International League for Peace and Freedom (WILPF), a nongovernmental organization founded in 1915 to challenge militarism, patriarchy and capitalism. She also represents WILPF on the International Steering Group of the International Campaign to Abolish Nuclear Weapons (ICAN), the 2017 Nobel Peace Prize laureate. She helped develop ICAN's strategy and was a leading civil society advocate during the negotiation of the Treaty on the Prohibition of Nuclear Weapons. She holds a BA Honours in peace and conflict studies from the University of Toronto and an MA in politics from the New School for Social Research in New York.

Kozue Akibayashi is International President of Women's International League for Peace and Freedom (2016–18) and Professor at Doshisha University, Kyoto, Japan. She received a doctorate in education from Teachers College, Columbia University. She has conducted participatory research on Okinawa Women Act Against Military Violence and has worked with them in developing transnational networks for demilitarization. Her research interests include gender, militarization/demilitarization, military training and learning for peace.

Ronni Alexander is Professor of transnational relations in the Graduate School of International Cooperation Studies, Kobe University, and Director of the Kobe University Office of Gender Equality. Living in Japan since 1977, she is a graduate of Yale University, United States, and in 1982 she received an MA (public administration) from International Christian University and a PhD (international relations) from Sophia University in 1989. She came to Kobe University as a research associate in 1989 and became a full professor in 1993, the first foreign woman to do so in a Japanese national university. A peace researcher, peace educator and peace activist, she began the Popoki Peace Project in 2006 and since March 2011 has been carrying out the Popoki Friendship Story Project in an area of Iwate Prefecture destroyed by the 2011 tsunami. In addition to her many academic publication, she has also published a series of picture books about peace.

Fatuma Ahmed Ali is Associate Professor of international relations at the School of Humanities and Social Sciences of the United States International University (USIU-A), Nairobi, Kenya. She is also a visiting faculty member and external researcher of the Interuniversity Institute for Social Development and Peace (IUDESP) of the Universitat Jaume I, Castellón, Spain. Ahmed Ali is a trainer and an independent consultant in the fields of social development, gender, security, peace, conflict, curriculum review, accreditation and countering violent extremism. She is an academic activist in the area of violence against women and has publications in both Spanish and English. Her latest publications include "Women's Agency and Violence against Women: The Case of the Coalition on Violence against Women in Kenya" in *African Conflict and Peacebuilding Review* (2017) and *Mujeres y Guerras: Deconstruyendo la noción de víctimas y reconstruyendo su papel de constructoras de la paz* (2015).

Mesfin G. Ayele, a PhD fellow in diversity management and governance at K. F. University of Graz/Austria, has worked and researched on intercultural dialogue, youth, racism and violence, peace education and developmental politics, migration and integration. From Ethiopia, he worked at the Ethiopian Ministry of Federal Affairs as a senior security expert, gaining experience in intelligence, security and conflict-related topics. He has worked as Operation Chief at a Counter Terrorism Intelligence Centre (CTIC) in Addis Ababa. His research focuses on human security, security sector reform, gender, peace education, ethnic conflicts and terrorism. Having conducted fieldwork in different parts of Ethiopia and the Horn of Africa, he has taught or conducted research at Addis Ababa University, the Centre for Intelligence and Security Training, the European Centre for Peace and Conflict Studies (EPU), the University of Innsbruck in Austria and the University of Jaume I in Spain. He is also affiliated with the European Research and Training Centre for Human Rights and Democracy in Graz. He holds a bachelor's degree in political science from the Addis Ababa University and a master's degree in peace, development, security and international conflict transformation from the University of Innsbruck.

Soumita Basu is Assistant Professor of international relations at the South Asian University, New Delhi, India. Her primary areas of research are the United Nations, feminist international relations, and critical security studies. Prior to joining SAU, she held the Hayward R. Alker and Mellon postdoctoral fellowships at the University of Southern California and Kenyon College, respectively. She has also worked with Women in Security, Conflict Management and Peace (WISCOMP) in New Delhi and Kashmir and the PeaceWomen project of the Women's International League for Peace and Freedom (WILPF) in New York.

Chloe Breyer has directed the Interfaith Centre of New York (ICNY) since 2009. ICNY is a nationally recognized nonprofit that works with hundreds of grassroots religious leaders from 12 faith traditions to catalyze partnerships with civic officials to resolve social problems plaguing New York City (NYC). Issues include police reform, immigration concerns and domestic violence. Breyer also serves as associate priest at St Philip's Church in Harlem and after 9/11 worked with NYC's Afghan community to rebuild a bombed mosque in Afghanistan – returning many times for health- and education-related projects. Breyer's publications include *The Close: A Young Woman's First Year at Seminary* (2000), along with chapters in *What Can One Person Do? Faith to Heal a Broken World* (2005) and *Challenging the Christian Right from the Heart of the Gospel* (2006). She is also a contributor to Slate (www.slate.com). She received a PhD in Christian ethics from Union Theological Seminary in New York in 2017.

Michele W. Milner is the director of learning and wellbeing at the Royal Veterinary College, University of London, United Kingdom. The department focuses on supporting student wellbeing through the development of innovative and inclusive practices in digital learning and educational development. Prior to coming to the United Kingdom, she worked as a linguist, teacher trainer and curriculum developer in higher education in Japan, Korea and China. While working in Asia, she developed and implemented strategic initiatives in transnational educational collaborations for UK and US universities. She is a principal fellow of the Higher Education Academy.

Bernedette Muthien serves part-time on South Africa's Constitutional Commission for Cultural, Religious and Linguistic Rights. She also serves on the Transnational Advisory Board of IIPE She is an experienced facilitator, researcher, poet and executive manager who designs, implements and evaluates projects for diverse institutions. She has over 200 publications, some translated from English into 16 other languages. She served on the Executive Council of the International Peace Research Association and is co-founder of the African Peace Research and Education Association. She works closely with the International Institute on Peace Education and the international journal *Human Security Studies*. Muthien was the first Fulbright-Amy Biehl fellow at Stanford University and holds postgraduate degrees.

Norma Nemeh has extensive experience in education. Her academic interests range within the fields of gender studies, human rights, peace, security and the political socialization of women. Awarded a doctorate of education from Teachers College, Columbia University, her research entitled 'A Feminist Perspective on Security in Jordan: A Study of the Interrelationship between Human Security and Peace Education' was awarded a Fulbright scholarship for field research. She has held positions as an academic director, then later, as a senior lecturer with the School for International Training – World Learning in Amman, Jordan; Adjunct Professor at Teachers College, Columbia University; and Senior Programs Manager at the Queen Rania Teacher Academy in Amman, Jordan.

Lisa S. Price is an independent researcher and writer, based in Canada, and was previously an instructor of women's studies at Simon Fraser University. She holds a PhD from the Violence, Abuse and Gender Relations Research Unit, Leeds Metropolitan University. She tracks both the broad area of violence against women and the specific field of international criminal adjudication of war rape. Her publications include *Feminist Frameworks: Building Theory on Violence against Women* and 'Finding the Man in the Soldier-Rapist: Some Reflections on Comprehension and Accountability'. Her activism incorporates both her scholarly interests and her wider social concerns, such as women's participation in the electoral process.

Albie Sharpe was awarded a PhD from the School of Public Health and Community Medicine at the University of New South Wales in Australia. His research focuses on exploring the complex interlinkages between human security and health promotion. He developed a conceptual model for conducting a human security evaluation and applied it to a non-communicable disease prevention project in post-war Sri Lanka, considering the relationships among health, peace, development and human security. These included complex recursive interactions among gender, employment, education, leadership, health and community wellbeing – areas critical to human security. He was formerly an associate professor in the International Institute, Ritsumeikan University, where he taught international health, development and peace studies. He has been involved in the organization of several peace education activities, including the Peace as a Global Language Conferences in Japan and PEACEworks, a group of photographers involved in a visual exploration of the concept of peace photography.

Suzuyo Takazato is co-founder of Okinawa Women Act Against Military Violence. She also founded Rape Emergency Intervention and Counseling Centre (REICO), the first rape crisis centre in Okinawa. After working as a social worker in Tokyo and in Okinawa, she was elected to Naha City Assembly in 1987 and served for four terms. She has been invited to speak at many international conferences since the 1980s and has led delegations from Okinawa to visit other countries. In 2006, she was chosen as one of the '1000 Peacewomen' for the Nobel Peace Prize, an international project to illuminate women's contribution to peace.

Valerie Zawilski is Assistant Professor of sociology at King's University College, London, and also teaches in the Social Justice and Peace Studies programme at the University of Western Ontario, Canada. She teaches courses on global social inequality, social justice and social change and edited a book (2009) on social inequality in Canada. She has written about the Soldiers' Mothers of Russia, Russian nationalism and war. She is currently writing the book *Geopolitics of War and Peace: Afghanistan, Chechnya and Kosovo*.

Foreword

Over the entire history of the human family, the voices of women have been raised in lamentation and protest over the economic waste, social destruction, political bankruptcy and human tragedy of war. Was it not women's role to keen at funerals and lament human suffering? Over the centuries of 'modern times', as monarchies gave way to democracies, political negotiation became preferred over civil war within nations, and law was envisioned as the essential mechanism of social order and arbiter of disputes, men's voices were also raised calling for an end to war, but it did not cease. In the 20th century, the United Nations, a global institution, was founded and developed to 'avoid the scourge of war' and to address the problems that gave rise to war and the injustices which belied democratic principles, including 'equality between men and women'.

As that institution became a platform upon which a global women's movement for equality, development and peace came to be a major force in the worldwide peace movement, women's lamentation became women's political argument and action. Informed by feminist analysis and energized by a commitment to the survival of civilization and the necessity of the nurturing of a culture of peace, that argument asserted that peace and women's equality were integrally related, calling into question the patriarchal orders that had governed the world from the ancient days of withholding love of Lysistrata to today's courageous public actions of Women in Black.

In the opening decades of this century, more men have been heard to voice the same arguments and to see the potential of their own liberation from the sexist repression of patriarchy in the achievement of authentic gender equality and in the abolition of war. Through recent years, as I have been an active participant in women's struggle for peace and an initiator of discussion of masculinities as an essential element in the formulation of concepts of and social action for a culture of peace, I have been privileged to witness firsthand the conceptual leadership and social courage of women and the men who have joined them in 'speaking truth to power'. Yet this truth is still – like the ancient laments of women expected to do the human family's mourning – condescendingly deemed by the present patriarchs (females among them) a plea for the impractical and impossible. Women from Ireland to Liberia have shown that what is necessary can be possible. The truth we now must speak to power is that armed might cannot and never will achieve human security. I welcome the plea that lies at the heart of *The Gender Imperative: Human Security vs State Security* as a call to look squarely at the horrendous gendered human consequence of militarized security systems and to begin serious consideration of the practical possibilities for alternative security systems. I am happy to join my voice with those of the women and men speaking truth to power in this volume.

Ingeborg Breines
Oslo, Norway
Former Director, Nordland Academy for
Arts and Sciences; Retired Co-President of
the International Peace Bureau, Former
Special Advisor on Gender to the Director
General of UNESCO; editor of *Male Roles,
Masculinities and Violence: A Culture of
Peace Perspective* (2000)

Introduction
Challenging patriarchal violence

It is past time to begin a serious consideration of alternatives to war and the multiple forms of state-sanctioned violence of the militarized political, economic and social structures that comprise the global security system. So, too, it is time to recognize that this global system of violence is the manifestation and mainstay of patriarchy. The well-being and survival of the human family make it imperative that this system be challenged. Approaching the imperative through the lens of gender, with particular reference to the experience of women, clearly reveals the multiple and severe human security deficits of the present international system of state security.

Many feminists and other peace advocates welcomed the emergence of the concept of human security as the idea that would instigate the long-awaited and much-needed scholarly and public discourse on alternative security systems. The notion of alternatives to the war system is one that has held the attention of a narrow sector of the international peace research community since its founding in the early 1960s. In the decades immediately following World War II, several serious plans for legally constituted international institutions capable of preventing war, and ultimately abolishing it, were circulated among academics and other citizens in proposals for a stronger United Nations advanced by such groups as the World Federalists, a movement that followed in the tradition of Western philosophy that had for several centuries explored the problematic of permanent peace. However, this same tradition of political thought also produced political realism and its assertion of the need for force to maintain order and resolve conflicts.

Tragically, the political realism so characteristic of patriarchal thinking that has governed the modern world has consigned these proposals – even the most practical and well detailed – to the political Siberia of Utopia. One of the core purposes of this book is to reclaim utopia in its original sense as a diagnosis, indeed as a denunciation, of the injustices and follies of the dominant order. It will approach this purpose through a challenge to the present international security system in an assessment of the systemic and constant insecurity to which it subjects the world's vulnerable populations, most particularly and universally, women. The myriad ways in which women have suffered gender-specific, negative affects of war and armed conflict have been thoroughly documented in the literature of women, war and peace, as will be seen in the references to the various articles.

This volume is an attempt to build on that well-laid foundation with an exploration of human security as a conceptual framework for an alternative to the present dangerous and destructive militarized state security framework. The articles included in this volume seek to contribute to opening discussions that go beyond the assessments and lamentations of imposed, unnecessary suffering under the extensive and excessive global system of militarization by encouraging inquiry into the achievement of human security through the demilitarization of the present system. Suggestions to facilitate such an inquiry appear in the conclusion to this book.

The contributors – female and male feminist scholar-activists – hope to widen and deepen the current discourse on human security by demonstrating that the welfare – perhaps the survival – of the world's vulnerable and most probably even of the powerful requires the demilitarization of state security. We hope to open discussion on the construction of systems of authentic national security based on the human security of peoples rather than on the protection and perpetuation of the interests of states. The present patriarchal state security system is at best prejudicial to women and at worst openly oppressive of half the human family. Through consideration of the most essential gendered aspects of security that derive from the multiple forms of the global patriarchy, this volume provides both challenging and promising perspectives on the most severe threats to the human future. The contributions are constructed within a comprehensive feminist framework of human security, the conceptual core and basis of the gender imperative.

This conceptual core is the assertion that human security derives from the experience and expectation of wellbeing of persons, communities and the planet which sustains them. Human wellbeing, it asserts, depends upon four essential conditions for the maintenance and continuation of human life: a life-sustaining environment; the meeting of essential physical needs; respect for the identity and dignity of persons and groups; and protection from avoidable harm and expectation of remedy for unavoidable harm. Each article addresses one or more of these four fundamental elements, demonstrating that women have unequal or no access to the elements addressed, and illuminates the integral relationship of these elements to human security, not only of women but also of all human beings.

The major assumption that influences the analysis and arguments for change presented here is that patriarchy, the hierarchy of power and privilege which advantages men over women, rich over poor and heavily armed over the defenceless, is the germinal paradigm from which most major human institutions, such as the state, the economy, organized religions and the social relations of the family and community, have evolved. The present security system functions to maintain this global patriarchal hierarchy, the most severe manifestation of which is constant, pervasive and often lethal violence against women. Gender violence is a daily occurrence in virtually all societies. Its severity and frequency is always heightened by regular presence of military, war and armed conflict.

A second significant assumption of the framework and analysis is that the fundamental inequalities inherent in the multiple contemporary forms of patriarchy, evident in most of the world's cultures and institutions, pose obstacles to the realization of the human security of such vast numbers of men and women as to threaten human survival. It is argued that these inequities must be challenged for the sake of survival, equality and security, each of which we assert to be integral to the other, and that the approach to that challenge so fundamental and essential to its success as to be imperative is gender.

A third central assumption is that the frustration of the experience and the expectation of human wellbeing is a continuing cause of armed conflict and war. War, in this time of weaponry of unprecedented destructive capacity that produces irreparable environmental damage and infrastructure destruction at enormous economic cost, poses the widest and most serious threat to wellbeing and to the very survival of all life on earth.

These assumptions lead to our central assertion that the present highly militarized global system of state security is not only incompatible with human security but also represents the foremost barrier to planetary security. Human security, we assert, cannot be achieved within this system. The challenge raised here is a call to the transformation of the present system into one intentionally and specifically designed to achieve human security.

The articles included in this volume highlight the assumptions, assertions and arguments of the framework by demonstrating the patriarchal nature of militarized security systems, documenting the system's gendered effects, offering examples of approaches to human security, identifying obstacles to its achievement and describing efforts and initiatives toward overcoming the obstacles.

It is our hope that this book will encourage people to think critically and systematically about militarized security, particularly the ways in which it threatens human wellbeing and survival; provide evidence to refute the utility and viability of the dominant patriarchal paradigm; and to offer a gender analysis that challenges the current system so as to encourage inquiry into ways toward transformation and change through consideration of alternatives to militarized security.

Toward the fulfillment of these purposes, we have organized the book into four sections. The three articles in the first section provide a theoretical foundation, focusing on the conceptualization of human security and outlining the comprehensive feminist security framework which provides the analytic lens for reflection on the following sections. The second section offers evidence from various societies, establishing the integral relationship between patriarchal violence and the state security system. The third section recounts instances of efforts to seek authentic security in actions and strategies to rollback the patriarchal violence of militarized state security. The fourth and final section describes alternative ways of thinking about striving toward human security, working within the constraints of the present system yet seeking to transform it.

We conclude with a sample inquiry to facilitate reflection on and discussion of the human security implications examined by suggesting the kinds of queries that might help to initiate a process of communal reflection and action of the kind we believe to be essential and integral to assessing possibilities and strategizing for transformational change toward the actual realization of positive visions of human security, liberating the concept from the Siberia of Utopianism into the reality of practical politics.

Part I
Confronting the militarized state security paradigm
Human security from a feminist perspective

1 Women and human security

A feminist framework and critique of the prevailing patriarchal security system

Betty A. Reardon

This is a revised version of an argument first published in Japanese as 'Toward Human Security: A Feminist Framework for Demilitarization' in *Women's Asia*, No. 33, 2003. It also contains arguments I have published in other journals.[1] A few updates have been added to this edition.

A core thesis on human security

The present discourse on human security, while broadening the components and definitions of security as it is pursued in the international system, has yet to face the core problematic of human security, militarized patriarchy. Within this emerging discourse, there has been no significant acknowledgement that human security can never can be achieved within the present highly militarized, war-prone, patriarchal nation state system. Neither, as I have argued for more than three decades, is it achievable within patriarchy which is the foundation of the war system (Reardon 1985). This collection of articles, exploring human security from a feminist perspective, is grounded in a set of assertions and arguments about what constitutes human security and what most obstructs it. Two propositions lie at the centre of these assertions and arguments: first, if human security is to be achieved, patriarchy must be replaced with gender equality, and second, war as an institution must be abolished in favour of non-violent structures and processes for resolving conflict and achieving national policy goals.

In short, concepts and modes of thinking about security must be transformed. This volume is intended to illuminate the consequences to human security posed by the lack of gender perspective that excludes women's experiences and needs from the wider security policy discourse and to encourage inquiry and discussion in which the necessary thinking about the dominant concept of security and its transformation might take place. Toward such transformation, we argue, a serious examination of security issues in women's daily lives in ordinary times and the gender particularities of their experiences in armed conflict are the primary and essential conditions for changing security thinking. We acknowledge, as does Bernedette Muthien in her article in this volume, that security itself, even as the notion of assurance of protection against great harms to the nation – that is, national security – is a contested term. That contestation, for the most part, concerns the issue of what constitutes security rather than the clarification of the term itself. In this article and in the contributions for which it is the foundation, both conceptual meanings and constitutive components will be addressed.

The purpose of this introductory discussion is to lay out arguments and assertions so as to make the case for the consideration of one proposed alternative concept of human security, a feminist comprehensive framework that addresses multiple, interrelated and essential foundations and sources of human security. Each of the remaining articles offers a deeper assessment of a particular aspect of security or case of insecurity to further illuminate the fundamental concepts that comprise this feminist framework for human security and demonstrate how women's experience reveals the ultimate futility of war and all forms of armed conflict. These assessments inquire into the policies and strategies that could produce the requisite transformation of the war system into an international system that is truly committed to the achievement of comprehensive human security for all peoples of the Earth.

The problem of human security in a militarized world

During the weeks in which the first version of this article was prepared (2009), the news media was rife with indications of a vision of a future in which national interests would be pursued by military force, examples being North Korea's testing of a nuclear weapon and American politicians raising the specter of threats to national security to rationalize the use of torture to obtain 'intelligence' from 'terrorists'. The *New York Times* reported on 9 June 2009, 'Global Arms Spending Up, Study Shows. World governments spent $1.46 trillion on upgrading their armed forces last year despite the economic downturn' (p. A6). We continue to live in a world in which our leaders, those charged with responsibility for our 'national security', perceive that security to be under constant threat, so severe as to necessitate the acquisition of ever more destructive weapons, so insidious as to convince normally democratic societies that the exigencies of security permit states to violate internationally agreed-upon standards of human rights. Nations and forces seeking entry into the higher levels of the global power hierarchy pursue the development of nuclear weapons, even in the face of the 2017 ban treaty – a proliferation of the possibilities for the total destruction of vast regions of the planet. We are constantly told we are under threat by other nations, justifying the violation of all standards of civility and frustrating impulses toward sociality and international cooperation, the conditions most conducive to human security within and among nations. Rather than engaging in the vigorous pursuit of such conditions, nations and some non-state actors – with ambitions to hold powers of state or who purport to represent the interest of particular peoples – continue to pursue military power in the name of national security or peoples' interests. Yet nations are not secure, and the interests of peoples are not served. The world, as our leaders persuade us, is dangerous. We contend, however, that the major dangers it holds are not the ones from which our states are prepared to protect us. The major dangers are in the daily insecurities of most of the peoples of the world, be they at peace or at war, a fact obscured by the priorities of current security policies and, as Michele W. Milner observes in her article, the media that report them.

For more than a year prior to 19 March 2003 – the day on which the United States invaded Iraq – the American people were instructed repeatedly that their security was severely threatened by Iraq, its association with terrorists, its development of weapons of mass destruction (never found) and its tyrannical leader. The British people were similarly instructed about these same threats to their national security that required pre-emptive military action. So, too, are the Pakistanis warned about India – indeed, it was stated that had the Indian Army been intervening within the country rather than the Taliban, the Pakistani government would have reacted with far greater haste to the advance of a political force seeking to impose an extreme patriarchal, misogynist regime; Indians are warned about Pakistan; North Koreans about South Korea and the United States and vice versa; Iranians about the United States and vice versa; the Israelis about Palestine: the list could go on.

The cumulative effect of these instructions from national leaderships about threats to security is an intense and pervasive sense of insecurity that persuades populations to maintain and support heavily armed states to protect them. Only with strong militaries, it is widely believed, can nations have any assurance of security. It is popular wisdom that before September 11, 2001, the American people, citizens of the most militarily advanced and powerful nation in world history, perceived their 'homeland' to be secure, a security based on the mightiest military the world had ever known. Although it was clear that even the mightiest military could not secure the nation against such attacks as crumbled the World Trade Towers and shattered the illusion of invulnerability held by so many Americans, the 'homeland security' discourse that ensued was largely limited to new methods of warfare, new forms of militarism and invasive surveillance to meet the 'new threats'. Consideration of how these new threats might affect the possibilities of progress toward the newly emerging concept of human security was not on the new national security agenda in the United States or in any of the nations involved in the War on Terror.

A pivotal question, seldom asked in the American security discourse, or indeed, in any nation, is 'Who among the citizens of the mighty state perceived and now perceives themselves to be truly secure?' Was it the single mother on minimum wage or welfare; a community on the edge of a toxic waste site; the black youth needing to walk through a racist neighbourhood; a young woman required, on returning from a late work shift, to walk alone on poorly lighted streets, blocks from the bus or subway to her home; the family living in a trailer park in a tornado area? Those whose loved ones and homes were swept away by Hurricanes Katrina and Maria? Is it the thousands upon thousands of Americans who in 2008 and 2009 lost their jobs and most of their retirement investments? Who among such vulnerable people of any nation are, in fact, secure? What is security? The advent of the concept of human security and the discussion of the relationship between national/state or strategic security and human or people's security is an opportunity to address these and other related queries.

To advance that discussion, we propose a feminist concept and framework of security to challenge the militarized state security system and to call attention to the gendered effects of that system, as they impact particularly on women. Many of these effects are chronicled in this collection of articles. The integral relationship between gender and militarism has been well explored and, feminists would argue, established in extensive literature on the topic.[2] Norma Nemeh, in telling us in her article of how the convergence of sexism and militarism impact Jordanian women, attests to the integral relationship between these two attributes of patriarchy. This collection attempts to build upon the current feminist discourse on women, war and peace, with an inquiry into alternatives to militarized national security within the context of gender as constructed in the present patriarchal order of world politics.

The essential significance of a feminist perspective is in its potential to illuminate the human security deficits imposed by the present system on virtually all vulnerable populations in all states, no matter their place in the global hierarchy. Through study of the gendered experience of women, a feminist perspective also sheds light on the ways in which human security is destroyed by armed conflict and is systematically weakened by all forms of militarized security. Feminists have attributed this systemic vulnerability to the power imbalance between men and women at the heart of patriarchy, still manifest in some form in most societies. I would also contend that the disadvantaged position of women in patriarchy puts in jeopardy the security of most of the human community – even the patriarchs. If women and those who depend upon them are not secure, to what extent can a nation, in the true sense of the word, meaning the people of a state or society, be secure? This is one of the central questions that informs this collection on gendered aspects of significant obstacles to and possibilities for the achievement of human security.

We intend to argue that authentic national security is human security, and we encourage readers to consider whether militarized state security can ever really assure it. Indeed, it is the militarized system of state security that seriously threatens human security in ways to be elaborated later in this article. This and other chapters will put forth some feminist assertions about security as a basis of our arguments and about a perspective from which to view the cases of insecurity and struggles for alternatives to militarized security described here.

Feminism asserts the equal human value of women and men and argues for the changes necessary to realize it. 'Feminist' here means as seen and analyzed from women's gendered perspective, a perspective influenced both by women's exclusion and marginalization from security politics and by their experience of struggle to provide day-by-day basic human security throughout history and still today throughout most of the world. This is the work that patriarchy has assigned them. In recent years the term 'masculinist' has begun to appear in literature dealing with various aspects of the gender problematic. I take this term to mean as seen from and interpreted in the light of men's gendered experience – now the subject of masculinities studies – particularly with regard to their public roles and also from the perspective of their purported human superiority to women and children (Breines et al. 2000). The term is often used to indicate, as well, the exclusion of women from the subject at hand or a discourse which does not consider others. The exclusionist male view of the masculinist perspective is in contrast with a feminist perspective which often also includes others as a consequence of the recognition of the organic and integral relationship between women and those to whom they relate. As noted by such scholars as Carol Gilligan (1982) and Mary Belenky (1986), many women think and behave in relational terms, nurturing relationships, while men tend to think in terms of separateness of themselves and the groups to which they belong, among them the nation state. The masculinist perspective tends also to be individualistic, an attribute I believe accounts for the fact that even the foundations of universal human rights are articulated only in terms of the individual, as is much of the current discourse on human security.[3] Neither forms of thinking are sexually – that is, biologically – determined, nor are they innate. Most gender scholars attribute these characteristics, as they do gender itself, to socialization, education and experience and therefore view them as subject to change through these same processes. Both these forms of thinking have security policy implications and consequences to be discussed next in a proposal for a feminist framework for human security and a critique of militarized state security.

'Gender', as the concept is generally used in works that deal with the differences and inequalities between men and women, is a socially derived concept, a culturally varied construct that assigns to men and women a set of cultural roles and social functions only minimally determined by their respective reproductive and sexual characteristics. However, the concept of gender that underlies the arguments articulated in this article is that it is the conceptual structure through which patriarchy has historically assured the psychosocial acceptance of the particular positions in the masculinist hierarchy to which patriarchy assigns men, women and children (Reardon 2008). Patriarchy has convinced most of humanity that the traditional gender roles and expectations that have governed relationships among men, women, children and society are the product of nature, designed by their 'divine creator'. Cultural practices regarding gender roles may vary, but the fundamental hierarchal structure is similar in all patriarchal societies. Gender is a system maintenance mechanism of patriarchy as manifest in the state, and the term 'gendered' as used here pertains to sex roles in the patriarchal order. This order we contend – in agreement with various scholars developing the field of masculinities studies – also severely restricts the human potential of men and exacts great costs from the majority of them, especially those in the ranks of the vulnerable, as observed elsewhere in this article.[4]

Patriarchy: a framework for human insecurity and a source of gender injustice

The present militarized system of state security is but a reification of the core political paradigm that has existed in most societies throughout most of human history. Patriarchy is likely to have preceded the state that is an abstraction for the power of governance, a depersonalization of power that allows those who hold and exercise it, to rationalize and obscure the harm they cause to those over whom they have power. What previously had been customary and viewed as cultural practice became sanctified and institutionalized in the nation state which claimed sovereign, often absolute, power over its peoples and based its claim to power on divine will. The state, it was asserted, was ordained by God – or the gods, among whom some rulers numbered themselves – and those who ruled were chosen by God to do so. Institutional religion reinforced the claim, and its institutions also reified the hierarchal order through which patriarchy organized itself. The state and institutionalized religion, the intermediaries between people or the gods, the armed forces mustered by these two institutions, the land which produced human livelihood and the law which ordered human relations were, with a few astonishing historical exceptions, all in the hands of men, some of whom maneuvered themselves to power over most other men and all others in the society, compelled by religion and the law to accept their rule. So it was and has been until the first changes in what R. W. Connell (2000), a founder of the field of masculinities studies, calls the global gender order. In 18th-century Europe, some noteworthy changes in the ordering of the hierarchy and procedures in the exercise of power began: changes that are purported to be the origins of modern representative democracy. As we have been well instructed in our school years, the changes emerged from developments in political thought that challenged divine right as the source and monarchy as the main form of governance and postulated 'the rights of man'. There were even some calls for the rights of women put forth by women and some men. Such men were usually liberal intellectuals, members of the literate, propertied classes at somewhat higher levels of the patriarchal hierarchy.[5] What was not included in our school texts was the fact that these steps toward representative government did not change the fundamental 'patriarchal power paradigm' (Reardon 2008).

Through the tenacity of patriarchal thinking, hierarchal arrangements of society based on race, class and gender; buttressed by inequitable access to benefits of production based on what has become global, corporate, free-market capitalism; psychologically reinforced by the fear of others engendered by fundamentalist religious precepts and ultranationalist xenophobia, patriarchy as the basic paradigm of human institutions continues to prevail. Varying in severity of the inequalities and oppressions it imposes from culture to culture and political regime to political regime, not withstanding what appears to be considerable progress in what the United Nations refers to as 'the advancement of women', the core characteristics of patriarchy are the mainstay of most societies.[6] Contemporary 'patriarchs' are heads of financial institutions, major transnational corporations and of the states that defend their interests, as well as the advocates of fundamentalism to be found among practitioners of all religions and in various cultures.

Paramount among these core characteristics of traditional patriarchy evident in its contemporary forms is the continued use and systemic threat of violence to maintain the power order. Among the various forms of violence that peace researchers – such as Johan Galtung, whose theory of violence is presented in Bernedette Muthien's article – have identified and defined, one ancient and universal form that has had currency in peace research and in some sectors of the human rights movement only in recent decades is gender violence. As I have argued elsewhere, there are multiple forms of gender violence, each performing a particular function in the perpetuation of patriarchy (Reardon 2008). So, too, as many feminists have argued since the conclusions of the first Consultation on Women and Peace of the International Peace Research Association, there is an apparent interrelationship among all forms of violence (IPRA 1983).[7]

However, this systemic interrelationship that makes most forms of violence integral one to the other is seldom addressed in any policy discussions relating to violence abatement, much less to war and national security, except by those feminists who have theorized an equally strong interrelationship between the oppression of women and the institution of war (Woolf [1938] 1966; Reardon 1985; Enloe 2000). We contend that this tendency toward separating what clearly should be considered together in an integral relationship, a characteristic of present security thinking to be addressed next, is a significant factor in limiting the more comprehensive approach to security issues that we see as essential to understanding the requirements and to designing the strategies for human security.

War and violence against women such as that documented in many of the cases recounted in this book are a primary and paramount manifestations of patriarchy, as is clearly seen in the organization of militaries and behaviour toward women (both civilian and military women) during armed conflict and in areas of long-term military presence. Our central line of argument is that so long as war is maintained as a legitimate instrument of national security policy, and preparation for war consumes resources that could be directed toward other essential ongoing needs of human security, human security cannot be achieved. Further from that argument is that if war is to be abolished, so, too, patriarchies must be replaced by gender-equal and humanly equitable societies, and militarized state security must be transformed into a people-centred system of non-violent institutions that provide for the wellbeing and protection of all sectors of the world's populations. It is the contention of those who have produced this volume that guidelines for such a system might be derived from feminist perspectives on human security and be designed along the institutional lines put forward by many who have envisioned amendments and changes in the international system that might reduce and ultimately eliminate socially sanctioned violence, assuring the full range of universal human rights and preserving the life of our planet. Some examples of these proposals will be noted in the section on confronting obstacles to human security.

A feminist framework of human security and a critique of militarized state security

The feminist framework of human security proposed here, first formulated in the 1980s from my observations of women's actions and movements for peace, human rights and environmental preservation, finds its foundations in women's gender roles and their socially assigned tasks of care for children, the aged, the ill, for most who are dependent on others for their wellbeing, in short, the vulnerable.[8] This gender role and the learning that is gleaned from performing these tasks have given women a distinct perspective on security different from that held by those in whose trust society has placed public affairs and the security of our nations. In that women's responsibilities call upon them to function in many spheres of human experience, their perspective on security is comprehensive, including factors overlooked by the state security paradigm.

The first of the core feminist assertions on the meaning of security, identifying the sources of its assurance, is that security is in essence the conditions that make possible the experience and expectation of wellbeing. This definition obtains in the cases of individuals and groups of all sizes and characters, including nations. Everything that is done in the name of security is ostensibly to fulfill those conditions. Yet the conditions are seldom, if ever, fully met, even in times of so-called peace – that is, little more than the temporary absence of active armed conflict. The three major problems with the present international security system that prevent it from assuring the conditions of comprehensive human security are (1) it is dominantly masculine rather than fully human in conception; (2) it is designed to achieve the security of the state rather than that of persons or human groups; and (3) what is most readily evident, it addresses only one of four fundamental sources of human wellbeing which are: a life-sustaining environment; fulfillment of needs for survival and health; respect for individual and group dignity and identity; and protection from the most severe effects of those harms the society cannot avoid, including assurance that the society will take care to mitigate the consequences thereof. The dominant masculinist concept – that is, men's gendered perspective – of security emphasizes protection of the state from harm by other states or political actors, including 'terrorists' at tragic cost to the other three sources of human security (Tickner 1992). The gendered differences in concepts of and perspectives on security are a significant factor in the debates that rage between peace activists and political realists; the latter, through the same form of thinking that leads to acceptance of gender roles as natural, still manages to keep the majority believing that the masculinist perspective provides a view of the world as it really is, not as we may wish it to be. Thus, prudence and practicality lead most citizenries to adopt the realist view, informing the opinions that sustain the present system.[9]

These three problems obtain because the security of peoples is primarily in the hands of the nation state that, as noted, is a creature of patriarchy which valorizes men over women and arrogates to them power over the public sphere. Thus, the control of resources and their use is in the hands of men, male elites who also control the state (through legal, constitutional and other methods). As a consequence of masculinist thinking, most of the ruling male elites see resources as finite and therefore to be acquired and defended against a distribution that might disadvantage their state as others benefit. Defence of resources, as well as the nation (to be read as the communal male identity), the elites contend, requires the capacity to apply armed force, even when this may disadvantage some, or even the majority of people, within the nation state. The future of the nation and of its people, they assert, depends upon the protection and preservation of the state and its ability to compete with other states. In patriarchal politics as in patriarchal business, every effort is made to maintain 'the competitive edge' – advantage over all others.

Most human beings have no competitive edge. They are not among the advantaged, and so they are regularly deprived of security in their daily lives, a situation frequently exacerbated by catastrophes or crises that call attention to the severe lack of daily human security among the vulnerable. Human security is everyday or quotidian security. Patriarchy assigns the major portion of the daily struggle to provide for the fundamental wellbeing and human security of families and communities to women. Consequently, women's approaches to security tend to be rooted in the daily work they do for the survival of others and in the struggles they conduct to improve the quality of life in their communities. Rather than in competing for and defending resources and power, women's behaviours and methods applied to meeting their human security responsibilities have tended to be cooperative and sharing: decisions to advantage one family member or neighbour over another are hard made by women. Their concerns tend to be for the wellbeing of the whole to which they belong and to increase the possibilities for more assurance of the future daily security of those in their care. On the face of it, this seems to me to be a far more promising survival strategy than competition and preparation for lethal conflict to gain or maintain an advantage. Certainly, this is so when the survival in question is that of the human species. Women's social and political activism stems from this concern with the conditions of the quotidian security of families and communities, the whole of the units to which they are affiliated. They have been active in environmental protection movements, efforts to overcome and compensate for poverty, the human rights movement for gender equality, the rights of the excluded and oppressed and the struggles against war and other forms of organized and physical violence.

Some women working in several or all these movements for human wellbeing have come to hold a comprehensive concept of security, such as that which informed the founding of the short-lived Women's International Network on Gender and Human Security (WINGHS), a group of women from various parts of the world, some of them from countries plagued by war. Academics and activists, most were working to overcome domestic and sexual violence and the effects of armed conflict on women. WINGHS used the framework and concept suggested here in their common preparation for an international conference on peace. Members of the network presented the concept of security as wellbeing and the comprehensive framework at The Hague Appeal for Peace Civil Society Conference in the Netherlands. In May 1999, a global congregation of 10,000 activists in such movements as those noted earlier came together to outline another comprehensive set of proposals for peace. The agenda devised there had many elements consistent with a comprehensive feminist framework and security as wellbeing concept. Human security, WINGHS argued and demonstrated in presentations on specific example cases from several countries represented in the network, should be defined as the expectation, perception and experience of human wellbeing. It derives primarily from the expectation that the four fundamental conditions or sources of wellbeing, as noted earlier, will be assured. Peoples and communities are secure if these four essential conditions obtain. We contend that all four conditions are undermined not only by armed conflict but also by militarized security per se, an argument well supported by the cases of Okinawa and Guam, where long-term military presence – as described by Ronni Alexander and Kozue Akibayashi with Suzuyo Takazato in their respective articles – has frustrated environmental preservation and civil economic development, abused the human rights of women and children and imposed, rather than protected against, various harms suffered by the local populations as a result of proximity to military personnel and activities.

A sustaining and sustainable environment

The first and primary fundament of human security is that the natural and constructed environments in which a people lives must be able to sustain human life and health. We cannot survive, nor in any way be secure, if our natural and human environments do not offer us the ecological conditions and economic means of survival or if the conditions of these environments put our lives and health at risk. The latter is clearly the case imposed by climate change and the current environmental crises of "super storms" floods, droughts and the like that have destroyed the means of survival of thousands upon thousands and threaten millions more with similar devastation. To a significant degree, this devastation is the result of human activity – industrial and military. The patriarchal drive for dominance over nature, its tendency to view Earth not as a living system, the source of nourishment for all other living things, but rather as a vast pile of resources to be extracted and exploited for its own purposes, has gendered, 'feminized' this planet. Earth has been factored into the ranks of the vulnerable in the patriarchal hierarchy, the property and raw material of the patriarchs.

War and preparation for war bring great destruction to the environment and create the conditions that together with extractive exploitative development have helped to bring about climate change and a series of 'natural' disasters. The environmentally disastrous consequences of militarism and colonialism are referenced in several articles in this volume, particularly, as noted,[10] those by Ronni Alexander and Kozue Akibayashi with Suzuyo Takazato, in which the authors inform us of the environmental damages caused by long-term military presence and the 'war games' that are rehearsals for war.

Since the completion of this draft in 2009, feminists and the authors of this volume have recognized climate change and nuclear weapons as threats to human security so extreme as to threaten the survival of humanity and this planet. We note that the 'climate science deniers' think and act within the patriarchal paradigm, 'realists' denying reality as they did in resisting the ban on nuclear weapons as documented by Ray Acheson in the one chapter new to this volume, on the negotiating of the UN ban treaty of 2017.

Fulfillment of fundamental survival needs

A second fundamental source of security is the meeting of basic physical and survival needs, what is often referred to as 'basic human needs'. Much modern development has ignored the needs of the poor and excluded women's perspectives, leading in many cases to increases in and new forms of poverty in neglected rural areas and overcrowded, under serviced urban areas. The excessive allocation of public funding to military expenditures frustrates the meeting of basic needs for a large percentage of the human population. Such spending priorities are also due to the dominance of masculinist thinking and the exclusion of women and the poor from policymaking. Human security thinking requires not only a comprehensive view of security, but also broader and more democratic and representative policymaking bodies to conceive and plan development as a human security process.

Imposed poverty produces social imbalances and disturbances that often lead to armed conflict and multiple forms of social violence. Mesfin G. Ayele, in his article on Ethiopia and women's struggles to overcome the limits imposed on them by patriarchy, provides ample evidence of poverty as a major obstacle to human security.

Respect for personal and group dignity and identity

A much overlooked third necessary source of human security is the fundamental human need for acknowledgement of our dignity and assurance that our personal and cultural identities are to be respected. Among all the human insecurities imposed by patriarchy, the denial of universal human worth may be the most instrumental in the maintenance of the war system; gender inequality and discrimination and gender oppression together with the assigning of human value in a hierarchal order provides the patriarchy with vulnerable and exploitable populations – poor youth as cannon fodder, men and women as field hands and factory and technical workers. The vast majority of the human family has lived in the fear that their identities – sexual, racial, ethnic, religious, even political if challenging the dominant order – could be the cause of traumatic physical and psychological insult, even death. Feminist human rights advocates have argued that patriarchy is the paradigm for racism and colonialism (Peoples Movement for Human Rights Education 2007). Susan Brownmiller (1975) has argued that rape is a strategy for keeping women in their subservient place. These oppressions comprise circumstances of constant human insecurity.

The most insidious aspect of the denial of this source of human security is that the vulnerable assigned to lower levels of social worth often come through long historic experience to believe in their own unworthiness (Fanon 1961). Racial minorities for centuries have lived in cultures that remind them daily of their inferiority to the majority. Women are persuaded that their own transgressions or stupidity account for their abuse and assaults. A well-behaved child is a submissive child. Submissiveness and silence are quotidian, imposed expectations, accepted as the price of survival, leaving the majority in a state of daily and constant human insecurity. When the silence is broken, often it is with violent, system-shaking retaliation, such as the attacks of 'terrorists'. This statement is not to rationalize or explain terrorism, but rather to pose the argument that in the face of this form of human insecurity even those who have privileged places in the power order are not secure.

The institution of war relies in large part on the willingness of peoples to deny dignity and respect to others identified as enemies (Reardon 1985). Military training often involves the dehumanizing of the adversary so as to assure that military personnel will not be deterred in the destruction of the other by any notion that an enemy can be worthy of respect. That an enemy – sometimes only a political adversary or people in the way of the goals of those who have armed power – is in any way the subject of universal human rights is a thought to be banished in the interests of the homeland or the state. Indeed, war is that condition in which human rights violations are sanctioned in the name of national security, the rights of the enemy and often the rights of the citizens of the nation whose security is said to be in need of defence. The articles by Lisa S. Price on the gender dimensions of the genocide in Darfur and by Fatuma Ahmed Ali on the gendered effects of armed conflict in Africa show how these physical and psychological insults to women's dignity and identity violate their claim to universal human rights, wielding devastating and often lethal blows to their human security.

Protection from avoidable harm

Early in the 21st century, a new precept of international order was promulgated by the United Nations, the 'Responsibility to Protect' (R2P).[11] When considering such conditions as those described in the article by Lisa S. Price, this is, indeed, an initiative of the international organization to be welcomed by all who hope to see developments in the international system, moving it closer to a capacity to assure human security. One circumstance, however, that limits the potential of this initiative to make substantial strides toward an alternative to the present cycle of inter- and intra-national armed violence characterized by large-scale killing of civilian populations is that it would be invoked only when the international community agreed that there was a crisis situation genocidal in nature. What is promising, however, is that the United Nations, in collaboration with international civil society, has taken this admittedly limited but potentially significant step toward a new view of state sovereignty by proposing intervention within states under certain circumstances as an international responsibility. This could be a step toward a wider range of possibilities to provide civilian populations with protection from avoidable harm. (It must also be noted, however, that some have expressed reservations with concerns that R2P could contribute to the militarization of the United Nations.)

Lamentably, there are no international standards or obligations to protect a nation's citizens from the consequences of natural disasters, resulting from the lack of environmental caution in the race for economic growth, or against the threats to their human security from narrowly based and misguided foreign and security policy decisions made by their leaders who resort to armed force to resolve conflict. In the United States, for example, although there was a strong international manifestation of opposition to what President Obama has called President Bush's war of choice, there was no international protection for the approximately 5,000 US military families who lost sons, daughters, brothers, sisters, husbands, wives and fathers and the countless Iraqi families, who suffered inordinately more losses to a war which could have been avoided. Many of these families, in addition to the devastating loss of a loved one, also suffered a significant loss in family income and capacity to meet economic needs.

Similar losses were faced by those who were deprived of loved ones, homes and jobs by Hurricanes Katrina and Maria. The same can be said of all the wars and disasters the world has known. They have had devastating effects on those involved during the trauma and for generations to come. Psychological scars, economic costs of loss of infrastructure and means of production, and in the case of war, now more than ever, caring for many who survived wounds that in previous wars would have been lethal but in our time leave victims totally dependent on others. Suicides and mental illness among the military and disaster victims add to the economic, social and psychological costs and limit the potential for the future human security of nations that survive wars. Neither holidays nor statues honouring these 'sacrifices for the nation' can make the nation secure. Neither can the mythology that sanctifies war provide authentic solace for the loss of what was and what could have been. (We note here that as of 2018 the 'war of choice' continues, and Hurricane Maria has had even longer-term and more devastating effects than Katrina, exacerbated by the colonial, i.e. vulnerable and exploitable status of Puerto Rico.)

War and militarized state security are the greatest of obstacles to the fourth source of human security, the expectation that our societies will take measures to protect us from avoidable harm and to care for us in cases of unavoidable crisis and disasters. This source of security is perhaps most seriously undermined by the present system in its failure to make clear distinctions between what is avoidable and what is unavoidable harm. Were we to fully examine the histories of the origins of all wars, we would likely find that not only so-called wars of choice were avoidable. Some argue that such is still the case.[12]

Human security is especially undermined by giving little attention to the unavoidable harms that are the real threats to our security, instead lavishing resources on preparation for and the conduct of the armed 'defense of the nation' in conflicts that in many if not most cases could be avoided through means of diplomacy and other forms of constructive conflict resolution, confidence building and cooperation. A dangerously narrow approach to this fourth security expectation, focused almost exclusively on the potential of militarily inflicted harm from other nation states or dissidents within a state, serves to prevent progress toward actual comprehensive human security.

A comprehensive and integrated approach to human security

All security issues, we argue, should be addressed within a holistic, comprehensive framework. The four fundaments of human security of the framework described here are interdependent one with the other and complementary in that denial of one to fulfill another can reduce not only that one but also all the others. Any security policy should be formulated so as to take into account all four of the fundamentals – that is, the potential consequences of the policy to each security source as well as the source toward which the policy is specifically directed. Special attention should be given to carefully assessing the effects on the vulnerable, projecting the security benefits and deficits they are likely to experience. Indeed, it is important to assess the potential impacts of policies on and each sector of whole populations, giving close attention to the equity of the potential results, asking who would benefit and who might suffer. Such assessment is rare in current security discourse which is confined mostly to strategic and military power issues, making it virtually impossible for the traditional mode of national security policy to be formulated so as to increase the human security of all a nation's people.

Separating out 'national security' policy – as the protection function is conceived within the present militarized state security system – from all the other fundamentals of security and privileging it over them is rationalized by the appeal to fear and sense of threat among the general population. The general citizenry is socialized to believe that ordinary citizens are incapable of understanding, much less participating in, security policy formation and application. Such decisions are best left to the wise and capable leadership who takes responsibility for the security of the nation. Although some may consider the nation to be the general citizenry – that is, the human beings who comprise it – national leaders consider it to be the state, reinforcing the security disadvantage to human populations. Such thinking in terms of hierarchies of the importance of some factors over others to the nation and separating issues one from the other, a practice that gives the leaders a greater sense of control, obscures most if not all secondary effects and glosses over security deficits suffered by the vulnerable. It is a form of thinking that consigns unintended loss of life in combat to the category of 'collateral damage', or even more devaluing of human life, 'friendly fire'. The vulnerable, like non-voting segments of the population, are given little valence in strategic and security policy planning.

So, too, the separating of state security from a comprehensive, people-centred national security such as we conceive to be human security led to what some feminists believe to be the two main flaws of the Ogata-Sen report (2003). The report deems human security to be a complement to national security, separating it from full integral relationship to the other security sources it discusses, a number similar to those included in the feminist framework we offer here. More disturbing still, although it calls for conflict reduction measures, it does not foresee a transformation of the militarized state security system, nor does it contemplate any significant alternatives or amendments to it. This lack of recognition of what the opening of this article asserted to be the main problem of current discussions of human security, failure to acknowledge that militarized state security is incompatible with human security and the two 'securities' cannot be accommodated in the same system, is a serious flaw of the report. So, too, is its lack of a gender perspective that we believe compromises much of what the report sets out to do in broadening the security discourse and making it more inclusive. Theories of security devoid of a gender dimension cannot be authentically people-centred. Neither can they produce effective human security policies.

Another consequence of these separations is the phenomenon of conceptualizing separate 'securities', acknowledging that there are various sources of the security of a people, but treating each as distinct and independent from the others and subject to separate and distinct policymaking. So we have a proliferation of securities: environmental security, food security, social security and, most recently, climate security, among others. This latter begins to appear in the narrative of the military. Long concerned with the effects of weather and climate on combat, and likely subject to some growing concern with climate change, there may now be some contemplation of interventions for strategic purposes. As each scientific and technological advance has been put to military use and the sophistication of weaponry, producing research into space war and cyber space war, each new concern for the public order and social welfare becomes 'securitized', taken into the service of military security in some way, a phenomenon cautioned against in a recent volume on human security (Shani et al. 2007).

Thus, we see the need for a profound change in thinking and for widening the pool of the educated, striving for greater sophistication of security thinking among ordinary citizenry as the military strives toward greater sophistication of weaponry. However, we seek to shift the thinking from contemplation of greater potential for destruction to contemplation of greater potential for human wellbeing. The patriarchs understand that their exclusive hold on authority could be challenged by a thoughtful, critically educated public. Fear of this challenge no doubt contributes to the prohibition of women's education by fundamentalist forces that lead to the murder of teachers and the burning of schools in Afghanistan, such as in the case recounted in Chloe Breyer's article.

Striving for human security calls us to transform the epistemology of patriarchy, the ways of knowing of the nearly universal system of male dominance that privileges a minority of powerful men and their interests, values and perceptions over those of most other men and all women, children, the aged and, for the most part, anyone who does not fit the identity profile of the patriarchs. Those of less social value in this order are described on the basis of their differences from the patriarchal norm to be less intelligent and incapable of exercising power. Wise men are those best equipped to think about important issues and to decide for the rest of the population. State power accrues to them, they assert, because they know how to use it, and it must be used so that the wise continue to keep it. For millennia human civilization in virtually all cultures has lived by some such system of knowledge and governance. It is such thinking that determines that the most significant threats to national security are from other nations or renegade forces within the nation who would usurp power from those who are rightfully entitled to wield it. Such thinking prevents states from fully dedicating themselves to a comprehensive security system that would seek to reduce all forms of harm to their citizens and keeps them from doing all in their power to mitigate the damage of what are still unavoidable harms. Should they focus adequate attention on protecting people from avoidable harm, they would, for example, view health and healthcare as presented in the article by Albie Sharpe as a fundamental requirement of human security. They would certainly take into account potential health effects before embarking on undertakings that might produce the consequences of such disasters, as described earlier.

Patriarchy as a sociopolitical structure, as the essential worldview and mode of thought within which most public policy is made, has never been and is not now conducive to the development of a human security regime in which all would reap benefits from society. Nor it is likely to become so. For it precludes wide public discourse on these issues, maintaining strong influence on reportage and the way in which the information media manage public security discourse to the continued advantage of the dominant security paradigm, as described by Michele W. Milner's article.

It thus follows that few societies have ever actually undertaken to devise a comprehensive human security regime. Societies that would aspire to meet the four security expectations for most of its population would be essentially secure and peaceful, for there would be less power contention within and between such societies. As a society intentionally seeks to provide the fundamental conditions of human security for all its population, it moves toward being a just society, acknowledging that justice and security are essential to peace in all societies – local, national and global. Judged by these standards, there are no really just and peaceful or truly secure societies in the world and probably none that are fully committed to achieving either justice or authentic human security. The human security of citizens in most nations is still secondary to the national interest as defined by the male elites who hold national power. It is the recognition of this fact of the daily insecurity of the human family that inspires feminist efforts to redefine, demilitarize, indeed, to re-conceptualize security, and that impels them to assert that we need to think in distinctly different terms from those that comprise the thinking of the present power elites. Most particularly, we must confront the problematic of demilitarizing the global security system so that it might better assure the conditions of human security. While the first of these two factors, the daily insecurity of most of the human family, led to the articulation of human security as a new perspective, the second factor, the undermining of quotidian security by militarized state security, has been given little public attention. This lack of attention is not for lack of possibilities.

Confronting the obstacles: toward demilitarization and gender equality

Various remedies are and have been advocated to overcome the consequences of the human imbalance of dominant masculinist security policies. Some of these remedies, feminist peace activists believe, could contribute to pushing the international system closer to a sustainable system of human security. Over the years since, and even before World War II, there have been, as well, some visionary, utopian – that is, a vision of the best and most desirable social conditions that can be conceptualized and described – proposals for institutional alternatives to militarized security and the abolition of war. Among these are the mid-20th-century Clark-Sohn proposals for *World Peace Through World Law* (1966) and at the end of the 20th century *The Hague Agenda for Peace and Justice in the 21st Century* (1999). As is outlined in a small and largely unknown publication, *The Conquest of War* (1989), there are multiple possibilities for alternative security systems to keep peace and to strive for justice. Most such proposals advocate as the core element of the demilitarization of security, reducing and eliminating national arms and militaries in favour of international peacekeeping and dispute settlement.

Visions and plans for a disarmed world also informed the proposals and work of peace visionaries, such as Bertha von Suttner, who from girlhood was concerned with the increase in the volume and destructive capacity of armaments. In 1905, she was awarded the Nobel Peace Prize for founding the Permanent International Peace Bureau that continues to be a respected voice for disarmament and diplomacy. That diplomacy and law might replace armed force in international disputes was the vision of the founding of the International Court of Justice (ICJ) in 1921 and the League of Nations in 1919. While the latter was overwhelmed by patriarchal nationalism and the lack of more creative responses to dictatorship and genocide, the ICJ was incorporated into the structure of the United Nations, established in 1945. At present and in recent years, the ICJ has been the scene of some of the special tribunals addressing some of the very kind of issues that led to World War II – genocidal crimes. That young men need not, generation after generation, risk and lose their lives in the national interest was the intent of the Oxford Pledge that circulated among the youth during the 1930s, committing university students to conscientious objection. In recent years, the right of conscientious objection has been given more public attention, and in the United States the bases for claiming the right have been broadened through practice and precedent. Civil society groups have constituted non-violent peacekeeping forces that interpose themselves between combatants in incipient or actual armed conflicts, offering an internationally replicable model for non-violent conflict intervention.

That all this could be undertaken in the reality of actual international politics is evidenced in the 1962 agreement between the Soviet Union and the United States that general and complete disarmament should be the ultimate purpose of all arms agreements and treaties.[13] Nothing would be more effective in limiting the destructive capacity of the state than depriving it of its most patriarchal characteristic, exclusive right to armed force, a primary symbol and enforcer of sovereignty. Few states fully acknowledge, much less live up to, the responsibility that rationalizes state sovereignty, providing for the welfare of the citizenry and protecting their rights. In recent years, the rise of patriarchal authoritarian governments has taken the world far from the political philosophy of the modern state as articulated in the American Declaration of Independence (1776) that governments are instituted to secure 'the right to life, liberty and the pursuit of happiness'. Happiness is taken to mean wellbeing, and thus, we would argue, states have an obligation to provide for the human security of the nation. Such is authentic national security. And such is the purpose of the International Covenant on Economic, Social and Cultural Rights, one of the two foundational treaties intended to implement the responsibility of states to assure the human rights of their citizens. It was in the name of the human rights obligations of government that the Soldiers' Mothers of Russia, as Valerie Zawilski informs us in her article, challenged the sovereignty of the state, as they sought to protect human rights and to assure the human security of their sons in the military who were serving in the Chechen war.

How, it is often asked, might we be assured of the power to overthrow oppression in a world without arms? Putting aside an acknowledgement that arms are among the primary mainstays of oppression, we can refer to a significant history of non-violent political change of the last century, so often overshadowed by the multiplicities of armed struggles that characterized the 20th century. Among the most outstanding of the major political changes brought about without recourse to arms are Gandhi's non-violent movement for the independence of India; the People's Power that toppled the Philippine dictatorship; the Velvet Revolution that overcame authoritarianism in Czechoslovakia; the ending of apartheid in South Africa; and the civil rights movement in the United States. These and many more historic experiences of specific and sophisticated non-violent strategies used for defence and liberation have been well documented in *From Dictatorship to Democracy* (Sharp 1993). Further, there are nations that have abjured military security. Most significant among these are Costa Rica which abolished its army in 1948 and consequently increased its budget for education and public health services. The constitution adopted by Japan during the US occupation following World War II renounced war in its Article 9 that has become a worldwide symbol for practical steps for peace. Although Japan actually maintains an advanced military capability in its Self Defence Forces, and right-wing forces are pushing for the abrogation of Article 9, there is strong support for it among Japanese citizens, and a vigorous campaign for its preservation has been mounted with significant international support. In May 2008, more than 3,000 people, many of them from other countries, gathered in the outskirts of Tokyo to manifest this support (Peace Boat 2009). A similar concept based on legal approaches toward demilitarization lies in the Luarca Declaration of the Human Right to Peace, fast becoming a worldwide movement (2006).

Although some remedial steps may and are being taken in the present system to reform a few of its most egregious effects – steps that reflect some vision of a more humanly secure system – little consideration has been given to possibilities for alternative security systems. Proposals for full-scale alternative security systems call for clear plans for alternative institutions and structures to replace the war system. Even more challenging, they also call for courageous commitment to transform the masculinist thinking that produces the prevailing security policies. Nothing short of political boldness and such transformation of thinking and policymaking will bring about the demilitarization of security. Such a goal is indeed viewed as utopian in the sense of the impossible – a departure from reality. Yet utopias can serve as models of a preferred, humanly secure world.

Many women and men see possibilities for the needed transformation and have, as noted earlier, put creative and critical human capacities to work in envisioning and designing – some in specific institutional detail – plans for alternative security systems. In the tradition of Bertha von Suttner, they perceive images of new realities: institutions for non-violent conflict resolution; a legal framework to maintain global order and to keep the peace with minimum force, applied only when needed to reduce violence and harm; strengthening of international law and legal institutions to resolve disputes and prosecute international crimes rather than wage wars; developing mutually beneficial relationships among all nations to cooperatively address the global problems that threaten the human security of all nations, overcoming relationships of competition and threat in favour of the constructive collaboration essential to survival; and involving women, the poor and other marginalized and vulnerable groups fully and equally in all security matters.

Indeed, there are possibilities for committing human talent and global resources, now expended on militarized state security, to the fulfillment of all security expectations in a world of cultural diversity, gender equality and human solidarity. But these visions can be achieved only when human needs are the primary concern of security establishments. As recognized in UN Security Council Resolution 1325 (2000) that Soumita Basu assesses in her article – one of the most promising remedial measures if fully implemented – this concern is not likely to be the focus of security policymaking without the equal participation of women. Neither is the achievement of authentic human security – that women peace activists assert to be essential to a just peace – possible absent the full representation of all the world's diverse peoples. Human security depends on gender equality and authentic democracy in all spheres of social organizations and political Institutions. Striving toward human equality and political democracy requires challenging the global gender order and transcending the patriarchal roles and hierarchies that deny equality and democracy.

Some see in the encoding of human rights standards in international law one of the most visionary and potentially most politically practical mechanisms to move the world toward the equality and democracy that would characterize human security. The arena of human rights is one in which struggles for gender justice and against many forms of oppression and deprivation are pursued. Most of what our feminist framework for human security includes as the sources of human security can be claimed by all human beings under the international human rights standards, especially as they have been extended to specify the rights of women and children. What the human rights standards miss in the framework can be found in the Earth Charter that articulates the ecological values that inform the framework's first fundament – manifest in the Paris Accords to resist cimate change – and the International Criminal Court (2002) which can hold legally accountable those who would repress the third fundament in crimes that deny human dignity and destroy persons so as to eliminate the identity of their groups.

Because human security lies as much in the expectation as in the experience of wellbeing, security is greater when the presence or perception of threat is lessened. In order for human beings and human communities to perceive and experience security, they must be able to expect some assurance of wellbeing in all of the four basic areas of environment, basic needs, human dignity and protection from avoidable harm. So, too, when these expectations are reasonably assured, peoples are likely not only to feel less threatened and less vulnerable, but also they are far less likely to threaten others for economic, environmental or political reasons. If nations are striving for authentic human security, they are not so likely to be preparing for or waging war but rather working toward peaceful, less costly resolution of conflicts and mutually beneficial solutions to common international problems, building constructive relationships with rather than threatening other nations. Authentic political will toward such transformed security policies and public intent to achieve human security would be the greatest possible assurance of the reduction of armed violence and the ultimate elimination of the institution of war. Women's peace groups are working to build such will and intent.

Millions of women throughout the world – as attested to by the joint nomination of 1,000 women peace activists from all over the world for the Nobel Peace Prize (2005) – are fully committed to the struggle for peace, human security and equality (Vermot-Mangold, 2005). Many of their struggles are recounted in this volume. Women's peace groups have been among the leaders in advancing transformational thinking through peace education, now a vibrant worldwide movement, and cultivating political will through various forms of action. Among such actions are those taken by the Women in Black who keep vigil at the sites of division and violence in many countries; action undertaken by the members of Code Pink in the United States, Iraq, Gaza and other areas of violent conflict; the challenge to the occupation of the West Bank and defence of the right of conscientious objections by the members of the New Profile in Israel, by the government for daring to challenge and claim the rights presumed to obtain in a democracy; and the lobbying of Voice of Women Canada at the United Nations for Security Council Resolution 1325, the Reaching Critical Will program for disarmament of the Women's International League for Peace and Freedom, Women Cross the DMZ, calling for a peace treaty between North and South Korea, and various steps toward the abolition of war. Women have been actively involved in conflict resolution and bringing an end to armed combat in many countries, Ireland, Sierra Leone and Liberia being a few such examples. As Asha Hans documents in her article – which also describes an actual experiment in implementing human security – women not only have suffered the violence of the India-Pakistan border conflict and the failure of their respective states to protect them, but also have courageously challenged the political powers that perpetuate the conflict.

Women, even more significantly, have been influential in policy campaigns and the formation of institutions and policies that can lead the way toward the demilitarization of the global security system, including – as we see in this volume – the resistance to militarization and armed conflict. Women have been leaders in all spheres of the struggle to make the possibilities for human security into probabilities. Much of this institutional work has been done in and around the United Nations. Voice of Women Canada, as noted, has launched various initiatives for disarmament at UN conferences and treaty body meetings. The women lawyers of the Gender Justice Caucus, leaders in the drafting of the statute that established the International Criminal Court, were responsible for including rape among the crimes stipulated for prosecution under the Rome Statute that came into force in 2002. Women and women's groups were among the strongest and most creative in the formation of *The Hague Agenda for Peace and Justice in the 21st Century*, a 50-point programme of specific steps toward the abolition of war, now an official UN document (*The Hague Appeal for Peace* 1999). Within that agenda and various other proposals are multiple possibilities for the global institutional changes that could demilitarize security, moving the world closer to a comprehensive human security paradigm such as that envisioned in the feminist framework put forth here. Among the most politically and institutionally relevant provisions of the agenda are those of Global Action to Prevent War, 'a comprehensive, multi-stage programme for moving toward a world in which armed conflict is rare' (*The Hague Agenda*, p. 10).

Among all the United Nation's steps to actualize the potential for human security, none are more significant than the Sustainable Development Goals (2015), the Paris Climate Accords (2015) and the Treaty on the Prohibition of Nuclear Weapons (2017). All recognize the common crises that threaten the peoples of the Earth and the planet they share, and all are a testament to the efficacy of communal action by global civil society in which women play a major leadership role. Such is attested to in the one new article in this edition, the description of the political process of the nuclear treaty conference by Ray Acheson of the Women's International League for Peace and Freedom. She shows that civil society working for a more secure common future was able to prevail, winning the majority of the member states and overcoming the opposition of the patriarchal realism of the nuclear states. That achievement and its promise were recognized in the awarding of the 2017 Nobel Peace Prize to the International Campaign to Abolish Nuclear Weapons. The prize was accepted by two women leaders of the campaign.

Conclusion: the imperative of a gender perspective and a comprehensive approach

The Hague Agenda and the other achievements noted earlier are but a few of the indicators that an alternative non-violent security system is possible. To transform these possibilities into realities, two important dimensions must be integrated into the review and assessment of existing suggested remedies and proposals and into the design of the new ones that may be found necessary. We have faulted *Human Security Now* for the lack of gender perspective and its advocating human security as a complement to state security. Although *The Hague Agenda* includes provisions on gender, advocating for the inclusion of women in peace matters, none of its other proposals, indeed few of the proposals mentioned here, promising as they are, have an adequate gender perspective. Without it, the fundamental obstacle to human security, patriarchy, is not likely to be overcome.

Equally imperative is a comprehensive approach. We cannot achieve human security in its complex multi-dimensions – even with the afore noted proposals or many more possibilities, including those with a more mature gender perspective – without finding ways to integrate them into a holistic framework, interrelating the various components into a comprehensive system directed to the purpose of eliminating violence and providing for human wellbeing. For this, in sum, is the essence of human security, wellbeing made possible through the elimination of all forms of violence, assured by institutions designed specifically to achieve and maintain wellbeing; in short, demilitarizing national security and bringing an end to patriarchy.

Notes

1 Among other journal articles on the topic most relevant to the discussions here is Reardon (1996).
2 A selected bibliography of such works is included in the references to this article.
3 It was a decade after the Universal Declaration and the two foundational human rights covenants entered into force before 'third-generation' rights or group rights emerged in the human rights discourse.
4 Among the important researchers in the field we recommend as relevant to the interpretation of gender as it is applied in this essay are R. W. Connell, Michael Kaufman and Michael Kimmel. Ian Harris has done some significant work documenting the costs patriarchy exacts from men. Mark Sommers, a pioneer in the field of masculinities, has also done work on alternative security systems, as cited in this article.
5 In the United States, some male abolitionists of the anti-slavery movement also supported women's suffrage. It was argued by some that the two issues were related as essential attributes of human freedom and democracy. A similar position was held by the English poet Percy B. Shelley, husband of Mary Godwin, daughter of Mary Wollstonecraft, author of *The Vindication of the Rights of Women* (1792). Also, at the end of the 18th century, Olympe de Gouges, a feminist bluestocking, issued a proclamation of the rights of women and was executed by the forces of the French Revolution for her prescience.
6 The term 'patriarchy' is still largely excluded from the United Nation's discourses on gender equality, as was the term 'feminist' for many years, even during the two International Women's Decades. Although the term 'gender' began to replace the word 'women' in some of the discourse and documents, it is only in the past few years that men's roles in the gender problematic have been addressed at all. UNESCO has been a pioneer in bringing the field of masculinities studies into the peace discourse (Breines et al. 2000).
7 A similar argument, concerning the interrelationships among various forms of violence, is made in the conclusion of a 1994 consultation organized by the UN Division for the Advancement of Women in preparation for the Fourth World Conference on Women held in Beijing in 1995 (Breines 2000).
8 This feminist framework for human security emerged through preparation for and participation in a speaking tour entitled 'Listen to Women for a Change' organized by the Women's International League for Peace and Freedom undertaken in 1985.
9 Much of the body of critical peace research and philosophy of peace education, such as work of Dale Snauwaert (2002), challenge the validity of this

view, as does the feminist critique of the field of international relations. J. Ann Tickner (1992) offers one of the most penetrating examples of this criticism.
10 It is significant that the concept of human security was first addressed in international discussions of social problems related to development. It became a formal part of the ongoing United Nations discourse through *The Human Development Report* published annually. It is now, as well, the subject of another annual UN report, *The Human Security Report*.
11 Responsibility to Protect (R2P) is a response to the proliferation of the genocidal character of so many of the armed conflicts that have raged since the 1990s. It is an initiative strongly supported by the UN Secretary-General. In a recent seminal work on the topic, *Preventing Genocide* (2008), David Hamburg advocates for several preventive strategies similar to the policies that have been suggested by many as elements of human security.
12 Scholars and advocates of non-violent defence, most notably Gene Sharp (1973, 1993), argue that in virtually all cases wars could have been prevented and conflict conducted without violence. Research on the development of a theoretical interpretation of conflict processes and resolution procedures has been the lifelong work of such scholars as Morton Deutsch et al. (2006).
13 The McCloy-Zorin Agreement was named after the negotiators for the United States and the Soviet Union were validated by the UN General Assembly in 1962 but later repudiated by the two parties. General and complete disarmament has not been seriously considered since them. However, the Secretary-General's Report on Disarmament and Non-Proliferation Education does make two minor mentions of it.

References

Belenky, M. 1986. *Women's Ways of Knowing*. New York: Basic Books, Inc.
Breines, I., R. W. Connell and I. Eide (eds.). 2000. *Male Roles, Masculinities and Violence: A Cultural of Peace Perspective*. Paris: UNESCO Press.
Breines, I., D. Gierycz and B. A. Reardon. 1999. *Toward a Women's Agenda for a Culture of Peace*. Paris: UNESCO Press.
Brownmiller, S. 1975. *Against Our Will: Men, Women and Rape*. New York: Simon and Schuster.
Clark, G. and L. Sohn. 1966. *World Peace through World Law*. Cambridge: Harvard University Press.
Conclusions of the Consultation on Women Peace and Disarmament. 1983. International Peace Research Association. Consultation in Gyor, Hungary. Unpublished.
Connell, R. W. 2000. 'Masculinities and Globalization', in I. Breines, R. W. Connell and I. Eide (eds.), *Male Roles, Masculinities and Violence: A Cultural of Peace Perspective*. Paris: UNESCO Press.
Deutsch, M., P. Coleman and E. C. Marcus (eds.). 2006. *The Handbook of Conflict Resolution*. San Francisco: Jossey-Bass.

Enloe, C. 2000. *Maneuvers: The International Politics of Militarizing Women's Lives*. Berkeley: University of California Press.
Fanon, F. 1961. *The Wretched of the Earth*. New York: Grove Press.
Gilligan, C. 1982. *In a Different Voice*. Cambridge: Harvard University Press.
Hague Agenda for Peace. 1999. *The Hague Agenda for Peace and Justice in the(21st Century*. Retrieved from www.haguepeace.org.
Hamburg, D. 2008. *Preventing Genocide: Practical Steps toward Early Detection and Effective Action*. London: Paradigm Publishers.
Hollins, H. B., A. Powers and M. Sommers. 1989. *The Conquest of War: Alternative Strategies for Global Security*. Boulder: Westview Press.
The Luarca Declaration. 2006. Luarca, Spain: The Spanish Association for the Advancement of International Human Rights Law.
Ogata, S. and A. Sen. 2003. *Human Security Now*. New York: United Nations.
Peace Boat. 2009. 'Global Article 9 Conference to Abolish War'. Tokyo. www. peaceboat.org.
Peoples Movement for Human Rights Education. 2007. 'Transforming the Patriarchal Order to a Human Rights System: A Position Paper'. Retrieved from www.pdhre.org.
Reardon, B. A. 1985. *Sexism and the War System*. New York: Teachers College Press. [Second printing, 1996, SUNY press, Syracuse, New York]
———. 1996. 'Women's Visions of Peace: Images of Global Security', in J. Turpin and L. A. Lorentean (eds.), *The Gendered World Order: Militarism, Development and the Environment*. New York: Routledge.
———. 1998. 'Gender and Global Security: Feminist Challenge to the United Nations and Peace Research', in *The International Journal of Cooperation Studies*. Kobe Japan: Kobe University.
———. 2008. 'Toward a Gender Theory of Systemic Global Violence: Exposing the Patriarchal Paradigm', a seminar presentation to be published by the University of Granada, Spain in 2010.
Secretary General of the United Nations. 2002. *Report on Disarmament Education and Education for Nonproliferation*. New York: United Nations A/57124.
Security Council Resolution 1325. 2000. New York: The United Nations. GENDOC/NO/720/18.
Security Council Resolution 1820. 2008. New York: The United Nations. GENDOC/NO8/391/44.
Sharp, G. 1973. *Politics of Non Violent Action; Part I Power and Struggle*. Cambridge: Albert Einstein Institute.
———. 1993. *From Dictatorship to Democracy*. Cambridge: Albert Einstein Institute.
Shani, G., M. Sato and M. Kamal. 2007. *Protecting Human Security in a Post 9/11 World: Critical and Global Insecurities*. London: Palgrave McMillan.
Snauwaert, D. 2002. 'Just War and Democratic Education Post 9/11', paper delivered at the Conference on Teaching and Learning in the New Global Era. Unpublished.

Tickner, J. A. 1992. *Gender in International Relations: Feminist Perspectives on Achieving Global Security*. New York: Columbia University Press.

Vermot-Mangold, R. G. 2005. *10000 Women across the Globe*. Geneva: A Kontrast Book published by the Association of 1000 Women for the Nobel Peace Prize.

Wollstonecraft, M. (1792) 1999. *The Vindication of the Rights of Women*. New York: Bartleby.

Woolf, V. (1938) 1966. *Three Guineas*. San Diego: Harcourt Brace Janovich.

2 Gendered insecurity under long-term military presence
The case of Okinawa

Kozue Akibayashi and Suzuyo Takazato

Introduction: a gender perspective on human security

When the 1994 *Human Development Report*, the annual report of the UN Development Programme (UNDP), proposed 'new dimensions of human security' (UNDP 1994), the peace activists' community welcomed this UN initiative of redirecting the focus of security discourse and policies to non-military aspects of security. The report further articulated the structural problems of militarized national security by pointing out that it causes insecurity of people around the world.

This chapter highlights the negative effects of militarized security on human security from a gender perspective by introducing the work of Okinawa Women Act Against Military Violence (OWAAMV), a women's peace movement in Okinawa, Japan. OWAAMV was officially established in November 1995 by women in Okinawa who spoke out and acted out against military violence (violence committed by military personnel against civilians and non-combatants, further defined next), namely gender-based violence committed by US soldiers who have been stationed in Okinawa for more than seven decades since the end of World War II. OWAAMV, which emerged as a convergent movement of different advocacy groups for the human rights of women in Okinawa, asserts the need for a gender analysis of the present global security system (Akibayashi 2002; Akibayashi and Takazato 2009).

The mainstream discourse on security has been conducted mainly in the arena of international relations in military terms, within the framework of the nation state. 'Security' or 'security policies' are thus almost synonyms to national security provided by the military, armed with bombs, missiles and combat personnel. Especially during the post–WWII period when the Cold War between the two most powerful nations prevailed, security referred to protection of the state from foreign attack; thus, arms and military power are the primary means of providing the security of the state. This conceptualization has been argued by feminist scholars to derive from the realist paradigm of international relations that has its origin in Western political theory (Tickner 1992; Peterson 1992).

Yet with the disintegration of the Soviet Union and the end of the Cold War in the late 1980s and early 1990s, the notion of the enemy against whom security policies were planned has changed. The military which prepares itself to defend against the presumed enemy and maximizes its preparedness with the weaponry and the training of its personnel may not be the best approach to security. The critiques of the military-exclusive security notion have appeared from different perspectives. A precedent for this critique can be found in the argument of a peace researcher, Robert C. Johansen, put forward even in the early 1980s (Johansen 1980). There he analyses US foreign policy from a perspective of human interest, suggesting global human interest may be undermined by the military-centred national interest.

Having been developed from the outcomes of the UN Social Summit in 1993 where the welfare of all human beings on Earth was the agenda, the 1994 *Human Development Report* emphasizes the need for a shift of focus on security from military security to people-centred security.

> The concept of security has for too long been interpreted narrowly: as security of territory from external aggression, or as protection of national interests in foreign policy or as global security from the threat of nuclear holocaust. It has been related more to nation-states than to people... Forgotten were the legitimate concerns of ordinary people who sought security in their daily lives. For many of them, security symbolizes protection from the threat of disease, hunger, unemployment, crime, social conflict, political repression and environmental hazards.
>
> (UNDP 1994: 22)

It further defines human security in two aspects: 'first, safety from such chronic threats as hunger, disease and repression. And second, it means protection from sudden and hurtful disruption in the pattern of daily life – whether in homes, in jobs or in communities' (p. 23). In this document, a comprehensive concept of human wellbeing is introduced as the focal point of security. The report provoked various discussions on security. In 2001, the United Nations launched the independent Commission on Human Security (CHS) with two co-chairs: Sadako Ogata of Japan, who served as the UN High Commissioner

Gendered insecurity under long-term military presence

for Refugees from 1991 to 2000, and Amartya Sen of India, the 1998 Nobel laureate in economics. The purpose of the CHS was three-fold:

> 1) to promote public understanding, engagement and support of human security and its underlying imperatives; 2) to develop the concept of human security as an operational tool for policy formulation and implementation; 3) to propose a concrete program of action to address critical and pervasive threats to human security.
> (Commission on Human Security 2002)

The establishment of the CHS posed a potential opportunity for the arguments long made by peace advocates in civil society whose work has been on re defining security from a people's perspective, critiquing the military security of the nation state, to be considered at last in the UN discourse on security. However, neither the institutional discourse of the CHS nor that of peace advocates considered gender as relevant – and we would argue integral – to human security.

Over the past two decades, with little acknowledgement from the international relations establishment, feminist scholars and women peace activists (Women's International League for Peace and Freedom, among others) have put forth a critique of military security from a gender perspective. Feminist international relations scholars, such as those cited here, have brought an alternative perspective to the realist paradigm of security since the early 1980s. By so doing, they bring 'gender' as a category of analysis to international politics and the security discourse. By pointing out the exclusion of women from international politics and the exclusion of feminine values to the overwhelming primacy of masculine views and values in the realist paradigm of international politics, feminists assert the inadequacy and limits of the present international security system.

J.A. Tickner (1992), an international relations scholar and political scientist, analyzes the traditional realist paradigm as follows:

> For realists, security is tied to the military security of the state. Given their pessimistic assumptions about the likely behaviour of states in an 'anarchic' international environment, most realists are sceptical about the possibility of states ever achieving perfect security. In an imperfect world, where many states have national security interests that go beyond self-preservation and where there is no international government to curb their ambitions, realists tell us that war could break out at any time because nothing can prevent it. Consequently, they advise, states must rely on their own

power capabilities to achieve security. The best contribution the discipline of international relations can make to national security is to investigate the causes of war and thereby help to design 'realistic' policies that can prolong intervals of peace. Realists counsel that morality is usually ineffective in a dangerous world: a 'realistic' understanding of a moral and instrumental behavior, characteristic of international politics, is necessary if states are not to fall prey to others' ambitions.

(ibid.:29)

She further asserts that 'the military, economic and ecological insecurity are connected with unequal gender relations' and argues that 'the achievement of peace, economic justice, and ecological sustainability is inseparable from overcoming social relations of domination and subordination; genuine security requires not only the absence of war but also the elimination of unjust social relations, including unequal gender relations'(Tickner 1992:128).

R.W. Connell (1995) argues, within the context of exploring the social organization of masculinity, that there is a link between the configuration of gender and the institution of the state.

The state, for instance, is a masculine institution. To say this is not to imply that the personalities of top male office-holders somehow seep through and stain the institution. It is to say something much stronger: that state organizational practices are structured in relation to the reproductive arena. The overwhelming majority of top office-holders are men because there is a gender configuring of recruitment and promotion, a gender configuring of the internal division of labour and systems of control, a gender configuring of policymaking, practical routines, and way of mobilizing pleasure and consent.

(ibid.:73)

In a similar vein, V. Spike Peterson's analysis of the state as a gendered institution opens up a discussion on the subject of security that has long been assumed to be primarily within the realm of the nation state. By looking at the historical processes of the state system and the 'protection' that the state system promises, Peterson (1992) examines the relationship of state and security by identifying the state as so 'gendered' as to account for the systemic insecurity of women. The dichotomy of protector-protected, she argues, is gendered, reflecting the masculine-feminine dichotomy, thus rendering the security it is constructed to protect in adequate. ' The dichotomy of protector-protected misrepresents the complexity of our "security" arrangements and especially the meaning of security in the context of human interdependence'(Peterson 1992:55–6).

Susan Brownmiller (1975) makes the case that rape is about the exercise of power over women. Her study of rape scrutinizes wartime rape that has existed throughout history in all locations. OWAAMV calls attention to the crime of rape as intrinsic to the military in and out of combat as a constant threatening reality for women in the areas of military presence and indeed within the military. Cases of sexual violence against female soldiers in the US military by other male soldiers, particularly the cases that occurred among those deployed in Iraq and Afghanistan, have shed more light on aspects of violence within the military (Wright 2008a, 2008b).

Members of OWAAMV have argued for more attention to military violence against women from a civil society perspective. Military violence against women can be defined as gender-based violence against women by the military or paramilitary; by individual soldiers or members of the military and paramilitary organizations; and by operations of military and paramilitary organizations. At the 1995 Huairou NGO Forum held prior to the UN Fourth World Conference on Women, OWAAMV presented a workshop on the theme and had exchanges with women from different parts of the world who shared OWAAMV's view of the importance of this concept. However, military violence against women was not a new phenomenon. Violence against women by the military has been experienced, as the Beijing Platform of Action (United Nations 1995) acknowledges, by women globally and throughout history.

Throughout the world women's peace movements are calling attention to the rise in military violence against women. The UN Security Council Resolution (UNSCR) 1325, 'Women, peace, and security', unanimously adopted in 2000, is a fruit of such calls and movements derived out of follow-up for implementation of the Beijing Platform for Action and an intensive lobbying by non-governmental organizations (NGOs) active around the United Nations. Although the adoption of UNSCR 1325 should be celebrated as the first Security Council resolution that incorporates the concept of gender in the security discourse and policy and acknowledges women's contributions to conflict prevention and resolution, as well as reconstruction of post-conflict societies, full implementation of the resolution remains a political agenda for the United Nations and its agencies as well as the member states. Another resolution related to gender and conflict was passed in June

2008. This resolution, UNSCR 1820, is more specifically focused on sexual violence in armed conflict. Some activists who have worked to promote UNSCR 1325 critically analyze the process of adoption of UNSCR 1820 by observing that it did not involve civil society efforts as was the case of UNSCR 1325; it is another tool to further visibility of violence by the military (Cook 2008).

In this vein, many are also challenging the military system itself and the integral element of misogyny that, they argue, underlies military training. Some are raising crucial questions about the prevailing realist concept of security that rationalizes the present proliferation of US military bases around the globe. Women in Okinawa who have lived with the presence of such bases for more than half a century were among the first and most active in posing the challenge and raising the questions: 'Whose security?', and Who and what is being made secure by this massive system of military might?

Women's peace movement in Okinawa: 'Whose security?'

Okinawa is the southernmost prefecture of Japan. The are a consisting of islands represents 0.6 percent of the entire territory of Japan. The population is approximately 1.36 million. Located at the midpoint between Tokyo and Manila, Okinawa is considered the 'keystone of the pacific' in US military strategy. Thus, under the bilateral security treaty between the United States and Japan (Treaty of Mutual Cooperation and Security between Japan and the United States of America) concluded originally in 1960, about 75 percent of all US military facilities exclusively used by the US military in Japan are located on the islands of Okinawa. The land area occupied by the US military is about 23,300 hectares, representing almost 20 percent of the land of the main island of Okinawa, where 90 percent of the entire population resides. Sea and air are controlled by the US military: 20 sea areas and 29 air spaces are designated as training areas where US military has priority. The air traffic of the airspace around Kadena Air Base, a 50-mile radius of 20,000 feet-altitude and around Kumejima Island, a 30-mile radius of 5,000 feet-altitude are under US military control (Okinawa Prefectural Government 2004). Currently, approximately 23,000 US troops are stationed there, plus 26,000 family members and dependents (Okinawa ken Chiji Koshits Kichi Taisaku-ka 2008). A characteristic of the demography of the forces stationed in Okinawa is a higher percentage of US Marines. Sixty percent of the troops belong to the Marine Corps, who are trained to be deployed to front-line combat. Okinawa hosts the largest number of marines outside the United States. This militarization of Okinawa is rationalized as essential to the security of the United States and its Pacific Allies in the global security system based on the realist paradigm which, as Tickner (1992) observes, equates security with the military security of states. It is argued that it is especially intended to defend the security of Japan which through the so-called sympathy budget carries the lion's share of the cost of the bases. Observers of US militarism view it as the major astern component of a worldwide system of bases that provides the United States with a strategic presence in every region of the world, a system that also has its eyes on outer space.

The United States began expropriating land and building military bases with the American occupation following World War II. Although governance of Okinawa reverted to Japan in 1972, the bases were neither removed nor reduced, effectively leaving Okinawa under continued American military occupation. This circumstance gave rise to the Okinawan anti-base movement that calls into question not only whose security is assured but also what constitutes security. The local people struggled for their political autonomy against unfair land expropriation, noise pollution, forest fires caused by live ammunition drills and other forms of environmental destruction caused by combat practice and training and the frequent occurrence of and US government collusion in the continued military presence and the various 'accidents' caused by military personnel. The Okinawa peace movements have been protests against the security policies of the Japanese occupation of Okinawa which undermines the human security of the people of Okinawa.

The Status of the US Forces Agreement (Agreement under Article VI of the Treaty of Mutual Cooperation and Security between Japan and the United States of America, Regarding Facilities and Areas and the Status of United States Armed Forces in Japan, SOFA) was concluded in 1960 when the US–Japan Security Treaty was signed. SOFA, which stipulates in detail the status of the troops and civilian workers stationed in the bases in Japan, the areas of training and soon, is often considered one of the major obstacles in achieving the daily human security of people in the host communities of the US military, reflecting unequal power relations between the US and Japanese governments, with the United States having much stronger power over Japan. Article 17 of SOFA has been particularly challenged by citizens of Okinawa and other places as it states that the US military authority has the primary right to exercise jurisdiction when offences are committed on official duty. This clause virtually gives a free hand to the US military for handling suspects because they can assert the personnel are on duty, even when they are not. There have been cases in which perpetrators were never apprehended by the Japanese/Okinawan authority and returned to the United States. There are provisions that pursue more equal relationships, yet the Japanese government had a secret accord with the US government that such provisions should not be strictly applied, as the *Ryukyu Shimpo*, one of the two major Okinawan newspapers revealed (*Ryukyu Shimpo* 2004).

In the mid-1990s, a stronger women's peace and human rights movement emerged in Okinawa, gaining more visibility by raising their distinctive women's voices against the rape of a 12-year-old Okinawan girl by three US soldiers in September 1995. The rape coincided with the UN Fourth World Conference on Women held in Beijing, China. Seventy-one Okinawan women participated in the NGO Forum in the city of Huairou organized in conjunction with the intergovernmental conference. One of the workshops offered by the Okinawan women presented their analysis of the consequences of the long-term military presence in their lives. The workshop was entitled 'Military: Structural Violence and Women'. At this workshop, they chronicled the history of sexual violence that the US military has committed against Okinawan women and demonstrated that the military is a violence-producing institution to which gender-based violence is intrinsic. They argued that because soldiers, especially marines, are prepared to engage in direct contact combat, they are trained to maximize their capacities to attack and destroy an 'enemy', a dehumanized other. Sexism that devalues the dignity and humanity of women is a primary process of dehumanizing the others, and denigration of women is integral to much military training. Soldiers acquire frustration, anger and aggression from intensive combat training, and these experiences are often vented against the women in their base locality (NGO Forum, Beijing 1995).

In putting forth this analysis of the nature of the military, they posed fundamental questions challenging the very notion of militarized security. Whose security does the military provide? Having lived in close proximity to an active foreign military whose presence is to assure 'security', they knew that the military has been a source of daily ubiquitous in security to local people, especially women and children.

When, upon their return from Beijing, they learnt of the rape of the 12-year-old girl, they immediately took action and protested, responding to the young victim's courage in reporting the crime to the local police. It was reported that she said she had reported to the police because she did not want to the same crime to be repeated. The Okinawa NGO Forum participants' public protests spearheaded island-wide protests against US military bases, among them the Citizen's Rally held in October 1995 that totalled about 100, 000 participants on the main island of Okinawa and other smaller islands of the Ryukyus.

As the focus of the protest movement began shifting from the human rights of women and children to the unfair bilateral treaty that conventional male-dominated peace movement had been insisting upon as the central issue, women realized the necessity to consolidate and develop their newly emerged movement to continue the focus of action on military violence against women. They also felt responsible for the voice that the young victim courageously raised by reporting the case to the police. In the Japanese criminal justice system, reflecting the patriarchal tradition, the police do not open investigation unless the victim files a complaint: this has hindered many victims of rape in coming forward. Victims of sexual violence in general often faced difficulties in reporting their cases to the police, as the UN Human Rights Committee points out in their recommendation, such as being required to prove resistance against the assault (United Nations 1995). Victims are, at times, blamed and scrutinized publicly as to whether they could justify their claims. In addition, the social stigma imposed on the victim, even as they gain justice, indicates that they are 'tainted' or 'shameful', leading the victims to be guilt-ridden. The young victim went to the police, it was reported, as she did not want the same thing to happen to other children. As many of the women have already addressed sexism in the criminal justice system in Japan and in Okinawa, these women were determined to continue their action.

They officially established Okinawa Women Act Against Military Violence (OWAAMV) in November 1995. The issues OWAAMV addresses stem from their concern about the wellbeing and daily lives of women and children. These issues include violence against women and children, especially the children of local women and US military personnel, frequently abandoned by their fathers, protecting human rights of women and children, and environmental destruction.

As introduced earlier, OWAAMV women have engaged in various actions that embody the nature and purpose of the OWAAMV movement. In the process of deciding on the name of the organization, the verb 'act' (*koudousuru*, in Japanese) was adopted by members to best describe their mission.

The OWAAMV movement not only demonstrates women's protest against military violence against women that identified patriarchy as the problematic of the militarized security system but also challenges the patriarchy within peace movements and Japanese and Okinawan culture as a fundamental obstacle to achieving peace. OWAAMV members repeatedly mentioned one incident at a protest rally in 1995: a male peace activist made are mark that denigrated women's assertion of the need for protecting the human rights of women and children.

> I have heard that a male peace activist even shoved a woman who was holding a sign saying 'Protect the human rights of women and children!' He was said to make a comment that this [the protest rally] is about the Security Treaty and that focusing on the issue of women and children diminishes the significance of the protest movement.
> (Minamoto 1995. Authors' translation from Japanese)

There is no official document that recorded the interaction, and some male peace activists have expressed disagreement on the occurrence of the incident itself. However, what is important to understand from the accounts of OWAAMV members is that women who stood up to protest against another occurrence of military violence against women felt that the existing peace movement dominated by men had not addressed the issue of military violence against women and children. They felt, again, that the human rights of women and children were not recognized as a central issue in the Okinawan peace movement that was first evoked by women's prompt actions. Thus, OWAAMV members were convinced of the necessity of solidifying the women's movement arising on the basis of the analysis of the interrelationships between sexism and militarism, which quickly emerged and gained public recognition. Their movement and argument then needed to remain visible and political, necessitating continuous political participation to overcome militarism and its source – patriarchy.

Security in the daily lives of women and children in Okinawa

In 1996, an OWAAMV delegation travelled to the United States to communicate with US citizens about issues related to the American military in Okinawa. In preparation for this 'America Peace Caravan', the members compiled a chronology of sexual crimes committed by US military personnel against women and children in Okinawa. Since then the chronology has been revised seven times, as more cases have occurred or come to light. The most recent version accounts for around 250 cases of different sorts of assaults against women and girls in Okinawa between 1945 and 2007: abduction; attempted rape;

rape, including cases of gang rape; and murder (OWAAMV 2008). The chronology represents only the tip off the iceberg of literally countless cases of violence. The social stigma against women victimized by sexual crimes has prevented many victims from reporting the crimes to the local police.

OWAAMV members describe clearly the relationship between crimes of violence against women in Okinawa by US soldiers and the organization and training of the military as 'structural (i.e., built into the institution) violence of the military'.

> The abduction and rape of an elementary school girl by three U.S. military personnel that occurred in September 1995 makes us realize that we must change the situation of living side by side with military bases and military personnel in an atmosphere of constant fear and tension, so that our children may grow up in a healthy environment. During the 50 years since the U.S. forces landed in Okinawa, untold numbers of girls and women have been attacked by U.S. military personnel. These crimes of sexual violence must be seen not merely as crimes committed by individual soldiers, but as crimes produced by the military system. We feel deep anger when we realize that most of these crimes have been ignored. At the same time, we issue a strong appeal for the implementation of a public system to heal the deep wounds of the victims and restore their human rights.
>
> (OWAAMV 1996:1)

The sex industry around the bases may be considered another form of military violence against women. The commander of the US forces in the Pacific, Admiral Richard C. Macke, made a remark before the trial of the three perpetrators of the rape of the 12-year-old girl that for the price the three paid for the rented car they used to abduct the victim, they could have employed a prostitute. The comment cost him his position, and he was forced into early retirement. But the comment encapsulates the fundamental patriarchal attitude that objectifies women and tolerates, even encourages, prostitution in Okinawa to serve US military personnel.

Women in Okinawa are fully aware of the presence of the sex industry for the military and relate it to the rapes and other sexual crimes committed by US military personnel. At the International Public Hearing on violence against women in armed conflict organized by a women's NGO, Women's Caucus for Gender Justice in the International Criminal Court, held in Tokyo in December 2000, a survivor of a gang rape by three US military personnel testified (Public Hearing 2000). In 1984, she was abducted and raped on her way home from school when she was 17 years old. She did not report the case to the police because she was reluctant to face a 'second rape' in the insensitivity of the police and the social stigma imposed on the victims of sexual crime that she had witnessed in the community. She noted that in her neighbourhood there had been many cases of rape by US military personnel, both reported and unreported, attributing these crimes to the presence of the US air base and prostitution for the military personnel located in the area.

Thus, OWAAMV members asserted that violence against women by military personnel should be understood within the problematic of a 'militarized' society that places a higher value on militarized security than on the human rights of women. They also argued that the US bases should be removed and that ultimately all military be abolished.

Amerasian children and the lack of legal protection of local women

Among the problems that women in Okinawa have faced is that of mixed-raced children fathered by US military personnel – Amerasian children. Some cases result from sexual crimes. In other cases fathers have abandoned their wives and children. Amerasian children often suffer discrimination because of their mixed-race appearance and the hostility against the US military. OWAAMV conducted a comparative research between SOFAs that Japan, Korea and the Philippines concluded with the United States and a similar one with Germany that provides for misconduct and crimes of US military personnel. It was found that the agreement with Germany meticulously stipulates the rights of the local women on marriage and the financial responsibility of the fathers in case of divorce. In contrast, SOFAs with Japan, Korea and the Philippines do not have such provisions. OWAAMV insists on the need for more comprehensive legal protection of Okinawan women and their Amerasian children.

Security for future generations: environmental destruction

US military operations and training, including live ammunition drills, have caused various health problems for many Okinawans and is also related to environmental destruction. Noise pollution, soil and water pollution from toxic substances and forest fires are among common cases of environmental destruction.

The effects of the use of toxic substances and chemicals are difficult to detect because often the detailed information is classified and not available to the local public. For example, it was only in 2007 that it was revealed to the Okinawan public that the US military used Agent Orange, the herbicide used during the Vietnam War for defoliation, in the Northern Training Area (the Jungle Warfare Training facility) (*The Okinawa Times* 2007; *Ryukyu Shimpo* 2007). It was also reported that the Vietnam veterans who were assigned the job of spraying the herbicide in the training area were diagnosed with prostate cancer. Although several genetic deformation cases appeared in later generations in Vietnam that were suspected to have been related to Agent Orange, there has been no research done in Okinawa or, as noted earlier, such information was not even available to the residents. In the vicinity of the Northern Training Area is located a major water dam that provides drinking water for the residents of the main island and It is imperative for the Okinawan public to be informed of such information. There are other cases of toxic contamination, including lead, mercury or PCB. Under the current policies, they do not have any means to protect their wellbeing against military operations that at times threaten their very survival.

Despite the Japanese government's official nuclear-free policy, researchers have found documents on the US side confirming secret deals between the two governments at the time of the reversion of Okinawa to Japan (Gabe 2000). The suspicions of people in Okinawa regarding the possibility of installation of nuclear weapons and radioactive contamination on the US bases in Okinawa turned out to be based on reality. Nuclear submarine visits are another source of environmental concern. In 2007, US nuclear submarines visited White Beach port located in Uruma city 24 times, the most frequent visits since the reversion in 1972 (Okinawa ken Chiji Koshits Kichi Taisaku-ka 2008), and it is continuing to increase. In 2008, the US media reported a nuclear submarine, *Houston*, leaked radioactive contaminated water, although the amount was small. It was after this report that the Japanese government was informed of the accident by the US government (*The Okinawa Times* 2007). Even then, the Okinawa prefectural government and municipalities were not given information about the accident, leading them to demand of the two governments more and prompt information. This action, however, can have only limited influence on assuring the safety of the residents.

The noise of military aircraft has long been a major issue, yet little or no progress has been made to reduce it. At The Hague Appeal for Peace Civil Society Conference held in the Netherlands in 1999,

Okinawa Hands for Peace, a youth group, spoke about the aircraft noise they are exposed to at school, noise so loud and disruptive that children and older students can hardly concentrate on their classes. Particularly in the surrounding areas of Kadena Air Base and Futenma Air Station, it is estimated that about 550,000 people are affected by the noise. Although there were restrictions agreed upon by the two governments on the hours of flying or testing engines during nighttime and early morning in 1996, there is also a provision stipulating that exceptions for necessary cases are admitted. On the grounds of this provision, restrictions are often not observed. Class actions have been brought to the Japanese courts to halt night flights and demand compensation. The courts admitted the damage done to the residents and ruled that they receive compensation; however, their demand for halting the night flights was dismissed (Okinawa ken Chiji Koshits Kichi Taisaku-ka 2008).

Reproductive health problems is another area of serious concern that needs more comprehensive and thorough research. A report issued in 1998 shows the significantly low birth weight of the babies in the locality of US air bases compared to the other parts of Japan that may be attributed to the noise (Research Study Committee of Aircraft Noise Influences to Health 1998).

In 1997, depleted uranium bullets were found offshore of uninhabited Torii Island. When the local government protested this discovery, the US military responded by declaring that these depleted uranium bullets were used 'accidentally'. Later, citizens' groups discovered that around the same period, the US military 'accidentally' used depleted uranium bullets in Puerto Rico and other practice areas (Okinawa ken Chiji Koshits Kichi Taisaku-ka 2008).

During the past decades or longer, citizens have protested against the building plan of a new military facility in Henoko, a small community in the northern area of the main island were US Marine Corps Camp Schwab is located. The controversial plan was announced shortly after the two governments agreed on closing the US Marine Corps Futenma Air Station in 1996, in part as a result of the strong public opinion against the US military evoked by the 1995 sexual violence case. Futenma Air Station, located in the midst of the highly populated city of Ginowan, has for a long time been symbolic of severe noise pollution and high risk of accidents. Instead of simply closing Futenma Air Station, the two governments selected Henoko as the replacement of Futenma Air Station. Henoko is a section in the city of Nago, an economically struggling area within Okinawa, which already suffers economic disparity with mainland Japan. In the city referendum held in 1997, about 53 percent of those who voted (the voting rate was about 82.5 percent) expressed objections to the plan of building a new military facility in Henoko. Environmental destruction is one of the major concerns about this plan, including protection of the dugong, an endangered sea mammal. Since then till 2009, residents have been protesting by staging sit-ins on the sea shore or even 'on the sea (on the platforms built to conduct drilling surveys)'. In 2003, a suit was brought to the US Federal Court in San Francisco to challenge the legitimacy of the construction plan in light of the US National Historic Preservation Act. This law suit is best described as *Dugong v. Rumsfeld*. In 2008, the court acknowledged that the ongoing environmental assessment was inadequate and ordered closer research on its implementation plan.

These are only a few examples of environmental destruction caused by US military operations. These damages are not only a present problem but also a problem that will last and affect generations to come.

Economic security

When discussing the possibilities of closing US bases in Okinawa, the economic issue is often brought up as a rationale for keeping the bases; it is argued that Okinawa could not survive without US military bases because they are a major source of employment and other economic activities. This is a myth believed by much of the Okinawan public. Okinawans did not have the opportunity to build a self-sustaining economic system because they were occupied by the US military for 27 years after the Asia-Pacific War ended. Under the occupation period, a currency that was directly linked to the US dollar was imposed upon them, separating them from mainland Japan. Having been deprived of opportunities to develop their own industry, they are now facing the worst unemployment rate and the lowest per capita income in Japan.

The Japanese government has used government subsidies as an incentive for hosting US military bases. Nago city received billions of yen, and large buildings were built. But even such construction business did not create sustainable jobs; rather, these state-of-the-art buildings in remote and rural areas are not in use, wasting more money in their maintenance and for utilities. The unemployment rate remains high, and the population keeps dropping. The sustainability of economic security is seriously undermined for a long period of time in Okinawa, perpetuating dependency on government subsidies and US military bases.

Transnational networks

All these problems over which OWAAMV and the people of Okinawa have challenged the US military and the Japanese government have yet to be included in the prevailing realist security discourse in which the human security of those negatively affected by military security is not a factor. Women in Okinawa have been tireless in their efforts to achieve authentic security for all people, to achieve a society in which the human rights of women and children on which their daily security depends are protected. They argue that in order to achieve authentic security, demilitarization is imperative because they know that militarized security does not provide security for women and children or, indeed, for all citizens of Okinawa and of the world.

One of the major goals that the OWAAMV movement is pursing is the achievement of a world without the military. To achieve this goal, OWAAMV members are keen about the importance of creating transnational networks on redefining security from a gender perspective. One of the outcomes of the 1996 America Peace Caravan is such a network of women working on the problems of the US military in the host countries and regions (Korea, the Philippines, Okinawa, Japan and Puerto Rico) and the US feminists, East Asia–US–Puerto Rico Women's Network Against Militarism. Since 1997, the Women's Network has developed solidarity actions, including international working meetings.

OWAAMV's argument for redefining security from a gender perspective also calls for a close reexamination of policy implementation for human security. The 1994 Human Development Report proposed a perspective on security discourse that takes the human dimension into account. The Japanese government is one of the major advocates of establishing a body on human security within and in association with the UN system, claiming that human security should be one of the main pillars at the G8 Summit 2000 held in Okinawa. Yet it was unclear whether the Japanese government's position on human security shared the original concept.

The decision to convene one of the working meetings, the International Women's Summit 2000 in Okinawa, was made to express OWAAMV's protest of the economic policies advocated at the G8 Summit because these economic policies support the present militarized security system. They also intended to appeal to a larger population who might turn their eyes to Okinawa and the US military base problem. OWAAMV members engaged in a process of articulating their proposed concept of human security. In conclusions agreed

Gendered insecurity under long-term military presence 53

upon during the process of preparation for the International Women's Summit 2000 organized by OWAAMV and the EA–US–PR Women's Network, they argued that there were four necessary conditions for human security:

1 the environment in which we live must be able to sustain human and natural life;
2 people's basic survival needs for food, clothing, shelter, healthcare and education must be met;
3 people's fundamental human dignity and respect for cultural identities must be honoured; and
4 people and the natural environment must be protected from avoidable harm.

(Final Statement 2000)

These conditions derive from the analytic framework of another network of feminist activists concerned with security, Women's International Network on Gender and Human Security (WINGHS), started in February 1999. The roots of the network stem from the International Conference on Violence against Women in War and Armed Conflict Situations held in Tokyo in November 1997 and the framework devised by Betty A. Reardon in the early 1990s and published in 1998 (Reardon 1998). The first network meeting was held in February 1999 in preparation for the presenting panels on 'Gender and Human Security' at The Hague Appeal for Peace Conference held in May of that year. The network comprised about 20 women from different regions of the world active in such fields as peace, the human rights of women and security. OWAAMV had close links to this network and to its successor, FeDem, the Feminist, Scholar-Activist Network on Demilitarization, a smaller group that continues to meet annually, usually in conjunction with the International Institute on Peace Education.

The OWAAMV movement continues to be actively connected with women in other parts of the world who share concerns about the human rights of women and the problems that the current militarized security system create. By so doing, the women of OWAAMV are struggling to disseminate their views on security.

Another development of transnational networks has two aspects. One is the global expansion of such a network, the International Network for Abolishing Foreign Military Bases, established in 2007 in Quito, Ecuador, resulting from the World Social Forum in Mumbai, India, in 2004, where one of the authors of this article, Suzuyo Takazato, was invited to speak at a session on US military presence and its impacts in the Asia-Pacific region. There activists attended the session and other related sessions and discussed and identified the need to create a global network for abolishing foreign military bases, as the existing campaigns were more of national character. At the Quito conference in 2007, together with the help of the government of Ecuador, about 400 international participants gathered and discussed further collaboration. In February 2009, peace organizations in the US convened a follow-up national organizing conference in Washington, DC. At the conference, the significance of a gender perspective was more widely recognized among participants that included EA–US–PR Women's Network members and Ann Wright, are tired US Army colonel working on sexual violence against female soldiers. Through this women's network within a larger international solidarity movement, there was recognition of the fact that addressing the problem of militarism itself, not only military bases, is imperative to transform the present security system.

The other aspect is in the Asia-Pacific region. As these women continue to explore opportunities for wider networks, they are reaching out to activists in Guam and Hawaii mainly through the EA–US–PR Women's Network and the International Network for Abolishing Foreign Military Bases. This connection with feminists in US territories illuminates more clearly the intersection of militarism and colonialism.

US military issues faced by people in Guam were brought to the closer attention of people in Okinawa when the US and Japan governments announced their agreement on the transformation and realignment of the military alliance of the two countries in 2005 and 2006: the US–Japan Security Consultative Committee revealed a plan to 'relocate' 8,000 US Marines and their family members to Guam in order to 'lessen the burden of Okinawa' and claimed that this was a long-time aspiration of Okinawa (Security Consultative Committee 2005, 2006). The small island of Guam, much smaller than the Okinawa main island, can hardly be associated with militarization by the general public. Guam is a resort place, like Okinawa, in a much closer location than Hawaii, another popular resort site, thus making it a competitor with Okinawa, whose economy is heavily dependent on tourism. The facts about the US military occupation of Guam are not well known.

The US–Japan SCC plan of reducing Okinawa's burden is a controversial package: the closure of Futenma USMC Air station promised in 1997 is now directly linked to the building of another facility in Henoko and to the transfer of US Marines to Guam. The transfer plan must be scrutinized for its impact on Okinawa and Guam as well as the financial responsibility of the Japanese government in building infrastructure in Guam in order to host more marines there (McCormack 2007).

During these years, a network was built between peace movements in Guam and Okinawa. It did not take too long for some Okinawan activists to realize the similarities of the colonization to the militarization of Guam by the United States. As an unincorporated territory of the United States (or a non-self-governing territory, in UN terms), people in Guam live with limited rights, and the indigenous people of Chamoro are struggling to preserve their culture and self-determination (Aguon 2006). Because of the solidarity developed through transnational networks, OWAAMV members were collectively one of the first and few unpopular critical voices of the transfer plan to Guam, contending that the plan would reduce the burden on Okinawa and calling for more attention to the analogy of the history and struggle of the Chamoro. Currently, OWAAMV is seeking closer ties among peace activists between Okinawa and Guam not only to address the transfer plan but also for demilitarization as a fundamental solution to the suffering of people of Okinawa and Guam.

The transnational networks that Okinawan women developed have shown multiple phases of militarism, and through the connection with feminist activists around the US bases, have analysed how militarism, dependence on power and a set of beliefs that security has to be provided by force operates in our daily lives. Their action challenges militarism and offers another view of the world – a demilitarized world where the security of all people is achieved.

Demand for demilitarized security

In the past decade, 'human security' has become one of the most popular concepts among researchers in such areas as political science in Japan. Despite the Japanese people's generally negative sentiment against militarism and Article 9 of the Japanese Constitution that renounces war as a means to resolve international disputes and the possession of arms, the Self-Defense Forces of Japan not only remains one of the most powerful militaries in the world but also is increasing its military capability to conduct military operations more fully with the US military.

The historical context of the 1994 HDR was the ending of the Cold War when possibilities for reallocation of worldwide military spending opened up the 'peace dividend'. Since then, however, as more intra-national conflicts broke out and 'terrorist' attacks, such as those in New York, London and Madrid, occurred, opportunities for the implementation of the possibilities offered in the 1994 report seem to have been lost. Reflecting the new context of pre-emptive war, the final report of the CHS, issued in 2003, concludes that human security is but a complement to state security. The very framework of militarized national security was left unchallenged.

The gender perspective on security that OWAAMV developed in cooperation with other women's peace movements around the world poses a challenge to militarized security, outlined in the comprehensive approach described here.

OWAAMV has analyzed the historical and daily experiences of women living under conditions of long-term military presence in Okinawa. This gender perspective illuminates the interrelationship between sexism and militarism and illustrates how militarized security undermines human security. For them, human security must be demilitarized security, a security system that is not dependent on armed forces and a system that does not place higher values on military strength than on the human rights of women.

References

Aguon, J. 2006. *Just Left of the Setting Sun*. Tokyo: Blue Ocean Press.

Akibayashi, K. 2002. 'Okinawa Women Act against Military Violence: A Feminist Challenge to Militarism', unpublished doctoral dissertation. New York: Teachers College, Columbia University.

Akibayashi, K. and S.Takazato. 2009. 'Okinawa: Women's Struggle for Demilitarization in Catherine Lutz', in C. Lutz (ed.), *The Bases of Empire: Global Struggle Against U.S. Military Posts*. London: Pluto Press.

Brownmiller, S. 1975. *Against Our Will: Men, Women and Rape*. New York: Bantam Books.

Connell, R.W. 1995. *Masculinities: Knowledge, Power and Social Change*. Berkeley, CA:University of California Press.

Commission on Human Security. 2002. 'Introduction to Human Security'. www.humansecurity-chs.org/intro/index.html.

Cook, S. 'Security Council Resolution 1820: A Move to End Sexual Violence in Conflict', *1325 Peace Women E-News*, issue 102. June 2008. 11 June 2009. www.peacewomen.org/un/sc/Open_Debates/Sexual_Violence08/Peace WomenAnalysis.pdf.

Gabe, M. 2000. *Okinawa Henkan to wa Nandattanoka* (What Did the Reversion of Okinawa Mean?). Tokyo: NHK Shuppan.

International Women's Summit. 2000. 'Final Statement'. 2000. Naha, Japan. 25 July.

Johansen, R.C. 1980. *The National Interest and the Human Interest: An Analysis of U.S. Foreign Policy*. Princeton, NJ: Princeton University Press.

Mc Cormack, G. 2007. *Client State: Japan in the American Embrace*. London and New York: Verso.
Minamoto, H. 1995. '*Okinawa no fukai ikidori*'(A Deep Anger of Okinawa), *Agora*, vol. 212(11):112–13.
NGO Forum Peking'95 Okinawa Jikko Iinkai (NGO Forum Beijing '95– Okinawa Committee). 1995. *Dai 4 Kai Sekai Josei Kaigi NGO Peking– Okinawa Unai Hou kokusho* (Fourth World Conference on Women NGO Beijing– Okinawa Unai Report), brochure. Peking, China.
Okinawa ken Chiji Koshits Kichi Taisaku-ka (Military Base Affairs Division, Okinawa Prefectural Government). 2008. 'Okinawa no Beigun Kichi' (US Military Bases in Okinawa). www3.pref.okinawa.jp/site/contents/attach/18016/shiryo1.pdf. Accessed 11 June 2009.
Okinawa Prefectural Government. 2004. 'U.S. Military Issues in Okinawa', brochure.
The Okinawa Times. 2007. '*Ho ku bude kareha zai sampu*' (Agent Orange Used in the Northern Area). 9 July. Evening edition.
Okinawan Women Act against Military Violence (OWAAMV). 1996. 'Okinawa Women's America Peace Caravan', brochure. Okinawa, Japan.
———. 2008. 'Post war US Military Crimes against Women in Okinawa', brochure. Naha, Japan.
Peterson, V.S. 1992. 'Security and Sovereign States: What Is at Stake in Taking Feminism Seriously?', in V.S. Peterson (ed.), *Gendered States: Feminist (Re) Visions of International Relations Theory*, pp. 31–64. Boulder, CO: Lynne Rienner Publishers.
Reardon, B. A. 1998. 'Gender and Global Security: A Feminist Challenge to the United Nations and Peace Research', *Kokusai Kyoryoku Ronnshuu*, vol. 6(1). June 1998.
Research Study Committee of Aircraft Noise Influences to Health. 1998. *Summary of the Second Interim Report of the Field Study on Public Health Around U.S. Bases in Okinawa*. March. www.jca.apc.org/HHK/Stat.Okinawa/PH9803E.html.Accessed 13 March 2010.
Ryukyu Shimpo. 2007. '*Hokubu Kunrenjode Karehazai*'(Agent Orange in the Northern Training Area). 9 July.
Ryukyu Shimpo Sha (ed.). 2004. *Nichibei Chiikyouteino Kangae-kata:Gaimusho Kimitsu Bunsho* (The Interpretation of US–Japan SOFA: Confidential Document of Ministry of Foreign Affairs of Japan). Tokyo: Kobunken.
Security Consultative Committee. 2005. U.S.-Japan Alliance: Realignment and Transformation for the Future. 29 October.
Tickner, J.A. 1992. *Gender in International Relations: Feminist Perspectives on Achieving Global Security*. New York:Columbia University Press.
United Nations. 1995. 'The Platform for Action and the Beijing Declaration', A/CONF.177/20(1995) and A/CONF.177/20/Add.1.15 September.
United Nations Development Programme (UNDP). 1994. *Human Development Report: New Dimensions of Human Security*. London: Oxford University Press.

United States-Japan Security Consultative Committee. 2006. 'United States-Japan Security Consultative Committee Document: United States-Japan Roadmap for Realignment Implementation.' 1 May. www.mofa.go.jp/region/n-america/us/security/scc/doc0605.html.Accessed 13 March 2010.

Women's Caucus for Gender Justice. 2000. 'Public Hearing on Crimes against Women in Recent Wars and Conflicts: A Compilation of Testimonies', brochure. Tokyo. 11 December.

Wright, A. 2008a. 'Sexual Assault in the Military: A DoD Cover-Up?', *Truthout*. www.truthout.org/article/sexual-assault-military-a-dod-cover-up. Posted 1 August 2008. Accessed 19 December 2008.

———. 2008b. 'US Military Keeping Secrets about Female Soldiers'"Suicides"?', *Truthout*. www.truthdig.com/report/item/20080826_us_military_keeping_secrets_about_female_soldiers_suicides/.Posted 26 August. Accessed 19 December 2008.

3 Human security and intersectional oppressions
Women in South Africa

Bernedette Muthien

Introduction

As a South African peace and gender researcher and human rights professional, I have come, as have many of my international colleagues, to question the prevailing notions of security as it is embedded in the nation-state paradigm. Being a country only recently governed under a democratic state that has finally enfranchised its African citizens, the South African experience teaches us much about the limits of this paradigm and the possibilities that may be found with the notion of human security. This article reflects that experience as it critically interrogates constructions of security generically, and human security specifically, in relation to women and notions of women's security. The constructs of national security and human security will be critiqued, questioning whose interests these constructs serve and how they are specifically gendered (and class-based) and neglect issues relevant to women specifically and other marginalized members of the international community.

Johan Galtung's (1996) triangular model of violence, with its antithesis, peace, will be examined in order to explicate violence generically, which will lead to an examination of gender-based violence more specifically, premised on a deconstruction of patriarchal ideology, deemed by the authors of this volume to be the source of human insecurity.

It will also propose possibilities that nonviolence offers to rethink peace and human security activisms, as exemplified by the work of Mahatma Gandhi and his South African granddaughter Ela Gandhi, Martin Luther King Jr, Nelson Mandela, Vera Brittain, Olive Schreiner, Wangari Maathai, Jody Williams, Shirin Ebadi, the Women's International League for Peace and Freedom (WILPF) and indeed this volume's Betty Reardon and Asha Hans, among a great many others.

State-centred security concerns itself with armies, guns and war, and it excludes people's basic needs. This article argues that the imperatives for peace and human security are nonviolence and justice.

Security as a contested and gendered terrain

What is security for women? In most cases it is perceived within the circumstances of women's daily lives. At workshops in South Africa, grassroots women identified their need for spouses or partners to be faithful and monogamous, especially in context of sexually transmitted illnesses that are fatal if left untreated. Given the high rate of generic societal violence, they also requested more mortuary vans and ambulances as well as safe passage for these critical services in gang-ridden marginalized communities. These women specifically called for an end to violence, an end to the gangsterism that plagues their communities, and critically, given the pervasiveness of gender-based violence in South Africa, an end to violence against women and children.

A well-known study on violence against women in metropolitan South Africa found that almost 60 per cent of women felt 'very unsafe' while walking in their own neighbourhoods at night, with only 5 per cent of women feeling 'very safe' in their neighbourhoods at night (Bollen, Artz, Vetten and Louw 1999: 75, 78). The alarming statistics on violence against women illustrate that a lack of women's security affects the entire Southern Africa region. Here we see the fact that women on the ground in South Africa, as in most regions of the world, experience insecurity directly, and that conditions of violence are generally ignored by security scholars and policymakers or are deemed to be unrelated to larger issues of national security.

Even the scholarly fields of security and peace studies have been dominated by men and men's interests, particularly their emphasis on armaments and war as areas of research. As with most fields of study, women's interests and needs have been largely neglected and ignored. Only in recent decades have feminist peace researchers finally been given a hearing in the scholarly discourses on security, peace and justice.

Feminists raised their challenge to peace research and peace studies in the same years that the concept of security itself became a matter of theoretical and political contestation (viz. Brock Utne, Betty Reardon, Dorothy Dinnerstein). Barry Buzan (1983) recognized security as an underdeveloped and contested concept. Buzan drew critical conceptual distinctions between defence and security, individual and national security, national and international security, violent means

Human security and intersectional oppressions 61

and peaceful ends. He applied his concept across a range of military, political, economic and social sectors. According to Buzan (ibid: 20), the national security problem is a systemic security problem in which individuals, states and the system all play a part. Thus Buzan (ibid: 187) anticipated the conceptual discussions that produced the notion of human security in proposing the holistic notion of systemic security so that the national security problem defines itself as much in economic, political and social terms as in military ones.

Political discussions of security have long centred mainly on issues of national security. So security has tended to be defined in terms of the nation state. Thus, the notion of national security, emanating predominantly from the field of strategic studies, is dominated by the neorealist mode of thought,[1] with its focus on power and institutions of power, especially the military. Neorealist thought and notions of the state derive from Thomas Hobbes ([1651] 1952). His infamous postulate that life in a state of nature is 'nasty, brutish and short' epitomizes the neorealist hypothesis of an international state system of anarchy. Classical American neorealist theorists, especially E. H. Carr (1939), Hans Morgenthau (1948) and Kenneth Waltz (1954, 1979) built on the Hobbesian notion of an anarchic state system, an argument that has rationalized the excessive military preparedness of the present state system. Reacting to this position, Maxi Schoeman (1998: 7, 22–23), who has extensively researched women's security in Southern Africa, criticizes Waltz in particular for 'de-historicizing' the international state system and assuming its 'inevitability, rather than admitting that it is a human construct and a product of a specific era and context'.

The British academic Hedley Bull (1977) tried to theorize a form of anarchy characterized by at least some interdependence and cooperation in his writings on an 'international society' of states. Bull's key contention centres on his notion of 'society' versus that of the traditional, more anarchic system, thus arguably placing his thinking between neoliberal[2] and neorealist thought. Issues about what constitutes cooperation, and whose interests it serves, can be derived from rudimentary studies of the world system's theory of Immanuel Wallerstein (1979). More recent critical theory is fundamentally concerned with historicizing the status quo and seeking structural transformation. The inclination toward structural change is to some degree due to raising the question of whose interests are served by the international state security system, a central component of feminist critiques.

What is clear throughout this theoretical work is that armed force and interstate violence are uncontested given the international security system in which each nation state independently pursues its own national security without regard, and often to the detriment of, the security of other states and peoples. When security alliances are formed, the same others-be-damned attitude toward those outside the alliance also obtains.

This traditional notion of national security, in terms of armies, guns and war, emphasizes the state as both the primary actor and the primary level of analysis. Narrow state-centrism excludes other important actors and levels of analyses, including individuals and groups (ethnicities and religious groupings, political and ideological groups, and non-state actors like corporate mercenaries and international non-governmental organizations [INGOs]), as well as other institutions (e.g. transnational corporations [TNCs] and multi-national corporations [MNCs], international financial institutions [IFIs] such as the World Bank, as well as the global arms trade – from manufacturers to marketers to purchasers). The modern move away from interstate war to intrastate conflict, in particular, stresses the importance of group and institutional analyses – for example, the conflict especially in central Africa involves regional, linguistic, economic group, state and international dimensions. It involves various political and military groups, especially diamond and oil TNCs, as well as other African states, notably Angola, Namibia, Rwanda, Uganda, Zimbabwe, as well as non-African states, such as Belgium, France and the United States. It includes non-state actors, such as INGOs, mercenaries, arms and other suppliers, locally and internationally.

The skewed focus on the state usually excludes the worst affected, women and children, especially in rural areas where women and girls are the ones who have to seek fresh water and wood for fuel, which exposes them to landmines (and sexual violence). Hence the irony of men who plant landmines to deter other men but which largely kill and maim women and children trying to survive during and after conflicts, another example of how the marginalized and vulnerable are deemed expendable under the present security system.

The traditional definition of security also emphasizes protection from harm for citizens of a country within national boundaries. National boundaries in Africa are colonial legacies, often arbitrary, and variously disputed – for example, the historic Kasikili/Sedudu Island conflict between Namibia and Botswana. Even Lake Malawi and its natural resources are cause for claims by Tanzania against Malawi. Sovereignty of borders is often bestowed, with little or no consultation, and with little regard by the international community to the impact on the inhabitants within the borders. This situation is made possible by the 'othering' and objectification of African peoples. As women are objectified under patriarchy, colonialism rationalized the theft of lands by claiming the inferiority of the colonized. Even within the colonial mind and structures, women are considered as less important than all others. Eritrea, for example, is deemed a sovereign state after its secession from Ethiopia, while Somaliland, where women contributed significantly to brokering peace, is not officially recognized.

The idea of protection from harm for citizens is narrowly defined and effectively means protection from foreign attack but does not preclude offensive measures deemed in the interests of citizens and state. Examples are South Africa and Botswana's military intervention in Lesotho during 1998 as well as Namibia's historic incursions into Angola against UNITA. So, too, the traditional definition of harm does not include other aspects of safety, security or wellbeing, including the environment, basic needs (e.g. food and housing), identity and dignity. A more holistic definition of protection from harm would mean more than the traditional protection from war and invasion by foreign armies. It would mean, to name a few examples, protection from hunger, protection from poverty, protection from sexual assault for women, children, some men and gender non-conforming people. In short, it would mean protections within the realms designated to comprise the foundations of human security.

The traditional national security definition of protection from harm refers to a state-level notion of harm and does not protect citizens from homelessness, illiteracy and unemployment. Nor does it protect citizens' fundamental human rights, as enshrined in the South African Constitution, to be free of discrimination on the grounds of race, class, gender, spirituality or sexuality. Negative peace, or the absence of war, conforms to traditional definitions of security in general and traditional protection from harm in particular. Positive peace, on the other hand, means both negative peace and the realization of even the most basic of social justice needs. As such, positive peace is also a conceptual antecedent to human security.

Traditional notions of security are based on conventional (though flawed) distinctions between public and private spheres. Community activists[3] assert that the state has traditionally been concerned with the male-dominated public realm. Thus, issues outside of the public realm, including domestic violence, job discrimination and the status of women, have not been viewed as concerns of national security. This public-private conceptual dichotomy, as well as the aforementioned male-dominated policymaking, are factors that have contributed to the exclusion of women's perspectives and experience, resulting in the systematic and global insecurity suffered by women.

64 Bernedette Muthien

A well-respected approach to peace that contests the national security model is proposed by Johan Galtung, whose theory matured from radical analyses of (under) development initiated in the 1960s into a groundbreaking conceptual scheme that became a core aspect of peace studies during the 1990s. Based on the work of other researchers (especially the work of Robert Johansen of the Peace Studies Program at Notre Dame [1975–96]) over two decades, Galtung (1996) took the debate into new realms of understanding the requirements for peace when he proposed what some have come to call a human security model. This model is taken into account when Betty Reardon asserts that human security should focus on environmental security, basic needs, issues of dignity and identity and, finally, protection from harm in an integrated, holistic framework for analysis and policymaking.

Galtung's paradigm is designed to provide a more holistic comprehensive definition of security and protection from *all* forms of harm. These include indirect or structural, cultural and direct or personal, and their respective antitheses, as postulated in Galtung's (1996) model. Structural violence (with its antithesis, structural peace) refers to, for example, discrimination based on class, race or gender, violence embedded in the very structure of society. Personal or direct violence implies a direct verbal or physical attack of one person on another. Cultural violence 'serves to legitimize direct and structural violence' (Galtung 1996: 31), as shown in Figure 3.1.

Although violence against women is direct and personal (e.g. a man assaults a woman) it also embodies structural sexism and genocide,

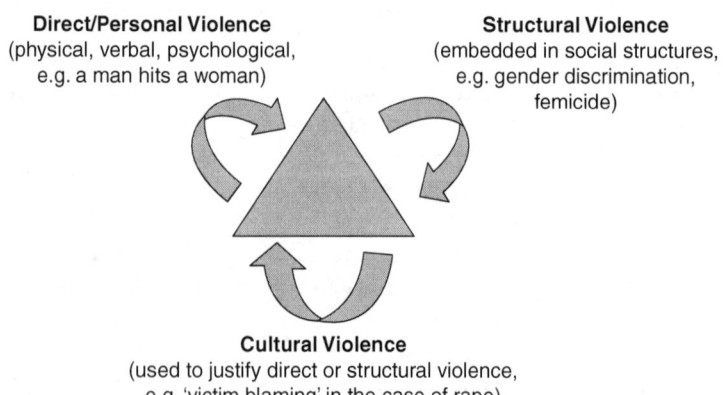

Figure 3.1 Johan Galtung's (1996) triangular model of violence, with its antithesis, peace (image by the author)

as well as cultural legitimization, which seeks its continuous replication. A subtle example of structural violence in this instance would be the victim blaming that occurs in cases of sexism and racism, which is institutionalized in law and legal practice. More pronounced forms include common practices which are sometimes codified in law, such as female genital mutilation, forced child brides and femicide/infanticide. In relation to cultural violence, it is evident, for example, when survivors internalize their personal and systemic brutalization. Cultural violence also relates to the sexist attitudes that keep women's opportunities limited.

The antithesis of violence, of course, is peace,[4] and the three forms of violence outlined earlier would also have corresponding forms of peace. If one eliminates physical assault (including physical forms of gender-based violence) one will experience personal/direct peace. If one eliminates structural violence (including sexism, racism and homophobia) and transforms institutions appropriately, one will experience structural peace. And if one eradicates cultural violence (including ways of thinking and being), one will experience cultural peace.

These three forms of violence and their antithesis, peace, comprise systems of violence and peace in which each form is interrelated with all the others. None can be isolated from the other. For example, one cannot eliminate gender-based violence without transforming institutions as well as ways of thinking and being. And if one changes cultures of violence into cultures of balance and harmony in line with egalitarian societies, one will necessarily eliminate gender-based violence because there will no longer be polar opposites, distrust and devaluation of others.

The Galtung paradigm comprises a holistic framework for peace and human security. Reactively, human security would include the absence of physical violence, or negative peace. But proactively, human security involves establishing mechanisms (policies and structures) that will ensure that individuals and communities enjoy personal, structural and cultural security – in other words, positive peace.

Within this paradigm, we might raise such questions as what comprises security and how it is constructed. The gender imperative, argued in this volume to be essential to human security, raises the question of how these constructions exclude women and other marginalized groups (e.g. indigenous peoples). Contributors to this collection, viewing present structures as essentially patriarchal, respond that the same structures that perpetuate war militate against the wellbeing of women, the poor and the marginalized, denying them access to the fundamental sources of human security.

Reardon, as outlined in her introduction to this collection, speaks of four sources of human security: a sustainable environment, the meeting of basic needs (e.g. food and housing), respect for identity and dignity and, finally, protection from harm. She asserts that the human security of groups and individuals derives from an expectation of well-being denied to women and others whom patriarchy consigns to continual and systematic vulnerability. A human security paradigm would seek to overcome systemic vulnerability.

Aspects of notions of security as based in positive peace and overcoming vulnerability can be seen in the departure from traditional practice of the post-Apartheid South African National Defence Force (SANDF), which, with assistance from civil society during the late 1990s, drafted their security legislation in a radically new way. They redefined security in terms of development and acknowledged the absence of an external aggressor and the very real threat of poverty to internal stability.

> In the new South Africa national security is no longer viewed as a predominantly military and police problem. It has been broadened to incorporate political, economic, social and environmental matters. At the heart of this new approach is a paramount concern with the security of people.
> (Department of Defence, Defence in Democracy: White Paper on National Defence for the Republic of South Africa, Department of Defence, Pretoria, 1996, page 5)

The significance of such non-military aspects of national security re-entered into the wider security discourse several years later with the publication of *Human Security Now* (2002), the report of the Independent Commission on Human Security chaired by Sadako Ogata of Japan and Amartya Sen of India. The Ogata-Sen report validated much of the human security framework advanced in this volume. However, it does not deal with the issues of the gender critique of militarized security's fundamental incompatibility with human security that this framework asserts. Neither does it deal with all three areas of violence that Galtung addresses.

Among various approaches to human security, I find Galtung's to be the most comprehensive in terms of inclusivity. He painstakingly demonstrates his respect for and desire to include women in his analysis. However, it is precisely the 'phallogocentrism' of generic knowledge and thought which precludes complete transcendence of his own masculine and other subjectivities. The term 'phallogocentrism' stems from the Greek words *phallos* (phallus) and *logos* (word) or *logy* (discourse) and thus implies that traditional (male-stream) knowledge and logic, constructed by men for men, is fundamentally imbued with male bias and will necessarily ignore the inclusion of women or women's perspectives. It follows that universal objectivity, constructed by male theoreticians throughout history, is neither universal nor objective but gendered and specifically male and hence serves particular (male) interests. Think, for example, of the founding fathers of modern democracy and social science: Greek philosophers (male) from Plato to Aristotle and European scholars (male) from Locke to Rousseau. An example closer to home is that of African griots (male), with Senegalese griots' strategic extrusion of Senegal's part in African slavery from their oral history.

Until the advent of the feminist critique of international relations theory, virtually all security theories and policies were essentially phallogocentric. Indeed, feminist critics, such as Barbara Roberts[5] (1942–98), analyzed the masculine fixation with weaponry as symbols and tools of power as phallogocentric (or 'machothink'). Reardon has argued that castration anxiety is in part responsible for the reluctance of nation states to disarm. Indeed, some form of masculinism prevails throughout the realms of political theory and practice and most Western thought in which the dominant paradigm was formed (1985).

Confucius, Gautama, Jesus and Muhammad were all male, too. The origins of the two major contemporary structures of authority and power, politics and religion, masculine in origin and worldview, have led us to prevailing masculinist notions of security. In spite of the efforts of some male theorists and policymakers to counter patriarchal security models, a system of security continues to prevail that seems incapable of even seeing women as human, and even less so, being sensitive to women's views and needs. To the detriment of the vulnerable, national security gives little or no priority to elements of human security as perceived by the women of Jordan, Okinawa, the Pacific Islands, Ethiopia, the borders of India and Pakistan or Darfur or indeed South Africa, many of whom are given voice in this collection. National security, however, seems deaf to, for example, the voices of grassroots women in Southern Africa who define security as

1   more than individual, and including families and communities;
2   more than physical, and including economics and health;
3   depending on gender justice; and
4   including the quotidian or everyday (from access to food to freedom from sexual assault).

Such a concept derives from women's lived experiences in all the realms of violence defined by Galtung but most especially from the personal, physical and sexual violence that most undermines their security.

During October 2017, the South African Police Services (SAPS) released the latest crime statistics of the preceding year (1 April 2016 to 31 March 2017). It showed that sexual offences decreased from 51,895 in the previous year to 49,660 in the year of the report. Included in the legal definition of sexual assault are rape, incest, bestiality, statutory rape and sexual grooming of children, among others. The majority of sexual offences are rape, of women, children and the gender non-conforming, by men. This amounts to 136 sexual assaults per day or five to six sexual assaults every hour in the country. Noting global and domestic incidence of under-reporting of especially sexual assault, one can extrapolate that many more unreported sexual assaults occur than that reported by the police. The rape statistic itself amounted to 39,828 for 2016–2017, down from 41,503 for 2015–2016. This is a decrease of 71.3 per 100,000 people compared with the previous year's 75.5. Thus, 109 rapes per day or four to five rapes every hour in South Africa are recorded by the police but are obviously much higher in reality. So, too, in South Africa a woman is murdered by her male partner every six hours (Mathews, Abrahams, Vetten, L Merwe and Jewkes 2004). This can be compared with developed countries like Belgium, Germany, Sweden and the United States, where at least 30 per cent of women are battered by their male partners. All forms of violence against women are asserted by various authors as the means of perpetuating women's secondary and submissive position in a patriarchal world. Violence against women has been the basis of a worldwide movement to criminalize and eliminate violence. The achievement of that goal, the eradication of violence against women, is essential to the achievement of human security.

Gender violence is at genocidal levels

What unites all women, across the world, in every village and every city? Gender discrimination, gender violence and gender oppression. This analysis is supported by international cross-country studies of gender-based violence (GBV) reported by Amnesty International[6] and the World Health Organization (WHO),[7] respectively, clearly showing that gender violence is pervasive in almost all societies across the world.

The 2002 WHO study on violence and health reports,

> In 48 population-based surveys from around the world, *between 10 and 69 per cent of women reported being physically assaulted by an intimate male partner* at some point in their lives. For many of these women, physical assault was not an isolated event but part of a continuing pattern of abusive behaviour . . . Data from a wide range of countries suggest that partner violence accounts for a significant number of deaths by murder among women. Studies from Australia, Canada, Israel, South Africa and the United States of America show that *40–70 per cent of female murder victims were killed by their husbands or boyfriends*, frequently in the context of an ongoing abusive relationship. This contrasts starkly with the situation of male murder victims. In the United States, for example, only 4 per cent of men murdered between 1976 and 1996 were killed by their wives, ex-wives or girlfriends.
> (2002: 114, 118, emphasis added)

Amnesty International's Facts and Figures report[8] of 2004 asserts that at least one-third of all women will experience some form of violence, and that *20 per cent of all women (one in five) are rape or attempted rape survivors*. Some of the statistics in this report include the following:

> At least one in every three women, or *up to one billion women*, have been beaten, coerced into sex, or otherwise abused in their lifetimes. Usually, the abuser is a member of her own family or someone known to her (Heise, M. Ellsberg, Gottemoeller 1999). Up to 47 per cent of women report that their first sexual intercourse was forced (WHO 2002). Up to 70 per cent of female murder victims are killed by their male partners.
> (WHO 2002; emphasis added)

The *Oxford English Reference Dictionary* (1996) defines 'genocide' as 'the mass extermination of human beings, esp. of a particular race or nation'. The Medical Research Council's 2004 policy brief on intimate homicide, or femicide, offers stark statistics: 'a woman is killed by her intimate partner in South Africa every six hours' (2004: 4). At least one woman is *murdered* every six hours entirely because she is a woman. There is a war being waged against our bodies and souls, and we are dying in droves. Just as the murders of Steve Biko and countless other activists were crucial for the survival of apartheid, and Patrice Lumumba's for global capital, so, too, the mutilation and murder of women daily, in every village and town in the world, serves to support hetero-patriarchy. As does our silence about this gross injustice, our deliberate ignorance of defaced bodies and serrated vaginas and anuses, infants' abdominal cavities destroyed by rape that is as old as patriarchy itself.

Amnesty International, in the previously mentioned report, estimates that at least 2 per cent of all girl babies born are subject 'to gender-selective abortion or died in infancy due to neglect' – that is, two in every 100 girl babies are deliberately killed because they are girls. Lloyd deMause draws his conclusion of the pervasiveness of child abuse from 'a lifetime of psycho-historical study of childhood and society'.

> The history of humanity is founded upon the abuse of children. Just as family therapists today find that child abuse often functions to hold families together as a way of solving their emotional problems, so, too, the routine assault of children has been society's most effective way of maintaining its collective emotional homeostasis. Most historical families once practiced infanticide, erotic beating and incest. Most states sacrificed and mutilated their children to relieve the guilt of adults. Even today, we continue to arrange the daily killing, maiming, molestation and starvation of children through our social, military and economic activities.
>
> (1998)

In his article deMause summarizes his 'evidence of why child abuse has been humanity's most powerful and most successful ritual, why it has been the cause of war and social violence, and why the eradication of child abuse and neglect is the most important social task we face today' (1998). The same applies to all forms of gender-based violence against women *and* children and against other marginalized people like homosexual, bisexual or gender non-conforming people[9] as well as against some men, especially in prisons and gangs and during formal conflicts.

Thus, the routine daily violence against *all* women and girls, children and some men prop up hetero-patriarchy as much as generic violence supports generic oppressions. A glaring question remains: If apartheid was overcome more than two decades ago, if we are moving toward an era of neoliberal democracies, where fascism and other recent past totalitarianisms are fading memories, why then has gender-based violence persisted for thousands of years? The answer: because heteropatriarchy survives, and GBV is critical to its survival; the oppression of one-half of human kind over the other ensures patriarchy's continuous replication.

To understand gender-based violence and why it happens, one has to understand violence and why violence happens. As a starting point, the following working definition of 'violence' is offered: *the harmful action or actions of one person or group against another person or group*. Looking at this definition, one can see that it speaks of one person or group versus or against another person or group. Us and Them. Us versus Them. Polar opposites. Binary oppositions, produced by a process of 'othering'.

The construction of binary oppositions may stem from a particular identity formation, the ways in which people are taught to view themselves and the world. The conventional modern formation of identity is premised on an understanding of 'I am because I am not'. So one can find such statements as 'I am female because I am not male'; 'I am black because I am not white'; 'I am African because I am not European or North American'. This construction of self fundamentally needs an 'other' against which to measure itself and its value. In a characteristically competitive environment, if the self is to succeed and to be valued, it needs to transcend or overpower the other, and if the self is to be valued and triumph, the other of necessity needs to be devalued. This process can be termed 'othering'.

Such identity construction premised on polarity or 'othering' fosters conflict over access to and control of resources. In this way power also becomes a resource, as in 'power to' and 'power over'. This belief system, based on 'I am because I have and you don't', can be juxtaposed with one in which there is a more equitable distribution of resources – that is, a more 'diffuse' form of power. Power as a relation between people became a contest over resources because it is premised on a flawed belief system centred on othering and the devaluation of the other.

Our understanding of the origins of othering and oppressions centres on the explication of two fundamental belief systems. Riane Eisler (1995), based on the work of anthropologist Marija Gimbutas, posits two models, the *partnership* model and the *dominator* model. When Eisler refers to the dominator model, she means 'patriarchy – the ranking of one-half of humanity over the other'. She describes the partnership model, on the other hand, as one in which social relations are primarily based on the principle of linking rather than ranking.

> In this model – beginning with the most fundamental difference in our species, between male and female – diversity is not equated with either inferiority or superiority.
>
> (1995: xvii)

Eisler continues to argue that the dominator model is based on domination and force and the power to take life (death, killing) rather than on the power to give life (birth) as in the partnership model, where actualization and maximization of individuals' potential is primordial.

Western and modern thinking and beliefs are premised on the dominator model. Societies based on this paradigm are intrinsically unequal, hierarchical and oppressive. A historical precedent is found in the shift in ancient Aztec society from partnership to dominator models. More recently, modern European imperialism, which constructed the present state system in Africa, provides further examples.

Significantly, the discourses of colonization similarly operate on a system of binary oppositions, such as female-male, black-white, infidel-believer or barbarity-civilization. This particular way of constructing personal and group identity fosters conflict rather than cooperation and, by its very nature, leads to violence. Think, for example, of the Hutu and Tutsi in the Great Lakes or any conflict in which enemy images compel the conflicting parties to violence.

However, while one bears in mind that colonization of Africa engendered much violence, one must also not forget that some African forebears traded in other Africans, as the histories of slavery evince. Some Africans, who operated on the construct of 'I am because I am not', also oppressed and waged wars against their kinsfolk whom they felt threatened by and whose property they wished to confiscate, practices which were exploited and exacerbated by colonization and which continue to this day. There are probably no modern societies in which exclusion and exploitation of others is absent; none without most or all of the three forms of violence in the Galtung paradigm; none without gender-based violence.

According to the Committee on the Elimination of Discrimination against Women (General Recommendation No. 12), gender-based violence is defined as

> violence that is directed against a woman because she is a woman, or that affects women disproportionately. It includes acts that

inflict physical, mental or sexual harm or suffering, and threats of such acts, coercion or arbitrary deprivation of liberty.

The Declaration on the Elimination of Violence against Women notes three key spheres in which gender-based violence may occur or which may perpetuate and/or condone such violence: the family, the community and the state. December Green adds one further site of gender-based violence, the economy. The concept of gender-based violence should accordingly be broadened to also include the notion of economic abuse, which has been defined in the South African Domestic Violence Act (1998) to include 'the unreasonable deprivation of economic or financial resources or the unreasonable disposal of household effects in which the victim/survivor has an interest'.

Gender-based violence therefore occurs through the act of *being gendered*. Through the kinds of identity construction where the self cannot exist without the other, and where the self cannot be valued without devaluing the other, women are valued as less than men. (It may be useful to note that men, too, get raped, especially during times of conflict. This is because these more vulnerable men are transformed into the other and are so feminized or turned into surrogate women. This happens in prisons throughout the world, in gangs and in areas of conflict. So, too, LGBTQI and gender non-conforming people are raped.)

The preceding CEDAW definition focuses on women as the subjects of gender-based violence; however, it should be recognized that such violence also affects men, not only as potential victims but also when they act as *perpetrators*.

It is ironic that the dominator model, and the ways in which it articulates itself in the construction of contemporary societies, brutalizes everyone, even the dominant or oppressor. If one is taught violence, control and domination as a way of life, one becomes brutalized by it on all sides of the equation. In this way even oppressors are victimized by the system and by their own violent behaviours (whether physical, institutional and/or cultural) because they cannot perceive of a more harmonious and compassionate existence. This is most readily evident in cases of family violence, especially in intensely patriarchal contexts where the role of father and provider turns on itself when the patriarch murders the entire family he is meant to protect. So, too, when fathers rape daughters as an expression of their right of ownership over female offspring. It is also commonly known that a large proportion of perpetrators of incest are themselves survivors of such violence. The same can be said about war, where no party involved in the conflict is left unscathed by the violence, murder and carnage.

Violence, murder and rape exact a toll on the psyche of both perpetrator and survivor/victim, and everyone is (re-) brutalized in the process, even spectators through vicarious trauma, as those working to combat gender-based violence will attest. As Jane Bennett puts it.

> Both women and men are vulnerable to the way dominant norms of gender relation, within their contexts, are working. Within South Africa, men are as likely to become blunt assailants of women (and often, of men), as women are to become victims of sexual abuse, domestic battery, economic abuse, and incest. Clearly, those who actively assault retain responsibility for their violence – that is a matter of principle and law. But the challenge for South Africans committed to the transformation of oppressive social norms is to untangle both 'victim' and 'perpetrator' from their terrible interlock of violence, no matter how shocking the 'perpetration' 'or how resonant the 'victimhood/survivorship'.
>
> (2000: 4)

Gender-based violence, as is commonly known, is not about sex or conflict. It is about control and power, in keeping with the dominator model. Vicky Randall asserts that 'if woman is associated with nature as opposed to culture, and culture is compelled to maintain itself, it follows that culture will devalue the nature it seeks to transcend, and hence man will subordinate woman' (1982: 23).

Gender-based violence is fundamentally premised on the ideology of male control over women's productive and reproductive powers, of male control over women's skills and resources and especially of control over our power to produce future generations of producers. It is also about male control over women's sexuality, which is the key aspect of reproductive power.

Women's productive powers include agricultural labour, wage labour in domestic service and other industries, as well as the informal sector (e.g. selling goods for small profits). Women's reproductive power centres on their ability to give birth and raise children, children who constitute the next generation of producers. Hence this particular function is of critical importance to patriarchy, and control of not only the present productive capacity but also that of future generations, too, is very important.

As consumers, women buy and use commodities in the home. Hence women are also caught up in the endlessly repetitive task of using (if not always producing) and reproducing (by baking, cooking, etc.) the commodity, and they are at least equally alienated from the product. Women also support the production process, apart from their 'invaluable' roles as consumers, through their domestic work, thus freeing men for labour in the production process and the public sphere. So, too, women reproduce the labour force by bearing the next generation of workers (and consumers or surplus accumulators).

A critical psychological dimension of the control of women's sexuality is male insecurity about the origins of their children. Women become impregnated, and without complex and expensive medical tests, a man will never know certainly whether he is the actual father of his female partner's children. This is prominent in male anxiety over and control of female sexuality. But far more fundamental in this dominator model is the need to limit women's mobility and choice to ensure their consistent producing and reproducing (of future generations of producers, reproducers and surplus accumulators).

So, too, with the kind of identity formation discussed earlier of self-other: with women devalued as lesser beings than men, women's sexuality is also devalued and of less consequence than that of men.

According to some writers, there are four clear indicators of gender-based violence. In societies where these circumstances prevail, gender-based violence is more likely to occur and/or to occur in more severe forms. The indicators are

1   economic inequality;
2   existing patterns of using physical violence to resolve conflicts;
3   male authority and control over decision-making (and excluding women from this process); and
4   restrictions on women's ability to leave the family setting.

All four indicators fit in with the dominator model, from inequality (economic and other forms), employing violence (physical, structural and cultural) as conflict resolution methods, male control over women and others to restrictions on women's (and others') mobility and freedom. In this sense, because violence generically, and gender-based violence specifically, function on the three axes of Galtung's triangle of violence-peace (personal or direct or physical, structural or institutional, and cultural), it is imperative that attention be paid to factors that exacerbate and contribute to violence, from issues of development and poverty to HIV and AIDS. Hence even the International Monetary Fund's Structural Adjustment Programmes, or SAPs (with decreased state spending on social security), contribute to gender-based violence, as Heidi Hudson (1998: 70) has shown in Zimbabwe, where the first two years of the introduction of SAPs led to health spending being cut by a third and the maternal mortality rate (a form of gender-based violence) doubled.

Gender-based violence, the most widespread and egregious threat to the human security of women and others, is a painful symptom of the dominator model and is, additionally, a major mechanism for the perpetuation of patriarchy. It is the most powerful argument for engendering security.

Rethinking transformation: realizing justice without violence and armed force

Among other transformative changes, engendering security will of necessity involve changes in the ways we think about the world and such issues as national and human security. Existing ways of thinking within the prevailing patriarchies are too often premised on polarity, the kind of thinking and activisms that engenders conflict rather than cooperation and which prohibits or inhibits efforts to seek true transformative solutions for social change.

Even social activism can be viewed as inherently conflictual and adversarial when two sets of 'enemies' square off in battle, with neither side able to claim victory without defeat of the other – in other words, a perpetuation of the dominator model which, by its very nature, perpetuates violence in a continuous cycle, as evinced by the current protracted conflict between Israel and Palestine. The emergence of active nonviolence as an effective strategy through which to struggle for structural and institutional change offers a practical alternative to violence for achieving political ends. Mohandas (Mahatma) Gandhi's concept of satyagraha (truth-force),[10] in which a non-violent mass campaign of non-compliance is waged, was originally conceptualized as an alternative to the idea of 'passive resistance', which implies passivity and victimhood over agency and action. Instead, *satyagraha* is designed as not merely an alternative to violence or force but as superior to it.[11] In the words of Geoffrey Ashe,

> The Satyagrahi – in theory – not only consents to suffer at the wrongdoer's hands, but conquers through suffering . . . Yet his [sic] victory is not the opponent's defeat. It is the opponent's conversion . . . Victory does not mean that one side triumphs at the other's expense, but that both sides are reconciled in a new harmony, with the Wrong cancelled . . . Gandhi, British-conditioned, believed in the reign of law as a moral concept. But – he insisted – some laws can and should be broken, in the name of a higher law with which they conflict.
>
> (1968: 101)

This expression of Gandhi's satyagraha is certainly in keeping with a partnership model and strategies appropriate to the movement for human security. Nelson Mandela, the first president of a democratic South Africa since 1994, transitioned from an adversarial position during the 1960s, with the formation of the African National Congress' (ANC) military wing, Umkhonto we Sizwe (MK or Spear of the Nation), to a philosophical and political perspective perfectly typical of the partnership model more latterly during his 27 years of imprisonment by the apartheid regime. Since the 1980s, Mandela consistently sought reconciliation through dialogue and negotiation with his erstwhile oppressors, eventually leading to a government of national unity based on proportional representation, including the former apartheid leader as one of two deputy presidents, and senior cabinet positions for leaders of opposition parties, in the first democratic government of national unity of 1994.

Mandela's selfless desire to seek alternatives to apartheid without wreaking vengeance on perpetrators of brutality led him to a search for common ground, reconciliation and nation building across ethnicities. Thus, both Gandhi and Mandela embody the principles of partnership, and both have proven to be formidable activists in the struggles for equity, justice and peace. Both viewed human rights through the prism of the partnership model, which allows for more creative ways of including human rights in activisms.

A key activist who historically embodied the principles of the partnership model in her struggle for justice and peace was Aung San Suu Kyi, who quoted her father during a speech to a mass rally during 1988: 'Democracy is the only ideology which is consistent with freedom. It is also an ideology that promotes and strengthens peace. It is therefore the only ideology we should aim for' (1991: 200).

Aung San Suu Kyi's methods of resistance included numerous hunger strikes while unlawfully imprisoned for 21 years (15 years under house arrest) by the military dictatorship in Burma. Her struggle for human rights was firmly located in the principles of democracy, non-violence and collective discipline, as Philip Kreager summarizes in Aung San Suu Kyi's book:

> These principles reflect the inspiration which Aung San Suu Kyi derived from her study and reflection on Gandhi's philosophy and practice of non-violent civil disobedience . . . Under such severe pressures [imprisoned, killed or driven into hiding], and against tremendous odds, Aung San Suu Kyi's reasoned insistence on the sole legitimacy of non-violent means and the priority of human

rights has proven the only enduring answer: by her example, and her prevention of bloodshed, she was able to establish a real alternative for the people, who otherwise face only submission.

(1991: 287, 288)

Aung San Suu Kyi also modeled her activism on the ideas espoused by Martin Luther King. Firmly rooted in the intrinsic egalitarianism of Buddhism, she noted the absence of hierarchical structures in pre-colonial Burmese society. She is a Nobel Peace Laureate (1991), along with other notable activists, such as South Africa's Albert Luthuli, Desmond Tutu and Nelson Mandela. However, once elected as president, Suu Kyi's mismanagement of the abuse of the Rohingya people in Burma has severely tarnished her contemporary reputation as a non-violent leader.

More quotidian examples are ordinary African women recorded throughout colonial history and since, in different African countries, who demonstrated by using what few instruments of resistance they had at their disposal, notably their bodies, by exposing their bare buttocks and other anatomical parts at police and government administrators. Thus, confronted with institutional violence and oppression, these African women literally put their bodies on the line for liberation and justice, without reciprocal resort to violence.

These examples of non-violent strategies illustrate that activism does not need to be violent in order to be effective. To achieve reconciliation between conflicting parties, one needs a redistribution of power – that is, one party has to voluntarily relinquish some of its power and resources. The dominant party may need to be *forced* to agree to redistributive justice. However, that force does not need to be violent, as argued earlier. We see more and more examples of non-violence being introduced to prevent or mitigate armed violence in cases of international conflict. The Dalai Lama's continued insistence on nonviolence as the main force in the struggle for Tibetan independence, as well as the civil resistance movement for the withdrawal of American military bases in various countries of the world, such as the cases of Okinawa and Guam reported in this volume, all attest to the potential of nonviolence as an alternative to militarization.

Conclusion

Although patriarchy and the dominator model have been around for thousands of years, evidence of societies modeled on partnership and egalitarianism clearly shows that patriarchal rule is not inevitable and that other, more cooperative possibilities do exist. Historical reflections of non-patriarchal societies and periods of rule help support a belief in, and conception of, forms of existence and societies that transcend patriarchal rule.[12]

The key to human security is to move away from the adversarial nature of the prevailing dominator system, with its inherent violence and oppression, and to move toward egalitarian partnership by embracing the timeless values of satyagraha. In the words of Aung San Suu Kyi,

> If a people or a nation can reach their objectives by disciplined and peaceful means, it would be a most honorable and admirable achievement . . . Those who have the greater strength should show restraint and tolerance towards those who have less strength . . . Democracy is an ideology that allows everyone to stand up according to his beliefs. They should not be threatened or endangered . . . Do not because of your greater strength be vengeful towards those who are of weaker strength.
>
> (1991: 201, 204)

This particular historic Suu Kyi quote speaks directly to the majority Buddhist Burmese people who are accused of abusing the minority Rohingya in Burma. It is experiences and sentiments such as these that inform struggles for justice that lead us to believe that a non-violent security system designed to achieve human wellbeing, and the wellbeing of women and other hitherto marginalized peoples, is not only possible but also decidedly necessary.

Notes

1 Maxi Schoeman (1998: 5) acknowledges that 'the literature (attempting to expand the existing narrow scope of Security Studies) is still rather thin to non-existing when it comes to broadening or exploring the agents of security'.
2 Maxi Schoeman (1998: 7), citing Robert Keohane, suggests that one objective of neoliberalism 'is to ensure that the state-system and the capitalist world economy function smoothly in their co-existence by diffusing any conflicts, tensions, or crises that may arise between them'. Hence the need to maintain the international states system, with Hedley Bull's (1977) idea of a loose society of states cooperating to perpetuate the status quo.
3 Interviews, Cape Town, 9–10 January 2000.
4 Conflict, which is not the same as violence, is not necessarily and intrinsically bad and may contribute to creative resolutions if peacefully resolved. All relations, and all societies, will invariably experience conflict at least

some of the time, in part due to difference(s). It is in acknowledging conflict (and differences), and dealing with them constructively and peacefully, that creativity and growth can be fostered.

5 Cf. e.g. Barbara Roberts (1984). Her book, *A Reconstructed World: A Feminist Biography of Gertrude Richardson* (1996), remains a feminist analytical staple.

6 'Making Violence against Women Count', 2004.

7 The WHO's 'World Report on Violence and Health', written by Henriette Jansen, includes two rates for intimate partner violence: 'In 48 population-based surveys from around the world, 10–69 per cent of women reported being physically assaulted by an intimate male partner at some point in their lives. In large national studies, the range is between 10–34 per cent . . . Physical violence in intimate relationships is often accompanied by psychological abuse, and in a third to over a half of cases by sexual violence'.

8 Readily available from their website: www.amnesty.org.

9 Lesbians and gender non-conforming people have been (throughout patriarchal time), and continue to be, raped as an ostensible 'cure' for their apparently aberrant sexualities. Much more ironic is the routine 'curative' rape of gay men. See Muthien (2004) for further discussion on this.

10 The originally Sanskrit and later Hindi word 'satya' simply means truth. A more subtle meaning of 'satya' is supreme consciousness ('Citsvaru'pa' or 'Purusha') or deity/deities/divine. A further complex meaning is mindfulness regarding others' welfare, or compassion and universal love, akin to the Greek 'Agape', love of the divine, others and self, a 'higher' form of love. Thus, truth and mindfulness in service of the greater good.

11 Cf. e.g. Ashe (1968). And one of many of Gandhi's own writings, including 'Civil Disobedience and nonviolence'.

12 Think also of the times when patriarchy did not exist – for example, the time of Amanitare of ancient Nubia (northern Ethiopia/southern Sudan). She was one of several ancient African queens who ruled but was eventually deposed by others hungrier for power (and more violent). Also see Douglas Fry and Graham Kemp's anthologies on 'societies of peace' as well as Amadiume (1997). See also Muthien's master's thesis, 'The KhoeSan & Partnership: Beyond Patriarchy & Violence', which analyzes an extensive list of past and present societies that are egalitarian (social and gender) and non-violent or more peaceful. Heide Goettner-Abendroth's groundbreaking collection, *Societies of Peace*, is also an invaluable resource on gender and social egalitarian societies that are concomitantly more peaceful, as are the scholarly and other books by Barbara Alice Mann of her native Iroquois, whom she characterizes as matriarchal and egalitarian. Many additional resources can be derived on gender and socially egalitarian societies around the world that exist to this day.

References

Amadiume, Ifi. 1997. *Reinventing Africa: Matriarchy, Religion and Culture*. London and New York: Zed Books.

Ashe, Geoffrey. 1968. *Gandhi*. New York: Stein and Day.

Bennett, Jane. 2000. 'Gender-Based Violence in South Africa', in *The African Gender Institute Newsletter*, Vol. 6. Cape Town: University of Cape Town, May.

Betty A. Reardon. 1985. *Sexism and the War System*. New York: Teachers College Press, pp. 34–35.

Bollen, Sandra, Lily Artz, Lisa Vetten and Antoinette Louw. 1999. *Violence against Women in Metropolitan South Africa: A Study on Impact and Service Delivery*, Monograph 41. Pretoria: Institute for Security Studies. September.

Bull, Hedley. 1977. *The Anarchical Society: A Study of Order in World Politics*. New York: Columbia University Press.

Buzan, Barry. 1983. *People, States and Fear: The National Security Problem in International Relations*. Sussex: Wheatsheaf.

Carr, Edward Hallett. 1939. *The Twenty Years' Crisis 1919–1939: An Introduction to the Study of International Relations*. London: Macmillan.

deMause, Lloyd. 1998. 'The History of Child Abuse', *The Journal of Psychohistory*, vol. 25 (3), Winter. https://ritualabuse.us/ritualabuse/articles/the-history-of-child-abuse-lloyd-demause-the-journal-of-psychohistory/ (last accessed 25 May 2018).

Eisler, Riane. 1995. *The Chalice and the Blade: Our History, Our Future*. San Francisco: HarperCollins.

Galtung, Johan. 1996. *Peace by Peaceful Means*. London: Sage Publications.

Gandhi, Mohandas. n.d. 'Civil Disobedience and nonviolence', *The International University Society Reading Course: The Commonwealth Story*, vol. 9: 248–55. Edinburgh: International University Society.

Gimbutas, Marija. 1963. *The Balts*. London: Thames and Hudson.

———. 1982. *Goddesses and Gods of Old Europe*. London: Thames and Hudson.

———. 1989. *The Language of the Goddess*. London: Thames and Hudson.

———. 1991. *The Civilization of the Goddess: The World of Old Europe*. San Francisco, CA: Harper Collins.

Heise, Lori, Mary Ellsberg and Megan Gottemoeller. 1999. 'Ending violence against women'. Report No.: Series L No. 11. Baltimore: Johns Hopkins University School of Public Health; Population Information Program.

Hobbes, Thomas. (1651) 1952. *The Leviathan*. Oxford: Oxford University Press.

Hudson, Heidi. 1998. 'A Feminist Reading of Security in Africa', in *Caring Security in Africa*, Monograph 20. Pretoria: Institute for Security Studies. February.

Mathews, Shanaaz, Naeema Abrahams, Lorna Martin, Lisa Vetten, L van der Merwe and Rachel Jewkes. 2004. 'Every Six Hours a Woman is Killed by her Intimate Partner'. MRC Policy Brief No. 5. June. http://www.csvr.org.za/docs/gender/sixhours.pdf (last accessed 25 May 2018).

Morgenthau, Hans J. 1948. *Politics among Nations: The Struggle for Power and Peace*. New York: Alfred A. Knopf.

Muthien, Bernedette. 2000. 'The Privatisation of War in Southern Africa', paper presented at the conference on 'Demilitarisation and Peacebuilding in Southern Africa', Pretoria. Bonn: International Centre for Conversion (BICC) and Centre for Conflict Resolution (CCR).

Muthien, Bernedette. 2004. "Strategic Interventions: Violence & HIV/AIDS". In Agenda. March 2004.

———. 2008. The KhoeSan & Partnership: Beyond Patriarchy & Violence. Master's thesis. Stellenbosch University. http://scholar.sun.ac.za/handle/10019.1/1879 (last accessed 7 December 2017).

Randall, Vicky. 1982. *Women and Politics*. New York: St Martin's.

Reardon, Betty. 1985. *Sexism and the War System*. Teachers College Press. New York: pp. 34–35.

Roberts, Barbara. 1984. 'The Death of Machothink: Feminist Research and the Transformation of Peace Studies', *Women's Studies International Forum*, vol. 7 (4): 195–200.

———. 1996. *A Reconstructed World: A Feminist Biography*. Montreal: McGill-Queen's University Press.

Schoeman, Maxi. 1998. 'An Exploration of the Link between Security and Development', in H. Solomon and M. Schoeman (eds.), *Security, Development and Gender in Africa*, Institute for Security Studies. Pretoria: Halfway House.

United Nations. 2002. *Human Security Now*. New York: United Nations.

Wallerstein, Immanuel. 1979. *The Capitalist World Economy*. Cambridge: Cambridge University Press.

Waltz, Kenneth. 1954. *Man, the State and War*. New York: Columbia University Press.

———. 1979. *Theory of International Politics*. New York: Random House.

World Health Organisation (WHO). 2002. World report on Violence and Health. Geneva: WHO. URL: http://www.who.int/violence_injury_prevention/violence/world_report/en/introduction.pdf (last accessed 25 May 2018).

Part II
Patriarchal conditioning to violence and human insecurity

4 Challenging the patriarchal national security paradigm

The role of Ethiopian women in peace and security

Mesfin G. Ayele

Introduction

Ethiopia's human security problems are mainly driven by the state's monopoly on violence, imposed by the patriarchal order of suspicion and paranoia under the cover of the protection of national security. This concept of national security emphasizes the security of the state at the expense of the security of individual citizens. When a state focuses on national security, it compromises the security of individuals, particularly women.

Under the agenda of national security, the state dignifies and secures the privilege and status of masculine role performers in the country's politics and military life. Ethiopian society is highly militaristic, hierarchical and patriarchal, like many others in the world. This deep-rooted patriarchy and militarism favours men's values in the political, economic and justice systems as well as in the religious institutions. Although the human security concept stresses that the fulfillment of all types of human rights and human needs are important for security, still the human security problems of women are numerous and sometimes beyond the human security perspectives.

Ethiopian women in particular have various types of security problems because of a masculine state-centric power structure which neglects and marginalizes women from the household to the country level. In a country like Ethiopia where there is no infrastructure for women's in/security analysis, in a country where 'Might is Right', where a state is everything but a provider of citizens' security, where paranoid men depend on their power rather than on people's will, it is difficult to think of security outside of military security. In this circumstance, patriarchy and hierarchy are considered normal and as a result marginalize and subordinate those who do not have power.

Ethiopia is also a multicultural, multi-ethnic and multi-religion society. Even today, in many cultures and religions in Ethiopia, women are considered to be objects, and their social status is very low. Women do not have equal property rights with men across many ethnic cultures in the country. They work long hours (between 13 to 15 hours a day) – the largest amount of time being spent on activities required to feed the family – and are still not considered as productive forces. HIV/AIDS is prevalent among young girls and commercial sex workers. The latter negotiate their livelihoods by selling their bodies in exchange for their survival needs. There is no reproductive healthcare or awareness, education or protection from the spread of HIV/AIDS within the military; no rehabilitation of those women who are exposed to this kind of insecurity; and no children's or maternal healthcare system (Habtamu Wondimu et al. 2004: 12).

Many women in conflict zones are not armed and cannot protect themselves, so they continue to be the main targets and victims of violence. On the one hand, women carry the maximum burden of economic, political and social injustices in the country. On the other, their problems are not addressed as a priority concern of the country simply because they do not have a voice in the decision-making processes.

The historical fact that the country has endured this culture of violence helps to question its concept of the security of its population, especially of women. It also shows the importance of bringing up the human security agenda in the context of Ethiopia. Therefore, this article focuses on the need for women's participation and challenging the existing gender asymmetry and patriarchal power institutions by describing the struggles and roles played by Ethiopian women in striving toward their rights.

Ethiopian women have long challenged the patriarchal system. In recent history, they showed their commitment and ability through participation in the armed struggle. According to a book published in Amharic, by one of the first woman fighters participating in the 17-year civil war (1974–91) (Yewbmar 2008) describes how the liberation groups marginalised women fighters during the struggle and after the fall of the military regime in 1991. Particularly, patriarchy prevailed even in those years of armed struggle. In her experience, the liberation struggle was predominantly controlled by men. Women did not have a decision-making role. Even though some women accomplished many heroic endeavours, participated in the battles and had the capacity and talent for leadership, they were not allowed to participate in the decision-making process conducted under the rubric of class struggle (ibid.: 42). Later the country formulated a new foreign and national security policy, fashioned according to the human security agenda. This policy denounces the old paradigm of suspicion and enmity toward other states and emphasizes the need to focus on domestic problems – for instance, the alleviation of poverty through rapid economic development and the cultivation of a democratic system. From this point of departure, this article will elaborate on the Ethiopian women's experiences in a militarized patriarchal society, their involvement in armed conflicts and liberation struggles and, finally, the human security threats evident in the new national security policy.

National security as a patriarchal paradigm and its effect on human security in Ethiopia

Ethiopia has a long history of statehood in Africa. Throughout this history, it has experienced several outside invasions – from the Egyptians, Ottomans, British, Italians and Somalis (Bahiru 1991). This history of independence battles has been deeply inscribed into the country's collective memory. An example is that every year in March the country celebrates the one-century-old national holiday, marking the Battle of Adwa Victory, in which the Ethiopian army defeated the invading Italian army on 1 March 1896. Ethiopia was the first and only country in Africa that defeated a European colonial power during the 'scramble for Africa', making it the only independent nation in Africa that has never been colonized. Its foundations were built within a patriarchal order of disinformation and distraction. Accordingly, the country's national security policy has been shaped more around suspicion and enmity than around taking opportunities for constructive and cooperative relationships and co-developments (Ministry of Information Press & Audiovisual Department (MIPAD 2002). This outlook resulted in a national security paradigm founded on paranoia and closed-door policies that have had a serious impact on the country's current problems.

The tendency toward oppression resulted from the unchallenged nature of masculine war making and ever-prevalent patriarchy. Any citizen can portray the patriot by demonstrating a deep knowledge of past wars. Ethiopians are proud of their long history of civilization, being the only country never to have been colonized in Africa, and talk about how they became different in African political history. This patriotic sentiment arising from century-old nationalist and militarist propaganda infused into the society through masculine role performance. This patriotic mental set has brought the country nothing but poverty and hunger.

This kind of worldview and paranoia consumed millions of lives over the last decades in the name of the protection of the *motherland*. According to Africa Watch reports, Ethiopia is said to be the country that fought the largest number of wars in the last half century (Africa Watch 1991). Through time, this patriotic history has brought about something we can call a militaristic national psyche within the country. Hence rulers formulated national security policies that were founded on the basis of suspicion and fear, again leading to vicious cycles of war. Parallel to these cycles, in its recent history the country has been frequently plagued by manmade famine and drought. Citizens have suffered from human rights abuse, lack of democracy and freedom (ibid.). The state for its part, as its foreign policy objective, has been prioritizing the defence of its territorial integrity and sovereignty based on abstract national interest and historical enmity with neighbouring countries. This has consumed a large amount of the country's wealth and human lives.

In this recent history of war, women have suffered the most. Women lost their loved ones because of war and, men being the farmers and breadwinners of the household when they went to war, women also lost their economic support as they did not have land ownership rights (Yewubmar 2008). At this point I would like to refer to some personal memories of the last three decades.

When I was four years old, my mother learnt of her brother's death on the war front. My uncle, younger than my mother, had been a very responsible person and very close to her. My mother used to tell me that the loss of her brother was hard to accept. Although my uncle had originally not been in the army but in the police force, nonetheless he was sent to the war front as part of the military.

It might have been from that time onwards that the question of the war system remained in my mind. My uncle had a young bride, having been married only two years. Of the huge number of mourners filling our house, women were the majority. My grandmother, my mother and my uncle's widow shaved their heads, wore black dresses for the next several years and slept on the floor without a bed (as the traditional practice asks of the Ethiopian woman when she loses her beloved one, relatives and family members). At that time, it was not only my uncle who died as a result of the nationalistic war waged all over the country but also many of my friends' fathers were sacrificed. Every other Sunday, there was a fresh mourning house in our neighbourhood. Many of the women/mothers were housewives and not educated or did not have their own income. Some were not legally married to their children's fathers. In many cases, they were forced to sell firewood, traditional homemade snacks (*Qolo*, *Dabo*) and beer (*Tella*) to raise their children. Sometimes they became prostitutes. As another impediment, in Ethiopia it is traditionally not possible for a woman to get married a second time, especially when she has children. I grew up seeing women in black, some of them wearing the same black clothes for many years. But there were also women fighters and army leaders who fought for their rights and their fellow women's rights in these years of civil war (Yewubmar 2008: 25–37).

Since 1991, Ethiopia has made significant advances in reforming and introducing democratic principles based on the current international trends. At the same time, Ethiopian nationalism or national sentiment is on the decline, along with the patriotic feeling and the war-mongering Ethiopian tradition, as I personally observed. In the 1995 constitution, the country introduced a new political dimension which was anchored in the principle of the 'unconditional right of nations, nationalities and peoples to exercise self determination, including secession' (FDRE 1995: Article 39). Accordingly, the 1995 constitution Article 8/1 states, 'All sovereign power resides in the nations, nationalities and peoples of Ethiopia' (FDRE 1995). This has brought in new progressive dimensions of nationalism, territorial integrity and sovereignty which in turn are the recipes of the national security paradigm.

The new concept of sovereignty is based on the principle of constitutionalism. In a constitutional government, it is the people ruling through a body of law that is sovereign. That is the form of government that commands legitimacy most commonly in the world today. However, the question of which people and when and how they give their sovereign consent still remains vague in the country's current political atmosphere, especially because most of the country's ethnic cultures are conditioned by a patriarchal order.

Some 20 years earlier, the issue of democracy and popular participation had no place in the Ethiopian society; under the motto of 'everything to the war front', citizens endured civil wars and dying for the motherland (Africa Watch 1991; Veale 2003). Wars and manmade and natural disastrous droughts resulting in famine have victimized millions throughout the country. It seems that the country has learnt a lesson from its own recent past. The current government formulated a new national security policy that recognizes in principle the dangers the country is facing: poverty, lack of democracy (the need of building up of democracy) and the lack of human security (MoFA 2007).

Because of the endless wars the country was engaged in for the last century, there was an absence of human security all over the country, and militarism and patriarchy were firmly entrenched within the society. Women benefited the least from this situation. The Ethiopian women understand that there is no practical solution to their problems produced by war and violence. There were times in history that they, too, fought wars and engaged actively in armed struggles for the survival of their nation and for bringing democracy to Ethiopia.

The next section of this article addresses Ethiopian women's participation in the armed struggles, especially the Tigrean women's participation as guerilla fighters in the 17-year civil war and their struggle against patriarchy inside the Tigrean Peoples Liberation Front (TPLF), and about how they fell short in bringing about women's equality in politics and in the decision-making arena.

Ethiopian women's roles and challenges in the traditional security paradigm

'Historically, women have been involved in conflicts, especially conflicts that arose because of attempts made by Europeans, specifically Italy, to invade and colonize Ethiopia' (Bahiru 1991). However, these contributions of women have always been invisible in major books of history. Recent studies show that as early as in the 14th century, women were taking up high positions and advising the kings on various important issues. It is also explained that some prominent women even sent for assistance from different foreign countries to avert various conflicts that arose (Minale 2001). However, whatever deeds were undertaken by these women were always presented as deeds done by either their husbands or their sons, which is why the performance of women does not occupy much space in history. In a patriarchal society like the Ethiopian, A. Minale argues that

> the talent and wisdom of women was accepted so long as it was an indispensable means to solve a major political crisis. But soon after the conflict was over, men were reluctant to give due recognition to women and their deeds because a prolonged period of acknowledgment could have meant giving women either their *proper* place in society or undermining the domination of men, which, in any case, was unacceptable to the males.
> (Emebet 2005: 114)

In this respect, Ethiopian women's experience is not any different from similar examples all over the world. However, this systemic downplaying of women's roles whenever society re-establishes its order always keeps women out of the security agenda, a part of countries' high politics. In the words of Jacklyn Cock,

> The role of women in militarization has been largely obscured and mystified by two competing perspectives – those of sexism and feminism. Both analyses exclude women from war on the grounds that they are bearers of 'special qualities'. Sexism excludes women from the ranks of the military on the grounds of their physical inferiority and unsuitability for fighting. As the weaker sex women must be 'protected' and 'defended'.
>
> (1992: 5)

As a consequence of this sexism, Ethiopian women serving in the military face these same challenges from their male comrades, even during the liberation struggle. According to Assefaw Yewubmar, sexism was part of the liberation struggle from the beginning; even though women had excelled in the military and physical training in the training centres and were able to show their capacities for combat and to lead military units, they were always considered to be the lower sex (2008: 39–43).

Ethiopia's recent experience in terms of women's involvement in armed conflict stems from the armed resistance of the Tigrean People Liberation Front (TPLF) waged against the Derg (the socialist government in power from 1974–91). Women were involved in the war directly by fighting on the battlefield and indirectly by providing supplies for the combatants. As combatants, women were thought to be equally aggressive, violent and reckless for the sake of showing their equality to their male colleagues (Yewubmar 2008). The involvement of women in armed conflict impacted their lives in different ways during the 17 years of civil war in Ethiopia. Although they fought hard all the way to victory, their systemic exclusion from the process of nation building was very much a lesson about the unchallenged nature of patriarchy in the society (Veale 2003).

Angela Veale researched the circumstances of women's participation in armed conflict. She shows that the TPLF was reluctant to recruit women combatants from the beginning because women were considered to be non-violent as compared to men. Later the TPLF/EPRDF started involving women fully in the fighting. The women she interviewed were on average 12.68 years old when recruited (Veale 2003). In other words, they were child soldiers when they joined the struggle. As children, it is obvious that they were easy to brainwash into a state of aggression.

The motivation of Tigrean women's involvement in the armed struggle was instigated by different factors. Many cases show that several women revolted against the domestic violence imposed on them, but the oppression of the majority of Ethiopian peasants under very few feudal landlords was not the reason for most young uneducated women to join the struggle. Yewubmar stated that those who joined the struggle in their youth were not mature enough to experience the feudal exploitation and the land tenure system at that time (2008: 36–7). To understand the motivation of the women who joined the fight, it is helpful to take a look at Tsegay:

> 36 per cent political motivation, 17 per cent socio-economic, and 47 per cent as 'emotional'. Political motivation refers to those who were motivated by political concerns such as by opposing the Derg, and its 'Red Terror' campaign, by nationalism or the ideology of socialism and the class struggle. This group, he argues, was mainly composed of university students, civil servants and teachers. In its attempts to crush the opposition rebel group, the Derg regime used torture to instill fear and social control and men and women were tortured for their political beliefs. Gender politics were an integral part of a broader liberation politics for many politically motivated women, thus ensuring gender equality as an issue was placed central to TPLF ideology.
>
> (Veale 2003: 2)

In Tsegay's findings, emotional factors were the greatest motivation for Tigrean women to join the struggle. I would argue that Ethiopian women constitute the majority of the poor because women traditionally do not have property rights. Land, oxen and production instruments belong to men. In many Ethiopian cultures, women are forced to marry an unknown person and without their consent (FDRE 1995). When the man, the breadwinner, dies or leaves the family behind, women and their children are exposed to extreme misery and starvation. Because of these sociocultural and economic inequalities, the *feminization of poverty* is an obvious threat to women. Being trapped in such hopeless situations, it is understandable that women, especially young women, trying to flee from this systemic oppression and dependence on men welcomed the alternative of joining the armed forces as a means to their personal liberation.

'Arguably, the recruitment and training of women within the TPLF was a means of capturing the hearts and minds of the community in its entirety, thus maximizing the impregnability of local structures to

Derg forces' (Yewubmar 2008: 4). As Yewubmar and Veale indicate, the TPLF/EPRDF used the image of women fighters to win the sympathy of the general public in the mobilization process. The means that were used for the politicization of women after recruitment were based on Marxist-Leninist ideology. This politicization included education up to the fourth grade before embarking on training as fighters. As Yewubmar described, it was also a women's association initiative within the TPLF that helped women to learn to read and write. The majority of the rural women who joined the struggle were not educated (Yewubmar 2008).

After the fall of the Derg and the change of government, the new government led by the EPRDF conducted a security and military reform that included all national defence structures to answer the World Bank's and International Monetary Fund's demobilization and security reform formalities. At this point, the fate of many of the TPLF/EPRDF women ex-fighters was demobilization. Mulugeta Tefera Emebet states what happened in the following way:

> However, once the conflict is over many of the women who have been active participants in the war and who had contributed significantly to the peace that resulted from the struggle are ignored during the rehabilitation and stabilization process. In fact many of them ended up in a worse situation than they had been in before they joined the struggle. Due to spending much of their time working for the army, many had their marriages dissolved, and as a result the number of female-headed households dramatically increased, which made women highly vulnerable to poverty. During demobilization women could not be equal beneficiaries of the 'fruits of victory', due to their poor educational background and other socio-cultural factors; many had difficulties adjusting to the patriarchal way of life in the community after experiencing equality with men during the wartime, and many felt depressed due to the realization that their chances of marriage and motherhood had been lost while they were in the war.
>
> (2005: 121)

Heidi Hudson's observation that 'feminist scholars have carefully reconstructed the gender-biassed formation and functioning of the state and its war machine' (2005) brings us back to the patriarchal construction of women who do not belong to the state and to the state and its business being viewed as only men's area.

In general, the participation of women in the civil war has brought about changes in favour of emancipation on the individual as well as the societal level. The EPRDF women's case shows that after the end of the war, women were either marginalized or excluded from political leadership and decision-making. After the demobilization, many women were socio-economically reintegrated on the basis of being employed by government offices as messengers and clerical workers or in the textile and other industry establishments by endowment funds. Another critical issue leading to women's further exclusion from the public sphere was that women were not able to continue high school and tertiary-level education after the war, unlike most of the male ex-combatants.

On the issue of political integration, women ex-combatants felt that, even though they were highly politicized within the Ethiopian society, they did not get enough representation in national politics. They felt that in the realm of politics and decision-making, women were moved aside.

At the transitional conference of 1991, the issues of women were not on the agenda, although they fought in the war. It is not clear as to what extent they were consulted in the development of the peace agreement on the formation of a transitional government (TGE). De Watteville argues,

> The participation of women, and especially female ex-combatants, in peace negotiations at an early stage is a prerequisite to the promotion of their interests and to their future participation in decision-making. It is at the peace table that the tone is set for the reconstruction of the country, and that the political, economic, social and institutional changes are initiated. It is also an opportunity for women to express their views and influence decisions.
> (Veale 2003: 12)

In conclusion, the ex-combatant women's experiences show that women in Ethiopia have challenged the masculinist idea of militarism through participation in armed conflicts. On the one hand, they challenged the domestic violence imposed on women, and on the other, they revolted against the totalitarian regime through armed struggle. In her research, Veale also observed that in the 17-year war the Tigrean women were highly militarized and politicized, similar to the case in some other African, Asian and Latin American countries. But finally, their attempts to participate in the decision-making process fell short because of the deep, structured patriarchal tradition in which women's actual place is in the house, while men take care of women. Different from their male comrades, the women's fate was demobilization, and they were again separated from their partners and husbands. Moreover, they were compelled to integrate into the civilian society without the proper and adequate infrastructure, especially without having defined their own role in the society or having gained economic empowerment.

The human security problems of Ethiopian women

The national policy on Ethiopian women accounts for the previously described situation of women by stating that Ethiopian women were compelled to play a unique role during the civil war (TGEOPM 1993: 6). Later, as a result of their struggle, the constitution recognized the basic rights of women, followed by the ratification of a women's policy, the establishment of the women's affairs ministry, the formulation of the new family law, the revision of the Ethiopian penal code to give serious punishment to persons committing violence/crimes against women and the issuance of many more policies and directives. The most important of these is the Ethiopian foreign affairs and national security policy which clearly notes the country's major threats as poverty and lack of democracy – in other words, it recognizes the absence of human security as the biggest challenge the country faces today. This policy is the result of the accumulation of all the preceding factors as well as global trends.

But the question now will be how much these policies are women inclusive, from formulation to implementation. Although Ethiopia is also a signatory of all gender-related international treaties, women in Ethiopia are still not equal partners in the peace process and policy negotiations. Rather, they are the main victims of gender-based violence and political, social and economic deprivation. This situation results from the institutionalization of the gendered construction of power and order which favour masculine values over feminine ones. The patriarchal institutions in the country are the cause or at least the instruments of women's in/security problems. It is obvious that the direct, structural and cultural violence embedded in the country's social, political and economic systems are responsible for the continuation of the exclusion and subordination of women.

The problems mainly emanate from the lack of women's equal participation in decision-making and law enforcement. Because of this, women still constitute the majority of victims of human rights abuses, HIV/AIDS and problems of maternal health, and they suffer from shortage of food, poverty and many more dangers to their personal security (Habtamu et al. 2004: 3–5).

'Women in Ethiopia occupy low status in society. In spite of their contributions to the wellbeing of their families and communities, women experience lower socio-economic status in general and hence are marginalized from making decisions at all levels' (WABEKBON 2006: 5). Despite women going unrecognized for their roles in society, they are still the bearers of the community identity and wellbeing across all ethnic and cultural groups. By the same token, it is clear that women's roles and contributions are critical for the promotion of the human security agenda, which is shifting the traditional emphasis from state security to a people-centred security. In relation to this shift, the human security emphasis seems to be a new development toward women's inclusion. Before critiquing the national security policy, it would be appropriate to analyze the human security problems of Ethiopian women in more detail.

In Ethiopia, poverty places a heavy burden on women who are denied access to and control over financial resources but who must disproportionately shoulder household management. This situation is true whether in rural or urban areas. Indeed, 'the Ethiopian peasant women are totally dependent on the income of their husbands with whom they labour under harsh conditions. Rural women work a much longer time than men, [spending 13 to 15 hours] in taking care of the children, animals, food processing and marketing' (Hirut 2000: 24–5). According to the Ethiopian Gender profile,

> The economy is mainly based on agriculture, and food insecurity is a common phenomenon. Industry is not developed. The leading industry is food and beverages, with women forming only 19 per cent of the employees, despite their engagement in traditional processing of all food stuff. Women's low status is expressed in their lack of decision making opportunities, asset ownership, overwork on farm and home which is not acknowledged, small percentage (30.8 per cent) of female employment in the formal sector, engaged in clerical and fiscal administrative position, earning below Birr 200.00 per month. Women are mainly employed in the informal sector, where earnings and security is low. The percentage of women in professional positions is only 29 per cent, compared to men of 71 per cent, because their educational attainment is also low.
>
> (Haregewoin and Emebet 2002: 3)

Similarly, in urban areas, 'the proportion of female workers in such low-or no-skill jobs as seasonal and short-term contractual work is found to be much higher than that of men. This shows the average salary of women is far less than that of men. Men mostly occupy the high-paying managerial and professional positions' (Ministry of Labour and Social Affairs 2004: xiii). All in all, a woman with inadequate or no income has no time and energy to think about and work for something that does not address her immediate survival and does not sustain her family for the following days.

According to WABEKBON, another human security problem for Ethiopian women is the lack of health coverage: women are affected disproportionately by HIV/AIDS, the poverty rate is high among women because they do not have their own livelihood and gender-based violence is rampant in the country.

> Health coverage is low at 51 per cent, and within this low health service coverage, the special health needs of women are not considered, with the exception of the reproductive health issues. HIV/AIDS awareness level for women is 8 per cent against 23 per cent for men. Unwanted pregnancy and abortion is a common problem in the youth, and female youth are more vulnerable to HIV/AIDS infection probably because of widespread practices like rape, early marriage and high rate of teenage prostitution.
>
> (Haregewoin and Emebet 2002: vii–viii)

Although women in Ethiopia are disproportionately affected by HIV/AIDS, little is being done to address ways to protect them from the disease. According to the latest report by Ethiopia's Federal HIV/AIDS Prevention and Control Office, the Single Point Estimate published by the Ministry of Health (MoH) and HIV/AIDS Prevention and Control Office (HAPCO), in 2007 it was estimated that 977,394 people were living with HIV/AIDS in Ethiopia. This results in a prevalence rate of 2.1 per cent (1.7 per cent among males and 2.6 per cent among females; 7.7 per cent urban and 0.9 per cent rural areas) for the total estimated population of 73 million. The number of new HIV infections was 125,528, including 14,148 HIV-positive births. Females accounted for 57.4 per cent of new infections (Federal Ministry of Health 2007). 'Women are more vulnerable to HIV/AIDS in Ethiopia, mainly due to a lack of know-how and control over how, when and where the sex takes place, particularly in rural areas, where culture and religion dominate the rights of women' (Plus News 2007). 'Many women also often lack information and access to services, and girls in the country often begin having sex early, either because of early marriage which can occur as early as age seven or eight' (UNICEF 2005).

According to Berhane Kelkay, coordinator of the National Association of Positive Ethiopian Women, female genital mutilation, widow inheritance, early marriage and rape put women at a higher risk of contracting HIV. She added that although organizations exist to support women and to encourage increased awareness about gender-based violence, support for such programmes is scarce, especially in rural areas (Plus News 2007).

In summary, despite policy gains, and despite efforts to utilize these government commitments to achieve legal and policy changes to protect and advance women's rights at the national level, many women, especially the poor ones, are worse off today than they were a decade ago. Ethiopian women's problems are numerous and interrelated with the societal problems which are in general within the human security threats definition. The issue here is: How can Ethiopia get out of these vicious circles of war and ethnic conflicts, environmental degradation, drought and famine? According to Bogalech Gebre, all these are interwoven, and the solutions are at the centre of the problems, spinning around women's problems.

> There is a relationship between peace, the environment, and the situation of women. The problems of bringing peace to Ethiopia, the difficulties of protecting the environment and women's inequitable participation in economic and political life, all have the same roots. To remove obstacles in the way of peace, to secure the survival of natural resources essential for the future, or to improve the situation of women in Ethiopia, those who make policy will have to look carefully at, and be willing to change, some fundamental assumptions and attitudes.
>
> (Bogaletch 1992)

Gebre Bogalech stated the importance of including women in the policy formulation and decision-making processes for the situation in Ethiopia to change at all.

For the purpose of analysis, I will consider the case of the new national security policy within the previously stated framework. In this analysis I argue that the Ethiopian government's intention is not clear: it has put the old security agenda under the rubric of human security, and it lacks the definition of women's security problems.

Ethiopian national security policy: human security and gender perspectives

The Ethiopian foreign affairs and national security policy is formulated within the human security framework. In the introduction of the policy document, it emphasizes poverty and lack of democracy as the country's primary concerns. It is fashioned in such a way as to mix the traditional security paradigm in tandem with the human security agenda. In its definition of security as serving the country's survival, it states,

> Our foreign relations and national security policy and strategy can only have relevance if it contributes to the fight against poverty and promotes speedy economic development, democracy and peace. If we do not realize our goals, one can predict that our country will be exposed to great instability and even collapse and our very security, and indeed survival, will be at stake.
> (MIPAD 2002)

This argument supports, on the one hand, the prioritization of state survival (territory and sovereignty), which is a traditional security agenda, focusing on national boundaries and existence as a state. On the other, the policy document seems to stress domestic problems like lack of democracy, good governance and poverty or absence of speedy economic development as priority problems of the country. One can see that this approach is inward-looking, different from the previous regimes which externalized domestic problems by prioritizing and exaggerating the external threats to the country. In fact, the intention of the policy paper was to define the human security threats of the country rather than jumping into the discussion of sovereignty and territorial integrity issues. At the same time, the policy paper also went further in defining the former government's limitations as follows:

> Former governments pursued external relations and national security policies that disregarded internal problems that were fundamental to our national condition. Rather, the effort was to focus on the outside world and to look in from the outside, as it were. Such an approach could not adequately protect our national interest and security. There is no point in trying to pursue a foreign relations and national security policy to be implemented externally without a major and effective in-country effort to realize our vision of development and democratization.
> (MIPAD 2002)

By saying this it highlights the problems of the former regimes by defining other countries as threats to Ethiopia, which results from the masculine, militaristic worldview based on the assumption that

Ethiopia is situated in a very dangerous, hostile geopolitical environment so that no country and no regime is friendly to it. The Ethiopian foreign affairs and national security document continues to explain,

> It should also be noted that the foreign policies of past governments were, in part, founded on a 'siege mentality' which considered the country to be surrounded by enemies. Its effects on the psychology of the people and its adverse impact on our relations with the outside world cannot be underestimated. This is, however, not to say that the country does not have external enemies or that all past policies directed against those who were arrayed against the country were wrong.
> (MIPAD 2002)

This statement is the antithesis of the traditional security paradigm which never tries to assess the opportunities but rather focuses on enmities. The policy paper does not deny that Ethiopia has experienced outside invasions several times in its history, but it underlines the importance of assessing opportunities rather than of exaggerating threats.

The foreign policy, which is a result of men's experience and knowledge, influenced by the competitive, suspicious, unrealistic and dangerous worldview, is in turn breeding a culture of violence. As Betty A. Reardon puts it, 'the culture of violence is the aggregation of world views, ways of thinking and problem solving that lead to the continuation of violence and armed forces' (2001: 21). In general terms, those views help(ed) the Ethiopian rulers to impose their fear and suspicion on the people, diverting attention from domestic problems of human rights violations to external problems of invasions and threats to national security, putting the economy at risk and multiplying Ethiopian enemies throughout the region.

In contrast, the current Ethiopian government states that domestic problems are the primary reason for our misery and obstacles for our survival in the world. In its description of its objectives, the Ethiopian foreign affairs and national security document puts it thus:

> There can be no doubt that the attainment of speedy economic development, democratization and peace is fundamental to the survival of our country which finds itself in a state of abject poverty and backwardness. That is why the Government gives priority to matters that are key to our survival and well-being.
> (MIPAD 2002)

Consequently, this policy paper includes the human security agenda – democracy, peace, poverty alleviation – as part of its formulation. Hence, under the subheading 'Basic Principles – The Foundations of Foreign Affairs and National Security Policy', it identifies and examines the sources and bases from which the policy springs in order to formulate a foreign affairs and security policy that addresses the preceding issues.

It says it is important to discuss the issues under the topic of development and the building of a democratic system as a basis for policies. For the Ethiopian people, benefiting from rapid development means living a life free from poverty, ignorance and backwardness, which is indeed in the primary interests of the people. Rapid development not only is important in raising the standard of living of the people but also is a guarantee of national survival, if rapid development that benefits the people could really be brought about. Here I would like to emphasize that the term 'people' sometimes excludes women which leads to the fact that 'bringing up a speedy economic development' does not necessarily mean development which benefits women. In other words, by continuing the discussion, establishing a democratic order in Ethiopia is the way to respect peoples' and individuals' rights, affirm good governance and assure stable working and living conditions. Democracy is an important instrument for mobilizing around common goals and for involving the people in nation building. Democracy guarantees that the members of the various nations, nationalities and religions in Ethiopia live in an atmosphere of tolerance. In the absence of a democratic order, national and religious divisions will inevitably intensify. The abuse of human rights would result in strife, and poverty would spread further, a recipe for disintegration and destruction. The realization of democracy will therefore not only help to attain development and good governance but also ensure national security. Without doubt, democratization is fundamental to safeguard the individual interests of every Ethiopian as well as to ensure the country's survival.

Compared to what the Ethiopian people have been through for a hundred years, the new way of defining national security was a surprise for observers and analysts.

> Some analysts are of the opinion that a public discussion of policies would be to divulge state secrets and serve the interests of the enemy. But we need to weigh the pros and cons of public discussion. Open discussions on policies empower the people to closely monitor the government's implementation of these policies, and

would ensure the introduction of a culture of transparency and accountability and indeed, democracy.

(MIPAD 2002)

According to this, it is not possible to hide the document from our enemies. Rather it helps to create a channel to our enemies and friends when they understand our intention and plan toward them. It is also a reflection of the emergence of a more democratic culture based on transparency. Although the public was not fully aware of it, the people lived under an 'iron curtain', without having ownership of the country's national issues. National politics was an area of a few personalities who had the power to do everything on behalf of the general public. This policy was a new beginning in the heart and mind of Ethiopia's political life.

A gender perspective

The worldwide trend in women's issues is moving forward; the last decades have been full of promises of change. Advancements in the recognition of women's full participation at all levels of decision-making have underlined the importance of women's participation in international peace and security. The EFANPS (Ethiopian Foreign Affairs and National Security Policy and Strategy), which seems noble in its formulation and objectives, has significant limitations concerning women's definitions of threats. It has been years since it was adopted, but the importance of gender mainstreaming from formulation to implementation has not been accomplished.

> The equal access and full participation of women in power structures and their full involvement in all efforts for the prevention and resolution of conflicts are essential for the maintenance and promotion of peace and security. If women are to play an equal part in securing and maintaining peace, they must be empowered politically and economically and represented adequately at all levels of decision-making.
> (Beijing Platform for Action 1995: para. 134)

This statement makes it clear that a gendered analysis of peacebuilding, one that truly addresses the nature of power relations between women and men, is essential to preventing and mitigating new violent conflict in societies while helping them to recover from past conflicts.

Since the 1991 government change in Ethiopia, much has been done to bring about women's active participation in the decision-making and political leadership arena, as mentioned earlier, although things are working to the contrary to the said policies and legislations (FDREMoWA 2006). In the case of the foreign and national security policy, there is an obvious problem of gender mainstreaming. The strategy does not include women's specific threats and experiences, their roles and empowerment, in an explicit way. Women's roles and contributions are critical for the promotion of the human security agenda, shifting traditional emphasis from interstate to people-centred security. The drafting of the document included the active participation of citizens from different levels, but still it lacks some views about threat definition and women's participation.

Due to the virtual absence of women from local and national power structures, several advancements were made toward the inclusion of women or women-centred policies, but these remained tainted by hypocrisy. The situation in security policy formulation and implementation is not any different. Women's priority issues are not addressed because women are not part of the policy formulation and decision-making process. The document did not take women's primary threats into account.

Despite policy gains, and efforts to use government commitments to achieve legal and policy changes to protect and advance women's rights at the national level, many women, especially the poor, are worse off today than they were a decade ago. The policy agenda of rapid development is not women-centred. The biggest part of the country's economy is agriculture-based: it is mainly connected to land ownership. Until recent constitutional reforms, Ethiopian women did not have property rights, so they were not entitled to land ownership in the land tenure system.

Generally, it seems that the policy is formulated to satisfy the interests of the Bretton Woods institutions for the purpose of obtaining financial aid. This situation is reflected in the ongoing privatization and investment projects which create more poverty because of labour layoffs and industrial development.

> The neo-liberal economic model and market-driven policies – particularly changes in trade and finance rules, and the deregulation and privatization of public goods and services – have exacerbated the poverty, food insecurity, and economic exclusion of the majority, while increasing the wealth and economic opportunities, and thus over-consumption, of the privileged few.
> (Zeitlin and Mpoumou 2004: 2)

This type of rapid economic development does not benefit the poor, especially women. Although it is well documented that women's empowerment is central to poverty eradication and national development, women still face significant barriers when it comes to access to resources, wage employment, and decision-making positions. As macroeconomic and national policies are too often gender blind, they are ineffective in addressing the needs of poor and minority women (FDREMoWA 2006).

The other important part of the policy is democratization as a foreign policy foundation. Feminists have traditionally been suspicious of what they see as the legacy of the Western liberal – democratic tradition that they claim is patriarchal and that, historically, has favoured men's over women's interests. In addition, because women have traditionally had less access to formal political institutions, the focus on state institutions by scholars of democratization may miss ways in which women are participating in politics outside formal political channels at the grassroots level.

On this point, the document talks about consensus building among the country's citizens. In Ethiopia, women constitute 49.8 per cent of the population, according to the gender profile data (2006). The Ethiopian foreign affairs document states, 'All said the benefits of public discussion on basic policies and directions in order to reach a common national understanding far outweigh the loss. Creating the possibility for such debate enables the people to make their own contribution; this should be a priority above all others' (MoFA 2007).

But the paradox of this statement is that women are totally absent from the policy formulation and implementation spheres. Without their participation, it will be difficult to bring about consensus. In the earlier discussion about Ethiopian women's participation in armed conflicts, it was shown how the masculinist tendency, which was hidden under the guise other agendas during the liberation movement, has come into the open again (Yewubmar 2008: 189). The demobilization scheme had pushed women from the decision-making sphere. In the process of formulating this national security policy and strategy, the question of why women are absent from the political and security business was raised by the public in discussion forums organized by the government in the preparation phase. The truth is, for peace to prevail and for global citizenry to gain recognition, women should play a significant role in peace and security issues on the domestic as well as the global stage.

Conclusion

The human security problems of Ethiopian women are not very different from women's security situation worldwide. Women constitute the majority of the poor, illiterate and victims of violence and disease. It does not seem realistic to talk about their role in the national security decision-making while they are denied access to education, justice and recognition within the existing patriarchal structure of the country. First and foremost, the question about women's security threats has to be raised. Women's security concerns/dangers are many, but the major ones are lack of access to political leadership and decision-making. Poverty, HIV/AIDS and environmental degradation are affecting women at an increasing rate. At this point, the importance of the inclusion of women in the security and strategic decision-making area becomes clear because the lack of women in decision-making is the source of all the grave problems they face.

Finally, with the continuing absence of women in policy formulation and implementation, and without the inclusion of the specific threats to women's security, it will be difficult to bring about a consensus on the definition and maintenance of Ethiopian national security.

I believe that without a structural change in society toward gender inclusiveness, human security as a concept will not be reflected on all societal levels.

References

Africa Watch. 1991. 'Evil Days: 30 Years of Wars and Famine in Ethiopia: An African Watch Report: A Division of Human Rights Watch'. New York.

Bahiru, Zewde. 1991. *A History of Modern Ethiopia*. 1st edition London: James Curry.

Beijing Platform for Action. 1995, www.un.org/womenwatch/daw/beijing/platform/. Accessed on 20 July 2007.

Bogaletch Gebre. 1992. 'Women Peace and Development in Ethiopia', *Life & Peace Review*, vol. 6 (3), Women: Today & Tomorrow. Life and Peace Institute. www.kmgselfhelp.org/peace.html. Accessed 20 February 2008

Cock, Jacklyn. 1992. 'Feminism and Militarism: Some Questions Raised by the Gulf War', *South African Defence Review*, (6).

Emebet, Mulugeta Tefera. 2005. 'The Invincible Invisibles: Ethiopian Women in Conflict and Peace Making', in Dina Rodriguez and Edith Natukunda Togboa (eds.), *Gender and Peace Building in Africa*. San Jose, CA: University for Peace.

FDRE. 1995. 'Constitutions of the Federal Democratic Republic Ethiopia'. Proclamation No. 1/1995. Negarit Gazzeta.Addis Ababa, Ethiopia

FDREMoWA (Federal Democratic Republic of Ethiopia Ministry of Women's Affairs). 2006 (July 2006) (In Amharic paper edition). 'Ethiopian Women Development and Change Package', *Addis Ababa*, Ethiopia

Federal Ministry of Health: National HIV/AIDS Prevention and Control Office. 2005. 'AIDS in Ethiopia: Sixth Report'. www.etharc.org/aidsineth/publications/aidsineth6th_en.pdf. Accessed on 25 May 2018.

Haregewoin, Cherinet and Emebet Mulugeta. 2002. 'Country Gender Profile Ethiopia'. Swedish International Development Cooperation Agency (SIDA).

Hudson, Heidi. 2005. '"Doing" Security as Though Human Matter: A Feminist Perspective on Gender and the Politics of Human Security', *Security Dialogue*, vol. 36: 155. International Peace Research Institute: Sage Publications. http://sdi.sagepub.com. Accessed on 1 July 2007.

Kefetewe, Konjit. 2004. *Gender and Cross Cultural Dynamics in Ethiopia: The Case of Eleven Ethnic Groups. Addis Ababa, Center for Research Training and Information for Women in Development (CERTWID)*. Addis Ababa University Press.

Minale, A. 2001. 'Women and Warfare in Ethiopia: A Case Study of their Roles during the Campaign of Adwa, 1895/96, and the Italo-Ethiopian War, 1935–41'. Addis Ababa, Ethiopia: Organization for Social Science Research in Eastern and Southern Africa (OSSREA).

Ministry of Information Press & Audiovisual Department. November 2002. 'The Federal Democratic Republic of Ethiopia Foreign Affairs and National Security Policy and Strategy'. Addis Ababa. https://chilot.me/nationa-policies-and-strategies/?download=5894. Accessed on 25 May 2018.

Ministry of Labor and Social Affairs. 2004. 'Report of the National Survey on Employment, Working Condition, Decision-Making Role, Knowledge, Attitude and Behavior of Reproductive Health and HIV/AIDS of Women Workers Employed in Establishments Administered by Labor Proclamation No.42/93'. Addis Ababa, Ethiopia.

Plus News. 2007. 'ETHIOPIA: Inequality, Gender-Based Violence Raise HIV/AIDS Risk for Women'. Addis Ababa. allafrica.com/stories/200701081446.html. Accessed on 25 May 2018.

Reardon, Betty A. 2001. 'Introduction to Education for a Culture of Peace', in *Education to a Culture of Peace in a Gender Perspective*, pp. 17–34. Paris: UNESCO.

Terefe, Hirut. 2000. 'Gender and Development', in Christian Fellner (ed.), *Ethiopia: An Introduction into Culture, Economics, Politics, and Cooperation*. Vienna, Austria: Mattersburgerkreis.

TGEOPM (The Transitional Government of Ethiopia: Office of the Prime Minister). 1993. 'National Policy on Ethiopian Women'. Addis Ababa.

UNICEF. 2005. 'Livelihood and Vulnerabilities Study'. Addis Ababa: Ethiopia.

Veale, Angela. 2003. 'From Child Soldier to Ex-Fighter: Female Fighters, De-Mobilization and Reintegration in Ethiopia', Monograph No. 85. April

2003. https://issafrica.org/.../monograph-85-from-child-soldier-to-ex-fighter-female-fighters. Accessed 25 May 2018.

WABEKBON Development Consultant PLC. 2006. 'Final Report'. Ethiopia: Country Gender Profile. www.jica.go.jp/english/our_work/thematic_issues/gender/.../pdf/e06eth.pdf.

Yewubmar, Asefaw. 2008. '(In Amharic) The Phoenix Will Arise after Her Death: The Unfinished Tigrean Women Struggle'. Addis Ababa: Far East Trading Plc.

Zeitlin, June and Doris Mpoumou. 2004. 'No Human Security without Gender Equality', *The Big Issues: Reports by Commitment*. Women's Environment and Development Organization (WEDO). unpan1.un.org/intradoc/groups/public/documents/APCITY/UNPAN018180.pdf. Accessed on 25 May 2018.

5 War and armed conflict
Threat to African women's human security

Fatuma Ahmed Ali

Introduction

As Africa has been plagued by a series of armed conflicts, the peoples of many African countries have been bereft of most elements of human security. These conflicts, largely internal civil wars, bring into sharp focus the realities of the incompatibility between militarized approaches to political ends and human security. Viewed as a reasonable assurance of human wellbeing, as human security is conceived of in this volume, armed conflict may be seen as the major obstacle to human wellbeing in these African countries. African women in particular have suffered denial of all four fundamental sources of human security set forth in the framework which binds these articles together. This article will illuminate the multiple ways in which war and armed conflict deny thousands of African women their fundamental right to human security.

General effects of armed conflict on African women

> It has probably become more dangerous to be a woman than a soldier in modern conflict.
>
> Major-General Patrick Cammaert (2008), former commander of UN peacekeeping forces in the eastern Democratic Republic of the Congo

When we analyze the impact of war and armed conflict on women, we see that there is a need for a serious reconsideration of the concept of security. It is imperative to pose the following question: Can we ever assure human security when women's bodies are used as battlefields and weapons in armed conflict and war? We can never talk in any depth about human security without discussing issues that threaten human security in the first place, starting with the masculine concept of security as best assured by armed force, a concept that has continually manifested in wars and armed conflicts. In this case, human security is not concerned with weapons. It is a concern about human dignity, security for people and their welfare. We live in a culture of violence in which the victims of the worst violence are most often women. Women work for peace and security because the absence of peace carries the greatest threat to their personal security and to all that they cherish and nurture. Women have a significant stake in peace and human security as they are inevitably victims of war and armed conflicts not of their making. Regardless of whether they actually participate in it, they suffer the most painful wounds of armed conflict: the violation of their bodies, the deaths of dear ones and the destruction of their lives' work.

African women would affirm the statement of the former UN Secretary-General.

> During the cold war, security tended to be defined almost entirely in terms of military might and the balance of terror. Today, we know that 'security' means far more than the absence of conflict. We also have a greater appreciation for non-military sources of conflict. We know that lasting peace requires a broader vision encompassing areas such as education and health, democracy and human rights, protection against environmental degradation, and the proliferation of deadly weapons. We know that we cannot be secure amidst starvation, that we cannot build peace without alleviating poverty, and that we cannot build freedom on foundations of injustice. These pillars of what we now understand as the people-centered concept of 'human security' are interrelated and mutually reinforcing. No shift in the way we think or act is more critical than that of putting people at the centre of everything we do.
>
> (Annan 2001)

Concepts of human security are, in principle, quite broad, taking the individual person as the nexus of its concern, the life as *lived*, as the most appropriate lens through which to view the political, economic and social environment. At its most basic level, human security means freedom from fear (McRae 2001: 15). Freedom from fear entails assurance of human rights. Human rights are a key constituent of human security, even in conflict situations; human security concerns not only rights but also the safety of civilians (ibid.: 16). Further, and more importantly, concepts of human security are premised on the need to assess security on the basis of the wellbeing of people rather than on the interests of states.

Tehranian (1999: xii) adds the idea that human security is also concerned with culturally constructed individual welfare conditions. The cultural perspective brings to light the fact that the role and status of women have kept them insecure based on their physical, social and economic conditions imposed by the dominant patriarchal systems. Reed and Tehranian (1999: 36) argue that human security has two central aspects: first, safety from such chronic threats as hunger, disease and repression, and second, protection from sudden and hurtful disruptions in the patterns of daily life, whether in homes, in jobs or in communities. According to the feminist human security paradigm that informs this volume, among the worst of these often avoidable disruptions are wars and armed conflicts.

Adding to these descriptors, this article argues that there is another important goal of human security: a world free from the largely unnecessary violence and suffering caused by armed conflicts. This would thus fulfill the need for protection from avoidable harm, one of the four fundamental requirements for human security identified in a feminist framework paradigm of gender and human security.

This article further argues that the construction and categorization of women primarily as victims of war exposes them as weak and vulnerable persons whose bodies and lives can be used as weapons of war through the imposition of fear, pain and shame. One consequence of constructing women as victims is their exclusion from formal peace negotiations and peacebuilding in their post-war societies. This denies women the recognition of their abilities, skills and rewards in contributing to peacebuilding.

During armed conflict and war, women and girls experience violence from many sides. These include armed groups, peacekeeping forces, families, police, civilian officials, government officials and rebels. Recently, there have been reports of sexual exploitation and abuse by humanitarian personnel and the misuse of humanitarian assistance for sexual exploitation purposes in West Africa and Democratic Republic of Congo (DRC). Violence against women has physical, psychological, economic and social aspects to it; their bodies become a battleground for those who use terror as a tactic of war (Ahmed 2007).

Women, however, are not just victims of armed conflict. As affirmed by Security Council Resolution 1325 (United Nations 2002), they also have active roles to play as negotiators and contributors to peacebuilding. That said, however, they have often been denied this possibility. The active role of women in war is downplayed by emphasizing the consequences women suffer in the aftermath of political violence, such as loss of family members, property, their refugee status and widowhood, physical, psychological and sexual abuse. Also, based on these consequences, women's participation in such activities as mobilizing for peace and contributing to their societies before, during and after armed conflict is not often recognized and acknowledged.

Despite the fact that women are primarily seen as victims of armed conflicts in patriarchal cultures, they have also emerged as tremendous human resources, often engaging in peacebuilding and organizing themselves in active networking through local, national and international non-governmental organizations (NGOs) and peace movements. They organize for health, education, economic, social and cultural survival, including the wellbeing of every individual in the community. Women's roles in reconstructing the society after the rampages of war show that women are more than ready and able to negotiate and participate in peace processes. War drastically changes the society. Many men are killed or are exiled from the country; therefore, women have had to shoulder many new and unaccustomed burdens outside their traditional roles in the family and household.

Armed conflicts are often the result of attempts to control such economic resources as oil, metals, diamonds, drugs or contested territorial boundaries and construction of identity or nation. In such countries as Sudan, for example, oilfield exploration has caused and intensified the impoverishment of women and men, leading to protracted conflicts. The control of resources, like the exercise of power, is gendered. Those who do not have power/resources or groups that are disproportionately, although by no means exclusively, made up of women, marginalized men and children are the ones who suffer the most and usually are not the ones who initiate wars. Also, unresolved struggles over resources combined with the severe impact of displacement, impoverishment and increased militarization in zones of conflict serve to prolong existing armed conflicts. Moreover, conflicts tend to cause and perpetuate inequalities between ethnic groups and discrimination against marginalized groups of women and men, thereby paving the way for the outbreak of future armed conflicts.

Gendered impacts of war and armed conflict on women

Contemporary conflicts have multidimensional gendered impacts on both men and women, but the most varied and complex are those that affect women. The relationship between women and war is complex, sensitive and contradictory, posing a complicated network of threats to women's human security. The experiences of people in armed conflicts and wars can in many ways be gender-specific. For instance, men instigate and conduct wars, are wounded and killed in combat. Women do not make security decisions, yet they comprise the majority of those who suffer more of the deprivations imposed by war; they are the caretakers of those who are wounded and mourners of the dead. Recently, it was reported that, in the African continent, around 100 million persons had been affected by the consequences of armed conflict (Estefanía 2006: 13). Children are included in the same category as women because they are dependent on women. Women are subjected to abuses as they are forced to flee conflict zones, and they are thus not only the primary victims of domestic violence in times of peace but also commonly are victims and casualties of the public violence of war. Violence against women during war often magnifies the inequalities that women face in their everyday lives. Gender violence and inequalities not only in Africa but also throughout the world pose a major obstacle to the human security of all vulnerable populations.

Although the exact numbers and gender proportions of killings in war are virtually impossible to determine, the assumption that more men than women are killed in warfare is plausible. However, when war reaches the civilian population, the proportion of the female population also rises (Skjelsbaek and Smith 2001: 3). In reality, in contemporary so-called new wars, the civilian population makes up 70 per cent of war-related victims. Therefore, Rajoo (2005: 17) argues that the impact of armed conflict and war on women is most severe as they are forced to experience conflict not only as future peace builders but also as victims, opponents and survivors.

Current armed conflict no longer resembles traditional interstate war. Wars in Africa are more often fought within states. The development of smaller, lighter, but still lethal weapons has made it possible to coerce both children and women into armed combat. These developments have clearly impacted the issues and problems of security, including political, social, economic, environmental and cultural security. All these aspects have gender dimensions. International Alert (2001) reports that the experiences of contemporary armed conflict are, in many instances, gender-specific. For example, men and boys are the usual 'carriers' and 'users' of portable weapons, and women and girls are often the 'caretakers' for those wounded by these weapons. These light weapons are also involved in many acts of sexual and other forms of violence committed against women by military personnel.

During war, women have always been targeted specifically because of their sex and gender roles. They are subjected to abduction, sexual slavery, rape and unique brands of torture. They are also forced to serve as cooks and nurses for combat troops. As will be discussed next, trauma for female victims of violence continues even when the conflict is over, as they are frequently shunned, ostracized and further stigmatized as a result of the violence they have experienced during armed conflict. This stigmatization exacerbates the basic social subjugation of women in African cultures. Both men and women are socialized to believe that women should be subservient to men. Men also internalize the ideology that they (men) have the right to subjugate women (Warsame 2002: 61).

In an era where it is not easy to distinguish between combatants and non-combatants, especially in wars where there are no frontlines, no uniforms, no recognized military structure and new categories of fighters like women and children, many African conflicts occur in villages, between different ethnicities, races and families, owing to the fact that the vast majority of these armed conflicts are intrastate more than interstate conflicts. The development of efficient war-making technologies by the military industry makes modern war and militarism extremely deadly. Given that technology does not distinguish between combatants and civilians, and that it allows for women and children to participate in combat, women and girls now constitute a high proportion of the casualties during war and armed conflict.

At an individual level, women experience the danger of constant physical insecurity. In addition to the dangers of torture, gunfire, bombings and landmines, women and girls are at particular risk of sexual violence used increasingly as a weapon of war (Jones-Demen 2009: 105). For example, after the 1994 genocide in Rwanda, possibly 500,000 women were raped (Skjelsbaek and Smith 2001). This event marked the first recognition of the use of rape as widespread or systematic attack against women on the basis of ethnic grounds in Africa. More recently, it has been reported that an average of 40 women are raped every day in South Kivu, DR Congo, as a result of the conflict.

The increase of domestic violence is another category of danger. It has been asserted that domestic violence rises in times of armed conflict and social stress. During times of conflict, women suffer domestic violence at the hands of their in-laws or caretakers as their husbands disappear into the war, die or are exiled. For example, as observed by Lisa S. Price in this volume, Sudanese women from Darfur and Somali refugee women in camps experience domestic violence at the hands of their protectors (father or brothers-in-law) who are their cultural guardians in the absence of their husbands. The health consequences of this gender violence are exacerbated by the lack of medical care.

The impact of the destruction of health services is enormous as injuries occur and diseases are spread: in Rwanda 80 per cent of the women after the genocide had contracted venereal diseases. Also, in Burundi, Liberia and DR Congo, there are high rates of HIV/AIDS, partly owing to the widespread incidence of rape committed against women by forces fighting on the ground (Jones-Demen 2009; International Alert 2005). Mental health is also affected by the loss of family members, homes, prospects for the future and the need to adjust to radically new circumstances. All such experiences exacerbate the psychological impact of the experience of war, social upheaval and displacement, such as occurred in Somalia and in Kenya during the 2007–2008 political violence.

The experiences of women and men in armed conflict are varied and take place in highly different contexts. In some cases, individuals become direct targets of violence, while in others whole communities may be indirectly threatened through insecurity, fear and loss of livelihood. In Africa, conflict may be short-lived – for example, in the Ivory Coast, Kenya, Zimbabwe, Guinea Conakry and Madagascar, while in other cases, such as Somalia, DR Congo, Sudan and northern Uganda, wars continue for years, giving rise to situations of long-term general insecurity. Displacement and flight are often important features but not consistently so. The gender impacts of conflict are therefore difficult to categorize, and the distinctions made will inevitably be subjective. Nevertheless, some trends are clearly documented, such as demographic shifts, changes in marriage practices and the sexual division of labour. This situation has been visibly noticed in Somalia, where a majority of the male population has either died or been exiled. Involvement in the fighting has impacted the marriage practices and sexual division of labour, forcing women to assume non-traditional roles within their societies (Warsame 2002; Gardner and El Bushra 2004). The long-term social processes that follow a conflict must be understood in their particular contexts. The impact of war on women can be distinguished at the personal or individual level, at the levels of household and community and at the broader societal level.

Within the household, family composition changes when large numbers of men and boys are absent. There is a clear tendency toward a greater proportion of female-headed and child-headed households in conflict and post-conflict situations (30 per cent or more). This new reality changes the division of labour. Whether the household is headed by a male or female, there is a strong tendency for women to take on additional productive roles, either because of the absence of men or because men have lost access to the resources they once controlled.

On a community level, conflict may create space to make a redefinition of social relations possible, but in so doing it rearranges, adapts or reinforces patriarchal ideologies rather than fundamentally changing them. At the same time, we should not forget that the consequences of conflict are, from society to society, varied and complex and often lead in turn to further various consequences.

Refugees and displaced persons are another group of direct civilian victims in armed conflict. People become vulnerable when they are displaced and removed from their daily livelihood. Women and children comprise the majority of refugees and internally displaced persons. Displacement as a gendered impact of armed conflicts is the clearest violation of human, economic, political and social rights and of the failure to comply with international law (Moser and Clark 2001). At the end of 2004, the UN High Commission for Refugees (UNHCR) estimated the number of the refugee population in sub-Saharan Africa as 2,748,400 – 30 per cent of the global refugee population. Of the world's estimated 25 million internally displaced persons (IDPs), for example, Africa was home to over half of the 13 million IDPs (Williams 2005: 17). According to El Jack (2003), displacement does not necessarily mean that people leave or are forcibly removed to destinations that are far from their homes during and after armed conflict. Millions of people were internally displaced during armed conflict in the 1990s. While forced to leave their homes, they are still living within the borders of their countries.

The UN Refugee Convention of 1951 protects refugees outside of native borders but does not cover IDPs. The United Nations 1951 Convention relating to the Status of Refugees and its 1967 Protocol identifies five main characteristics that should be used to determine individual refugee status: a refugee is a person who leaves her or his country of residence to escape persecution on account of race, religion, nationality or membership of a particular social group or political opinion (UNHCR 1992: 8).

In Africa, the 1951 Convention is complemented by the 1969 Organization of African Unity (OAU) Convention that recognizes a refugee as 'every person who, owing to external aggression, occupation, foreign domination or events seriously disturbing public order in either part or the whole of his country of origin or nationality, is compelled to leave his place of habitual residence in order to seek refuge in another place outside his country of origin or nationality' (Williams 2005: 14–18). IDPs, unlike refugees, do not have a specific body of international law governing their protection. Over the past years, armed conflict has been the leading cause of displacement. However, the international community has limited options to protect displaced people within their borders if their home country is not willing to cooperate. In this way, the legal status of IDPs continues to be a serious concern.

Displacement is often viewed as a temporary or transitory phenomenon; however, the experiences in such countries as Somalia and Sudan show that it is actually a prolonged process. Furthermore, displacement disproportionately disadvantages women because it results in reduced access to resources to cope with household responsibilities and increased physical and emotional violence (El Jack 2003). Thus, displacement also implies social exclusion and poverty – conditions that are themselves likely to prolong conflict, constituting another barrier to the human security of African women.

Even in times of so-called peace, forced displacement is frequently used as a strategy of war that targets gender relations through family breakdown and social destabilization. Therefore, it can be argued that displacement does not affect all women the same way. In Sudan, for instance, ethnic groups, such as the Dinka, Nuer, Nuba, as well as other groups in the south and the Nuba Mountains, are marginalized due to their minority status. Women from these groups constitute an increasing number of war fatalities and casualties. Furthermore, the added responsibilities women have in productive, reproductive and community work are often transferred to younger girls and boys within the family, such as caring for the children, the elderly and the sick, along with managing burdensome domestic work. This shift of responsibility impacts the welfare and future of female household members (El Jack 2003).

Scholars who have closely studied the phenomenon of IDPs argue that the world of displaced women remains a challenge. However, displaced women continue to demonstrate resilience and try to live life as 'normally' as possible, given the circumstances. Positive examples include the Saharawi women who have lived in Algeria as refugees for 30 years. These women have played an essential role in the running of the camps from the beginning and have made incredible strides in some aspects of their lives. The literacy rate is estimated at 90 per cent, child mortality has decreased sharply, and they have established such services as day care. Saharawi women look forward to playing an integral role in the society on their return to Western Sahara (Williams 2005).

Women and girls often face sexual violence in refugee camps and in safe or resettled locations. They also face gender discrimination while seeking asylum. They confront many problems related to their biological make-up, including menstruation, gestation, parturition and lactation. Far more children and women die as a result of disease and malnutrition caused by war than from direct attack. Lack of necessities, such as healthcare, and insufficient food and rest in the refugee camps impel women and girls to take desperate measures, such as prostitution – for instance, in South Kivu, DR Congo, illegal trading and becoming perpetrators by participating in armed groups for survival purposes (Turpin 1998: 4–10; International Alert 2005: 26).

Many scholars acknowledge that women and girls experience conflict and displacement in different ways from men because of the division of gender roles and responsibilities. Furthermore, Williams (2005: 18) argues that the protection of IDPs and refugees is not only a human rights issue but also given the role women can play in state reform and peace processes, the protection of women is essential to Africa's development and on a broader scale for global security. Contemporary wars engulf the whole community, fundamentally affecting everyone's daily life by turning it upside down. What was known becomes unknown, what was safe, unsafe and what was familiar becomes unfamiliar (Bonnin 1998). In this way, war and armed conflict constitute a serious threat to women's human security because they experience its direct and indirect impact.

The general phenomenon in wartime is that men go to the battlefield and women stay at home. Losses in war reduce the number of men, and the consequence is that the number of war widows rapidly increases. War widows not only lose their loved ones but also lose a source of income, as they have to take up the burden of raising children and taking care of the elders as well as becoming the new social protectors. In many cases, they face economic burdens and security threats. In some societies, widows experience discrimination and difficulties in social integration. Besides, some cultures prevent widows from land entitlement and holding other properties in their own names.

Wherever and whenever armed conflict occurs, there is a high level of gender-based violence regardless of age, race, class and ethnicity. For instance, Africa has experienced many protracted intrastate wars where violence against women has been used as a weapon of war. The Declaration on the Elimination of Violence against Women (DEVAW) defines violence against women as 'any act of genderbased violence that results in, or is likely to result in, physical, sexual or mental harm or suffering to women, including threats of such acts, coercion or arbitrary deprivation of liberty, whether occurring in public or in private life' (UNIFEM 2005: 10). Violence is also considered to be a private issue, both within and beyond armed conflict. Therefore, violence against women and girls is physical, psychological, economic and social as their bodies and status become a battleground for those who use terror as a tactic of war. Furthermore, violence against women, such as sexual violence, has not only been used for ethnic cleansing but, given the stigma associated with such violence, also to cause the deliberate erosion of a people and their culture. Women do not only flee war zones in search of food and to escape being killed but also to prevent abduction, rape, enforced pregnancy, sexual trafficking, infection with sexually transmitted diseases and HIV/AIDS (Williams 2005: 19).

The various general effects of armed conflict on African women might be summarized in the following six categories:

1. The first way in which women suffer is as collateral victims of conflicts. They are attacked and molested by both sides in a conflict. For example, in the northern Ugandan conflict, the Acholi women are assaulted by both the Ugandan army and a rebel group, the Lord's Resistance Army (LRA).
2. Women suffer as fighters, participants or combatants. As participants in hospitals or in domestic services, they suffer the agony of seeing suffering every day and a feeling of helplessness or hopelessness regarding the situation. Women combatants also experience all types of discrimination, sexual and psychological violence as well as physical assault. Being in a non-state or unofficial military, such rebel or paramilitary groups do not guarantee security for women fighters once they are taken as prisoners. Women combatants are not treated like their male counterparts when taken prisoner of war because they are easily used as domestic and sexual workers. As members of guerrilla forces or militias, they do not enjoy the protection granted under the international conventions to all combatants that is guaranteed under the Geneva Conventions for prisoners of wars because they are not accounted for as official combatants. This is a direct violation of the Geneva Conventions for Prisoners of Wars (POWs). For example, many former girl child soldiers from Mozambique, Sierra Leone, Liberia, Burundi and Democratic Republic of Congo have reported discrimination and violence against them during their combatant roles.
3. Women suffer as politicians. As politicians, women suffer politically from threats of death and assassinations. For instance, Agathe Uwilingiyimana was a Rwandan political figure who served as the prime minister of Rwanda from 18 July 1993 till her death on 7 April 1994. Her term ended when she was assassinated for being

a moderate Hutu during the opening of the 1994 Rwandan Genocide by the presidential guard. These threats also extend to women's families and friends. Women politicians are easily threatened by guerrilla or paramilitary groups because they are considered to be 'vulnerable', a soft target for men, used as bargaining tools, especially in countries where rebel groups operate by kidnapping politicians. They also suffer from family pressures and at times cannot continue with their work. In this situation, an interesting example involves Dr Specioza Naigaga Wandira Kazibwe, who was the elected vice president of Uganda from 1994 to 2003, the first woman in Africa to hold that position. After finding it difficult to perform her political duties and deal with an increasingly messy divorce case due to the domestic violence she suffered, she resigned from her position in government. Ellen Johnson-Sirleaf, elected president of Liberia in 2007, may be the one exception.

4 Women suffer because of their relatives. Women who have families as active members – either in the government forces, in official positions or in rebel movements – are tortured for the purposes of exposing information on the whereabouts of their loved ones.

5 Women also suffer as peace builders or campaigners, especially in their desire to bring about peace and justice. They suffer because they have generally been denied the possibility or the opportunity to participate in peace processes as they are seen as *poor victims* who need masculine protection. As peace builders, they encounter opposition and oppression from the very system they are challenging in order to secure their rights for the purpose of building a better future for their children and for society at large. For example, the first African woman Noble Peace Laureate, Professor Wangari Maathai, experienced political violence in the early 1990s in her endeavour to campaign for the freedom of political detainees and the protection of the Karura Forest in Kenya.

6 Finally, women suffer many and varied forms of physical violence during conflict. These include torture, mutilation (such as in the cases of Sierra Leone and Liberia where people's limbs were cut off), forced prostitution, slavery, assassination/ murder, abduction and forced pregnancy. They may also be infected with sexually transmitted diseases, such as HIV/AIDS, as occurred in DR Congo. Women and children are reported to be victims of anti-personal landmines in Angola and Mozambique. They are forced to take up arms, kill and torture. They are detained, humiliated, given inhumane treatment and suffer from fear due to insecurity. In some cases they are sterilized. Moreover, women are often forced

to witness the murder of their family members (Ross-Sheriff and Swigonski 2006: 130). Women and children are adversely affected due to these experiences, and as a result, the entire society undergoes trauma that often causes irreparable damage to human security.

Armed conflict destroys individuals, families, communities and the economy. For instance, the war in northern Uganda between the LRA and the government of Uganda has led to the collapse of agricultural production, livestock and looting of property. During this conflict, prolonged insecurity also disrupted trade, leading to poverty. Furthermore, conflict situations considerably increase the trauma of gender-specific physical insecurity for women and girls. This is particularly true in remote rural areas far away from general media coverage. Hence such violations are often either ignored or unreported (FAO/WFP 2000: 2).

Gender-based violence increases during armed conflict

We argue in this collection that such effects as just described, especially violence against women, must be central to any constructive discussion of human security. Such violence is integral to the war system that comprises militarized state security. Gender-based violence (GBV) has become an intentional strategy of armed conflict. There are multiple causes of GBV that occur in times of peace as well as in armed conflict. GBV is physical, sexual and psychological violence against both men and women that occurs within the family and the community and is perpetrated or condoned by the state (Bouta and others 2005: 33). This kind of violence has been predominant within and between adversaries in postcolonial conflicts in Africa, The Balkans, Latin America and Asia. Although it is most often women who are targets of GBV, both women and men may be subjected to rape and the consequent increased rate of HIV/AIDS infection as well as other sexually transmitted infections (STIs); damage to physical and psychological health; and disruption of lives and loss of self-confidence and self-esteem (El Jack 2003: 16). The purpose of GBV in inter-group conflict includes desecrating the honour of the enemy and creating fear of the threat of rape toward defeating the enemy as a whole. In general practice, it is considered that men are protectors of women. That is why, in many African cultures, when women are attacked by the enemy, it is a factor in demoralizing the men because it signifies that their honour and function as the protector has been destroyed. In an attempt to escape the harm and the dishonor, a mass flow of migration takes place, producing a large number of women and children refugees. For example, Lisa S. Price notes that the tactic employed by the Janjaweed in Darfur, Sudan, of raping, killing and burning property is designed to deliberately force people out of their homes, particularly women as the producers and reproducers of society.

Scholars (such as Bouta and others 2005) assert that, in conflict situations, GBV is committed against both civilians and soldiers. It is not an accidental side effect of war but an intentional act against an individual and a criminal act of aggression against the entire community or nation. They agree that women are more vulnerable to GBV than men because of prevailing oppressive gender relations and the fact that more women than men lack mobility and are unarmed and unprotected (ibid.: 33). In most armed conflicts in Africa, such as those in Somalia, Sudan, DR Congo and northern Uganda, this situation makes women more vulnerable and, hence, they become the majority of victims of GBV. As mentioned earlier, GBV does not occur 'accidentally' or as a side effect of warfare as is sometimes suggested, but rather, it is consciously planned and targeted. GBV is strategic violence that is aimed at intimidating and demoralizing the enemy. It is a crime against the individual and the entire community, targeting women: symbolic bearers of ethnic, caste and national identity, they are systematically violated. From a cultural perspective, the entire community is affected by this violence (ibid.: 35).

GBV is frequently rooted in pre-conflict conditions, but it increases and often becomes an accepted practice during conflict and in the post-conflict period when a shift in GBV seems to take place from the public to the private domain through an increase in domestic violence by the immediate family members or neighbours. Identifying domestic violence during conflict is difficult because, usually, the men are away from home, fighting, or taking refuge in another country. In this situation, many women suffer domestic violence at the hands of their in-laws, guardians or neighbours in whose care they have been left.

Domestic violence is common during peacetime, but it tends to increase in conflict and post-conflict situations because of the wide availability of weapons, the violence that male family members have experienced or meted out, battle trauma, frustration and lack of jobs, shelter and basic services (Lindsey 2001; Rehn and Sirleaf 2002). In the aftermath of conflict, trauma that male combatants have suffered may be transformed into domestic violence. Domestic violence not only affects the victim but also damages the fabric of society, creating fear in women's lives and socializing children into a culture of violence, which undermines social cohesion and transmits violence to the next generation (Bouta and others 2005). Amnesty International (2004: 52) also reports that women living through conflict not only have to endure assaults or threats of assault by the other side but also have to face increased levels of violence from within their families at the same time as they are depended upon to rebuild their communities from the ground up.

Sexual threats from the enemy force women to become combatants in their own groups to protect themselves, often changing their roles from victims to perpetrators of violence. They think that they will be safer from the enemy if they join in the conflict as combatants. However, whether women are the victims or perpetrators, they are not safe. Women also take part in conflict to take revenge for the atrocities committed on them and their families by enemies. For instance, in Liberia many women fought to protect themselves and other women from rape and murder and to avenge the ill treatment meted out to themselves and other women. For example, Ellen, now about 30 years old, said she enlisted at age 16 after being raped by the same men who killed her mother and father right before her eyes (Jones-Demen 2009: 108–9). There was also the famous Black Diamond, a female rebel commander, said to have controlled about 1,000 women fights against Charles Taylor. She was feared by friends and foes (ibid.: 117). In many instances, a conflicting party abducts adolescent girls, rapes women and girls and commits other sexual abuses against them.

Some types of GBV are experienced almost entirely by women and girls during and after conflict, such as forced prostitution, sex work, trafficking for sexual or other types of slavery, and forced pregnancy. Women often resort to forced prostitution as a coping mechanism to survive conflict, as it offers a source of income and bargaining power. For example, currently, more women than men are forced into commercial sex in a desperate attempt to survive in the DR Congo. They may become sexually involved with members of armed groups or with people who provide food, shelter, safe passage and other needs in exchange for sex as well as with relatively well-off international agency personnel (Rehn and Sirleaf 2002; El-Bushra 2003; Bouta and others 2005).

GBV tends to increase in conflict situations because it has become a means of warfare as a result of a general breakdown in law and order and a policy to demoralize the enemy (Byrne 1996). Moreover, sex can come to be seen as a form of reward or war booty that unpaid, underfed and drugged or intoxicated fighters demand. This is largely because troops are usually young, sexually active, male and single, and in some armies, actively discouraged from marrying (Bouta and others 2005: 26–37). Although GBV affects men, male GBV survivors generally have been overlooked. Men and boys are raped during conflict, and men become targets of sexual abuse, torture and mutilation to attack and destroy their sense of masculinity or manhood (United Nations 2002). In most African countries and cultures, it has been difficult to address and recognize the problems of male GBV victims because their sense of masculinity or manhood is very important in defining their identity, gender roles and relations in their societies. This aspect of exploiting shame as a means of intimidation of men extends far beyond Africa. The full disclosure of sexual abuse as torture in American camps holding prisoners taken in the so-called War on Terror attested to the widespread use of this criminal practice.

The impact of GBV also has distinct consequences for women and girls, including sexual mutilation, sterility, chronic reproductive/gynaecological health problems and, above all, marginalization from family and community due to stigma associated with sexual abuse (United Nations 2002). Their experience is gender-specific in three important respects, involving rape, women's vulnerability and the HIV/AIDS stigma (International Alert 2001). Due to a lack of security, women and girls are also vulnerable to GBV as they go about their daily activities. Women leave their homes in search of security, only to arrive in camps and find themselves vulnerable to serious atrocities and GBV (Williams 2005: 19).

The most serious type of GBV is rape because it is used as a weapon of war in many armed conflicts, as most recently witnessed in Democratic Republic of Congo, Darfur in Sudan and South Sudan. Rape as a gender-based form of violence has been used to infect people with diseases, such as HIV/AIDS, to make a mark, such as producing babies of a certain tribe or ethnic group, or to prove to the men on the enemy's side that they cannot protect their women, thus shaming the protectors on their failure to protect.

Furthermore, we can argue that the protector/protected roles are important in armed conflict because the bodies of the women have become the venue where the battle between the protectors is waged. Rape is a gendered weapon of war, and it occurs in many contexts. For example, refugee women fleeing war are raped by border guards, refugee camp officials, rebels, family members and others who hold power over their escape (Epp 2002). Rape has been defined as sexualized violence that seeks to humiliate, terrorize and destroy a woman based on her identity as a woman (Snyder and others 2006). In war, it is not simply gender that makes women a target for such violence. It is also the intersection of gender with a variety of multiple identities that allows groups of women to be differentiated between 'theirs and ours' (ibid.: 193). Rape as a gendered weapon of war is as old as war itself. Many scholars agree that wartime rape is as much, if not more, about the war on women as war between ethnic groups and states. Moreover, rape as a war on women is the longest war in history. This is so because of the traditional image of women as victims of war who should be protected by their male counterparts. Cases of systematic rape and sexual violation occur frequently during war through both individual and gang rape. Women have been raped in armed conflicts around the world, including Sierra Leone, Chechnya, Uganda, Liberia, Kuwait, East Timor, Vietnam, Indonesia, Kosovo, Democratic Republic of Congo, Bosnia, Sudan, Angola, Mozambique, Peru, Algeria, Korea, Colombia, South Sudan and Somalia and have experienced sexual assault by the insertion of such objects as umbrellas, firewood, sticks and batteries in their private parts.

The achievement of human security for women requires the elimination of gender-based violence. In order to eliminate GBV, Bouta and others (2005: 34) recommend that awareness needs to be raised to ensure that GBV in conflict is acknowledged and addressed in post-conflict reconstruction and that local capacity to provide psychological counselling is strengthened to reach all actors involved (survivors, survivors' families, witnesses and perpetrators). These scholars further affirm that women and men should have similar protection against GBV, have the same information on and access to GBV medical services and receive equal assistance from a same-sex health worker (and translator) during medical examinations. Moreover, one major breakthrough is a legal mechanism for dealing with GBV. This is the newly adopted UN Security Council Resolution 1820 (18 July 2008), which recognizes that rape epidemics in war and other forms of sexual violence can constitute war crimes, crimes against humanity or a constitutive act to genocide. This resolution is important for both African men and women living in conflict situations, such as in Somalia, South Sudan, Darfur and DR Congo, among others, because it is a sign of global renunciation of rape as a weapon of war against them which jeopardizes their human security.

The brutalities of war, death or separation from loved ones and family, forced migration, rape and sexual abuse, starvation, extreme violence and cruel acts leave deep scars on the psyches of both women and men. Women and children significantly become victims and are traumatized by conflict. The psychological consequences are far more severe than the physical ones due to the high level of stress and anxiety in their daily lives. The reproductive systems of women are damaged through rape, sexual assault and exploitation. Social health, including the education and development essential to the wellbeing of society, also deteriorates in times of armed conflict (Turpin 1998; Lindsey 2001).

Violence against women is a complex dynamic, often hard to fully comprehend. It is usually conceptualized as an interpersonal crime, either within families or between strangers. Thus, stereotypes and ideals surrounding the fertility and virginity of women are a basis for analyzing why the victimization of women in times of war not only hurts women but also destroys the ties of women to their families and communities of origin (Milillo 2006: 199). Perhaps the representation of women as the pure preservation of the society, as maternal symbols in many African societies, leads to their victimization during wars and armed conflicts.

Such scholars as G. G. Jansen (2006) have studied and documented the effects of armed conflict on the physical and mental health of women. This is reported to be one of the long-lasting effects of armed conflict due to the undetectable nature of suffering on the individual. Her findings include the recognition that post-traumatic stress disorder, as well as anxiety, depression and increased homicide rates, are the by-products of atrocities that are perpetrated and endured by many during war, flight and refugee situations. As a result, Rehn and Sirleaf (2002) argue that psychosocial support and reproductive health services (emergency contraception and treatment for STIs) for women should be an integral part of emergency assistance and post-conflict reconstruction, especially for those who have experienced physical trauma, torture and rape.

El Jack (2003) asserts that conflict worsens existing patterns of sexual violence against women in two main ways. First, the incidence of 'everyday' violence, particularly domestic violence, increases as communities break down during and after conflicts. Second, 'everyday' violence escalates in the context of masculinized and militarized conflict situations. Conflict breeds distinct types of power relations and imbalances. In the context of conflict, for instance, violence against women is more than the exercise of power over women. By raping women, who represent the purity and culture of the nation, invading armies are also symbolically raping the nation itself (2003: 16).

Gender relations in war and armed conflict

Armed conflicts have influenced and modified gender relations. In Africa, such wars as those in Liberia, Sierra Leone, Rwanda, Mozambique,

Burundi, northern Uganda, Angola, Somaliland, Sudan, Somalia, South Sudan and DR Congo have changed the traditional roles of women. Generally, armed conflict and war affect the life of everyone and change traditional roles in the family, community and 'public domain'. The changes are normally unplanned as the men disappear into war. The changes force women to assume new roles, bearing full responsibility for their children, elderly relatives and the community in general. They become the heads of households and the breadwinners, taking over responsibility for earning a livelihood, caring for farms and animals, trading and being active outside the home – activities often traditionally carried out by men. The very fact that many of the menfolk are absent often heightens the insecurity and danger for women and children left behind, especially in countries that are currently in conflict, such as Somalia, Sudan (Darfur), South Sudan and DR Congo. This accelerates the breakdown of the traditional protection and support mechanisms upon which the community previously relied.

Because war and armed conflict are gendered activities, women and men have different access to resources, power and decision-making before, during and after conflicts. In this sense women and men, therefore, experience armed conflict and war in very different ways. Men are the decision makers and usually the primary combatants. Meanwhile, the experience of women may centre on ensuring survival for other family members. Hence their needs and the resources tend to be different. But these differences receive little attention. By failing to consider gender relations and inequalities, in many post-conflict countries, for instance, in Liberia and Sierra Leone, potential resources or possible tensions in reconstruction initiatives are overlooked.

Changes in women's traditional roles

Examining the role of women as perpetrators in relation to gender can reveal negative or positive consequences. In such countries as Angola, Sierra Leone, northern Uganda and Mozambique, girl soldiers were subjected to constant sexual aggression by the armed group they belonged to (Price 2004). Many argue that the role of women soldiers has been both to increase the number of soldiers in general – even in supportive roles, such as administrative positions. Therefore, war experiences may offer many women soldiers a meaning and purpose in their traditional lives that peacetime may lack. However, when the war is over, men and women are often encouraged to take different roles or to go back to their previous socially prescribed roles. In this case, it is argued that the men do not have a break in their gendered socialization, whereas the women do.

For that reason, female ex-combatants, who have broken the rules of traditional behaviour and gender roles, are marginalized during the reconstruction process. Female soldiers who have broken ties with their families and participated in a war on terms similar to those are very often socialized out of their local settings and traditions. This was the case in countries like Liberia, Burundi, Mozambique and Sierra Leone, where girl child soldiers were required to undergo a cleansing ceremony in order to be accepted back into their societies. They tend to face difficulties when the conflict is over because there is pressure on them to return to more traditional ways of living soon after their roles as active participants in the conflict is over. Another obstacle that female ex-combatants face is the overall reluctance of society to recognize the importance of their contributions to the war effort and the consequent social change. Men also have been unwilling to share veteran status with women, especially where women have been denied their roles in direct combat. Among the negative and positive aspects that have been mentioned here, it should be noted that, although the role of women as participants allows them to escape from their traditional roles, it also exposes them to traumatic experiences, such as rape and GBV, as described earlier. In discussing women as victims of military and gender violence, the idea of women as perpetrators of military violence is introduced to demonstrate that armed conflict and war always generate more costs than benefits for women despite their participation.

Sometimes armed conflict promotes development of new abilities in women and girls which can be witnessed during the conflict and in post-conflict reconstruction. For example, during the Eritrean struggle, those fighting for national independence established a school curriculum which reflected a commitment to socialist equality and the rights of women. Classes were co-educational, and girls were encouraged to fully participate in all fields, particularly the technical ones. In Liberia, this led to the first elected female president of Africa, mentioned earlier. Ms Johnson Sirleaf is committed to supporting issues that affect women and to reforming all laws in order to protect and promote women's human rights in accordance with international human rights treaties to which Liberia is a signatory (Jones-Demen 2009: 101–4). Rwanda is another inspiring post-conflict example, particularly in the field of political participation where women constitute 36 per cent of cabinet positions and 41 per cent of legislative seats (ibid.: 112).

Unfortunately, on the other hand, war more often discourages girls from attending school because it is unsafe for them to leave home. In the case of Somalia, girls dropped out of school when it became too dangerous to attend classes. In some cases, this accelerated their early marriage. Meanwhile, in some wars, particularly religious conflicts, certain factions with strong patriarchal views believe that girls should not be educated at all under any circumstances. As described by Chloe Breyer in her article in this collection, this has been the situation in areas of Afghanistan taken over by the Taliban or under the control of other fundamentalists.

El Jack (2003) further claims that one reason gender awareness initiatives lack support is the division in thinking between technical and social support. She says that technical support refers to assistance with immediate results, such as re-establishing running water, sewage systems, health facilities or the electricity supply. Social support, by contrast, refers to assistance with longer-term issues that are harder to tackle and provide fewer quantifiable results and that are therefore considered to be lower priority, such as schooling, training and social service provision – developments most needed to move toward gender equality. Both types of support, however, bring into question social, cultural and religious practices. But during periods of conflict, it has been considered inappropriate to address gender relations. The result is that the effect of technical interventions, such as large-scale sanitation projects, on the dynamics between men and women are not considered (2003: 14). Also, due to the political and social context of armed conflict, it is difficult to access food, health, education and other basic goods and services. During conflict, direct violence, such as rape, intimidates and represses women; structural violence (poverty, inequality) institutionalizes repression; and cultural violence (accepted norms and values) internalizes the repressive relationship in the minds of women and men (Rajoo 2005: 18).

Even though women assume non-stereotypical roles as combatants, policymakers and/or heads of household, attempts to have their voices heard in official processes are often dismissed (El Jack 2003: 9). Thus, in a violent, militarized world where abuse and victimization are prevalent, everybody belongs to either the category of victim or abuser or both. There is an internal contradiction between the different roles of victim, victimizer, bystander and rescuer that the individual is invited or forced to play. Only when she or he understands and acknowledges this is it possible for the person to move forward. Women have shown greater ability to reflect on themselves and to differentiate their own experience from the conflict at hand, thus recognizing more deeply the complexity and hypocrisy of war (Wimble 2003: 90). It may be this capacity to reflect and understand more profoundly the costs and contradictions of war and armed violence which leads so many women to mobilize against all forms of organized violence. This plays a significant role in the struggle to transform the militarized security system into one that might better assure human security for all vulnerable populations.

El Jack (2003: 6) remarks that the inequality experienced by women during and after conflict in all societies derives from a dominant view of gender roles. During armed conflict and war, the traditional gender roles assigned by patriarchy change, and these changes are usually irreversible. Under such circumstances, women and men adopt new gender roles as a means of survival. A central argument being made in this collection of articles on gender and human security is that the survival of the whole human family may well depend and a worldwide transformation of gender roles as essential to the transformation of the militarized system of state security now being challenged by women throughout the world. If gender roles are changed in armed conflict, might it be possible also to develop peaceful means to move toward a more just and equal gender relations?

Although it has been witnessed that conflict affects women and men differently, both suffer during war. Both have a high stake in achieving peace and human security. Many scholars have acknowledged that gender relations in pre-conflict situations often set the stage for the options for women and men during armed conflict and war. Thus, the dominant social, political and economic norms often influence the scope and potential women and men have for action in actual conflict situations (Woroniuk and Schalkwyk 1998). For example, if women are not active in political structures, they will find it hard to influence political decisions that precipitate increased military tension. However, other scholars, such as El Jack (2003), argue that gender relations are always characterized by unequal access to, or distribution of, power. Her argument is that, given that gender discrimination is so prevalent, it influences other dynamics of armed conflict. More specifically, gender analysis of armed conflict and war highlights the difference between men and women in terms of their gendered activities, their needs, their acquisition and control of resources and their access to decision-making processes in a post-conflict situation (ibid.: 11). She remarks further that a gender analysis must extend beyond addressing women's immediate needs, such as food, water and health services, and toward their longer-term comprehensive human security needs, including equal representation in decision-making processes and leadership roles. Hence, it should also recognize how shifts into non-traditional roles affect power balances and gender relations. Here are arguments in favour of promoting women's equality as an essential basis for peace and a necessity for their human security.

As has been described, during war, gender relations can be subjected to stress and change; survival strategies often necessitate a change in the gender division of labour. In this situation, women may become responsible for an increased number of dependents. Also, unequal gender relations in the pre-conflict era shape the ways in which families and households allocate resources, influencing the distribution of entitlements, responsibilities, work and leisure between male and female members (UNRISD 2005: 65). It can be argued that inequalities based on sex are a pervasive feature of all societies; they are the product of socially constructed power relations, norms and practices (ibid.: xx). It can further be argued that, whether in peace or conflict, the global political economy changes the role of women. As a result, women face structural and cultural violence, the most common and widespread of all obstacles to their human security. However, the social upheaval caused by conflict creates the potential to redefine gender relations (El Jack 2003: 41). Given the present global environmental and economic upheavals, perhaps we are now at a historic moment conducive to the transformation sought by women and all who strive for peace.

Conclusion: changing gender roles for human security

The influence of war on gender and the changes in the traditional gender roles during conflict and post-conflict periods show that gender roles can and should change. For the sake of human security, gender roles and relations have to be renegotiated or reshaped so that they become flexible to both male and female. One such change should be in the traditional perception of women in armed conflict and post-conflict situation as 'victims of war', taking into account recent gender studies that have underlined how women play a pivotal role in conflict and post-conflict. One of the aspects that has not yet received due recognition has been women's role in peace processes and their abilities as peace builders. It is important to acknowledge that gender hierarchies constantly change as old forms dissolve and recreate. Hence, we may actively participate in that dissolution and recreation so as to move toward gender equality and human security.

The situation of women in armed conflict may not be easy to understand except by women themselves who have experienced the consequences and know the threat that war poses to their human security.

There is not a single country in the world where violence against women is not a significant problem and a disturbing reality, whether in war or peace. It is time to discuss human security not only for the female half of the world's people but also for all those made most vulnerable by the present order.

References

Ahmed Ali, F. 2007. 'Women and War: Deconstructing the Notion of Victim and Reconstructing their Roles as Peace Builders', PhD dissertation. Spain: Universitat Jaume I, Castellón.
Amnesty International. 2004. *It Is in Our Hands to Stop Violence against Women*. London: Amnesty International Publications.
Annan, K. 2001. 'Foreword', in R. McRae and D. Hubert (eds.), *Human Security and the New Diplomacy: Protecting People, Promoting Peace*. Montreal: McGill-Queens's University Press, pp. xix–xx.
Bonnin, D. 1998. 'Not a Male Affair: Women and Conflict in South Africa', *Arena Magazine*, (4): 35–28. June–July.
Bouta, T. and others. 2005. *Gender, Conflict, and Development*. Washington, DC: World Bank.
Byrne, B. 1996. 'Gender, Conflict and Development'. http://www.bridge.ids. ac.uk/sites/bridge.ids.ac.uk/files/reports/re34c.pdf. Accessed 15 August 2007.
Major-General Cammaert, P. 2008. 'Meeting the Protection Challenges in Contemporary Armed Conflict: Women Affected by War', WP914th WILTON PARK CONFERENCE: Women Targeted or Affected by Armed Conflict: What Role for Military Peacekeepers? Tuesday 27 May 2008. www.wiltonpark. org.uk/wp-content/uploads/wp914-report.pdf. Accessed 20 May 2018.
El-Bushra, J. 2003. *Women Building Peace: Sharing Know How*. London: International Alert.
El Jack, A. 2003. *Gender and Armed Conflict: Overview Report*. Brighton: BRIDGE, Institute of Development Studies (IDS), University of Sussex.
Epp, M. 2002. 'Women, War and Rape', *The Other Side*, vol. 3 (38): 42. May–June. InfoTrac Web: Expanded Academic ASAP.
Estefanía, J. 2006. 'África, sorprendente objeto de deseo (o no)', *El País, Economía: Agenda Global. Uso de las materias primas*. 19 November.
FAO/WFP. 2000. 'Socio-Economic and Gender Analysis in Emergency Operations, Abstract SEAGA'. www.reliefweb.int/library/GHARkit/.Docfiles/ SUMMARYSEAGA.doc. Accessed 15 August 2007.
Gardner, J. and J. El Bushra (eds.). 2004. *Somalia: The Untold Story: The War Through the Eyes of Somali Women*. London: Pluto Press.
International Alert. 2001. *Protection of Civilians: Gender Considerations for Disarmament, Conflict Transformation and the Establishment of Human Security*. London: International Alert.
———. 2005. *Women's Bodies as a Battleground: Sexual Violence against Women and Girls During the War in the Democratic Republic of Congo, South Kivu (1996–2003)*. London: International Alert.

Jansen, G. G. 2006. 'Gender and War: The Effects of Armed Conflict on Women's Health and Mental Health', *Affilia: Journal of Women and Social Work*, vol. 21 (2): 134–45.

Jones-Demen, A. 2009. 'Dynamics of Gender Relations in War-Time and Post-War Liberia: Implications for Public Policy', in K. Omeje (ed.), *War to Peace Transition Conflict Intervention and Peacebuilding in Liberia*. Lanham: University Press of America Inc.

Lindsey, C. 2001. *Women and War*. Geneva: International Review of the Red Cross.

McRae, R. 2001. 'Human Security in a Globalized World', in R. McRae and D. Hubert (eds.), *Human Security and the New Diplomacy: Protecting People, Promoting Peace*. Montreal: McGill-Queens's University Press, pp. 14–27.

Milillo, D. 2006. 'Rape as a Tactic of War: Social and Psychological Perspectives', *Affilia: Journal of Women and Social Work*, vol. 21 (2): 196–205.

Moser, C. and F. Clark (eds.). 2001. *Victims, Perpetrators or Actors? Gender, Armed Conflict and Political Violence*. London: Zed Books.

Price, S. 2004. 'Use of Girl Soldiers Condemned', BBC News Africa. 4 March. http://news.bbc.co.uk/2/hi/africa/3531641.stm. Accessed 2 August 2007.

Rajoo, K. 2005. 'Sexual Abuse and Exploitation: Power Tools in Peace Keeping Missions', *The African Centre for the Constructive Resolution of Dispute* (ACCORD), vol. 4: 17–23.

Reed, L. and M. Tehranian. 1999. 'Evolving Security Regimes', in M. Tehranian (ed.), *World APART: Human Security Global Governance*. London/New York: I. B. Tauris Publishers.

Rehn, E. and E. J. Sirleaf. 2002. *Women, War and Peace: The Independent Experts' Assessment of the Impact of Armed Conflict on Women and Women's Roles in Peace-building*. New York: United Nations Development Fund for Women.

Ross-Sheriff, F. and M. E. Swigonski (eds.). 2006. 'Women, War and Peace Building', *Affilia: Journal of Women and Social Work*, vol. 21 (2): 129–32.

Skjelsbaek, I. and D. Smith (eds.). 2001. *Gender, Peace and Conflict*. Oslo: International Peace Research Institute (PRIO).

Snyder, C. S. and others. 2006. 'On the Battleground of Women's Bodies: Mass Rape in Bosnia-Herzegovina', *Affilia: Journal of Women and Social Work*, vol. 21 (2): 184–95.

Tehranian, M. (ed.). 1999. *Worlds Apart: Human Security Global Governance*. London/New York: I. B. Tauris Publishers.

Turpin, J. 1998. 'Many Faces: Women Confronting War', in L. Lorentzen and J. Turpin (eds.), *The Women and War Reader*. New York: New York University Press, pp. 3–18.

UNHCR. 1992. *UNHCR'S Handbook on Procedures and Criteria for Determining Refugee Status Under the 1951 Convention and the 1967 Protocol Relating to the Status of Refugees*. Geneva: UNHCR. www.unhcr.org/home/PUBL/3d58e13b4.pdf. Accessed 10 August 2007.

UNIFEM. 2005. 'Violence against Women', UN. www.unifem.org/filescon firmed/149/213_chapter01.pdf. Accessed 24 March 2005.

United Nations. 2002. *Women, Peace and Security*. Geneva: United Nations. www.un.org/womenwatch/daw/public/eWPS.pdf. Accessed 2 August 2007.
UNRISD. 2005. *Gender Equity: Striving for Justice in an Unequal World*. France: UNRISD.
Warsame, A. M. 2002. *Queens without Crowns: Somaliland Women's Changing Roles and Peace Building*. Horn of Africa Series 4. Nairobi: SOWRAG/ Life & Peace Institute.
Williams, H. 2005. 'Protecting the Vulnerable: The Case of Displaced Women in Africa', *The African Centre for the Constructive Resolution of Dispute* (ACCORD), vol. 3: 17–22.
Wimble, N. 2003. 'Recovering Herstory: Looking at Women in Kosovo through an Alternative Lens', MA dissertation. Spain: Universitat Jaume I, Castellón.
Woroniuk, B. and J. Schalkwyk. 1998. *Conflict, Peace-Building, Disarmament, Security*. Stockholm: Swedish International Cooperation Agency (SIDA).

6 Sexual violence and genocide, the greatest violation of human security
Responses to the case of Darfur

Lisa S. Price

> It happened last August when we were in our farms outside the village. We saw five Arab men who came to us and asked where our husbands were. Then they told us that we should have sex with them. We said no. So they beat and raped us. After they abused us, they told us that now we would have Arab babies; and if they would find any Fur woman, they would rape them again to change the colour of their children.
> –Three women (25, 30 and 40), October 2004, West Darfur (Médecins Sans Frontières, 2005: 1)

If we stand in the shoes of an African woman in Darfur, what does human security look like? It does not consist of lofty words spoken in great chambers. Rather, security (and its opposite) are measured in daily calculations which can be literally life-and-death decisions: Can I leave the displaced persons' camp to collect firewood and water at the risk of rape by roving soldiers and militiamen? If I don't, how will I cook for my family? Do I return to my village to pick up provisions or are men waiting there to capture women into sexual slavery? Is it safe to send my daughter to school when schools have been targeted? Do I speak of the sexual violence done to me and risk social and familial ostracism? Do I report the violence to the police and risk being arrested for adultery? Five years into the genocide, Darfuri women know about human security because they know the contours of its absence. Those contours describe not just direct physical threat but also attacks on economic wellbeing and social cohesion.

It is axiomatic to say that the war system impoverishes human security. When the object of armed conflict is genocide and its implements include rape, sexual mutilation, sexual slavery and forced pregnancy, the battleground is women's bodies, and the stakes can be the survival of a whole people.

States have as one of their mandates the protection of their citizens from internal and external harm. That is why most states have a police force and military. States are also tasked with guaranteeing rights and freedoms set out in international covenants, such as the Universal Declaration of Human Rights. Yet too often the perpetrators of rights violations are the selfsame states. When that happens, how should the international community respond?

This article examines the role of sexual violence in the Darfur genocide and the range of international instruments which could be deployed to protect and promote the security of Darfuri women. I maintain that what is needed is a robust, adequately resourced intervention force with a specific mandate to protect civilians and to rebuild civilian infrastructure. Examples of the former include the firewood patrols initiated by African Union (AU) troops which protect women from rape and abduction when they leave villages and camps. An example of the latter is digging bore holes to replace wells poisoned by the Sudanese Armed Forces (SAF) and the *Janjaweed*.

Sexual violence (I mean the phrase to cover a range of violations, not just rape) is a prominent tactic in the government and Janjaweed campaign of extermination in Darfur. Before proceeding to a discussion of possible forms of international response, it is necessary to appreciate the acts, meanings and consequences of the sexual violation of Darfuri women. These, then, are the facts.

Genocidal rape in Darfur

The first Sudanese civil war, which ended in a ceasefire in 2005, pitted the Muslim north against the Christian and animist south and did not involve the western (Darfur) provinces. In contrast, in Darfur, the conflict is not religious, as almost all residents practice Islam. The opposition is both racial (light-skinned Arabs versus dark-skinned Africans) and occupational (settled agrarians versus nomadic herders). It is animated by resource competition due to drought and by a political system which is both repressive and highly preferential. Open armed conflict began in 2003 when Darfuri rebel groups, such as the Sudan Liberation Army (SLA), began attacking government facilities. Within months the Sudanese military and government-supported Janjaweed (the name means 'devils on horseback') militia were targeting civilians, and the conflict became a genocide. Over 400,000 civilians have been killed, over 3,000,000 have been forcibly displaced and 90 per cent of their villages have been destroyed. This is out of a total population of 6,000,000, both Arab and African, who lived in the three Darfur provinces, roughly the size of France.

As to sexual violence, it is impossible to set the number of victims. Since 2005, detailed information from within Darfur has been nearly impossible to obtain as a result of the Sudanese government's blockade against media and researchers. In addition, in 2005 the government arrested a *Médecins Sans Frontières* (MSF) worker in response to a report by that organization on the prevalence of sexual violence in the conflict. The result has been to create a 'chilly climate' in which aid organizations keep silent on sex crimes in order to avoid government retaliation. Notwithstanding these logistical and political barriers, in its 2007 world report, Human Rights Watch indicated that 'tens of thousands of women have been subject to sexual abuse' (quoted in Bastick et al. 2007: 63). This is at best a gross estimate, for several factors restrict the reporting of sexual assault. Drawing on the work of the International Rescue Committee in the Democratic Republic of Congo, each reported assault potentially represents 30 others (cited in Ginerich and Leaning 2004: 16–17). In addition, in Sudan, as in many countries, rape victims are severely stigmatized, so if they can, most keep silent about what has been done to them. Women who have been sexually murdered or die as a result of sexual torture and women held in sexual slavery obviously cannot report attacks. Finally, in Darfur, one-third of the people in need are beyond the reach of aid organizations and hence also cannot make reports. In light of these considerations, we can appreciate one aid worker's conclusion that 'the number of women in Darfur that have faced horrible [sexual] traumas is *unimaginable*' (emphasis added, quoted in van Zeijl 2007: 12).

Tara Ginerich and Jennifer Leaning identify three settings in which most reported rapes in Darfur take place. The settings correspond to temporal progress. First, in the days prior to an attack on an African village, Janjaweed militiamen and government soldiers attack women and girls who have left the village to collect firewood and water. Second, during the attack, women are hunted down in house-to-house searches; they may be raped where they are found or taken to a central location to be raped in view of other villagers. Third, following the destruction of their village, women and girls may be pursued as they flee to what they hope is safety (2004: 14). To these it is important to add a fourth setting: areas around internally displaced person (IDP) and refugee camps. As in their own villages prior to attack, women and girls are especially vulnerable when they leave the camps in search of water, wood, food and fodder.

Another form of sexual abuse found in Darfur is sexual slavery. The UN Commission of Inquiry and various non-governmental organizations (NGOs) have accumulated many accounts of girls and women being captured and held as sex slaves. Some are released within a few days or weeks, others have been held for years and the fate of many remains unknown. Women who have escaped or been released described being forced to perform domestic labour during the day and being raped nightly, often by multiple soldiers and militiamen. Some describe being forced into sham marriages. Most disturbingly, some survivors recount being transported and sold to Arab men. The Darfur Consortium interviewed a 21-year-old woman who was captured with 43 others. They were driven by Land Cruiser for two days to a central staging area where, with women from other villages, they were flown to Khartoum. The soldiers were given money after which 'each woman was given to a soldier, now I do not know where any of them are. I was given to an Arab soldier, taken to his house and locked inside. Every night he used me like a wife. For two months I did not see the outside' (2008: 10).

According to a briefing paper prepared by MSF in early 2005, only 4 per cent of sexual assaults have occurred during active combat (MSF 2005: 3). Almost all the rest happen as the women are fleeing their home villages. MSF researchers also found that 81 per cent of the victims describe their assailants as members of the military or militia 'who use their weapons to force the assault' (ibid.). The presence of weapons makes escape impossible. Justin Wagner gives as an example a 17-year-old girl who resisted: '[she] was killed and her naked body was left on the street for the entire village to see' (2005: 205). Weapons also heighten victims' fear, especially when accompanied by threats of murder. One victim, who was raped by four Janjaweed, described having a gun pointed at her head as she was raped: 'It was so painful, but fear was even more than pain' (quoted in Human Rights Watch 2005: 6). Finally, weapons combined with threats are used to prevent onlookers from intervening (see, for example, Amnesty International 2005: 7).

In Darfur, the strategic use of sexual violence conforms to patterns seen in other genocides. Many women are raped in the presence of family members, both to increase the woman's sense of humiliation and to underline the powerlessness of victims' husbands and fathers. In other words, sexual violation of women is a means of communicating defeat to men of the subordinate group. When, out of their own feelings of shame, men abandon their families and communities, the Darfuri social structure is further weakened. One example is that of the father of a 16-year-old rape victim: 'Her father became very ill, since that time. He never goes out with the rest of the men and he does nothing but staying (sic) inside the room' (witness testimony recorded in Human Rights Watch 2005: 11).

Women are also raped in front of whole villages, again increasing their violation while also intimidating the onlookers, thereby prompting all villagers to flee. Inasmuch as the object of genocide is not so much the physical death of a people as it is social and territorial death, rape in public is a powerful tactic. For most peoples, national identity encompasses not only such intangibles as language and religion but also physical connection with a particular place. When that place becomes a site of torture, it ceases to be a home and instead becomes a place of horror, to be fled both in fact and in memory.

Community bonds are further broken not only because, as previously noted, male relatives of rape victims depart but also because onlookers experience shame at having witnessed rape as a kind of pornography, unwanted yet no less unforgettable. Their sense of themselves as a people of worth is undermined. Furthermore, their own shame can be displaced onto victims who after the fact are often ostracized, sometimes literally forced to live apart from others of the group. Seen as damaged goods and lacking the status and protection of a family, these women may be targeted for sexual assault a second time, the difference being that the assailants come from the same ethnic group as the victims and are in physical proximity within the camps. Victims may also themselves choose to withdraw, whether because of their own sense of shame or in order to avoid the shame and accompanying hostility of their community.

The authors of Refugee International's 2007 report maintain that in order for rape victims to be reintegrated into their communities, men need to address their own feelings of powerlessness in failing to protect their families and also that men need to directly address community attitudes toward survivors. In addition, survivors' attitudes toward male relatives need to be aired, as is evident in this woman's view: 'These men were supposed to protect their families. Instead, the women are turning against them for failing to help them. They will not respect them' (Refugees International 2007a: 13).

A significant proportion of victims are gang raped. They describe assailants taking turns, one raping the woman while others stand guard or simply watch, and then changing roles. Compared to rapes by an individual assailant, gang rape can be more violent, more injurious and more humiliating for the victim. It can also serve to forge bonds among the gang members, heightening their sense of themselves as both sexually and ethnically dominant. In their own eyes and in the eyes of their fellows, this display of sexual violence reconfirms their identity as masculine and Arab.

Whether working singularly or in groups, many soldier-rapists go beyond 'simply' raping their victims. They beat them, torture them and mutilate them, often in sexually specific ways. Some women report having had their legs broken or ankles shot, apparently to make it difficult for them to escape, a practice also seen in Rwanda. Other women are marked, literally branded or their faces and/or having their thighs slashed to create scars that serve as permanent emblems – readable both by the victims and by their communities – of their status as rape victims. Pregnant women have had their bellies cut open and their fetuses killed, sometimes because it is male and paradoxically, other times because it is female. As has happened in previous genocides, some women in Darfur have been genitally mutilated. What I have found most disturbing, however, are reports such as this: 'The men didn't just rape them but afterwards they cut their sexual parts and sewed them up' (quoted in Human Rights Watch 2005: 4–5). I can only speculate that this represents a kind of deranged mimicry of female genital mutilation, a harmful cultural practice and form of gender-based violence known to be practiced in western Sudan outside the parameters of the genocide.

Of course, as in all wars and pogroms, some rape is opportunistic, although in creating fear and uncertainty it, too, is a weapon of terror. It is sometimes difficult to distinguish personal from political motives for war rape, and indeed, few attacks are purely one or the other. Whether opportunistic or part of a planned attack, sexual atrocities afford pleasure, as described by a witness-survivor from Mukjar: 'They are happy when they rape. They sing when they rape and they tell [us] that we are just slaves and that they can do with us how they wish' (quoted in Amnesty International 2005: 5). However, while enjoying themselves, soldier-rapists may also express genocidal intent: 'You, the black women, we will exterminate you, you have no god' (quoted in ibid.: 1).

Finally, some rape is genealogical, with the rapists stating their intention that their African victims give birth to light-skinned babies. Sometimes referred to as 'military occupation of the womb' (Fisher 1996: 124), the tactic is based on a common assumption that ethnicity passes through the male line only. Regardless of being borne by an African woman and presumably raised in an African social milieu, the child (who is always assumed to be a boy) takes on the ethnicity of the rapist only – biological, cultural, social, behavioural – and is imagined to one day grow into his heritage, including ethnic enmity toward the people who nurtured him. One example is a Janjaweed rapist who told his victim, 'I will give you a light-skinned baby to take this land from you' (Refugees International 2007a: 2). In another case, a young woman who was gang raped attested that her attackers said, 'Black girl, you are too dark. You are like a dog. We want to make a light baby. You get out of this area and leave the child when it's made' (Wax 2004: 1). Inasmuch as the motive for forced impregnation is 'the desire to populate the region with Arab children and to hinder the ability of certain African tribes to repopulate themselves' (Wagner 2005: 205), it can be said that forced impregnation meets the definition of one of the constituent acts of genocide: imposing measures intended to prevent births within the group (Genocide Convention Article II [d]).

Some soldiers and militiamen describe genealogical rape in farming terms, such as 'plant[ing] tomatoes' (Refugees International 2007b: 19 n. 4), with tomatoes representing the lighter skin tone of Arabs which is called red. This description echoes Serb rapists who claimed to be sowing 'the seeds of Serbia in Bosnia' (UN Commission of Experts 1994: paragraphs 285–301). As I have previously written, 'it seems that for [assailants] rape and forced pregnancy are not simply a means of achieving territorial conquest but actually *are* territorial conquest, women's bodies being viewed as fertile soil, no different from farm fields' (Price 2001: 220).

Children born of rape (in Rwanda they were called children of bad memories or devil's children) threaten social cohesion and also serve as constant reminders of the violence done to their mothers. All this is made worse by the belief in Sudan that a woman cannot get pregnant from rape, and some pregnant rape victims have been imprisoned for 'adultery'. Furthermore, the idée fixe that children inherit only their fathers' ethnicity is shared by Darfur's African peoples. Although some mothers are able to claim, 'I will love the child [b]ut I will always hate the father' (Wax 2004: 3), for others the babies will always be Janjaweed and therefore unwanted (see, for example, Human Rights Watch 2005: 11). And regardless of the mothers' views, the attitudes among their husbands, fathers and male community leaders that the children are enemies predominate. It is little wonder, then, that rape victims sometimes abandon their babies.

The women and girls rejected by their families are often more vulnerable to exploitation, including being forced into survival prostitution: compelled trade sex for food and other goods or coerced by either male camp residents or camp guards to provide sex in exchange for 'protection' (Human Rights Watch 2005: 9), presumably from other men. Not only are they at risk when they leave the camps but also vulnerable within them, whether from male camp inhabitants, camp guards or foreign peacekeepers and humanitarian aid workers. Women who have been raped previously by government soldiers or militiamen may be particularly targeted in the camps because they are seen as 'damaged goods'.

Female vulnerability is also heightened by traditional gender roles. Wagner points out that because women are responsible for the care of children and the elderly, they are 'less mobile during flight' (2005: 203). Gendered economic roles also make women primarily responsible for gathering needed resources, such as water and firewood, which takes them out of the relative safety of villages and camps. Finally, there is an awful kind of calculation: men who leave the camps are vulnerable to being killed while women are 'only' raped.

There can be no doubt that the pain, humiliation (personal, familial and communitarian), social disruption and indeed children of ethnicized rape are not unexpected or unwanted side effects. They are, rather, the point of it. Genocidaires act as they do because they know it works in achieving their genocidal purposes. As Catharine MacKinnon puts it,

> Sexual abuse, in reality, is a perfect genocidal tool. It does to ethnic, racial, religious and national groups what has been done to women as such from time immemorial in one of the most effective systems of domination-to-destruction in history. The perpetrators have not failed to notice.
>
> (2006: 233)

MacKinnon's analysis is borne out by a passage in the Amnesty International report.

> In the social context of Darfur, rape is a widespread cultural taboo of which all groups are aware. The *Janjawid* [*sic*], by raping and abusing women, *know the effects that these would have* not only on the women themselves, both in the short-term and in the longer-term, but also on their communities as a whole. Violence done in public, such as raping women in front of their relatives or their community or gang rapes, point to an attempt to humiliate both women and men.
>
> (2005: 18, emphasis added)

Finally, Wagner quotes Astrid Aafjes on the durability of war rape as sourced in its efficaciousness: 'sexual violence persists in armed conflict because it works. It makes the perpetrators feel dominant, and it makes the nation of the victims feel humiliated. Effective strategies against sexual violence in armed conflict require an understanding of this basic dynamic' (quoted in Wagner 2005: 214).

The use of sexual violence as an instrument of genocide is revealed in an attack described by Halima Bashir (2008). A Darfuri doctor, she was one day called to attend to more than 40 girls and two women who were sexually assaulted and mutilated when their school was attacked. The rapists were Janjaweed supported by Sudanese soldiers who encircled the school, preventing the children from fleeing and the villagers from coming to their aid. There is no military importance to a girls' school. The attack was aimed at ethnic cleansing, as revealed by the words of one attacker.

> We will let you live so you can tell your mothers and fathers and brothers what we did to you. Tell them from us: if you stay, the same and worse will happen to you all. Next time, we will show no mercy. Leave this land. Sudan is for the Arabs. It is not for black dogs and slaves.
>
> (ibid.: 257–58)

The adult villagers got the message: the attack was meant to instill maximum terror immediately and in the longer-term. It made their future in that place untenable. It underlined to the men of the village that they were powerless to protect their children. Appallingly, Bashir describes as the 'saving grace' that nearly all the girls assaulted were 'too young to have been made pregnant by their attackers' (ibid.: 255). For many, their torn bodies will not heal, and for all of them, the psychological torment will last a lifetime.

In Darfur, as elsewhere, there is ample evidence that sexual violence is not the random, isolated act of a few randy soldiers. It is, rather, widespread and systematic, planned and coordinated, enacted at the direction of government and the Janjaweed leaders. One victim attested that, as she was being gang raped, 'They said, "The government gave me permission to rape you. This is not your land anymore, *abid* [slave], go"' (Wax 2004: 2). In another case, Janjaweed fighters claimed to have the permission of the *muhaez* (provincial commissioner) to beat and rape African women. One of their victims reported the assault to the local police and identified the men involved. The perpetrators were arrested and disarmed, but the next day they were released with their weapons. The complainant was told that cases of violence would no longer be addressed by the Sudanese courts (Amnesty International 2005: 17). Thus, it appears the men were correct in their claim of government permission to abuse women. These examples demonstrate both that force is a principal tool for the maintenance of patriarchy and that, as such, its use is licensed by male *élites*.

Wagner quotes from a Sudanese government document obtained by Human Rights Watch which instructs officials in North Darfur 'to overlook minor offence by the *mujahedeem* [militia members] against civilians who are suspected members of the rebellion' (2005: 199). Even the Sudanese foreign minister, Mustafa Osman, has admitted, 'the government may have turned a blind eye toward the militias' (ibid.: 200). Perhaps most tellingly, the International Criminal Court prosecutor has presented evidence that Ali Kushayb, a leader of the Janjaweed, directly supervised the sexual abuse of some African women. As described by Femke van Zeijl, 'The prosecutor's evidence puts him in Arawalla, West Darfur, in 2003. During the attack on that village, he was seen personally inspecting a group of naked women tied to trees before they were raped by men in soldiers' uniforms' (2007: 12).

I emphasize the issue of state licence because it evidences a genocidal intent on the part of the Sudanese government and demonstrates the use of sexual violence as a political/military strategy aimed at destroying the African presence in Darfur. Nicholas Kristof maintains, 'Sudan's government dispatches rapists the way other governments dispatch the police, the better to terrorize black Africans and break their spirit' (2008). John Hagan, Wenona Rymond-Richmond and Patricia Parker characterize the overall campaign of attacks in Darfur as 'racially motivated, lethally destructive, state supported and militarily unjustified' (2005: 552). We may say the same of the component sexual attacks.

The sexual abuse of Darfuri girls and women can be imagined as cascading victimhood. The woman herself is the first and most direct victim; the violence is visited upon her body. Her family endures secondary victimization, for the woman may be lost to it through death, abduction or ostracism. Next, community bonds may be strained or broken, particularly if the community's men experience shame at not being able to protect 'their' women. Finally, if the woman becomes pregnant as a result of rape, her child may be marked, spreading victimhood to the next generation. Seen as a contagion of suffering, it becomes clear that widespread and systematic sexual violence is a powerful tool for effecting genocidal intent. It negates any notion of human security.

International mechanisms of response

For some years now, my primary research interest has been the international criminal adjudication of wartime sexual violence. Although cognizant of their limitations, I have regarded international tribunals as important vehicles for both justice and deterrence. In preparing this article, however, I began to ask myself whether other instruments of international humanitarian law might be usefully deployed *while atrocities are taking place*. Here the object would be less judgement and punishment and more prevention. What follows is an exploration of some of the textual bases for intervention directed at halting the sexual and gender-based violence currently being committed in Darfur.

UN Charter

The UN Charter, agreed to in 1945, is that body's foundational document. It is not, properly speaking, a constituent element of international humanitarian law inasmuch as it does not address the treatment of civilians by enemy forces. It also makes scant reference to human rights, and what comments are made are largely 'promotional and programmatic' (Steiner and Alston 1996: 119) rather than specifically obligatory. In short, the UN Charter is little concerned with relations between states and individuals (whether nationals or aliens). Rather, it focuses on interstate relations and on the role of the United Nations as arbiter and enforcer of said relations.

With regard to armed conflict, the charter's decisive provisions are contained in Chapter VII (Articles 39–51). Entitled 'Actions with Respect to Threats to Peace, Breaches of the Peace, and Acts of Aggression', it attends to circumstances in which, notwithstanding the ideal commitments to the peaceful resolution of conflicts, the reality of war or its threat arises. Chapter VII, especially Articles 39–42, gives sweeping powers to the Security Council first to determine that a threat to peace or act of aggression exists and then to direct actions to be taken in response. These powers are problematic, especially given the realpolitik of the five permanent members of the Security Council.

Both because it is intended as a peace institution and due to hostility from many states to the notion of a supranational permanent military, the United Nations does not have its own army. Instead, it must rely on member states to contribute forces and *matériel*. This, too, requires political negotiations both among and within states. After the debacle of Somalia, the United States in particular has been loath to commit its troops to UN peacekeeping and peacemaking operations.

This reluctance is juxtaposed by some developing world states, such as Bangladesh, which look to the UN missions as a way to equip and pay the salaries of their militaries. There are also occasions where larger geopolitics is at play: Sudan's insistence that the bulk of troops for the hybrid force must come from African countries is one cynical example.

Invoking Chapter VII to authorize peacemaking and peacekeeping missions is a relatively new development. Like everything else within the United Nations, such application is subject to political debate and backroom bargaining. For example, China and Russia – both permanent members of the Security Council – are ideologically opposed to any infringement on state sovereignty. Their opposition also has practical grounds in that both states are engaged in violent repression of independence movements (Chechnya and Tibet) and both are doubtless guilty of mass human rights abuses. Their governments rightly fear that if a precedent is set on humanitarian intervention, one day it may be their turn. Regarding Sudan, China is further disinclined to approve international military action because it relies on Sudan for oil, paid for with military equipment. In 2006, a plan was developed to increase the number of African Union troops in Darfur from 7,000 to 20,000. After negotiations, China agreed not to use its Security Council veto – it ultimately abstained from voting – on the condition that a paragraph be inserted in the resolution requiring that the Sudanese government must approve the troop increase. The resolution passed, but Khartoum withheld approval, so in the end nothing came of it.

We should not write off the potential of the UN Charter to change into an instrument of human security. Precedents set in the 1990s, particularly using the charter as an authorizing text of the International Criminal Tribunal for the former Yugoslavia (ICTY) and the International Criminal Tribunal for Rwanda (ICTR), demonstrate that crises within state borders can come under the rubric of threats to peace and aggression. In the instance of Darfur, it may be additionally claimed that the genocide is now spilling over into Chad, making it an international crisis.

Responsibility to protect

After the international community's bumbling intervention into the former Yugoslavia and its almost complete passivity in the face of the Rwandan genocide, it became evident that Chapter VII is an inadequate frame for intervention, particularly in non-international armed conflicts. The roadblock to further change and human security is the doctrine of state sovereignty which seemed to trump all other principles.

Seeking to circumvent this impasse, in 2005 UN member states committed themselves to a doctrine known as 'responsibility to protect'. The doctrine arose out of a kind of institutional soul-searching occasioned by the 10th anniversary of the Rwandan genocide. It commits individual states to protect their populations from 'genocide, war crimes, ethnic cleansing and crimes against humanity' (UN 2005: paragraph 138). If individual states are unwilling or unable to so protect their peoples, then the doctrine calls for the international community, through the United Nations, to assume protective responsibility. Initially, this is to be accomplished by 'diplomatic, humanitarian and other peaceful means' (paragraph 139). Should those fail, then 'collective action' – by which is meant military action, although it can also include sanctions and arms embargoes – is to be initiated through the UN Security Council. Although now two years old, 'responsibility to protect' has yet to be tested. Certainly there have been opportunities, Burma, the Democratic Republic of Congo and, of course, Sudan among them. Whether the doctrine will ever amount to more than just fine words remains a question. British Conservative Shadow International Development Secretary Andrew Mitchell has said about Darfur: 'The International Community is itself on trial. The much-vaunted responsibility to protect so enthusiastically embraced last year by world leaders in New York is looking more and more like a piece of meaningless mumbo-jumbo' (quoted in Suleiman 2007: 2). Past experience makes me doubtful as well; however, currently the Montreal Institute for Genocide and Human Rights Studies is conducting research into what they are calling the will to intervene. This research may provide direction on how words may be translated into action.

Paul D. Williams and Alex J. Bellamy (2005) identify a fundamental disjunction between international actors' words on the responsibility to protect and the (in)actions with regard to Darfur. They see Western states in particular using the language of responsibility to protect 'to enhance their own humanitarian credentials' (ibid.: 29) while not actually taking any action. They attribute this refusal to act to three factors: 'increased scepticism about the West's humanitarianism, especially after the invasion of Iraq; the strategic interests of the permanent members of the Security Council in Sudan; and the relationship between the Darfur crisis and Sudan's other civil wars and peace processes' (ibid.).

The first of these is particularly germane for women. The US-led invasion and military occupation of both Afghanistan and Iraq have been justified in part with a claim that the forces are there to liberate women. This pretext has been revealed as deception, particularly given that the occupying forces target civilian populations – women, children and non-combatant men. The effect is an Orwellian 'war is peace' played out on the bodies of women. More broadly, Williams and Bellamy contend that the invasions have raised suspicions that 'the West's humanitarian justifications mask neo-imperial ambitions' (2005: 36) and power the most overt face of patriarchy. In relation to Darfur, critics suggest that humanitarian intervention is simply 'a facade for gaining access to Sudan's oil' (ibid.: 37).

We come back to the same problem seen in other doctrines reviewed in this article: the failure of political will to accept the political risks (domestic and international) and material and personnel costs of non-violent intervention in the name of human security.

Genocide Convention

The term 'genocide' was coined by Polish jurist Raphael Lemkin to describe the exterminationist policies of the Axis powers. It derives from the ancient Greek *genos* (race, tribe) and the Latin *cide* (killing) and is analogous to such words as homicide. The Genocide Convention, based on Lempkin's definition although more restricted in terms of definitions, came into being in 1948. It prohibits attacks on national, ethnic, racial or religious groups but omits the most basic of identities, namely gender. Proscribed acts are killing; causing serious bodily or mental harm; deliberately imposing conditions of life calculated to bring about the group's physical destruction; preventing births within the group; and forcibly transferring children of the group to another group.

A finding of genocide requires two elements: (1) a prohibited act such as causing serious bodily or mental harm; and (2) a specific intent to destroy all or part of the targeted group. The latter is what distinguishes genocide from crimes against humanity and war crimes. There is no numerical threshold for genocide, but it is commonly understood to mean widespread attacks on significant numbers of group members.

Feminist writers, such as Joan Ringelheim (1985, 1997) and Andrea Dworkin (1994), have pointed out that genocidal policies and practices have differential effects on the men and women (and children) of the targeted group. Brief examples from the Nazi Holocaust (the most thoroughly researched genocide to date) serve to demonstrate some of these differences. Among Jews, women were disproportionately subject to killing both because they were often the larger group available for selection and because the selections followed both gender and age criteria (Ringelheim 1997: 31). Jewish and non-Jewish women were subjected to sexual humiliation, rape and other forms of sexual assault and sexual enslavement – treatment rarely meted out to men. Because their childbearing capacity presented a threat to the Nazi ideology of race superiority, Jewish and Roma women were experimented upon in hopes of discovering a quick and inexpensive alternative to surgical sterilization (Lentin 1997: 9). Forced pregnancy, forced abortion and infanticide (forced or 'voluntary') are all manifestations of the genocidal project which touch women but not men of the targeted groups. The reality of genocide, then, is gender (and age) specific in many of its forms, actions and consequences. In its gender blind language and in its failure to (at least partially) enumerate particular genocidal practices, the convention, as with so many other international humanitarian law instruments, renders women's experiences invisible.

Although the Genocide Convention omits gender as a group identity, and the definition of genocidal acts does not explicitly name acts of sexual violence, it is not irrelevant to our discussion. In a case before the ICTR (the prosecutor versus Jean-Paul Akayesu), the jurists made several pertinent points, including that when committed with the requisite intent, rape and other forms of sexual violence constitute serious bodily and mental harm; that the rapes resulted in the physical and psychological destruction of Tutsi women, their families and their communities; that the rape of Tutsi women was systematic and was perpetrated against 'all Tutsi women and solely against them' (Judgement, paragraph 732; that propaganda concerning Tutsi women amounted to the 'sexualized representation of ethnic identity' (Judgement, paragraph 732); and that sexual violence was a step in the process of the destruction of the Tutsi group.

Given this ruling, it should be possible to interpret the Genocide Convention as covering sexual violence, thereby triggering the international community to intervene in the Darfur conflict on the basis of what is being done to women. Realistically, that can never be the sole basis for intervention, as violence against women continues to be seen as relatively less important than crimes done to men. But certainly it could be one basis among many justifying such intervention.

Human security

By each criterion for human security set out in this book, the situation in Darfur is a crisis. In attacking a village, Janjaweed fighters and SAF soldiers destroy water pumps and poison wells by dumping corpses in them, thereby destroying the biosphere. They rape, mutilate, kill and enslave seemingly at will, thus subjecting Darfuris

Sexual violence and genocide, the greatest violation 149

to avoidable harm. They steal livestock and burn or carry off food stores, undermining human needs. And by their use of sexual violence against civilian women, they negate any sense of human dignity. As Bashir writes, 'They came not only to kill us but to destroy our ability to live' (2008: 292).

Michael Barnett argues that following the end of the Cold War (usually dated at 1989), the United Nations shifted its focus of concern from state security to human security (1996: 135). He draws attention to changes in the nature and scope of UN peacekeeping activities: 'If prior to 1988 peacekeeping concerned interpositioning lightly armed UN troops between two states that had agreed to a ceasefire, they were now involved in a myriad of activities associated with nation building and humanitarian assistance' (ibid.). Barnett attributes this change to UN officials being 'unshackled' from the Cold War. He overlooks what may be a more proximal cause, namely that the typology of war changed such that the previous model of peacekeeping was no longer operable. Consider, for example, that in the period from 1991 to 1994, there were 82 armed conflicts worldwide (conflicts being defined as those in which more than 1,000 lives were lost). Of those 82, 79 were within states and only three were between states (Mahbub ul-Haq in Brazier 1994: 20). In any event, an ambitious and initially successful programme of humanitarian intervention was launched, and to at least some within the United Nations, it appeared that the organization was 'on the verge of fulfilling its initial but long-delayed promise' (Barnett 1996: 135). However, within only a few years, the success of UN interventions in Cambodia, El Salvador and Haiti were outweighed by the debacles of Somalia, Bosnia and Rwanda.

In considering whether the concept of human security as currently understood may ameliorate women's experience of genocidal rape, I have examined a foundational document, *Human Security Now* (2003), which is a report sponsored by the United Nations and written by a commission of experts co-chaired by Sadako Ogata, former UN High Commissioner for Refugees, and Amartya Sen, Nobel laureate in economics and a social development theorist who has written on gender inequality. In the preface to this report, the authors identify the subject matter of human security as 'safeguarding and expanding people's vital freedoms' (p. iv). Accomplishing this requires both protection ('shielding people from acute threats') and social development ('empowering people to take charge of their own lives'). They juxtapose state security, which for too long has been the sole subject and enactor of security, with security of people, arguing that the latter should take precedence. And while the state remains the 'fundamental purveyor of security' (p. 2), it is also the case that often 'individuals require protection from the arbitrary power of the state' (p. 3).

Taking note that human security is 'more than the absence of violent conflict' (p. 4), the commission usefully lists at least some of its constituent parts: 'human rights, good governance, access to education and healthcare and ensuring that each individual has opportunities and choices to fulfill his or her own potential' (p. 4). These may be accomplished by what are described as building blocks: 'freedom from want, freedom from fear and the freedom of future generations to inherit a healthy natural environment' (ibid.).

Absent from both the constituents of human security and their building blocks is any mention of gender-based violence. It is impossible for a woman to, say, exercise opportunities and choices if she is subject to violence from an intimate partner, strangers and/or enforcement agencies of the state. Similarly, the prospect of want – for herself and for her children – is often what keeps a woman from leaving her battering husband. As to freedom from fear, it seems to me that fear of male violence can be the defining characteristic of women's lives. As Elizabeth Stanko comments, 'All women have some experience of male violation... *To walk the streets warily at night is how we actually feel our femininity*' (1985: 157, emphasis in original).

For women, security is always primarily personal. Its presence or absence is measured in degrees of safety from violence, especially gender-based violence; degrees of food and shelter security for themselves and their families; degrees of freedom of movement and freedom from limiting or harmful cultural practices; and, when necessary, degrees of access to legal remedies when personal security is threatened. For most of the world's women, states are linked positively to security when they act to guarantee women's physical, economic and social security. States are linked negatively to security when they condone – by silence or by active promotion – violation of women's security, most extremely, when agents of the state are directed or given licence to perpetrate violence against women.

For women living in war zones, the elements of human security and their building blocks are precisely what are absent from their quotidian existence. This leads me to wonder whether the model of human security is an attainable or indeed a useful one for women in Darfur and other conflict zones. In failing to acknowledge women's situatedness, the authors of this report screen out key components of women's lives and challenges to their attainment of human security. Having said that, next I continue to envisage how feminists could shape the language of human security to encompass women's experiences within and outside armed conflict.

In a short essay included in the report, Frene Ginwala suggests that Africa's experience of colonialism and neocolonialism gives rise to debates around 'whose security matters and under what conditions, and what are the moral, ethical and legal bases for what is termed a 'just war' (p. 3). Although it may not have been Ginwala's intent, the former is centrally important for women. In a later chapter, the authors acknowledge that in conflict situations women and girls are particularly vulnerable, and their abuse often carries a 'political and symbolic message' (p. 35). They also call attention to the fact that incidents of gender-based and sexual violence increase immediately following armed conflict. Taken together these lead me to ask: Whose security, whose peace, whose justice?

Inasmuch as human security shifts the emphasis away from states, it focuses on the protection of people, not 'borders or territories' (p. 33). In so doing, it not only expands attention beyond interstate wars to internal and communitarian conflict but also, and more importantly, in attending to individuals at the grassroots level, human security has at least the potential to make women's experiences, understandings and priorities visible on the world stage. For example, the report notes that 'control over people is often the objective of fighting' (p. 21). As evidenced by Darfur, for women this control can take the form of sexual slavery, forced pregnancy and being targeted for rape as a means of terrorizing a community. Certainly any doctrine which prioritizes civilians over states and their political and military apparatuses has at least the potential to increase awareness of women's experiences of armed conflict.

The challenge for feminists is to ensure that gender is not subsumed under race, religion, ethnicity or other male-defined and male-led (i.e., patriarchal) collectivities. These categories of association tend to be treated naturalistically, whereas speaking of women *qua* women is considered 'political' in the pejorative sense. Yet if we do not foreground gender specificity, then the differential effects of armed conflict on women are too easily overlooked. In relation to security, the struggle is a familiar one: on the one hand, to have 'women' included in 'human' and therefore for women to be accorded the same rights to security as men; and on the other, to have women's particular social and material locations recognized and treated differently from those of men.

More fundamentally, all too often, the rights-bearing person is imagined to be male (see, for example, MacKinnon 1989: 157–70). If 'human' is assumed to be 'man', then the doctrine of human security may indeed conflict with or undermine the security needs of women, and the liberal feminist project of claiming 'women are human too' is revealed as inadequate, even counter-productive. If the male standard is left unproblematized, then women's situatedness and concomitant perspectives and aspirations are rendered invisible. As feminists have learnt to speak of 'women's rights' to draw attention to the specificity of women's being-in-the-world, so should we supplant the language of human security and specify our subject as 'women's security'? I am drawn to recall Audre Lorde's oft-quoted perception, 'The master's tools will never dismantle the master's house' (1984: 110). This means that whether the topic is rights, security or liberation, not only our objectives but also the forms our social change activism take must be informed by a standpoint grounded in women's ways of seeing (Frye 1983) and knowing (Belenky et al. 1986).

In a presentation critiquing the Canadian government's approach to human security, Rosalind Boyd offers a set of questions intended to evaluate the gender-sensitivity of any such programme.

> Does it make the lives of women and their families safer?
> Does it contribute to women's sense of security within the community? Does it address the needs and rights of women as full citizens?
> Does it recognize the different ways men and women are affected? Does it deal with the source or root causes of women's insecurity?
> How far does this agenda go in making the world less militaristic or less violent?
>
> (2003: 3)

These simply stated criteria could go a long way toward the creation of enlightened and effective interventions into wartime sexual violence. The criteria could also be applied to other sources of women's insecurity, such as poverty and healthcare. Even when not fully realized, the questions themselves could serve to point out lacunae in national and international human security initiatives. Boyd's list of interrogations could act as a tool of consciousness-raising for the political, diplomatic, bureaucratic and military *élites* (still overwhelmingly male) who make policy and design intervention strategies. Just as importantly, seeking answers to the questions necessarily requires decision makers to attend to the experiences and perspectives of women 'on the ground', those most affected by their actions and inactions, their definitions and resource allocations. And inasmuch as the questions decentralize the state as actor, agent and recipient of human security initiatives, they would benefit all non-combatants – women, men and children – and cover all acts, not just those of sexual violence.

In Darfur, there has been some recognition by peacekeepers of the specificity of violence and the specific needs which arise from it. In the later stages of its peacekeeping mission, the AU launched 'firewood patrols' in which its soldiers seek to protect Darfuri women when they leave the IDP and refugee camps in search of firewood. These patrols are nowhere near frequent enough, and the complement of AU peacekeepers is inadequate to the job, both of which mean women are still being targeted for rape in their scavenging expeditions. Nonetheless, the patrols evidence a new awareness among peacekeepers of the specific dangers women in conflict zones face.

As can be seen, the Ogata-Sen model of human security is an inadequate tool for protecting Darfuri women. It has almost nothing to say regarding women's unique and specific security needs, such as the need for secure housing. I have demonstrated that the doctrine can be *interpreted* to serve women's needs, but that is a poor substitute for explicit language. Ogata and Sen also have little to say about extrastate enforcement of the principles they advocate. In turn, this is rooted in their choice to leave the state unproblematized. Furthermore, Ogata and Sen do not challenge the state security perspective, nor do they problematize the differential effects of state violence on women and men. Perhaps they decided to work within 'the system' rather than to challenge its foundation. Perhaps they deliberately set their sights low in hopes of stimulating incremental change, starting, for example, with small arms reductions rather than with full disarmament. But we cannot cross a chasm in two steps. In the end, then, Ogata and Sen reinforce the state as guarantor of human security, thus abandoning the majority of the world's people subject to violence and insecurity by their own state apparatuses. At best, the doctrine of human security may be used as a tool of moral suasion and political shaming. It will take bolder voices to challenge statist violence.

Resolution 1325 on Women, Peace and Security

The UN Security Council Resolution 1325, entitled 'Women, Peace and Security', is a remarkable document if for no other reason than the swiftness with which it moved from an informal proposal of a network of NGOs in 1998 to a formal resolution, unanimously adopted on 31 October 2000. It is more remarkable for being the first occasion in which the needs and experiences of women in conflict zones were debated by the Security Council. It was initially envisioned as an advocacy tool, a measuring stick against which efforts at 'gender mainstreaming' by various UN bodies – especially those engaged in aspects of international peace and security – could be evaluated. The NGO network, working with women located in UN agencies and in some member state missions, saw to it that the resolution became an instrument of institutional change, setting out positive duties for the United Nations and its member states.

In this volume, Soumita Basu gives a detailed analysis of the history and subject matter of Resolution 1325 which I will not repeat. Instead I will consider how 1325 *might* be applied to the plight of women in Darfur. I stress the word 'might' because, notwithstanding its status as international law, the resolution is fundamentally a political document, its potential utilization subject to posturing and sub rosa negotiation among male *élites* at both the national and the international levels.

Ancil Adrian-Paul and Sanam Naraaghi Anderlini categorize the substantive provisions of 1325 into four themes: (1) women's participation in decision-making and peace processes; (2) integration of gender perspectives in peacekeeping; (3) protection of women; and (4) gender mainstreaming (2004: 15). For women living in Darfur and in refugee camps in Chad and the Central African Republic, the third is the priority, although it cannot be fully realized without the other three.

Adrian-Paul and Anderlini summarize the positives of 1325's protective measures as first requiring state and non-state actors to be responsible for protecting women and indicating that actors can be held accountable for harms done to women, and second, that the United Nations itself, together with humanitarian agencies, can be held accountable for inadequate protection of women and girls in refugee and IDP camps (2004: 16). They caution, however, that in the absence of effective monitoring, evaluation and incentives for compliance, change is unlikely (ibid.). This criticism applies to all of Resolution 1325: the words are progressive, but no provision has been made for translating them into action, except perhaps the rather vague threat of possibly one day being held accountable.

In 2005, the NGO Working Group on Women, Peace and Security published a report evaluating progress made toward the realization of the ideals set out in 1325. They conclude that 'while some progress has been made, there is still a great deal of work to be done' (2005: viii). They point out, for example, that 'only a fraction of people around the world' are aware of the provisions and obligations put down in the resolution (ibid.: ix). Obviously, if women are unaware of their rights, they cannot demand that those rights be respected. Within the UN system, the working group finds that 'the lack of directly allocated resources has impeded progress and implementation' (ibid.). And although some states have developed National Action Plans for implementing 1325, they are very few – the working group identifies only five. However, progress being made at the level of civil society. In Sri Lanka, for example, women's groups have been active in translating the resolution and disseminating it to women in villages. They have also hosted seminars and workshops (including for politicians), and one group – the Association of War-Affected Women – has organized public demonstrations to 'generate momentum around SC 1325 and inspire new women leaders' (2005: 73).

In a section entitled 'Moving Beyond Rhetoric', the working group opines,

> For women, peace and security concerns to be truly addressed, the Resolution's provisions must be active at the local level, as useful, understandable and accessible for women's activism, as a structure informing peace negotiations, and as a framework for women to demand rights.
>
> (2005: 99)

This requires money and personnel at all levels. It also requires structural change. Those in turn require political will on the part of national and international *élites*, most of whom are men. It seems, then, that although 1325 is a historic step forward in its articulation of the needs and perspectives of women in conflict zones, it is not yet sufficiently operationalized to be of immediate benefit to the women trapped in the Darfur genocide. But perhaps the experiences of Darfuri women can inform feminists' advocacy on 1325, and by comparing actuality to text, point the way forward.

Commenting on the protection measures in Resolution 1325, Cynthia Cockburn states, 'You could say that "protection" emphasizes women's passivity, their victimhood. In the absence of a strong statement against war, this could be seen as simply trying to "make war safer for women"' (2007: 147). This may be a little harsh, for the realities 1325 attempts to address are that war exists and in war women are made targets for specific forms of violence, including sexual violence. But Cockburn does identify a worrying characteristic in speech about war: the tendency to depict women as both innocent and helpless.

In Darfur as in all other zones of conflict, women are not just victims of masculinist political and sexual violence. Some women take up arms; a few commit atrocities. In the absence of men – through death, flight or mobilization – civilian women hold their families and communities together. They care for the young, the elderly and the wounded. They organize the gathering and distribution of food and other resources. Crucially, women act as change agents. For these reasons, it is vital that women have a voice in the administration of IDP and refugee camps and, in the longer-term, in peace negotiations and post-conflict reconstruction. Yet this happens far too infrequently. The authors of the Amnesty International report found that the male leadership of the rebel groups have set themselves up as the 'sole representatives of the people of Darfur' (2004: 14). A similar situation in south Sudan led to an increased risk of violations of women's rights. The authors conclude, 'Women, who bear the brunt of the burdens of the conflict, have rarely participated in political decision-making regarding the conflict or peace' (ibid.).

UN Declaration on the Elimination of Violence against Women (DEVAW)

Passed by the UN General Assembly in 1994, the DEVAW is another historic document, not least in its recognition that such violence is socially constructed and is a 'manifestation of historically unequal power relations between men and women' (preamble, paragraph 6). The declaration identifies violence as 'one of the crucial social mechanisms by which women are forced into a subordinate position compared to men' (ibid.). The preamble also identifies a reciprocal relationship between discrimination and violence, each reinforcing the other (preamble, paragraph 3) and characterizes violence as an obstacle to women's attainment of fundamental rights and freedoms (preamble, paragraph 5), such as equality, security, liberty, integrity and dignity (preamble, paragraph 1).

DEVAW's most important contribution is its definition of violence against women. Article 1 gives a broad definition:

> For the purposes of this Declaration, the term 'violence against women' means any act of gender-based violence that results in, or is likely to result in, physical, sexual or psychological harm or suffering to women, including threats of such acts, coercion or arbitrary deprivation of liberty, whether occurring in public or in private life.

Article 2 expands this definition by giving examples of some of the forms violence against women can take, such as battering, rape (both inside and outside marriage), female genital mutilation and sexual harassment at work and in educational institutions. The three sub-articles of Article 2 identify three locations in which gender-based violence commonly occurs: in the family (Article 2 [a]); in the community (Article 2 [b]); and the 'physical, sexual and psychological violence perpetrated or condoned by the State, wherever it occurs' (Article 2 [c]).

In relation to sexual violence in armed conflict, the latter sub-article is pivotal. Also important to the subject is the declaration's list of categories of women who are particularly vulnerable to violence, including those who belong to a minority group (presumably ethnic but potentially also political or sexual), refugee women, women in detention and 'women in situations of armed conflict' (preamble, paragraph 7). Subsequent sub-articles call for specific measures to be adopted by member states (Article 4 [1]) and by the UN system (Article 5 [c]) for the protection of such vulnerable populations of women. Finally, within a longer list of human rights, DEVAW specifies the right to life (Article 3 [a]), the right to liberty and security (Article 3 [c]) and the right 'not to be subjected to torture, or other cruel, inhuman or degrading treatment or punishment' (Article 3 [h]), all of which are particularly germane to the subject of women in conflict zones.

In spite of – or, more likely, because of – its progressiveness, to date DEVAW has had little impact on practices of violence against women, either domestically or internationally, in war or in 'peace'. Part of the problem is its form: unlike conventions, UN declarations have no legal force. They are more akin to statements of aspiration – good intentions lacking any requirement for implementation. Feminists can use DEVAW as a tool of political suasion, pointing out where the actions of the United Nations and its member states fall short of or conflict with the principles enshrined in it, but embarrassing governments and intergovernmental bodies is a poor substitute for compulsory implementation.

Hilkka Pietilä and Jeanne Vickers, in their work on women and the United Nations, explain a common process wherein a declaration 'which can only offer recommendations' (1996: 25) is prepared first; only later (and only in some cases) are its principles transposed into a draft convention. Of course that process is imbued with politics – with contestation and negotiation and bargaining – as member states pursue wording which accords with their priorities, often at the expense of the people for whom the particular convention ostensibly is meant. At times this can amount to little more than impression management: the text says, 'Look what we are doing for women' while the subtext says, 'We won't do anything to undermine systems of patriarchal privilege, including the unfettered right to anti-woman violence'. That is the pessimistic view. More optimistically, we can say that both as an advocacy tool and as the groundwork for a hoped-for future convention, DEVAW is a valuable document. For the women currently suffering war rape in Darfur and elsewhere, though, it has little to offer.

The International Criminal Court

Instead of intervention, the world community covers its complicity and expiates its guilt through the medium of post-genocide war crimes tribunals. The ad hoc tribunals established for Rwanda and the former Yugoslavia at the close of the 20th century served to reanimate the moribund movement toward a permanent body of criminal adjudication, and in 2002 the International Criminal Court (ICC) came into force. Its mandate is to try individuals accused of war crimes, crimes against humanity and genocide when the relevant home government is unable or refuses to try them. The question I wish to address is: Do potential trials at the ICC sufficiently discharge the international community's responsibilities to the victims of genocidal rape in Darfur?

The ICC shows great promise for adjudicating sexual violence as a war crime and as a crime against humanity. It specifies crimes of sexual violence, such as forced pregnancy, which, while prevalent in the former Yugoslavia and Rwanda, were not identified in the relevant statutes. The ICC's statute, however, has the same problems as the Genocide Convention: it does not list gender as a group identity, nor does it list sexual violence as a constituent act of genocide. The latter is especially troubling, for it reverses the decision of the Akayesu case before the ICTR. Still, in recognizing such crimes as sexual slavery, it is an improvement over previous tribunals.

In the case of Darfur, the court has so far issued three indictments against a Janjaweed leader, the government minister for humanitarian affairs (how ironic) and the Sudanese president Omar Hassan Ahmad Al-Bashir. All three have been charged, inter alia, with command responsibility for crimes of sexual violence perpetrated by men under their command. The Janjaweed leader has also been charged with direct participation in the rape of Darfuri women.

Sudan is not a party to the ICC. Its government, therefore, refuses to recognize its jurisdiction. However, the Rome Statute includes a provision allowing referral to the court when the UN Security Council determines that a threat to peace or an act of aggression exists. The referent authorizing text is Chapter VII of the UN Charter, the same as was employed for the Yugoslav and Rwandan tribunals. It is an interesting legal authority, for, in essence, it makes events within a state matters of international concern, thereby modifying the principle of the sovereignty of states within their borders. The Rome Statute also sets out that a situation can be referred to the ICC when the relevant national government is unwilling or unable to prosecute war criminals.

Because the ICC lacks an enforcement arm, it cannot directly arrest indictees. Instead it relies on member states to do that. Sudan is not going to arrest its own president, so, barring a change in government, arrest warrants can be executed only if the indictees travel outside. Sudan

Sudanese human rights lawyer Saliah Mahmoud Osman has noted that from the day the ICC prosecutor announced his office would be launching an investigation in Darfur, 'there was a decline in the commission of crimes for more than three or five months – because the perpetrators were panicked that they could be held accountable' (quoted in Murphy 2007: 1). But the investigation dragged on, and it became clear that the chances of genocidaires being held to account are slight. Then, Osman states, 'by the time they felt there was nobody any longer talking about justice, then the situation erupted again' (quoted in ibid.). Osman is replying to those who argue that indictments by the ICC can prolong conflicts because government and military leaders fear that a negotiated peace could result in their arrests. In contrast, Osman argues, 'Justice can play the role of a deterrence mechanism' (quoted in ibid.).

The international community has a long history of unenforced treaties and conventions. The ICC at least has a structure, a budget and personnel. It cannot directly intervene to halt atrocities while they are happening, but, as Osman attests, the threat of exposure by ICC investigators may rein in the worst acts of brutality. That threat, though, must be credible. In the end, then, whatever deterrence effect the court has applies more to future potential war criminals; that is, if Janjaweed commander Ali Kushayb is eventually tried and convicted of rape as a crime against humanity, it may forestall acts of sexual violence in later conflicts. But that can be little comfort to today's victims.

Returning to my question, plainly potential trials before the ICC are not sufficient to discharge the international community's responsibilities toward the victims of gender violence in Darfur. Post hoc adjudication is no substitute for timely intervention. That said, the ICC is more than a symbol of justice. Symbolism, though, is an important role for it communicates to victims, perpetrators and bystanders that the international community will not tolerate some actions in armed conflict.

The ICC is a young institution. It has yet to complete one trial. Until there are convictions, many genocidaires will feel secure. What is needed is a body of case law based on convictions. They do not need to be state specific: if the leaders of the Lord's Resistance Army in Uganda are convicted of torture as a crime against humanity, that ruling could stay the hand of militias in the Democratic Republic of Congo. In short, the court must demonstrate its reach and its seriousness. Early trials will set precedents for later ones. For this reason, it is crucial that crimes of sexual violence, up to and including genocidal rape, be prosecuted in the earliest of trials. From the start the court must demonstrate its willingness to take crimes against women as seriously as it takes crimes against men. Accordingly, feminists need to monitor court proceedings, from investigation all the way through sentencing, to ensure that gender violence is not ignored or glossed over. The ICTY and ICTR set precedents in determining that sexual violence in armed conflict constitutes crimes against humanity, war crimes and, in certain situations, an act of genocide. The ICC, with a statute which enumerates sexual crimes more fully than the ICTY and ICTR statutes, has potential which must be capitalized upon.

I am acutely aware that even as I write, women and girls in Sudan and across the border in Chad are being subjected to forms of sexual violation I can barely imagine. The same is true in Burma, Chechnya and other sites of genocide and armed conflict. The international community's responsibilities toward them hold in the present, not just away in some distant day when a court in The Hague begins compiling dossiers, issues arrest warrants and perhaps (but only perhaps) launches a few hopefully representative prosecutions of genocidaires. For feminists certainly, but also for others who profess a commitment to international justice, it is not enough to lobby the ICC to take up the myriad crimes of sexual violence occurring in Darfur. We need to be applying pressure – loudly and publicly as well as with quiet lobbying – on our home governments and on international agencies to act swiftly and decisively to protect the remaining Darfuri women from sexual violation at the hands of government soldiers and Janjaweed. Post hoc international criminal adjudication is no substitute for timely and effective intervention while a genocide is being conducted. Yet the possibility of being called to account, if it is credible, surely must give some genocidaires pause. That is a fit purpose for all law. But let us first forcefully remind the politicians, diplomats and bureaucrats that they have the tools – the Genocide Convention, the doctrine of responsibility to protect, Resolution 1325, the Declaration on the Elimination of Violence against Women and the regime of human security – to intervene immediately. And when the next attempt at genocide comes along, as surely it will, may the international community take up those tools swiftly, before the lives of thousands of women are lost to sexual violence and its sequelae. That is our final responsibility to the women of Darfur.

In the calling to account and attempts at post-conflict justice, women's experiences and perspectives must be sought, for without them, reconciliation is illusory and too often sows the seeds of future conflict. More than just an appeal for fairness, then, the demand that women be included in national and international tribunals – up to and including the ICC – is based on an understanding that crimes against women wound all members of a society. It is often noted that without justice there can be no lasting peace. Surely now it is evident to both state and non-state actors, and to those of us who stand outside as observers, that without justice for women there can be no peace for anyone.

Human rights, human security, gender and genocide

The realms of human rights and human security are so entwined, so interdependent, that it is reasonable to say we cannot have one without the other. Consider the following three representative examples from the Universal Declaration of Human Rights.

Article 19 guarantees freedom of opinions and expression. This human right cannot be exercised in the absence of security of person; indeed, in war and warlike settings, to speak one's mind can easily lead to torture and death. The right to marry and found a family (Article 16) has no meaning to a woman raped in war and subsequently shunned by her family and community. Third, the declaration's most basic promise, in Article 3, is the right to life, liberty and security of person. It embodies the guiding principles of the doctrine of human rights yet is debased and ignored in total institutions, such as war, genocide and apartheid.

If we look otherwise, focusing on human security, we see the same pattern of interdependence. Human security elements cannot be achieved in the absence of a culture of human rights. Access to a sustainable environment, for example, means little if at any time one may be subject to arbitrary arrest, detention or exile (declaration, Article 9). Similarly, protection against avoidable harm is just so many words if the declaration's prohibition against slavery and servitude (Article 4) is not respected. This example is especially pertinent to the Darfuri women captured and sold into sexual slavery.

From a feminist perspective, human rights, human security and their interdependence all have differing meanings and impacts for women and men. This fact has directed feminist activism in two directions. One has been an attempt to 'count women in'. Here feminists attempt to reinterpret instruments, such as the Universal Declaration, to be truly universal, applying equally to women and men. The second direction is to advocate stand-alone instruments which speak exclusively of women's rights and needs, such as Resolution 1325. The modus here is to emphasize the unique rather than the universal.

Both directions have merits and both have drawbacks. The universalizing programme highlights women's equal humanity but leaves untouched the male standard of what it means to be human. Highlighting women's uniqueness brings to the fore the gender specificity of rights and needs but at the risk of ghettoization and potential marginalization. Perhaps as with rights and security, there is an interdependence between the universal and the unique. It is vital that the understanding of 'human' be expanded to encompass gender equality. But equality itself requires gender specificity in language and action.

Genocide seeks the destruction of a people as a people. Methods include physical extermination (murder, starvation); institutional destruction (bombing mosques and libraries); and cultural annihilation (banning native languages and cultural practices, such as potlatches). Some genocidal practices, such as carpet-bombing villages, strike without distinction, while others, such as sexual slavery, are directed at only the women of the targeted group. The effects of genocidal actions can also be both generalized and specific, sometimes at the same time: a daylight attack on a village is likely to harm more women than men if the latter are out of the village tending livestock, working away or have joined a military force.

Genocidaires do not see their victims as worthy humans or even as human at all. Accordingly, they have no reason to respect the human security and human rights of their victims. Indeed, in genocidal campaigns the former are attacked while the latter are abrogated. In this, too, women are differentially targeted and differentially affected. They are attacked in their sexual beings (rape, forced nudity); in their reproductive beings (genital mutilation, forced pregnancy); and in their social and economic roles in sustenance, housing, healthcare and childrearing.

The genocide taking place in Sudan is directed at all African Darfuris – men, women and children. Within that broad programme, some strategies and tactics utilized by the Sudanese Army and Janjaweed are directed at Darfuri women in their economic and social roles generally and in their sexual and reproductive capacities specifically. Victims are targeted not just because they are Darfuri and not just because they are women but specifically because they are Darfuri women. It makes sense, then, that any attempt at restoring human security in Darfur must be similarly specific. Gender specificity may begin with protection, recovery and reintegration of sexually victimized women, but it should not end there. It must extend to such areas as education, healthcare and provisioning, all of which reside mostly in women's remit. Finally, gender specificity must extend longitudinally to peace-making and post-conflict restoration.

Conclusion

Gayle Smith, one of the founders of the ENOUGH Project, which is directed at ending genocide and mass atrocities, maintains, 'There are three ways that genocide can be brought to a halt: the international community can intervene; its victims can militarily defeat its perpetrators; or the actions of the international community can force the perpetrators to alter their calculations' (2007). There is, of course, a fourth way: the genocidaires can be successful in their project. In any event, if the international community acts at all, it is only well after genocide has been initiated. The folly of such an approach is attested to by Roméo Dallaire (2004), the UN commander in Rwanda in 1994. With solid evidence of planned ethnic slaughter, Dallaire requested permission to confiscate arms held in depots around Kigali, the Rwandan capital. His UN superiors, including Under Secretary-General for Peacekeeping Operations Kofi Annan (who later became the UN Secretary-General), refused permission. Up to a million Tutsis and moderate Hutus (as well as 12 UN peacekeepers) died as a result of this hesitation. The international community seems to have learnt little from this experience for, 13 years later, foot-dragging and dilatory negotiation characterize plans for a peacekeeping force to be deployed in Sudan.

There can be no doubt that a preventable catastrophe is taking place in Sudan. For all Darfuris, but especially for women and girls, daily life is conducted in the almost total absence of even minimal standards of human security. Barring a change in political leadership, the genocide will continue. Accordingly, any remedial action will have to come from outside Sudan.

Relying as it does on norms of precedent, the United Nations grounds its actions in authorizing texts – previously agreed-upon doctrines and conventions – and evidentiary texts – those describing the situation at issue. It should not be difficult to frame the rape and sexual mutilation of prepubescent schoolgirls as an act of genocide. Such characterization should then trigger action of the basis of, inter alia, the doctrine of responsibility to protect. We have the evidence (e.g. Bashir's first-person account) and the authority (e.g. the Rome Statute). What is missing is political will among the politicians, diplomats and bureaucrats who haunt the halls of the United Nations and national capitals.

It is a cliché to say that an injury to one is an injury to all, but like all clichés, it holds a grain of truth. If the international community does not act to meet minimal human security needs in Darfur, where violations of international humanitarian law are blatant, what hope is there for the Palestinian, Tutsi or Tamil women subject to state-sponsored sexual violence?

If we are serious about the project of advancing human security, then we must begin with women's security, including, most basically, the right of women to be safe from gender-based and sexual violence during the wars of men.

References

Adrian-Paul, Ancil and Sanam Naraghi Anderlini. 2004. 'Key International Policies and Legal Mechanisms: Women's Rights in the Context of Peace and Security', in International Alert and Women Waging Peace (eds.), *Inclusive Security, Sustainable Peace: A Toolkit for Advocacy and Action*, pp. 15–27. London: International Alert and Women Waging Peace.

Amnesty International. 2005. *Darfur: Rape as a Weapon of War: Sexual Violence and its Consequences*. New York: Amnesty International.

Barnett, Michael N. 1996. 'The Politics of Indifference at the United Nations and Genocide in Rwanda and Bosnia', in Thomas Cushman and Stjepan G. Mestrovic (eds.), *This Time We Knew: Western Responses to Genocide in Bosnia*, pp. 128–62. New York: New York University Press.

Bashir, Halima. 2008. *Tears of the Desert*. London: Hodder and Stoughton.

Bastick, Megan, Karin Grimm and Rahel Kunz. 2007. *Sexual Violence in Armed Conflict: Global Overview and Implications for the Security Sector*. Geneva: Geneva Centre for the Democratic Control of Armed Forces.

Belenky, Mary Field, By the McVicker Clinchy, Nancy Rule Goldberger and Jill Mattuck Tarule. 1986. *Women's Ways of Knowing: The Development of Self, Voice, and Mind*. New York: Basic Books.

Boyd, Rosalind. 2003. 'The Canadian Human Security Approach: A Gender Sensitive Strategy?', 'Human Security = Women's Security', conference sponsored by the Feminist Institute of the Heinrich Böll Foundation, Berlin, 24–25 October.

Brazier, Chris. 1994. 'The New Deal: Interview with Mahbub ul-Haq', *New Internationalis*, no. 262, pp. 20–3. December.

Cockburn, Cynthia. 2007. *From Where We Stand: War, Women's Activism and Feminist Analysis*. London: Zed Books.

Commission on Human Security. 2003. 'Human Security Now', chairs Sedako Ogata and Amartya Sen. New York: United Nations.
Dallaire, Roméo. 2004. *Shake Hands with the Devil: The Failure of Humanity in Rwanda*. Toronto: Vintage Canada.
Darfur Consortium. 2008. *Darfur: Abductions, Sexual Slavery and Forced Labour*. Kampala, Uganda: Darfur Consortium.
Dworkin, Andrea. 1994. 'The Unremembered: Searching for Women at the Holocaust Memorial Museum', *Ms*: 52–58. November–December.
Fisher, Siobhán. 1996. 'Occupation of the Womb: Forced Impregnation as Genocide', *Duke Law Journal*, vol. 46: 9–133.
Frye, Marilyn. 1983. *The Politics of Reality: Essays in Feminist Theory*. Freedom, CA: Crossing Books.
Ginerich, Tara and Jennifer Leaning. 2004. 'The Use of Rape as a Weapon of War in the Conflict in Darfur, Sudan', study prepared for USAID. October 2004.
Hagan, John, Patricia Parker and Wenona Rymond-Richmond. 2005. 'The Criminology of Genocide: The Death and Rape of Darfur', *Criminology*, vol. 43 (5): 525–62.
Human Rights Watch. 2005. *Sexual Violence and Its Consequences among Dis-Placed Persons in Darfur and Chad*. New York: Human Rights Watch.
International Criminal Court for Rwanda. 1998. "Judgement in the Trial of The Prosecutor versus Jean-Paul Akayesu, Case No. ICTR – 96-4-T." Decision of 2 September, 1998.
Kristof, Nicholas. 2008. 'Tortured But Not Silenced', *New York Times*. 31 August. www.nytimes.com/2008/08/31/opinion/31kristof.html?_r=1&oref=slogin.
Lentin, Ronit. 1997. 'Introduction: (En)gendering Genocides', in Ronit Lentin (ed.), *Gender and Catastrophe*, pp. 2–17. London: Zed Books.
Lorde, Audre. 1984. *Sister/Outsider: Essays and Speeches*. San Francisco: Crossing Press.
MacKinnon, Catharine A. 1989. *Toward a Feminist Theory of the State*. Cambridge, MA: Harvard University Press.
MacKinnon, Catharine A. 2006. *Are Women Human? And Other International Dialogues*. Cambridge, MA: Belknap Press of Harvard University Press.
Médicins Sans Frontières. 2005. *The Crushing Burden of Rape: Sexual Violence in Darfur*. London: MSF.
Murphy, Kim. 2007. 'Justice Sought for Darfur War Crimes', *Los Angeles Times*. 12 June. www.latimes.com/news/nationworld/world/ladarfur12jun12,1, 6265299.satory?coll=laheadlines-world&ctrack=1&cset=true.
Pietiliä, Hikka and Jeanne Vickers. 1996. *Making Women Matter: The Role of the United Nations* (3rd edn.). London: Zed Books.
Price, Lisa S. 2001. 'Finding the Man in the Soldier-Rapist: Some Reflections on Comprehension and Accountability', *Women's Studies International Forum*, vol. 24 (2): 211–27.
Refugees International. 2007a. *Ending Sexual Violence in Darfur: An Advocacy Agenda*. Washington: Refugees International.
———. 2007b. *Laws without Justice: An Assessment of Sudanese Laws Affecting Survivors of Rape*. Washington: Refugees International.

Ringelheim, Joan. 1985. 'Women and the Holocaust: A Reconsideration of Research', *Signs: Journal of Women in Culture and Society*, vol. 10 (4): 741–61.
———. 1997. 'Genocide and Gender: A Split Memory', in Ronit Lentin (ed.), *Gender and Catastrophe*, pp. 18–33. London: Zed Books.
Smith, Gayle. 2007. 'Genocide and the Rule of Law', Testimony before the House Committee on the Judiciary Subcommittee on Crime, Terrorism and Homeland Security. 23 October. www.americanprogress.org/issues/2007/10/smith_testimony.html.
Stanko, Elizabeth A. 1985. *Intimate Intrusions: Women's Experience of Male Violence*. London: Routledge and Kegan Paul.
Steiner, Henry J. and Philip Alston. 1996. *International Human Rights in Context: Law, Politics, Morals*. Oxford: Clarendon Press.
Suleiman, Mahmoiud A. 2007. 'Too Many UN Resolutions on Darfur Too Little Action', *Sudan Tribune*. 28 December. www.sudantribune.com/spip.php?page-imprintable&id_article-25342.
United Nations. 1994. *Final Report of the Commission of Experts Established Pursuant to Security Council Resolution 780*, submitted 27 May. New York: United Nations.
———. 2005. *Report of the International Commission of Inquiry on Darfur to the Secretary-General*. 31 January 2005. New York: United Nations.
van Zeijl, Femke. 2007. 'War against Women', *New Internationalist*, no. 401, pp. 10–12. June.
Wagner, Justin. 2005. 'The Systematic Use of Rape in Darfur: A Blueprint for International War Crimes', *Georgetown Journal of International Law*, vol. 37 (1): 193–243.
Wax, Emily. 2004. 'Militiamen in W. Sudan Use Rape as a Weapon of Ethnic Cleansing', *Sudan Tribune*. 30 June. www.sudantribune.com/spip.php?article3680.
Williams, Paul D. and Alex J. Bellamy. 2005. 'The Responsibility to Protect and the Crisis in Darfur', *Security Dialogue*, vol. 36 (1): 27–47. March.
Working Group on Women, Peace and Security. 2005. *From Global to Local: Making Peace Work for Women*. New York: Working Group on Women, Peace and Security.

7 Security discourses
A gender perspective
Michele W. Milner

Introduction: views of security

The concept of security has become ever more prevalent in the media and the public imagination since the 9/11 attacks and the start of the ensuing War on Terror. However, there are many definitions and understandings of the word 'security', making it an essentially contested term across a variety of disciplines and in the popular discourse of the media. Within the field of international relations, it has been associated with the idea of national security and conceptualized as the ability of the nation state as a sovereign entity to protect and secure itself from outside or foreign threats. This traditional view of national security, derived from Hobbes's realist paradigm, developed coherency and legitimacy after World War II and during the Cold War period. It focuses on state interests by promoting military defence, government stability and economic development, and as such, it represents the interests of power-holders in society, which, feminist researchers note, are embedded within a patriarchal system.

From a feminist perspective, this conceptualization has been criticized as excluding the voices and concerns of women as part of the society that is being protected (Tickner 2001). Feminist researchers have pointed out that when security policies that are discussed in public debates are embedded within the framework of patriarchal societies, this essentially serves to mask the concerns of women. It begs the question of exactly who in a society is being protected and by whom (Blanchard 2003). It also sets up gendered identity distinctions, which equate notions of heroism and protectionism with masculine identities. As Tickner (2001: 49) explains, these fixed and gendered notions of identity make a fundamental connection between the masculinity of strategic security discourse and how it is understood by the public.

> Feminists have examined how states legitimate their security-seeking behavior through appeals to types of 'hegemonic' masculinity. They

are also investigating the extent to which state and national identities, which can lead to conflict, are based on gendered constructions. The valorization of war through its identification with a heroic kind of masculinity depends on a feminized, devalued notion of peace seen as unattainable and unrealistic. Since feminists believe that gender is a variable social construction, they claim that there is nothing inevitable about these gendered distinctions; thus, their analyses often include the emancipatory goal of postulating a different definition of security less dependent on binary and unequal gender hierarchies.

When alternative visions of security are presented without unpacking the gendered masculine constructs that support the dominant discourse of national security, they run the risk of being easily dismissed for being utopian because they are often seen as representing feminized and static notions of peace.

Human security

Betty A. Reardon (2004) notes that other possibilities for achieving security, that encompass different definitions, have limited potential until the fundamental nature of the connection between the current highly militarized system and patriarchy is recognized and replaced with a system based on gender equality. The concept of human security, as noted in the article by Kozue Akibayashi and Suzuyo Takazato, is an alternative vision that was put forward in the 1990s by both feminist and international relations scholars. At the Millennium Summit in 2000, the UN Secretary-General Kofi Annan declared the need to prioritize a vision of security that recognized the necessity of freedom from want and fear and that recognized 'individual sovereignty must take precedence over state sovereignty' (Lee 2004). The concept of human security has many definitions, but generally speaking it is more comprehensive and inclusive than the national military definitions. Human security has been conceptualized as having minimum security ideals, which include provisions for basic needs in terms of food, water, protection from natural and forced displacement and protection from direct and structural violence. These constitute fundamental needs and human rights. It also has maximum security ideals, such as ensuring people's access to a dignified life and a sustainable civil society (ibid.). These protect and promote individuals' wellbeing by striving to eliminate insecurities in such areas as health, income, the environment, politics and communities. In this sense, human security's comprehensive approach is preventive and empowering to individuals not only in terms of survival but also human dignity.

The feminist human security framework presented in this volume derives from a concept of human security presented at The Hague Appeal for Peace Civil Society Conference in 1999 which prioritizes the experience and expectation of wellbeing. In order to do so, four essential conditions for human life must be met: a life-sustaining environment; basic survival needs; fundamental dignity and respect for personal and cultural identities; and protection from avoidable harm. The fundamental interdependence of these conditions forms the basis for authentic security, which is a prerequisite for societal transformation based on non-violent structures and gender justice.

Human security is a conceptual paradigm shift away from the concept of national military security, which is ubiquitous in most mainstream media debates. As with any concept, its meaning does not rest on a predetermined essence but is socially produced and contested through discourse, making the relationship between language and patriarchal power structures an essential area of scrutiny and a site of possibility for transformative action. Any responsible exploration of this relationship, in the context of contemporary possibilities for transformative action, would give primary attention to the language employed by the information media in their presentation of security issues.

Canadian troops in Afghanistan

The debate about the role of the Canadian troops in Afghanistan has centred on whether the purpose of their role should be development or combat, and as such, it provides a site for exploring how different conceptions of security are constructed in the media. The American-NATO occupation of Afghanistan occurred right after 9/11 in 2001 and was justified by the US government and the media in a variety of ways. While initially seen as a way to strike back at Al-Qaeda, an enemy that does not have a nation state identity, the discourse of retribution was soon subsumed in the notion of a humanitarian mission that would bring human rights and dignity to the Afghan people. Operation Enduring Freedom put great emphasis on ending the suffering of the Afghan people under the cruel and repressive Taliban regime. The justification drew much of its rhetorical force from the discourse of imperialism, in particular evoking the narratives of a noble protection scenario and Orientalism (Stabile and Kumar 2005: 766).

> It constructed the West as the beacon of civilization with an obligation to tame the Islamic world and liberate its women. This served to erase not only the political struggles of women in Afghanistan against both the Northern Alliance and the Taliban, but those of the women in the West as well who, contrary to Orientalist claims about the eternal virtues of Western civilization have had to organize and fight for what rights they enjoy today.

This gendered discourse of justification focused on the concept of military security as a source of protection for the weakened nation state of Afghanistan in order that it became 'thinkable, doable and to an extent inevitable that the USA would bomb Afghanistan, the main base of the Islamist militant movement, Al-Qaeda as punishment for crimes attributed to Al-Qaeda' (Shepherd 2006). The need to secure the rights of Afghan women from the Taliban, as a key argument justifying the intervention, omits a great deal of the historical and material context that is relevant to the situation of Afghan women. By simplifying it in this manner, the enemy of the Taliban can also be stereotyped as part of a demonic Islamic character, which in turn justifies the need for intervention and protection by the successful nation states and is linked narratively to many other colonial invasions which purported to save the lives of women from savages. But as Cohn and Enloe (2003) have pointed out (and as is observed from the African experience by Bernedette Muthien in this volume), military action in the name of imperialism never improves the lives of women and children. As passive recipients of protection from gendered power structures, they are disempowered and denied agency in how they live their daily lives. In the case of Afghanistan, this was made even clearer by the fact that little if any media attention was paid to the situation of Afghan women prior to the time when they became rhetorically useful as a justification for military intervention. In recent years their situation has again been of little consequence to the political considerations of American and NATO security policymakers.

The complex constructions of gender and protection that were initially used to justify the war have also been seen in the Canadian media in its debate on the purpose of their troops' mission in Afghanistan. Canada's involvement began with 750 troops in 2002, as part of their commitment to NATO's multilateral intervention to assist the United States in searching for 'terrorists'. Originally conceived as a short-term intervention, this time-limited idea changed in 2003 when troops increased to over 2,000. The purpose of the mission began to seem more like a long-term peacekeeping mission (such as Yugoslavia, where Canada remained through most of the 1990s) where Canadian troops were to work with Afghan national government agencies on development that would increase the overall stability of the region. Yet in 2005, when more troops were sent and then relocated to the dangerous southern city of Kandahar, the number of casualties increased and many wondered if Canada's mission was essentially one of combat rather than of development. Canadians questioned how long their troops should be involved in a costly and ambiguous mission that entailed such a high loss of life.

Although Operation Enduring Freedom was orchestrated by the American military, it was heavily supported in terms of troop involvement by both the Canadian and the British militaries as well as other members of NATO. As such, increasing numbers of casualties in both countries have prompted more public debate as to the role and appropriateness of their troops in this conflict. Because Canada's former prime minister was not supportive of the Iraq invasion, no Canadian troops were sent to that country. This has meant that public debate regarding Canada's international role in the War on Terror has centred on Afghanistan and has developed in intensity as the mission has been extended and casualties have increased.

Language and power

The role of language is important in understanding social issues because it constitutes and stabilizes concepts relating to human activity over time. Certain conceptual frameworks that entail ideologies and belief systems (such as patriarchy and national security) are given legitimacy through communicative patterns that emerge in discourse by power elites and state structures (Chilton 1996). Critical discourse analysis (CDA) seeks to unpack these patterns in order to increase the awareness of the social function of language with regard to creating, maintaining and reinforcing relationships of power. CDA views the relationship between concepts and how they are expressed in language as being fluid and having ideological underpinnings. It is concerned with the representation of various aspects of the social, such as events (people, places, actions) and structures (organizational and institutional) and how these relate and interact with one another in terms of their relation to power structures. These representations both shape and are shaped by various patterns of discourse, which relate to one another in dialogic relationships (Fairclough and Wodak 1997).

Such concepts as the 'nation state' or 'military security' are not naturally occurring organizing principles but rather are created and maintained through discourse. In this sense, language has the capacity to structure the nature of policy formulations and the arguments that justify them. This in turn has a profound impact on the presentation and shaping of events that relate to concepts like security. When discussing a contested concept, such as security, this means that gendered aspects and ideological assumptions that have become naturalized in patterns of discourse about national military security need to be identified in order to appreciate the effect they have on justifying various courses of action to the public (Fairclough 2003). Unless these patterns of discourse are made explicit, they may go unchallenged and leave little room for alternative ways of understanding complex social problems. Similarly, just as the concept of human security itself constitutes a paradigm shift, the language that is used to discuss it must change and gain rhetorical force or else its transformative possibilities cannot be fully understood.

These types of relationships between gender and military security systems have been probed in the work of Cohn and Enloe (2003) in which they identified the masculine discourse of US security experts as being dominant and therefore considered the only legitimate form of expression when discussing the concept of security. Similarly, studies by Milliken and Sylvan (1996) have shown how the gendered discourse of policymakers in relation to the US bombing of Indochina constructed a reality based on notions of masculine strength that legitimated the bombing campaigns. For both, the words of policymakers and defence experts had the power to reinforce polarized dualistic definitions of masculine and feminine, which are tied to security decisions, and also to limit the participation of alternative ideas and concepts that did not conform to these patterns.

Metaphors and security

Lakoff and Johnson (1980) have argued that metaphors are fundamental to how people understand and live in the world. They provide both a physical and a social orientation to concepts and ideas by linking two ideas or objects. This allows us to understand one concept in relation to another and creates a web of conceptual mappings that link the ideas in our imaginations. Metaphor analysis draws on cognitive semantics and emphasizes the relationship between source domains, which tend to be concrete, simple and familiar, and target domains, which are abstract, complex or difficult to define. For example, in the conceptual metaphor ARGUMENT IS WAR, the source domain (war) is used to map certain characteristics of the more complex target domain of argument. These mappings of certain characteristics onto another entity also entail a variety of values and evaluations that construct a particular representation of that event, person or idea.

Chilton (1996) has taken a cognitive approach to his analysis of the ideological meanings of metaphors in security discourse and recognized the importance of long-term mental schemata or conceptual frameworks to the negotiation of meaning that occurs in the understanding of political communication. As Chilton notes, metaphor is not merely a literary ornamentation but is part of what constitutes the thinking concerning political discourse and provides 'communicative cohesion, and . . . a means for both consensus and conflict'.

In terms of abstract phenomena like security, within international relations discourses, Chilton has identified four systems of conceptual meaning or schema, which have been pervasive when discussing the concept of national security: the *container* schema, the *path* schema, the *force* schema and the *link* schema. The use of metaphors constitutes the discursive production of an object, such as security, by linking it to other objects and ideas (Mutimar 2005) in a way that becomes conventionalized and is therefore seen as objective. As Chilton (1996) states, this

> is partly because the discourse of realism, which has yielded concrete policies, has created the world which it claims exists as an objective and independent entity 'out there'. Realism, in the sense in which it is used in international relations theory, contributed to creating the political reality which it purports to describe objectively.

These cognitive structures systematically link various meanings (such as the nation state as a *container* that needs to be secured and protected) which are used by specialized discourse communities like defence analysts and policymakers (Chilton, 2004). These mental models can also be understood from a feminist perspective as being culturally embedded in patriarchal power structures which then prioritize certain understandings of security and form a point of connection between specialized discourses and the general public.

Charteris-Black (2004) has examined the emotional and rhetorical potential of metaphor in political communication and described it as a 'cognitive heuristic' which makes complex social issues more intelligible while providing emotional resonance with various symbolic representations. The effect of these heuristic devices can be to justify and persuade particular ideological perspectives.

Dominant media discourses

Media texts draw heavily on the presentation of ideas and discursive patterns of other texts in order to maintain dominant discourses (Karim 2003). From a gender perspective, this would mean that alternative discourses that question the patriarchal values of the dominant discourses would be given less, if any, prominence. As Hall (1979) notes, the prevalence of the dominant discourses serves to make them seem naturalized and conditions the audience/readers to accept the orientation to the issues that is supplied by the worldviews of socio-economic and intellectual elites who perpetuate them.

> This is not a single, unitary, but a plurality of dominant discourses: They are not deliberately selected by encoders to 'reproduce events within the dominant ideology', but constitute the *field* of meanings within which they just choose. Precisely because they have become 'universalized and naturalized', they appear to be the only forms of intelligibility available; they have become sedimented as the 'only rational, universally valid ones'.

As Hall correctly emphasizes, dominant discourses, often derived from patriarchal systems, are ubiquitous in media arguments, but this does not imply that the media conspires to create this effect. Rather, they are produced and maintained through hegemonic processes which constitute frames, definitions and reference points for understanding by audiences (Karim 2003). They also are 'excellent examples of socially poignant representations . . . (and) constitute verbal evidence for an underlying system of ideas – or ideology – whose assumptions may be ignored if we are unaware of them' (Charteris-Black 2004). The use of metaphors as a dominant and convenient linguistic resource provides coherence to this process and becomes an example of how gendered linguistic mechanisms, rooted in patriarchal societal values, serve to limit how the concept of security is understood. With respect to how language is used and understood by various discourse communities and groups (such as policymakers, the media and their audiences), it is necessary to examine the cognitive structures that produce various word associations used in metaphoric expressions. As Chilton (1996: 91) notes,

> If metaphors were necessary categories corresponding uniquely to objective entities, the use of metaphor would not vitiate the claim

to objectivity; but metaphors as argued earlier, are selected, specified and formulated in discourse, according to interests. Although many of these metaphors have their source in recurrent commonly shared image schemas, the diverse way they are formulated and deployed is neither inevitable nor trivial, but part of a conceptual framework which gives meaning to the various possible descriptions of the international political domain.

In this way, the dominant interests and values of patriarchal organizational systems become naturalized to the extent that their use in various public discourses is so commonplace that it is not questioned, nor are its ideological roots or emotive persuasive aspects fully appreciated. This then naturalizes and gives preference to various political realities and justifications while marginalizing or omitting others.

Method

In order to investigate how metaphors were used to structure the complex interaction between gender and security in the Canadian media, I collected a corpus of articles on Afghanistan from the weekly Canadian newsmagazine *Macleans* during the period from 2006 to 2008. *Macleans* has a wide national readership of middle- to upper-class readers who are interested in current affairs; therefore, it serves as a barometer of public debate. As Canada's only weekly newsmagazine, it represents a uniquely Canadian perspective through its content, as opposed to other newsmagazines, such as *Time* (Canadian edition), which offer a more American point of view. Although the small sampling of articles cannot be considered representative of all media coverage in the Canadian mainstream media, it gives an indication of the type of security discourses that have been commonly found.

I was interested in how the gendered nature of the military security system was revealed through the metaphors used to describe it. Because the Canadian debate about the troops' role contrasted their purpose in terms of development or combat, I also wanted to see if there was evidence of novel metaphors being used to describe more authentic notions of human security that might show evidence of a conceptual paradigm shift in language.

Metaphoric schema in Canadian security discourses

The conceptual metaphor of the STATE AS PERSON occurred frequently in the corpus and serves to confer validity on the nation state concept by personifying it and endowing it with a set of values, beliefs and attitudes.

> Gen. Rick Hillier, the charismatic chief of defence staff, *who is deeply committed to helping Afghanistan find its feet as a democracy*, recently admitted the obvious: the Taliban resistance in the south has been stiffer this summer than anyone expected.
> (*Macleans*, 26 August 2006, emphasis added)

In the case of Afghanistan, because it is seen as a failed state, the metaphoric expressions used to refer to it are different types of weakened people, such as children, who are not sufficiently developed to look after themselves. This also fortifies the need for help by stronger nation states as parents that need to nurture and help the child. This in turn constructs a moral high ground, based on patriarchal power associations, of MORALITY IS STRENGTH upon developed nation states in their relationships with the developing world.

> The document I saw shows the work that must be accomplished, not only by soldiers but also by civilians and governments, *if Afghanistan can ever be safe enough to stand on its own*.
> (*Macleans*, 12 November 2007, emphasis added)

Safety and security are conflated with maturity and strength, which is further associated with male children, so that even when a nation state is weak or naughty, it is still masculine.

> One high-ranking ISAF military officer had a similar thought. 'I have long thought the message we should send to the Afghan people should be the image of a *coalition soldier holding a rifle in one hand and a shovel in the other and saying, 'I've got the will and the capability to use either. Which would you have me use?'* Now I think it's time to replace the rifle with a crescent wrench. And the message now should be, to the Afghan leadership, '*We are gonna take the training wheels off this bicycle. You boys had better start pedalling*'.
>
> 'Six years have been spent on *baby steps with this government*', Sultanzoy said. '*You've been spoonfeeding them and they don't even want to chew*'.
>
> This nation has never had a smooth transition of power. *If we once again push this guy [Karzai] down the nation's throat*, we won't even be able to buy time and say better leadership is coming.

By this point, a lot of readers must be wondering whether there is any point Canadian troops even sticking around for the end of this film.
(*Macleans*, 12 November 2007, emphasis added)

The weakness of a failed state is also characterized as a person not in charge of all his mental capacities, although this may not be a specifically gendered portrayal. However, it reinforces the masculine concepts of heroism and assistance that are implied as being necessary to secure and democratize the failed state.

The Taliban's current Ramadan offensive may not live up to its moniker 'Nasrat' (Victory), but it is throwing the crisis in Afghanistan into harsh relief. Despite a half-decade of NATO-led fighting against the stubborn insurgency and billions in development aid, *the country is closer to a basket case than a beacon of democracy in the troubled Middle East.*
(*Macleans*, 22 October 2007, emphasis added)

However, the gendered distinction between failed (female) and non-failed (male) nation states becomes salient when Afghanistan is referred to as a victim of sexual violence at the hands of its president. This justifies the use of military strength as necessary to rescue it from enemies either within or neighbouring the country.

Sarah Chayes is a former National Public Radio reporter who has lived in Kandahar for five years, working with NGOs and running a small co-operative business, Arghand, that makes and sells fancy soap. 'People's anger with the government is just absolutely overflowing', she said. 'I think Karzai tried very weakly, in the beginning, to rein a bunch of these guys in. He's totally buckled. *He's presiding over the gang rape of his country*'.
(*Macleans*, 12 November 2007, emphasis added)

The SECURITY AS CONTAINER metaphor has a variety of entailments that include the hardening of national borders through military force in order to maintain the sovereignty of nation states. This is a constant point of reference when discussing Afghanistan because its border with Pakistan is seen as fluid, both in terms of national security and with regard to democratic and fundamentalist ideologies.

> With much of the leadership now slipping into Pakistan, it will be difficult for NATO to do any lasting damage to the Taliban command structure. 'The border is a concern to us', Grant says, adding, in a veiled message to Pakistani authorities, *'Any sovereign state should ensure that its border is secure'*.
> (*Macleans*, 15 January 2007, emphasis added)

Containment also implies spatial concepts, which keep certain forces in and others out in order to secure and protect a society. This can be seen as not only securing, through containing, national boundaries but also areas within a country, which are defined as being morally repugnant, such as the distinctions made between the cities and countryside in Afghanistan. This again plays on the gendered construction of MORALITY/DEMOCRACY AS STRENGTH, which justifies the use of force to intervene within national and interior boundaries.

> AFGHAN AUTHORITIES ARE TRYING TO RID KABUL OF ITS SEEDY REPUTATION BY RE-INJECTING ISLAM INTO THIS CITY OF SIN
> Since the fall of the Taliban in 2001, Kabul has transformed from an *austere fulcrum of religious zealots* into the pre-eminent red-light district of the Muslim world.
> So now, four years after *Kabul's theological iron curtain was pried open by the U.S.-led invasion of Afghanistan*, the capital is *teetering on the brink* of another revolution, as authorities try to mount a crackdown against excess. But *making over* this new City of Sin is proving to be a real challenge.
> (*Macleans*, 3 April 2006, emphasis added)

In this case, the city of Kabul is first seen as a container for Muslim austerity that has turned into a container for Western vices. However, the need for military force to 'make over' the city rests on external forces and has little to do with the citizens who inhabit it.

As Chilton (1996) points out, there was an expansion of the container notion of national security from the US perspective during the Vietnam War which expanded the perimeter of what needed to be secured in order to support US and democratic interests. Thus, US national security included Asian territories, such as South Korea and later Vietnam. In a similar way, the War on Terror expanded the perimeter of national security interests to include the securing of the base of operations for Al-Qaeda in Afghanistan, and later Iraq, through the use of the NATO alliance. Although NATO is associated geographically with the Northern Atlantic region, its expansion to fight the War on Terror makes it a container of Western ideals, which can be mobilized and expanded through the multilateral intervention in Afghanistan.

> Canada deployed military forces overseas *to confront or contain violence that could threaten Canada and her allies*. Our society is based on free markets and individual liberty. Radical Islam is the latest variant of a mindset that seeks to destroy the individual and subordinate it to the state or, in this case, it is a twisted variant of Islam used as *a tool for control by charismatic leaders who view our political, economic and social system as an obstacle to their designs*.
>
> They never believed *that the West would storm this rugged citadel*, and believed that the track record of failure in previous attempts to control Afghanistan would serve as a deterrent. They were wrong. The coalition effort, Operation Enduring Freedom, destroyed the Taliban government shielding al-Qaeda and *ripped out the terrorist infrastructure*.
>
> Together, *'hunting' operations and 'building' operations* counter the Taliban's attempts to coerce the Afghan people in the province to join their cause.
>
> (*Macleans*, 11 September 2006, emphasis added)

The metaphor of SECURITY AS FORCE is also used as a justification for military action as opposed to any other type of action that might be used in order to achieve the goals for spreading Western ideals and containing anything opposed to it. The justification for the use of military force is further legitimized by making distinctions of 'otherness' about the enemy, such as portraying the INSURGENTS AS ANIMALS or GARBAGE that need to be disposed of. This less-than-human portrayal legitimizes the use of force to achieve these goals and to provide a secure environment.

> Gordon O'Connor, the retired general Harper named defence minister, played down the likelihood of combat. In an interview, he said rather vaguely that the Canadian task force in Kandahar was there *'to provide a security environment'*. What about fighting the Taliban? 'Our role is not to conduct combat operations', O'Connor stressed, although there might be some *'rooting out of insurgents'*.
>
> (*Macleans*, 20 March 2006, emphasis added)

You clear out the enemy, leave, they come back, and you have to clear them out again. Canadians are getting a crash course in what a counter-insurgency war is all about.

The flow of a counter-insurgency war is very different from the linear battles of Vimy or Normandy, *and this is connected to how success is measured.* Insurgency wars do have territorial aspects, but also have important social and psychological 'terrain'.

Fighting an insurgency cannot be measured linearly. Pashmul is not Vimy: we move in, clear it out, leave (because we cannot be everywhere all the time, and the Afghan government is not yet able to exert a permanent presence), *the enemy comes in, and we have to remove them again. It is like taking out the garbage . . . you have to keep doing it.*

(*Macleans*, 25 September 2006, emphasis added)

The metaphorical schema of the PATH or JOURNEY structures the process of arriving at security as a goal to be reached, but it may imply that the way to reach it is unclear because the emphasis is on the end point and not on the specific means being used. Similarly, the force driving the journey may be derived from powers, which make the agency of security-seeking behaviour opaque and ubiquitous. This again points to the power behind the nation state as driving the journey, as opposed to individuals. These characteristics can be seen in the metaphorical expressions used to discuss the plans or pathways that would lead to peace in Afghanistan.

Afghans need *security*, but that's slow in *coming*. How long will our soldiers really have to stay in their country? Just because there is no *master plan* for getting Afghanistan on its feet doesn't mean *nobody plans*. But the planning is a *furtive, piecemeal business*, better suited to pointing out the contradictions of this bizarre conflict than to tracing *a dependable path through them to peace.*

One of the surprises when I visited Afghanistan last month is that there is simply no *commonly endorsed road map for helping the country until it can govern itself* and everyone else can go home.

Well, there's the Afghanistan Compact, *a five-year plan that came out of an international summit in London last year, but it is sketchy and already outpaced by events.*

Instead of a plan there is Babel: 37 foreign countries, including Canada, contributing troops to NATO's 41,000-soldier International Security Assistance Force (ISAF); international umbrella groups with their own agendas, like the United Nations and the

Security discourses 181

European Union; hundreds of non-governmental aid organizations like CARE and Doctors Without Borders; and the *fractured and factious institutions* of Afghan civil society itself. Often these groups don't get along. Most NGOs won't talk to soldiers for fear of becoming insurgents' targets. The assorted troop-donor countries define the conflict differently.
(*Macleans*, 12 November 2007, emphasis added)

Noticeable is the lack of agency in terms of who is planning the journey, which conceptualizes it as ineffective because it is not unilateral. Because this coalition of interested parties is not prioritized hierarchically as is the military, it is also seen as ineffective, and little attention is paid to the idea of cooperative interaction in order to achieve alternative visions of security.

The two stated purposes of Canada's troops in Afghanistan, development and combat, are conflated and militarized with such expressions as 'developmental warrior'. The notion of security as meaning only military security, or freedom from direct violence, is also reinforced by the use of the container metaphor to refer to military bases operating within Afghanistan and the safety they represent. This clearly prioritizes the value of military security, reinforcing its masculine and protective qualities, which is needed by development workers.

Military planners are playing a tricky balancing act in Afghanistan: taking a measured approach while soldiers die risks damage to the morale of Canada's fighting men and women. Phrases like '*the developmental warrior*', used by Lt.-Col. Ian Hope, commander of First Battalion of the Patricias, when he addresses troops at Gumbad, often fall on deaf ears for soldiers who have seen friends hit by attacks. '*How much longer are we gonna be taking it from behind?*' one soldier asks Hope – a question he has difficulty answering.

But for now, a fissure remains: combat soldiers say they are not getting enough respect from other Canadian troops whose job is reconstruction, and they're beginning to grumble. 'That will change', says Hope to frustrated battalion members. '*When they see you come onto the base from outside the wire*, they will respect you. Eventually. In the meantime, remember, you are professional soldiers'.
Stirring words (*Macleans*, 24 April 2006, emphasis added)

This rape metaphor equates the presence of development workers with females and the risk they pose to maintaining secured and contained bases of military operation. This weakens the concept of development and constructs it as being less important than military security. This is strengthened by the notion of balancing military security and development as 'fantasy'. The FORCE schema, which is associated with the balancing of strong and weak forces, again feminizes the human aspects associated with the goals of development, in favour of the masculine qualities associated with 'hard fighting' in a mission named 'Mountain Thrust'.

> But that sort of *talk of a balanced effort in which the army supports the work of diplomats and aid workers soon began to sound like a fantasy*. Instead, this spring and summer brought all but *uninterrupted hard fighting*, punctuated increasingly by suicide bomber attacks, as Canadian and other NATO forces, mainly American, British and Dutch, pressed into Taliban strongholds in an offensive called *Operation Mountain Thrust*.
> (*Macleans*, 28 August 2006, emphasis added)

> *It has come to dominate the two main dimensions of Ottawa's outlook on the world: managing our bilateral relationship with the U.S. and leveraging our position in multilateral organizations. On one hand, Canadian boots on the ground in Afghanistan lend Ottawa much of whatever credibility it boasts in today's terror-obsessed Washington. On the other, the growing UN-sanctioned NATO role in Afghanistan makes this the key test for a new sort of muscular but benign multilateral intervention.*
> (*Macleans*, 28 August 2006, emphasis added)

Distinctions relating to power are further made in military operations where cooperative multilateral interventions that are 'muscular but benign' exhibit less credence then traditional unilateral operations.

As we can see from these patterns of discourse about development, the concept is diminished in validity and in fact is portrayed as being a deterrent rather than as a necessary condition to more comprehensive definitions of security. The fact that the term 'development' itself is undefined in the discourse does not unpack various approaches of ideological significance. By treating it as a monolithic concept within the discourse of military security, it is more easily dismissed as having a cooperative role. However, one occurrence of a novel metaphor endeavoured to capture an alternative vision that could be compatible with some of the conditions set out in the feminist definition of human security integral to this volume. SECURITY AS MULTIPLE BOXES encapsulates a visual alternative to the hierarchical nature of military security.

Dozens of agencies would *need to sign off on the chart in question* before it could have any official weight. That's just never going to happen.

The document I saw shows the work that must be accomplished, not only by soldiers but also by civilians and governments, if Afghanistan can ever be safe enough to stand on its own. *Boxes with labels like 'Independent Media' and 'Progressive Governance Extended to Districts' are sprinkled across the page. Events soldiers may help with, but can never deliver alone. At the left hand of the chart is today, late 2007, in an Afghanistan where violence is increasing and social and economic progress is measurable, but halting. Dates unfold across the top:* 2010, when it would be nice if conditions had improved in a dozen measurable ways; 2011, when six or eight other criteria should be met; and a final state of blessed normality, when the Afghan government delivers fair service without violent harassment to all 34 provinces and the country's army and police are its own best defence.

The date at the right hand of the chart reads, '20??'. Not even a maverick planner dares to pretend he can know when the job will be done.

How long will this take? Ten years was at the short end of the betting pool.

Nobody on the ground *puts much stock* in predictions, including their own. I asked *the officer with the unclassified-but-unreleased chart* whether his *timeline to a peaceful Afghanistan was getting longer or shorter* as he put the *planning exercise through successive iterations. He said any box on the timeline could move left or right depending on the assumptions behind it.* Military planning in an environment of radical uncertainty *is a thought exercise, not a stone tablet from the mountaintop.*

'But here's an interesting thing', the officer said. He pointed to a box, currently positioned late in 2009, which read: 'Narcotics Influences Isolated from GOA' – the Government of Afghanistan. Of course it's a laudable goal: an Afghanistan in which the *billions of dollars in opium traffic are reduced or walled off to the point where they have no influence on the country's politics.*

This box and the assumptions behind it were the object of an interagency meeting with what the officer called 'robust UNAMA input', which meant that somebody from the United Nations Assistance Mission in Afghanistan gave him an earful.

(*Macleans*, 12 November 2007, emphasis added)

The boxes on the chart not only refer to a variety of sources of shared agency for the security plan, including civilians and government, but also include a variable timeline that allows for flexibility and interactivity between agents and events. This presents a cooperative notion of both the process and the goals of security that cannot be achieved through military intervention and therefore puts emphasis on the dignity of individuals, not only the state.

A different metaphor for comprehensive security is seen with SECURITY AS A BUILDING; however, this one does not encapsulate the same possibilities of authenticity as the one referring to multiple boxes. This is because the visual nature of the metaphor of three distinct pillars to hold up a building precludes the ability for them to interact with one another and therefore continues to isolate the goals and functions of different aspects of society for achieving security.

> Coalition planners like to talk about a '*comprehensive approach*' to Afghan self-sufficiency that *emphasizes three pillars*: '*security*', delivered essentially by soldiers, first ours and then eventually Afghanistan's; '*reconstruction and development*', the work of soldiers, NGOs, Afghans and outsiders working together, sometimes clumsily; and '*governance*', the consent of the governed in a society ruled by laws, not by bribes and threats. The problem, as NATO's latest classified Periodic Mission Review says, is that '*progress in security operations is outpacing progress in the other pillars*'.
>
> (*Macleans*, 12 November 2007, emphasis added)

The analysis of metaphors in *Macleans* reveals the gendered assumptions that are implicit in the metaphors used to describe the intervention of NATO forces for security in Afghanistan and a one-dimensional nature of security. Security, in this sense, is defined primarily in terms of the military objectives to protect and nurture the containment of the nation state and does not embody the FeDem definition of human security to any extent. Despite the media debate in terms of the troops' role being for combat or development, and the historic role of peacekeepers that Canadians identify with their military, the actual debate is heavily skewed toward a narrowly defined military security that prioritizes national security. This is evidenced through the extensive use of military metaphors, such as the containment metaphor. Its various entailments reinforce and justify the role of the state to control threats to security by military means, based on gendered distinctions of males as protectors. Female, and therefore weaker, identities are associated with the failed state of Afghanistan and its need for protection and rescue from fundamentalist Islamic forces that threaten the prominence of Western morality associated with democratic principles. In this sense, democracy as a value also takes on a gendered identity because it is secured, reinforced and protected from values of difference that would challenge it by national boundaries. The ideological and military dimensions of these values of difference are mutually reinforced by drawing metaphorical boundaries between US and THEM as can be seen in the metaphors which dehumanize THEM (the insurgents as enemy) as rodents. This justifies their extermination but does not answer fundamental questions of where they will go, or in the case of Afghanistan, how they would be integrated into a democratic society. Given that the Taliban insurgents have deep-rooted cultural ties in Afghanistan, this dualistic and overly simplified portrayal of the enemy is useful only in terms of justifying military action and thus continues to promote political and community insecurities through this confrontational orientation to threats.

The use of this metaphoric schema to define military security is also problematic in that the political resolution entailed by containment is unclear. As argued earlier, not only does the pervasive use of this metaphor schema polarize and dehumanize the enemy but also, in this case, it reinforces the idea that Islam and terrorism are a united enemy. Containment of 'insurgents' becomes containment of Islam and evokes other entailments of this metaphor, such as the anger and instability of Islamic values that might boil over if they are not controlled by military power. All this does little to offer any kind of resolution in terms of civil society or integration of diverse views in one society. It promotes a winner-take-all attitude that marginalizes the dignity of the members of Afghan society by only addressing threats to national security in a top-down approach. Less hierarchically organized systems of security based on the securing of political, social and economic human needs through development are devalued in the context of this discourse and problematized as interfering with the goals of military security.

Just as the enemy is dehumanized and one-dimensional in conventional military security discourse, so becomes the concept of development within this debate over the future of Afghanistan, rendering it of secondary importance and to some extent dismissible. The concept of development is usually associated with the idea of progress and the entailments of technology and democratic values. This is often conveyed metaphorically through journey metaphors where PURPOSES ARE DESTINATIONS (Chilton 1996). What is noticeable in this media security debate is that the journey again seems skewed to the destination of national security, with very little attention paid to what the process of development could bring in terms of promoting individual dignity and wellbeing. Although one novel metaphor, that of various boxes, is used to construct a more comprehensive and less centralized notion of security, its rhetorical force is undercut by its isolation in the discourse. As a novel metaphor, it has yet to gain recognition through repeated use in various discourse communities.

Because the security metaphors of *containment*, *path* and *force* are so bound up with national security discourses which are embedded with a patriarchal military system, it is worthwhile to ask what other metaphors might be used to construct the notion of human security in the public imagination. Human security can be related to Maslow's hierarchy of needs, and this conception gives it a pyramid-like physical space dimension. However, a metaphoric conception of human security would also need to be diffuse and wide-ranging, which would bring more focus to cooperative and interdependent forms of interaction between a variety of individuals and state actors. In terms of agency, the container metaphor serves to limit the force of what is being contained in favour of the strength of the container, thus rendering the inside or the power of individuals passive in comparison to state forces. Metaphoric expressions of more authentic definitions of security and gender would need to pay more attention to the notion of diffuse agency by allocating power across a broader spectrum of participants so that a balance of interests is less polarized between traditional gendered dichotomies.

Language is a powerful communicative tool that shapes abstract concepts, contributes to policymaking and structures the terms of engagement for public debate. Language is not a benign tool. How it is used is part of the power structures and systemic patterns of inequities and injustice that give coherence and prominence to military security while masking the insecurities that it causes. For these reasons, the consideration of how it is used to define concepts in the broader culture is more than just an academic pursuit of discursive features but is central in understanding its transformative role for conceptualizing and constituting the concept of human security. This concept of security which places emphasis on the individual as opposed to the territory of the nation state, is new and has not worked its way into people's imagination in the coherent ways that military security pervades most cultures. Yet many recognize that security threats come in the form of pervasive and systemic social, economic and cultural insecurities. Language is key in the articulation and persuasion of the importance of these more humanistic values and ideologies so that transformative possibilities can be understood and debated. The meanings of these transformative possibilities are shared meanings that need to be defined and interpreted by cultures. However, for this to happen, there needs to be an awareness of how the debate continues to be structured by naturalized and gendered uses of language that maintain and support existing power hierarchies.

References

Blanchard, E. M. 2003. 'Gender, International Relations, and the Development of Feminist Security Theory', *Signs: Journal of Women in Culture and Society*, vol. 28 (4): 1289–312.

Charteris-Black, J. 2004. *Corpus Approaches to Critical Metaphor Analysis*. Basingstoke: Palgrave Macmillan.

Chilton, P. A. 1996. *Security Metaphors: Cold War Discourse from Containment to Common House*. New York: Peter Lang.

Chilton, P. A. 2004. *Analysing Political Discourse: Theory and Practice*. London: Routledge.

Cohn, C. and C. Enloe. 2003. 'A Conversation with Cynthia Enloe: Feminists Look at Masculinity and the Men Who Wage War', *Signs*, vol. 28 (4): 1187–208.

Fairclough, N. 2003. *Analysing Discourse*. London: Routledge.

Fairclough, N. and R. Wodak. 1997. 'Critical Discourse Analysis', in T. A. Vdijk (ed.), *Introduction to Critical Discourse Analysis*, pp. 258–84. London: Routledge.

Hall, S. 1979. 'Culture, Media and the Ideological Effect', in J. Curran (ed.), *Mass Communication and Society*. Beverly Hills: Sage Publications.

Karim, K. H. 2003. *Islamic Peril: Media and Global Violence*. London: Black Rose Books.

Lakoff, G. and M. Johnson. 1980. *Metaphors We Live By*. Chicago: University of Chicago Press.

Lee, S. W. 2004. *Promoting Human Security: Ethical, Normative and Educational Frameworks in East Asia*. Seoul: Korean National Commission for UNESCO.

Milliken, J. and D. Sylvan. 1996. 'Soft Bodies, Hard Targets and Chic Theories: US Bombing Policies in Indochina', *Millennium: Journal of International Studies*, vol. 25 (2): 321–59.

Mutimar, D. 2005. 'Waging Wars in Iraq: The Metaphoric Constitution of Wars and Enemies', *46th Annual ISA Convention* 'Dynamics of World Politics: Capacity, Preferences and Leadership'. Honolulu, Hawaii.

Reardon, B. A. 2004. *Toward Human Security, a Gender Approach to Demilitarization: Women in Asia*. Tokyo: Asia-Japan Women's Resource Center.
Shepherd, L. J. 2006. 'Veiled References: Constructions of Gender in the Bush Administration Discourse on the Attacks of Afghanistan post 9/11', *International Feminist Journal of Politics*, vol. 8 (1): 19–41.
Stabile, C. and D. Kumar. 2005. 'Unveiling Imperialism: Media, Gender and the War on Afghanistan', *Media, Culture and Society*, vol. 27 (5): 765–82.
Tickner, J. A. 2001. *Gendering World Politics*. New York: Columbia University Press.

Part III
Militarization/demilitarization
Eroding and promoting human security

8 Seeking human security in a militarized Pacific
Struggles for peace and security by Pacific Island women[1]

Ronni Alexander

> I am one of the victims of army abuse. A military policeman named Robin Monai raped me. He buggered me and raped me wearing a coffee mug handle on his penis . . . This caused me internal damage. This man is still here on Buka and nothing has been done to correct this injustice. This is a man who used to cut the ears off and then kill our men. He is still here. Nothing has been done; there is no justice. There are many women's organizations, but they are of no help. They have funding but I do not know what they do with this money. They do not fight for our women's rights and they do not help us, the victims. Today we must try to forgive and forget.
>
> (Sirivi and Havini 2004: 65)

Introduction

Human security is an approach to security that seeks to place persons and communities, rather than states, at the centre of the security discourse and to open up the concept to various kinds of security and insecurity within the broad framework of freedom from want and freedom from fear. In so doing, it not only allows us to name a wide variety of forms of structural and cultural violence as insecurity but also enables us to consider how various kinds of insecurity relate to gender, and in particular, here, to women. At the same time, there is still work to be done. For example, the human security discourse is, I believe, still grappling with finding ways to enhance personal and communal security that are not in the end dependent on states, even though they might not entail military action. This is an extremely difficult issue, and as the following pages will show, one reason for that difficultly lies in the fact that due in part to the institutionalized gender hierarchies in states themselves, women can engage in effective resistance while at the same time contributing to the reproduction of traditional cultural practices that marginalize women. Similarly, although human security recognizes difference, there is much variation in just how much difference is to be acknowledged. For example, human security is theoretically applicable to queer people, but in practice, for reasons of space as in this article or otherwise, they are often left out. The social transformation required to achieve human security involves a reworking of gender relations, part of which would include affirmation of variations and combinations, including transgender. Although the discussion here will as a first step focus on women, an important area for further work is to explore the implications of human security for multiple gender identities, including transgender and queer people in the region.[2]

This article will explore how current cultural governance which emphasizes gender (in this case generally meaning women) both creates spaces for resistance to violence and recreates the patriarchal militarism and the culture of violence in the Pacific Island Countries and Territories (PICTs) region, an area comprised of 14 independent small island states, several self-governing territories, Australia and New Zealand. The objective is to begin to look at human security in the region through the intersection of militarization, gender violence and resistance in its gendered and militarized spaces. The Pacific Islands region is often considered by scholars of international relations to be too small and/or weak for serious consideration, but as in other postcolonial states, global trends, such as globalization, militarization and gender violence causing human insecurity, have had serious implications. Marginalization due to size is yet another aspect of the ways in which traditional thinking about security is 'inhuman'.

Following a short overview of human security in the region from the perspective of Pacific women, the article will look at regional and national frameworks for addressing women's issues and violence and will introduce some organizations working toward that goal. This will be followed by two case studies, both examples of the consequences of militarized security. These cases will focus on efforts for resistance and transformation, discussing the implications for human security. The first will look at an armed conflict – the Bougainville Crisis – focusing on the role played by women in peacemaking. Although this conflict occurred before the adoption of Resolution 1325 (see Soumita Basu in this volume), it is typical of the kind of conflict that resolution hopes to address. The second will look at a problem beyond the realm of Resolution 1325 – the question of military bases. Local women in Okinawa have long opposed the US presence on their island, but it is only recently that they have begun to join with others opposing US bases elsewhere. Here we will look at how a relationship is growing between women in Okinawa and Guam, prompted by government plans to remove 8,000 US Marines and their families to Guam from US bases on Okinawa. The article will conclude with some thoughts on the implications of these struggles for reconciliation and progress toward human security in the region. In the Pacific, militarization has threatened not only human security but also the very existence of indigenous cultures, economies, ways of life and even at times the islands themselves. Thus, in order to be effective, human security must deal not only with gender but also with militarization. The exploration of ways that demilitarization can be achieved may be one key to transformative resistance.

Human security from the inside: Pacific Island women's views of a militarized Pacific

Pacific Island women live in militarized and colonized spaces, which have provided harbours and bases for foreign and domestic military forces, as well as access to fisheries and other marine resources, including the minerals which lie beneath the ocean surface. These relationships have been maintained in the postcolonial Pacific, linking the Pacific Island countries and territories not only with the regional powers but also with countries at the centre of the world economy and the militarized global security system. As such, they continue to suffer the human security deficits integral to militarized security.

The colonization and militarization of Pacific spaces provide a clear example of the patriarchal colonial order and contemporary patriarchalism as defined by Betty A. Reardon in this volume. Militarization has not been limited to physical spaces, but has created militarized cultures, identities and bodies. Military coercion has become embodied through the intergenerational effects of nuclear and/or toxic contamination on Pacific peoples, their forced migration/relocation due to the contamination of their living spaces and the Amerasian and other children of mixed background living near military bases.[3] The pollution of bodies and lands in the Pacific in the name of security is an extreme example of 'inhuman security'. It is visible as well in the Pacific Islanders serving overseas in peacekeeping forces or working for private security companies, and the families those soldiers are supporting both through wages and sometimes through death.[4]

Militarized security in the Pacific since the end of the Cold War is visible in the increase in intra-regional and internal conflicts: four coups in Fiji, armed conflicts in the Solomon Islands, Papua New Guinea,

Timor Leste and West Papua and political violence in Tonga and New Caledonia. In addition, civil society movements in Asian countries, such as the Philippines and Japan, attempt to reassert their sovereignty and oust US bases; the relative importance of military facilities on US Pacific territories has grown. An example that will be considered here is the current US plan to relocate roughly 4,000 marines and their families from Okinawa (Marine Corps Air Station Futenma) to Guam.

Colonized spaces are controlled not only through military coercion and economic regulation but also through the creation and management of identity. The creation and maintenance of gendered identities plays an important role in this cultural governance which often seeks legitimacy in militarism, patriarchalism and capitalist modernity. Colonization creates new and often artificial borders; after independence, postcolonial states take over the attempt to align territorial and cultural boundaries. Cultural governance is a tool in this endeavour, moulding personal and collective gender and other identities into forms supportive of patriarchal hierarchies. For example, colonization created not only individual national identities but also 'the Pacific', an entity composed of islands in a far sea, dry surfaces far from power centres, but 'the Pacific' is also a sea of islands, a holistic totality of oceans and islands. Similarly, in the binary world of the West, the Pacific Islands are neither Orient nor Occident, neither East nor West, although the mission of 'civilizing' the 'savage' islander was a powerful tool in the colonization process. Unlike the Caribbean, where indigenous island cultures were essentially exterminated, indigenous Pacific Islanders have remained, although the experience of colonization brought many changes to the nature of that 'indigeneity'. In those islands that remain under foreign rule, the indigenous peoples are a subordinated and often unrecognized minority, such as the Native Hawaiians in Hawaii and the Chamorus in Guam.

Military bases are one place where the priorities of patriarchal cultural governance, militarization and militarized spaces are visible. Bases bring military activities and create military economies, but military and militarized cultures remain even after the bases are gone. Often resistance to this violence seeks to be transformational, aiming at alternative cultural production, but much of it actually serves to promote hegemonic militarism and militarization.

When societies and institutions commit themselves and their resources to the waging of war, they are engaging in militarism (see Reardon 1985). In order to mobilize vast social and economic resources for military purposes, people must recognize the need for doing so. This is accomplished through militarization, a mechanism which privileges military concerns, giving 'value' to aspects of ordinary life normally not directly related to the military, such as fashion design, and making people accept military values and solutions without their necessarily being aware of what is happening.

In the present global order, militarism and militarization happen in all countries, but like patriarchy, militarism is a hegemonic project which is 'constituted through systematic power relationships that privilege certain ways of knowing, being and acting and that give voice to only certain people's experiences and agendas' (Nayak and Suchland 2006: 469). Militarization is a powerful tool of cultural governance and uses gender to further its goals. The archetype of women as mothers, wives and caregivers commits women to bearing and raising sons to send off to war to fight for their nation. When caregiving institutions are militarized, the people who work in them (largely women) are serving military aims, even if they do not consciously support them.

Cultural governance, patriarchy and militarization also work to define gender violence, as they marginalize women in general and certain women in particular, thereby legitimizing some forms of gender violence but not necessarily others. For example, the construction of masculinity in the military is a major factor in prostitution and the gender violence which surrounds military bases, but the military often disregards and/or fails to give importance to that violence. In the words of Cynthia Enloe,

> Feminists from India, Zimbabwe and Japan to Britain, the United States, Serbia, Chile, South Korea, Palestine, Israel and Algeria all have found that when they have followed the bread crumbs of privileged masculinity, they have been led time and again not just to the doorstep of the military, but to the threshold of all those social institutions that promote militarization.
>
> (Enloe 2000: 33)

While Reardon holds that all militarisms are essentially patriarchal,[5] Laura Kaplan explains the relationship between privileged masculinity and militarization with what she calls patriarchal militarism. One aspect of patriarchal militarism is that it encourages men to create images of women as 'devalued others' and then to use those images as a 'model for training and inspiring masculine warriors to devalue and distance themselves from enemies' (Kaplan 1994: 124).[6] The devalued images of women employed by the military encourage gender violence, often so much so that it is disguised or made invisible. This 'invisibilization' makes it difficult for the victims to tell even their families and friends, let alone speak out in public. When victims and others do speak out, invisibilization' means that often their voices go unheeded or that their claims are not given serious consideration.

Patriarchal militarism uses dual images of male and female, masculine and feminine, to enhance male violence at the expense of women. In so doing, it both negates and makes invisible those who identify as transgendered or queer and who contradict both the binary itself and the stereotypes necessary to create these two categories. In general, both men and women play their respective roles based on this binary view of gender and so become part of the process. To the extent that they do not question the binary, they are also part of the process of invisibilization and delegitimization of queer lives and the reproduction of gender violence.

One role for women in many cultures, including the island of Bougainville, is that of peacemaker, based on their caretaking role. It is important to consider how this traditional role fits into the larger system of modern-day warfare. As we will see, although this role as peacemaker may contribute to the establishment of peace over the short-term, it may also affirm that 'which they seek to avoid: marginalization of the other, which leads to the divisions between people on which wars are predicated' (Kaplan 1994: 128).

Militarization and militarized mentalities do not necessarily take the form of direct violence. Often they constitute a form of structural violence which is not only violent in and of itself but also under certain circumstances results in direct violence. Quite often this takes the form of gender violence, most often directed against women (and sometimes 'feminine' men) by men. Gender violence is

> a systematic, institutionalized and/or programmatic violence (sexual, physical, psychological) that operates through the constructs of gender and often at the intersection of sexuality, race and national identity. Gender violence comprises the acts and practices that systematically target a person, group or community in marginalized communities or any other perceived threats to dominant political structures and practices.
>
> (Nayak and Suchland 2006: 469)[7]

Here conflict and gender violence in the Pacific are seen first as being in part a legacy of colonial rule which institutionalized male privilege through systems for control over social and economic resources, such as land and social position, as well as recreating and reinforcing gendered roles. This has contributed both directly and indirectly to the militarization of the region as these systems prioritize military/security concerns. Colonization and cultural governance also created ethnic tensions as different ethnic and/or tribal groups were brought together, often in ways that suited the needs of the colonizers rather than the colonized, and later to local elites. This occurred both through the drawing of what eventually became national boundaries and through the movements of people, such as the British importation of sugar plantation workers to Fiji from India. The pyramid of colonization privileged white over non-white, male over female and some ethnicities over others, generally ensuring white men a secure spot on top and relegating indigenous women to the bottom. In terms of gender, modern cultural governance within the hierarchical global gender order denies legitimacy to some more than others, privileging men over women and giving transgendered and queer people virtually no place all.[8]

Human security in the Pacific Islands is undermined by this hierarchal militarized cultural governance, particularly in the ways it combines with development agendas that affect the distribution and use of land and resources. Pacific women identify the following as the major causes of conflict in the region:

> Increasingly unequal access to land, paid employment and economic resources, particularly when inequality is based on ethnicity; centralization of resources and services; lack of involvement in decision-making and authority; a weakening of traditional methods of dispute resolution; and the growth of a 'Rambo' culture of violence and guns among young unemployed men.
> (Thomas 2005a: 157)

These causes occur against a background of changing demographics, including migration and urbanization and a growing gap between a small wealthy minority which has profited from 'development', and an increasing number of impoverished and/or poor people. Pamela Thomas identifies a lack of information about political processes as exacerbating the situation and draws links between the influence of media violence, domestic violence, a growing culture of violence and national conflict (Thomas 2005b: 3–4).

Local violence is manifested not only in an increase in armed conflict but also in direct violence by armed youth gangs or increasing domestic violence. It is also visible as structural/cultural violence in such forms as gender and ethnic discrimination, lack of access to social resources for women and particular ethnic groups and discriminatory legislation. The outbreak of armed conflict in the region, and the use of peacekeepers to contain that conflict, as well as participation by Pacific Island forces in international peacekeeping, has helped spread the culture of violence within the islands, reaching more and more people, further undermining human security and causing more and more pain.

Particularly in recent years, international development and security communities have attempted to address some of these issues of gender violence. One example of this can be seen in the adoption of Resolution 1325 by the UN Security Council in 2000. This resolution encourages member states to 'ensure increased representation of women at all decision-making levels in national, regional and international institutions and mechanisms for the prevention, management and resolution of conflict' and calls on all involved actors, 'when negotiating and implementing peace agreements, to adopt a gender perspective' (UNSCR 1325 2000). The adoption of Resolution 1325 led to an increase in cooperation among governments, international governmental organizations (IGOs) and non-governmental organizations (NGOs) at transnational as well as local levels. This should have had enormous implications for organizations working with women in conflict situations, yet although we do hear more about the ways conflicts are affecting women, there is still a long way to go before those situations are rectified in the Pacific Islands region as well as elsewhere. The case studies that follow suggest that one reason for these failures is that often peace efforts, including those by women, are conducted within the contours of entrenched patriarchal remnants of colonialism.

Another aspect of the seeming inability of transnational networks to end gender violence may be that the liberal gender perspective and its concomitant focus on women adopted by most agencies working in international development and human security seek to find solutions in increasing the number of women involved rather than changing structures which adversely affect women, often conflating the terms 'gender' and 'women'. This approach can be effective in getting more women jobs, but the focus on individual choice rather than on institutionalized gender hierarchies makes it unable to address other power imbalances, gendered and otherwise. As such, it can serve to assist in the reproduction of traditional gender/power roles and their accompanying violence, even while trying to eliminate it (see Connell 1990). Transformation requires calling attention to, and changing, the power imbalances and patriarchal structures that underlie gender roles. Substituting the word 'gender' for 'women' is not enough.

Seeking human security in a militarized Pacific 199

Working for peace and opposing violence in the Pacific

As we have seen, threats to human security have become a feature of the landscape of the Pacific Islands region. Such measures as Resolution 1325 have provided an impetus for work at the regional and national levels to deal with gender(ed) violence, and the following is a brief summary of efforts in the PICTs. This will be followed by two contrasting examples of militarization, both of which include gender(ed) violence: the Bougainville Crisis and the relocation of US Marines from Okinawa to Guam.

Beyond the broad implications of human security, at first glance, there may be little to connect the examples offered here. Cultural governance has taught us that Japan (but not necessarily Okinawa) is outside the 'Pacific Islands region' (but a part of the Pacific). The political status of Guam is that of an unincorporated territory of the United States, putting it, like Japan, outside the purview of regional organizations in the Pacific Islands region.[9] The Bougainville Crisis was a prolonged internal conflict which ended before Resolution 1325 was enacted; US military bases in Japan are not generally regarded as being within the intended realm of that resolution in the first place. This dissonance allows us to consider the trans-border implications of human security and to recognize some of the ways militarized cultural governance works to impose boundaries and how resistance can work to change them. It is hoped that these examples will help to promote discussion of the relationship between gender(ed) violence and militarization and to illustrate the ways in which cultural governance influences both.

Gender equality should be a prerequisite for human security. Between 1982 and 2008, the organization responsible for coordinating gender mainstreaming and equality at the regional level in the Pacific region was the Pacific Women's Bureau (PWB), an intergovernmental organization operating within the auspices of the Pacific Community. The PWB was the sole regional organization recognized by governmental and non-governmental women's organizations as advocating gender awareness, gender mainstreaming and the needs of women in the region. In 2008, the PWB was merged with the Community Education and Training Centre (CETC), the former Cultural Affairs Program and the Pacific Youth Bureau to form the Human Development Program (HDP). At the time of this writing, the HDP belonged to the Social Resources Division of the Secretariat of the Pacific Community (SPC; former South Pacific Commission) and had as its mission to 'To maximize the development potential of Pacific Island people in health, culture and information and enhance the empowerment of women and young people' (SPC-HDP).[10] Following the work of the PWB, the HDP endeavours to improve the status of Pacific women through the monitoring of the implementation of the Pacific Platform for Action on the Advancement of Women and Gender Equality (PPA)[11] and the Millennium Development Goals (MDGs).

All Pacific Island countries and territories have established institutions for women at the national level, and 13 countries have ratified the Convention on the Elimination of All Forms of Discrimination against Women (CEDAW), but resources for these institutions are scarce; few countries mainstream gender, and compliance with CEDAW is minimal in some countries. The levels of women's participation in political and public decision-making is generally low, and reduced budgets due to regional/local conflicts, structural reforms and financial crises have served to further marginalize women and women's issues. Women are under-represented in business, particularly in senior management positions, including the media, and only a few countries have specific measures to foster women's economic participation.

With regard to gender violence, violence against women and domestic violence are prevalent, as are teenage pregnancies, school dropouts and broken families. These trends are linked to alcohol and substance abuse, which remains common (Secretariat of the Pacific Community 2006: 2–3). In addition, of particular concern with regard to the freedom from the want side of human security are the continued exploitation of women migrant workers and the impact of trade liberalization policies.

The regional structure for response to security issues is based on the 2000 (PIF) Biketawa Declaration (Secretariat of the Pacific Islands Forum 2000) which mandates response to security issues at the regional level and reiterates the rule of law, individual freedoms, equal rights regardless of gender, race, colour, creed or political belief, and the right to participation in political processes. In 2005, the Pacific Plan adopted a broad definition of security which listed human security as one of four priority goals for the region and included gender equality as a crosscutting strategic objective. The implementation of Resolution 1325 in all countries, including those that have not experienced recent violent conflict, is considered useful as it provides a framework to ensure consideration to gender dimensions of peace and stability, as 'violence, instability and conflict have had devastating effects on the lives of women and girls including physically, emotionally and psychologically and in their ability to achieve their basic rights and freedoms' (Secretariat of the Pacific Islands Forum 2012: 7). Women and young women have also played an important part in conflict prevention, management and recovery in the region.

Numerous civil society organizations in the region are also working to oppose violence and to create peace. Women, often at great risk to themselves, have engaged in vigils and peace marches, lobbied political leaders, talked with soldiers and armed fighters, networked to provide information, shelter, food and other assistance and worked to restore their communities once the direct violence has ceased. In some ways, these activities have been possible for Pacific women precisely because they are women; gender roles and gendered power relations have given them the space to resist. However, those same power relations have meant that their work has not necessarily been widely heard or acknowledged.

> What is seldom given adequate consideration is the role that Pacific Island women have played, and continue to play, in establishing communication channels between warring parties, in restoring and maintaining peace, in rebuilding communities and in working to overcome the physical and psychological trauma of conflict.
> (Thomas 2005a: 155)

Case studies in gendered peace activism

As we have seen, the militarized Pacific poses a threat to both the freedom from want and the freedom from fear of people in the region. Here we will consider two contrasting examples of militarization: the Bougainville Crisis and the militarization of Guam and Okinawa, including the relocation of US Marines from Okinawa to Guam. These two very different situations offer some insight into the threats to, and possibilities for, human security in the region.

Case study 1: Bougainville

> One thing the army did was to make men strip and commit anal sex with each other at gunpoint. People were afraid of the gun and would do these things to avoid being shot.
> – Sirivi and Havini (2004: 64)

> Violence is glamorous masculinity in Melanesia.
> – Macintyre (2005: 42)

Bougainville Island, together with the neighbouring Buka Island and several small atolls, forms one of the 19 provinces of Papua New

Guinea (PNG). Although it is geographically and ethnically closer to the Solomon Islands than to PNG, the continued use of the huge open-pit Panguna copper mine in central Bougainville was an essential element of the PNG government's plan for development after independence in 1975. The development of the mine disrupted the social fabric not only through the presence of ethnically and culturally different workers but also through destruction of the land itself and forced relocation. Moreover, the PNG Constitution provides only for compensation for the surface of the land, giving complete ownership of everything else to the PNG government. Compensation for use by the mine was made once and only once (if at all); there was no renegotiation.

The Bougainville Crisis (see Garasu 2002) which began in 1989 was initially centred on the mine, which was soon closed. The conflict became a 10-year internal conflict between the secessionist Bougainville Revolutionary Army (BRA) and the Papua New Guinea Defence Forces and their supporters, the local Resistance. By its conclusion, between 15,000 and 20,000 people had lost their lives.

Bougainvilleans traditionally live by gardening, hunting and fishing, and society is built around land. The mine, by its very nature, was intimately connected with the use (and abuse) and possession of the land. As such, it had a particularly strong impact on women because they are the traditional custodians of the land, and it is the woman's line that determines inheritance and use. Reflecting this relationship, a term often used to describe women is 'mothers of the land'. This phrase is invoked frequently in discussions of the roles women played as traditional peacemakers during and after the conflict.

For some women, the conflict was as much about land as it was about independence. 'I can't pass the land on now because most of it has been covered up by the mine', Patricia Dave said in 1988 as she stood among her grandchildren. 'The traditional system will never work again. The company has only paid the parents for this. What Ona is fighting for is that everybody, right down to the last born, should get compensation because our traditions have been broken and we will not be able to pass anything down to them'. It was this loss – the loss of land not to just one generation but to all the generations to come and all those that had been – that the miners did not seem to comprehend.

Another impact that the conflict had on the human security of all women and men on Bougainville was a blockade of Bougainville Island instigated by the PNG government with Australian assistance. The blockade prevented even humanitarian supplies from being brought in, depriving local communities of medical and other supplies. This affected not only the wounded but also inhibited access to food, medicine and other necessities. Women, even those in government-controlled areas, were unable to go daily to their gardens due to restrictions and fear of violence, and this in turn affected the health and wellbeing of their families. Shortages of human and material resources, including medicine, and the breakdown of services affected women's reproductive health, and the interruption of the supply of sanitary protection made it difficult for women to leave their homes during menstruation.

Militarization and the presence of weapons brought rampant sexual violence to Bougainville. Women were torn from their land, in the absence of traditional and/or modern cultural restraints; murder, rape and robbery in the name of the 'war' became everyday occurrences. Rather than being in the hands of chiefs, power was in the hands of groups of young men because they had guns. Women were raped and tortured, often in front of their husbands and children (Hakena 2005: 162). Women in care centres were subject to sexual abuse by PNGDF and Resistance Force soldiers and were frequently required to pay for necessities with sexual acts. These problems were compounded for women in the BRA-controlled areas, as they not only suffered from sexual violence and harassment from the government and resistance forces but also from the BRA as well (Garasu 2002).

The breakdown of traditional social rules and conventions made childrearing difficult; many mothers complained that their children were growing up without any socialization and were just running wild.

> Men, women and children as young as nine mix fruit juices with yeast and sugar, ferment it, and a few days later, drown their sorrows . . . Children who have seen close relatives die make their own homebrew because they have learnt from their mothers. Absenteeism from school is high and exam results are poor. Prior to the crisis the people were well-educated and went to university. Now, 80 per cent of children don't go to school . . . Children who were eight or nine when the crisis started are in their late teens now. They have joined the fighting and they don't even know why they are fighting.[12]

As the blockade prevented necessities from coming in, women in the BRA-controlled areas who fled into the bush had to create their own tools for planting new gardens, building shelters and surviving. They figured out how to make 'blockade soap' from cocoa pods, run their cars and trucks on coconut oil and store the hydro-electric power they generated from mountain streams in used car batteries. Women supporters of the BRA became 'mamas' for the men when they came to the villages, and in exchange for feeding and caring for them, the men brought smuggled supplies or smuggled sick children out to the Solomon Islands for treatment (Havini 2004: 70).

Women also tried to organize. Before the conflict, there had been two women's organizations on Bougainville. In the 1960s, the Churches' Women's Organization held programmes for self-reliance in the villages, and the Northern Solomons Provincial Council of Women was active in the 1970s and 1980s. The latter was trying to form a network of women's organizations when the conflict began, putting an end to their efforts (Garasu 2002).

The divide-and-conquer strategy of the PNGDF and Resistance Forces made networking difficult, and peace groups had to begin work within their own communities in isolation from one another. Women formed church and other groups to provide aid and assistance to one another and their children. Sometimes women used their traditional role as peacemakers to go into the bush and bring their sons back from fighting; high-status women served as go-betweens to help negotiate peace, sometimes going into the jungle to negotiate with the BRA. Using prayer meetings, reconciliation marches, peace marches, petitions and international support through contacts in Australia and New Zealand, women were able to influence the peace negotiations. For example, peace marches led by women in 1993 and 1994 led to peace negotiations, and in 1995, women from both sides sent delegations to the Beijing Women's Conference. The Bougainville Women for Peace and Freedom[13] was a group of BRA and Bougainville Interim Government supporters who worked for peace and unity from the BRA side, networking with non-governmental organizations (NGOs) in other countries (Havini 2004: 71).

In their traditional capacity as peacemakers, women were able to organize and participate in the peacebuilding process. The extent of their success, however, is a subject for debate. According to one of the founders of Bougainville Women for Peace and Freedom, Ruth Saovana-Spriggs, one of the reasons they were able to be persuasive was their emphasis on unity. 'Women have made it our mission to speak with one voice, a far larger voice than individual women's groups previously achieved, on separate issues of unity, reconciliation, an end to war, and rebuilding our lives and homes' (Spriggs 2004: 123).

At the same time, critics suggest that even when they speak, women are not necessarily heard, and the actual negotiations and decisions were carried out by men (Garasu 2002). 'Women's public status, condoned male violence, the law – both formal and traditional – and the ways in which it is interpreted and implemented, are crucial elements in the lack of attention paid to women's views and opinions' (Macintyre 2005: 41). Moreover, while some extol the role of women, Martha Macintyre claims,

> Men listened to women when they finally got sick of fighting – not when their wives died in childbirth because of the lack of hospital facilities; not when women were being routinely raped by soldiers, police and other Bougainvillean men; not when women had to struggle to find food for their families away from their villages. Women had no political presence when so-called peace talks were foundering. Violence by men was constantly met by counter-violence. Rapes were avenged by rapes, killings by killings.
> (ibid.: 43)

Macintyre goes on to say that in post-conflict Bougainville, the reality of women in reconstruction is that 'women's organizations are heavily dependent on outside funding, and that, in projects aimed at reconstruction and development, men are the major decision makers and beneficiaries' (ibid.).

The Leitana Nehan Women's Development Agency (LNDA), founded in 1992 and the recipient of the first UNIFEM Millennium Peace Prize in 2001, is one of the women's organizations working for peace and reconciliation. LNDA recognized that the violence experienced by women during and after the crisis did not arise solely as a result of the conflict but rather was related to violence that existed in peacetime, too. Moreover, they recognize 'a strong connection between violence against women and militarization of Bougainville society' (Hakena 2005: 165). As a result, they are currently working with entire communities, including men, youth and ex-combatants. The influence of the international development community is visible in LNDA's belief that gender mainstreaming needs to be improved and strengthened. They give evidence with such examples as the fact that when they began to work on arms disposal, they were told 'bluntly that arms control was not a women's issue' (ibid.: 168–69).

LNDA is facing the dissonance between traditional and transformative roles for women. During the conflict, the success of women in peacemaking in Bougainville was through use of their traditional gender roles as women, combined with an acknowledgement from outside that women are important in reconstruction and rehabilitation. In other words, women used their gender in a form of cultural governance to promote peace. Whether they will also be able to contribute to demilitarization remains to be seen.

A feminist analysis of this use of traditional women's roles would conclude that it limits the opportunities for peacemaking. However, an anti-militarist approach to peace would suggest the failure to challenge the ways traditional images of masculinity and femininity contribute to maintaining patriarchy, invoking those understandings in fact reinforces sexism as well as militarism.[14] Hence, efforts for peacemaking might in fact be successful but only in so far as they stay within the general confines of established gender roles. Unless the conceptions of masculinity and femininity that sustain systems and structures of domination and oppression are transformed, post-conflict society will return to pre-conflict modes of gender expression and domination. Perhaps what we are seeing in Bougainville today is a version of continued oppression due to the inability to totally dismantle and rebuild traditional gender and power relations after the war ended. In other words, the walk down the path to demilitarization may have begun, but it has yet to be completed.

Case study 2: Okinawa/Guam (Guahan)

> In times of war, the military takes people's lives. In times of peace, the military takes the dignity – and often lives – of women.
> – Mikanagi (2004: 97)

It is imperative that human security be concerned not only with what happens in war but also with the ways societies prepare for war in the name of peace. Militarization is one such way, and although it is enhanced and exacerbated by actual fighting, it is more a product of preparation for war than of war itself. Preparing for war has enormous economic benefits for weapons manufacturers, but it may wreak havoc on the people and environments where the actual preparation takes place. The case introduced in this section focuses on two islands: Okinawa and Guam (the indigenous name is Guahan). Colonization and war have served to seriously threaten the very existence of indigenous culture in both locations, but until recently, people have not worked together to oppose militarization. Gender violence, particularly the rape of a young girl by US military personnel in Okinawa, provided the impetus for women in Okinawa to begin to join with others in opposing American military bases. Okinawa and Guam were further drawn together when a plan was revealed to relocate US Marines from Okinawa to Guam. The women in Okinawa realized that the so-called solution being offered to the problem in Okinawa would merely offer different victims for sexual violence and would also further marginalize indigenous people and culture in Guam. As a result, opposition to the planned relocation has created a new site for resistance to US and Japanese cultural governance, as it has brought women of both islands together in a united stand. This has led them to view the question of militarization as one of structural violence and has forced them to look at the violent intersection of militarization, gender and racism. Here we will focus on how a group of women opposing the bases in Okinawa has changed to incorporate the struggle in Guam/Guahan.

Guam

Guam, the southernmost island of the Mariana Islands, is home to the indigenous Chamoru (Chamorro) people, a matrilineal society dependent on the ocean and gardens for survival. As in other island societies, men were responsible for ocean travel, fishing and war, while women cared for children, cultivated gardens and saw to the details of everyday living. Motherhood was extremely important, and women exercised power in decisions about family, marriage, property and inheritance.

Guam was first visited and claimed for Spain by Magellan in 1521, but it was not until 1668 that the first Jesuit missionaries and soldiers arrived and began activities in earnest. Colonization, coupled with some serious typhoon damage late in the 17th century, decimated the indigenous population, leaving many of the northern islands unpopulated. By the 19th century, the population of Guam had begun to grow again, but people were of mixed Chamoru, Filipino and Spanish origin. The oral traditions of the Chamoru people, as well as much of their language, had been lost. Guam came under US administration in 1898 as a result of the Spanish-American War (Rogers 1995: 113)[15] and was occupied by the Japanese Imperial Army in 1941.

World War II brought Guam and Okinawa together. Guam was occupied by the Japanese, and like Okinawa, it was the site of fierce fighting between US forces and the Japanese, followed by US military occupation. The US bombardment of Guam beginning on 18 July 1944 was 'the most intense crescendo of conventional firepower ever inflicted on any locality in the Pacific War' (Rogers 1995: 181). It eroded the last vestiges of discipline in Japanese soldiers and policemen. In Agana, 11 Chamoru men, women and young children were bayoneted to death. In a cave near Agat, more than a dozen teenage girls were raped by Japanese soldiers, and in another cave, an unknown number of Chamoru men were killed by Japanese (ibid.). US military records show 18,377 Japanese dead on Guam, of whom about 200 were civilians. An additional 1,250 Japanese surrendered. American casualties numbered 1,747 dead (1,520 US Marines) and 6,053 wounded. About 600 Chamorus are reported to have been killed during the Japanese occupation (Rogers 1995: 194).

The US Navy quickly reinstated its authority on Guam and proceeded to use the island as an entry point from which to invade other Mariana Islands and the Japanese mainland. Most of the Chamorus were put in refugee camps run by the United States, and their lives were governed by the needs of the US war, although the United States did put some effort into providing education and employment. After the war, the number of military personnel on Guam was greatly reduced, but the island remained under the administration of the US Navy until 1950, when the passage of the Organic Act made Guam an organized unincorporated territory of the United States, and the Chamoru population of Guam became US citizens. Guam continues to house important US military, primarily naval, facilities.[16] Recently, there has also been discussion that it might be used to house Iraqi refugees.

What has the US military presence on Guam meant thus far? The testimony of Victoria-Lola Montecalvo Leon Guerrero (Guahan Indigenous Collective) to the UN Committee on Decolonization in 2006 is both moving and informative. The following is a lengthy quotation from her testimony:

> Since World War II, the US military presence on Guahan has been devastating to the survival of our language and culture as a Chamoru people, our right to create our own form of government, our right to own the land that was passed down to us by our ancestors, our civil right to vote for all our leaders including the US president that is the Commander in Chief of the military that occupies 30 percent of our island, and our basic human right to survival. The legacy of World War II has led to the toxic pollution of our land and surrounding waters from nuclear and other carcinogenic waste and has increased the amounts of cancers and deaths among Chamoru people. And the legacy of World War II has meant that our Chamoru sons and daughters are forced to leave Guahan, their homeland, because the United States has limited our economic resources to tourism and military spending.
>
> There is a shortage of competitive jobs for young Chamoru people, who choose to enlist in the US military because they are told it will give them a brighter future. Yet, in every war the US has

fought since World War II – Vietnam, the Gulf War and the current 'War on Terror' – more Chamorus have died per capita than any other soldiers. And what do Chamoru families get when they lose a son or daughter to war? What do we get when we lose a life we poured 21 years and our hopes for the future into? We get a small sum of money, a US flag and a free burial spot to visit at the veteran's cemetery. What about that life? How do we get that back?

How do we get back the lives we've lost, the Chamorus who have been forced off their homeland, and the land we need to build on so that they can return? We do not get these resources back with an increased military presence on our island. But without the right to self-determination, we have no power, no legal recourse in which to stop this military build-up that will further displace the Chamoru people.

Earlier this year, the US Department of Defense unveiled its plan to move 8,000 Marines and their 9,000 dependents from Okinawa and Japan to Guahan, and to increase the existing population of Navy and Air Force personnel on the island. By 2014, there will be an estimated population increase of at least 35,000 people, which will greatly impact the island's current population of 168,000 and change our cultural, political, social and ecological environment.

(Perez 2006: 11, emphasis in original)

As this account makes clear, cultural governance, particularly the interplay of colonization, religion and militarization, has had serious implications for Chamoru culture. Through colonization, people were separated from both the sea and the land, changing forever the traditional way of life. The Catholic religion, brought by Spanish priests supported by soldiers, became a way of life, and the church became the focus for indigenous women's community activities. The demands of cultural governance under Spain, Japan and the United States delegitimized the Chamoru language and culture – for example, penalizing children in school for the use of their first language. Gradually Chamoru 'motherhood' became conflated with the Catholic Virgin Mary, and the role of indigenous women was reconstructed in that context. Interestingly, in the late 1970s, the alliance of religious fundamentalists with neoliberal politicians in the United States was manifested in Guam in the form of a debate over an abortion bill. Arguing for the 'protection of our unborn children' and conservative Catholic Chamoru right to life, women on Guam joined forces with anticolonial women who wanted to 'save the Chamoru people'. Although pro-choice forces eventually won out, this debate has served to divide

Chamoru women and to further contest the meaning of identity and gender in the context of the debate around self-determination (Dames 2003: 370–2).

Chamoru women have watched their land and harbours be converted into US bases. Those bases contain bombing ranges where the land is destroyed and places where it has been poisoned by toxins used by the military (see n. 3). The bases house nuclear and nuclear-capable weapons. Chamoru women have seen their daughters and their Amerislander children abandoned by their military husband/fathers. They have seen their sons and husbands, and now daughters, too, leave for Vietnam, for Saudi Arabia, for Iraq. They have prayed for their safety, and sometimes those prayers have been answered. They watch their children move to the US mainland in search of a better life and have seen them treated as second-class citizens there. Is it any doubt they wonder what it means to be a woman, a Chamoru, and Guamanian and an American?

These concerns mirror those of local residents in Okinawa, where most of the US bases in Japan are located. Let us now turn to the Okinawa side of the question.

Okinawa

The Okinawan Islands are located in the southernmost part of Japan. Although they have been long under Japanese rule, the Okinawan people have a distinct ethnic heritage and history. Although they have become incorporated into mainstream Japanese society, the Okinawan people joined the northern Ainu to form Japan's indigenous population. Efforts on the part of Okinawan people in recent years have resulted in the preservation and revival of many aspects of traditional culture, although unlike the Ainu, Okinawan culture is not officially recognized as indigenous by the Japanese government.

Although they are, of course, very different, Okinawa and Guam share a history of colonization and militarization. Along with Guam, Okinawa currently houses some of the most important US military facilities in the Pacific. Like Guam, Okinawan people have lost their land to US bases and live daily with the possibility they will be inadvertent victims of military accidents or targets of violence, including sexual violence, from US soldiers. Women in Okinawa share many of the same concerns as those outlined earleir for Chamoru women, but in spite of these similarities, until recently there has been little solidarity between those opposing US bases in Okinawa and those working for self-determination and opposing the bases in Guam. Here it is suggested that one reason for this is that cultural governance has kept them from seeing those similarities, emphasizing instead the differences as Japanese or American. Activism after the rape of a young Okinawan girl began to change that view.

US military bases in Okinawa have their origin in the Battle of Okinawa, the only land battle on Japanese soil during World War II and one in which the toll in civilian casualties was extremely high; one out of every three Okinawan civilians died. Although the Okinawan Islands were returned to Japan in 1970, they still house 75 per cent of the US forces in Japan. These take up more than 10 per cent of the total land area of the islands, and 19 per cent of that of the main island, Okinawa, and include 12 US Marine Corps installations. One of these is the Marine Corps Air Station Futenma (MCAS Futenma), located in midst of an urban area, Ginowan City.

US soldiers stationed on Okinawa have been sent to fight in the Korean, Vietnam, Gulf and Iraq Wars, and bases in Okinawa have served as logistical backup. On the main island, one cannot avoid the US bases; the sound of planes taking off and landing interrupts school lessons, military vehicles clog the roads and military personnel roam the streets. In spite of the current economic downturn, the bases are surrounded by bars and shops with large signs in English advertising their desire to attract military customers. One significant consequence of those businesses is military prostitution; another is rape and other forms of sexual violence, incidents of which often occur in these areas. Needless to say, the bases contribute to the human insecurity of the people of Okinawa and have long been the target of local resistance.

In 1995, a 12-year-old Okinawan girl was kidnapped and repeatedly raped by three American servicemen. This incident brought to the surface the smouldering anger at the presence of the bases in Okinawa, and a month later, an anti-base rally drew 85,000 people.[17] In 1996, in what was initially seen as an attempt to quell the anger of the Okinawan people, the Japanese government announced that the Futenma Base was to be returned. It soon became clear, however, that the base was to be relocated to an offshore location in Henoko Bay in the northern part of Okinawa Island (SACO 1996). The new base was to be built in a beautiful section of ocean, rich in marine wildlife and home to the endangered dugong, as well as the Okinawa woodpecker and Okinawa rail. Plans call for filling in a huge section of ocean, 2,500 metres long and 730 metres wide. It would be used for helicopter flight training as well as other activities.

Shortly after plans for the relocation became known, a sit-in was begun at Henoko, organized by the Henoko Society for the Protection of Life. This sit-in is still continuing today, more than ten years later. In 2004, authorities attempted to begin construction of offshore towers to be used for boring the seabed. Protesters in kayaks and other small craft engaged in non-violent resistance, impeding construction of most of the planned towers. Although plans had called for boring in 63 locations, the protestors succeeded in completely preventing it. In 2005, the towers that had been successfully installed were removed.

In October 2005, US and Japanese authorities announced a change in plans. The designated area for the relocation was changed to a section of Henoko that was already included within the area of Camp Schwab, another Marine Corps facility. The base is to have two runways in a V shape (see appendix). The reason given for the change was that it would make construction easier, although members of the Society for the Protection of Life believe that the real reason was the success of their protest. So far, these and other tactics have successfully delayed the construction of the new base. News reports in Japan on the implications of the election of Barack Obama have speculated on whether the new administration will respond to demands from the Okinawa Prefectural Government regarding the Futemna and Henoko bases, but it is, at the time of writing this, too early to tell.

From the perspective of most of the people of Okinawa, moving US bases and military forces to locations outside of Okinawa is considered to be desirable. Although US bases do bring some opportunities for employment, tourism and some businesses, these supposed advantages are offset by the reality of accidents, sexual and other violence, various kinds of pollution and other hazards. Moreover, the psychological cost of having US bases in Okinawa is very high; many Okinawan people strongly oppose their forced role in hosting US troops who provide logistical support for foreign conflict or train on Okinawa and then leave to kill people in other parts of the world.

Suzuyo Takazato is one Okinawan who is strongly opposed to US bases. In 1995, after the rape of the Okinawan girl by US soldiers, Takazato and her supporters established Okinawa Women Act Against Military Violence (OWAAMV), an association with the objective of stopping military violence and military power (see Takazato in this volume). At the same time, they opened the Rape Emergency Intervention Counseling Centre – Okinawa to support victims of sexual violence. One of their activities was to compile a record of reported acts of sexual violence committed against women by US soldiers. The record vividly illustrates how pervasive that violence had been. In addition to the many unwanted and forced pregnancies which resulted from the frequent raping of women and girls at gunpoint after the war, they found instances of a nine-month-old baby who was a victim of sexual violence in 1949 and a six-year-old girl who was raped and killed in 1955. During the Vietnam War years, it is reported that two to four people were strangled to death every year by US soldiers. The violence continued even after Okinawa was returned to Japan in 1972, where rape and/or attempted rape victims included both a 10-year-old and a 14-year-old girl.[18]

When the rape of the 12-year-old girl occurred in 1995, Takazato and some of the Okinawa NGO delegation had just come back from the Fourth World Conference on Women in Beijing, where she had given a presentation with other women from Okinawa on 'Military Violence against Women in Okinawa'. She was furious when she heard the news and took immediate action to mobilize women to protect themselves and their families, taking the position that the very existence of the military bases on Okinawa was an example of structural and direct violence against women (Takazato 1996).

The initial objective of OWAAMV was to break the silence surrounding sexual violence by US soldiers and to oust US bases from Okinawa. They soon learnt that most Americans knew little or nothing about the sexual violence committed by US soldiers abroad, and so Takazato organized a peace caravan to the United States to educate interested American women about the problem. OWAAMV's research and networking revealed that the problem did not concern just Okinawa and the United States, but actually involved women wherever US bases were located. This awareness led to the formation in 1997 of the East Asia–US–Puerto Rico Women's Network Against Militarism, with women from the Philippines, Korea, the United States and Puerto Rico. Through the network, the women realized that violence against women not only is a violation of human rights but also is fundamentally related to the racism, patriarchy, sex discrimination and economic oppression brought by militarism and globalization (Takazato 2003: 185).

After a conference in Seoul in 2002, the anti-base network further expanded to include Hawaii and Guam. This expansion of participation brought a new issue to the fore. Although there were similarities in the situations of women in the different countries, there was no direct and obvious link between what happened in Japan and what was going on in other places. This changed, however, with the inclusion of Guam and the growing awareness that the relocation of US soldiers from Okinawa to Guam might mean relief for Okinawan women but would at the same time threaten the very existence of the Chamoru people because the plans for Futenma include the relocation of 8,000 US Marines and their families from Okinawa to Guam. For OWAAMV, this realization reinforced their commitment to solidarity with others opposing bases elsewhere; it was not enough to simply oppose the American military presence on Okinawa. They increased their efforts to strengthen their international links and to argue that in order to oppose bases on Okinawa, they must oppose them everywhere, including Guam.

In February 2008, OWAAMV sponsored a study tour to Guam led by Takazato. One result of this visit was the endorsement of a 'Letter to Bush from the Women of Okinawa' (Peace and Justice for Guam), protesting sexual violence by US soldiers and calling for the withdrawal of US troops as the only way to end this violence. The letter also recognizes the violence inherent in the military as an institution, and thus its very presence is a threat to the human security of the people of Okinawa. Moreover, they have recognized that the bases, particularly because of the realignment in Japan, will affect Guam and other places, and that human security is possible only with full demilitarization. As such, they are calling for a security policy based on abolishing the military and weapons rather than being based on military strength (Akibayashi 2003: 175). This transnational alliance of citizens embodies an effort for human, rather than national, security.

Conclusion

The intersection of cultural governance, militarization and gender(ed) violence in the Pacific poses a challenging situation for the achievement of human security in the region. The links that connect three very different aspects of the Pacific human security problematic – regional structures for gender mainstreaming and implementation of Resolution 1325; women in the Bougainville Crisis; and resistance to US bases and the relocation of US Marines from Okinawa to Guam – illuminate the hegemonic militarism that prevails in the region. The US presence in the region is a particularly strong manifestation of this hegemony. This article has demonstrated how hegemonic militarism and its demands for the governance of gender threaten the human security of women in the region.

Human security, as defined in this volume, has four fundamental components: sustainable environment, meeting human needs, respecting universal human dignity and particular human identities and protection from avoidable harm. The Bougainville Crisis and the Okinawa/Guam situation clearly encompass all these components. Leaving the implications of actual war aside, military bases and open-pit mines are a direct negation of the principles of environmental sustainability. Neither bases nor large-scale development projects contribute to the meeting of human needs or protection from the avoidable harm that results from their presence. Moreover, as we have seen, militarized cultural governance threatens the human dignity and bodily integrity of all women through increased gender violence and some women in particular through the compromising of certain ethnic identities.

These cases have thus shown how cultural governance manipulates gender in the pursuit of 'inhuman security' toward the maintenance of patriarchal structures. For example, traditional roles and gender mainstreaming combine to involve women in every aspect of the conflict resolution process, but in reality, the voices of women are given relatively little notice, even when they play an active and constructive role in bringing armed conflict to an end. Moreover, the establishment of 'peace' has not necessarily included demilitarization or new roles for women. Here it is suggested that the traditional roles of women as peacemakers, and gender initiatives which fail to recognize the gender(ed) and structural violence upon which they are predicated, fall short of fully involving women in the processes of governance and peacebuilding. In order to produce human security, these processes must redefine the terms of cultural governance, making gender(ed) violence visible and engaging in demilitarization so as to prevent and avoid the continuation of the cycles of armed violence which unleash renewed epidemics of gender violence.

In the Bougainville Crisis, women on both sides paved the way for the official peace talks by recognizing the importance of unity and arranging for discussions among Bougainvilleans. In the case of Okinawa/Guam, the requirements of cultural governance from the perspective of Tokyo call for the incorporation of Okinawa into Japan, glossing over its history of colonization and different culture. A similar process occurs with Guam, which Washington treats as being essentially a part of the United States. Opposition to the planned relocation of US Marines from Okinawa to Guam has created a new site for resistance to US and Japanese cultural governance, as it has brought women of both sides together in a united stand. They have recognized that the cost of development for their islands will be increased militarization, no doubt accompanied by gender and racial violence.

Women in international organizations, as well as those on Bougainville and Okinawa/Guam, have used their gender identity as an entry point for opposing violence and militarization. In the liberal feminist approach of the international security/development community, measures such as Resolution 1325 use gender mainstreaming to increase the participation of women and to focus on their needs. In theory, these measures seek to address both 'gender violence' and 'gendered violence', but in practice, the conflation of gender with women has kept attention on the former to the detriment of the latter, limiting their potential for being truly transformative. In Bougainville, women used their traditional roles as peacemakers to call for unity among the warring parties and to pave the way for official peace talks. In so doing, they were able to transcend their allegiance to one side or the other in order to recreate and re-embody themselves as 'Bougainvilleans'. In the case of Okinawa/Guam, the rape of a 12-year-old girl became the catalyst for a growing international network of women in opposition to militarization and military violence which is calling for a redefinition of the basic concepts of security. In both of these cases, mobilization became possible only once they had overcome the binaries imposed by cultural governance. In both cases, 'unity' could not have become a goal without a rejection of militarization and military means to problem solving.

What remains unclear, however, is the extent to which unity and the rejection of militarization in a particular situation leads to a more generalized stance in opposition to structural violence and ultimately to non-violent work for peace. Without such an analysis, the success of 'women's efforts' in such situations may in fact lead to the reproduction of factors underlying the violence in the first place, giving temporary relief without providing a long-term solution.

This article has shown that for the concept of security to become 'human' and to overcome gender(ed) violence, it must have at its core an analysis which not only rejects patriarchy, racism and militarism but also allows for the transformation of 'gender' to accept a range of sexualities and microbiologies, affirms our mutual vulnerabilities as humans and our dependence on the earth which sustains us. This involves the recognition of various forms of difference and also the acknowledgement that we are both similar to, and different from, our friends and adversaries. Efforts to resist cultural governance, create alternatives and 'humanize' security must include such work if they are to be truly transformational. Focusing on women, or gender, or even 'unity' is not enough.

Notes

1 This article has been adapted from an earlier version which appeared in Ronni Alexander. *Journal of International Cooperation Studies*, vol. 16 (1), July 2008, pp. 71–104, as 'Confronting Militarization: Struggles for Peace and Security by Pacific Island Women'. It is used with permission.

2 It is evident that those who are seen to be *women*, whether by virtue of their own choice or otherwise, are affected differently by violence than those who are identified, or who identify as, *men*. The subjugation of women is the most evident injustice of the global gender order. At the same time, in focusing on women, discussion is almost exclusively limited to two gender categories, *women* and *men*, and it fails to seriously address the needs of transgender, queer or others who do not fit easily into these categories. Transgender people often face violence not only due to what others perceive as their gender but also because the are seen to be deviating from gender(ed) expectations. I wish to acknowledge these struggles with *gender* and to recognize the violence to which those involved are subjected.
3 For example, on 19 March 2009, a bill was introduced in the US House of Representatives (HR1630 2009), calling for an amendment to the Radiation Exposure Compensation Act to include the territory of Guam in the list of areas affected by the US atmospheric nuclear testing in the 1960s. This was based on a report by the National Research Council in 2005 which concluded that Guam received considerable fallout from the nuclear testing. The first confirmation of disease as a result of the use of toxic herbicides by the military on Guam was a ruling in 2005 by the US Court of Appeals for Veterans. Citation No.: 0527748; Decision Date: 10/13/05; Archive Date: 10/25/05, DOCKET NO. 02–11 819. Similar claims of illness by veterans who had been stationed in Okinawa have also been approved. For example, Citation NR: 9800877; Decision Date: 01/13/98; Archive Date: 01/21/98, DOCKET NO. 97–05 078. As far as Amerasian children are concerned, see, for example, Sims (2000).
4 In 2005, it was believed that about 1,000 Fijians are working as private security contractors in Iraq and another 2,000 ex-Fiji soldiers are working for the British army. See, for example, Inter Press Service News Agency (2007); Fijians have been killed. The number of military personnel from American Samoa killed in Iraq on a per capita basis is almost 13.5 times the US national average (US Department of the Interior, 2006).
5 See Betty A. Reardon in this volume. Reardon argues that patriarchy is the dominant organizational paradigm in most human societies and in all where power differentials are evident and exert primary influence over governance and human relations.
6 Laura Duhan Kaplan lists two additional features of patriarchal militarism:

> 1. Since war is seen by many to be a creative masculine act, the commitment of social resources to war is a male project; and 2. the public is convinced that militarism is necessary for safety because those who are different must be dominated for the good of both themselves and the dominators.

7 For a definition of violence against women and 'For the purposes of this Declaration, the term "violence against women" means any act of gender-based violence that results in, or is likely to result in, physical, sexual or psychological harm or suffering to women, including threats of such acts, coercion or arbitrary deprivation of liberty, whether occurring in public or in private life' (see the Declaration on the Elimination of Violence against Women).
8 Some Pacific cultures do have a so-called third sex, or traditional cultural practices, that include sexual acts between men. These cultural roles and

practices still exist but have been marginalized through the processes of colonization, modernization and militarization. Militaries have little room for men who are not 'masculine'.
9   Technically speaking, Japan is an observer in the Pacific Islands Forum and other regional organizations, and some regional bodies include non-independent entities, such as Guam, American Samoa, New Caledonia and French Polynesia.
10 The change in emphasis can be seen in comparing this mission with that of the PWB, which was to foster 'Empowered Pacific Island women and young people and strong cultural identities'.
11 The Revised Pacific Platform of Action (PPA) on the Advancement of Women and Gender Equality 2005–2015 is the result of a +10 review of the PPA approved at the sixth Regional Conference of Pacific Women and the Ministerial Conference on Women and Sustainable Development, both held in Noumea in 1994. The original plan formed the basis for the Pacific region's contribution the 1995 World Conference for Women in Beijing and the current PPA incorporates the Beijing +5 outcomes and commitments under CEDAW.
12 Helen Hakena quoted in Arthur McCutchan, 'The Bougainville Experience', *Pacific Women's Network Against Violence*, September 1997, p. 1.
13 The Bougainville Women for Peace and Freedom (BWPF) is an organization that developed a human rights programme in the formerly blockaded areas of Bougainville. Their meetings for women also attracted large crowds of men and chiefs. During the war, BWPF members recorded human rights abuses, often risking their lives to send their information to Sydney. These lists have been recognized by both the Bougainville Interim Government (BIG) and the BWPF as their own documents, even though they contained information of abuses committed and suffered by all sides in the conflict (www.converge.org.nz/pma/bouwom.htm, accessed 20 February 2008).
14 Burguieres, Mary K. 1990, 'Feminist approaches to peace: Another step for peace studies', *Millennium*, 19(1), 1–18.
15 The Chamoru people were not consulted in the transfer of sovereignty from Spain to the United States, and the ensuing treaty did not recognize indigenous sovereignty, nor did it oblige the United States to protect indigenous rights, promote their political, economic or social wellbeing or bring them to self-government.
16 For more on the Marine Corps in Guam, see the Marine Corps Activity Page at www.marforpac.marines.mil/Units/Marine-Corps-Activity-Guam/.
17 On 18 August 2008, one of the perpetrators of the rape, Kendrick Ledet, committed suicide after strangling a 22-year-old co-worker to death (*Japan Times*, 25 February 2008). The number of protestors was exceeded on 29 September 2007, when a rally protesting the Japanese government's plans to take out of textbooks all mention of the role played by Japanese soldiers in the mass suicides in Okinawa attracted 110,000 people. In February 2008, Japan was shocked by two more accusations of rape, both incidents perpetrated by US military men in Okinawa. The victim in one was a 14-year-old girl. In response, the United States imposed a curfew on all military personnel and vowed to take mid- and long-term

measures. For more on the response to military sexual violence, see Kozue Akibayashi and Suzuyo Takazato in this volume.

18 In Japanese, refer to www.space-yui.com/koudou.htm.

References

Akibayashi, Kozue. 2003. 'Anzen Hosho no Saiteigi wo Mezasu Josei no Rentai: Higashi Ajia-Beikoku-Puerto Rico Gunjishugi wo Yurusanai Josei Network to ha', *Asojie*, vol. 11: 172–8.

Bates, Prue A. 2005. 'Women and Peacemaking', Development Studies Network, Women, Gender and Development in the Pacific: Key Issues. Conflict and Peacemaking: Gender Perspectives. https://crawford.anu.edu.au/rmap/devnet/devnet/gen/gen_peace.pdf

Burguieres, Mary K. 1990, 'Feminist approaches to peace: Another step for peace studies', *Millennium*, 19(1): 1–18.

Connell, R.W. 1990. 'The State, Gender and Sexual Politics: Theory and Appraisal', *Theory and Society*, vol. 19 (5): 507–44. October.

Dames, Vivian Loyola. 2003. 'Chamoru Women, Self-Determination and the Politics of Abortion in Guam', in Shirley Hune and Gail M. Nomura (eds.), *Asian/Pacific Islander American Women: A Historical Anthology*, pp. 365–84. New York, NY: New York University Press.

Enloe, Cynthia. 2000. *Maneuvers: The International Politics of Militarizing Women's Lives*. London: University of California Press.

Garasu, Sister Lorraine. 2002. 'The Role of Women in Promoting Peace and Reconciliation', *Accord: Weaving Consensus: The Papua New Guinea: Bougainville Peace Process*. www.c-r.org/accord-article/role-women-promoting-peace-and-reconciliation. Accessed 27 December 2007.

Hakena, Helen. 2005. 'Papua New Guinea: Women in Armed Conflict', in Rawwida Baksh, Linda Etchart and Elsie Onubogu (eds.), *Gender Mainstreaming in Conflict Transformation: Building Sustainable Peace*, pp. 160–70. London: Commonwealth Secretariat.

Havini, Marilyn Taleo. 2004. 'Women in Community during the Blockade', in Josephone Tankunani Sirivi and Marilyn Taleo Havini (eds.), *Mothers of the Land: The Birth of the Bougainville Women for Peace and Freedom*, pp. 69–72. Canberra: Pandanus Books, Research School of Asian and Pacific Studies, Australian National University.

Kaplan, Laura Duhan. 1994. 'Woman as Caretaker: An Archetype That Supports Patriarchal Militarism', *Hypatia, Special Issue: Feminism and Peace*, vol. 9 (2): 123–32. Spring.

Macintyre, Martha. 2005. 'Violence and Peacemaking in Papua New Guinea: A Realistic Assessment of the Social and Cultural Issues at Grassroots Level', Development Studies Network: Women, Gender and Development in the Pacific: Key Issues. Conflict and Peacemaking: Gender Perspectives (web collection), pp. 41–45. https://crawford.anu.edu.au/rmap/devnet/devnet/gen/gen_peace.pdf. Accessed 15 May 2009.

Mikanagi, Yumiko. 2004. 'Okinawa: Women, Bases and US: Japan Relations', *International Relations of the Asia-Pacific*, vol. 4 (1): 97–111.
Nayak, Meghana and Jennifer Suchland. 2006. 'Gender Violence and Hegemonic Projects', *International Feminist Journal of Politics*, vol. 8 (4): 467–85.
Perez, Craig. 2006. 'The World Heard the Testimonies of.' https://craigsantosperez.wordpress.com/2006/10/09/the-world-heard-the-testimonies-of/. Accessed 27 December 2017.
Reardon, Betty A. 1985. *Sexism and the War System*. New York, NY: Teacher's College Press.
Rogers, Robert F. 1995. *Destiny's Landfall: A History of Guam*. University of Hawaii Press.
Sims, Calvin. 2000. 'A Hard Life for Amerasian Children', *The New York Times*. 23 July.
Sirivi, Josephone Tankunani and Marilyn Taleo Havini (eds.). 2004. *Mothers of the Land: The Birth of the Bougainville Women for Peace and Freedom*. Canberra: Pandanus Books, Research School of Asian and Pacific Studies, Australian National University.
Spriggs, Ruth Saovana. 2004. 'Unity and the Peace Process', in Josephone Tankunani Sirivi and Marilyn Taleo Havini (eds.), *Mothers of the Land: The Birth of the Bougainville Women for Peace and Freedom*, pp. 122–4. Canberra: Pandanus Books, Research School of Asian and Pacific Studies, Australian National University.
Takazato, Suzuyo. 1996. *Okinawa no Onnnatachi: Josei no Jinken to Kichi*. Tokyo: Akashi Shoten.
———. 2003. 'Okinawa no Kichi, Guntai no Genjou to Undo – Dai 4 kai Higashi Asia-Beikoku-Puerto Rico Gunjishugi wo Yurusanai Josei Network 2002. 8.15–20 Seoul Kaigi de no Okinawa Hokoku', *Asojie*, vol. 11: 179–85.
Thomas, Pamela. 2005a. 'The Pacific: Gender Issues in Conflict and Peacemaking', in Rawwida Baksh, Linda Etchart, Elsie Onubogu and Tina Johnson (eds.), *Gender Mainstreaming in Conflict Transformation: Building Sustainable Peace*, pp. 155–9. London: Commonwealth Secretariat.
——— (ed.). 2005b. 'Women, Gender and Development in the Pacific: Key Issues', online collection of papers. Development Studies Network. https://crawford.anu.edu.au/rmap/devnet/devnet/gen/gen_peace.pdf. Accessed 15 January 2009.

Documents

House of Representatives 1630 (11th Congress, 1st Session) to amend the Radiation Exposure Compensation Act to include the Territory of Guam in the list of affected areas with respect to which claims relating to atmospheric nuclear testing shall be allowed, and for other purposes. 19 March 2009. http://thomas.loc.gov/home/gpoxmlc111/h1630_ih.xml. Accessed 19 May 2009.
Secretariat of the Pacific Community. 2005. 'Revised Pacific Platform for Action on Advancement of Women and Gender Equality 2005 to 2015', 9th

Triennial Conference of Pacific Women, 16–19 August 2004 and 2nd Pacific Ministerial Meeting on Women, 19–20 August 2004. Nadi, Fiji Islands. PDF. www.spc.int.

Secretariat of the Pacific Islands Forum. 2000. *Biketawa Declaration*. https://www.forumsec.org/biketawa-declaration/. Accessed 7 December 2017.

Secretariat of the Pacific Islands Forum. 2012. 'Pacific Regional Action Plan: Women, Peace and Security 2012–2015'. https://endvaw.ca/wp-content/uploads/2015/12/pacific_regional_action_plan_on_women_peace_and_security_final_and_approved.pdf. Accessed 21 May 2018.

Special Action Committee on Okinawa (SACO). 1996. Final Report. 2 December. www.mofa.go.jp/region/n-america/us/security/96saco1.html. Accessed 24 December 2017.

UNSC Resolution 1325. 2000. www.unfpa.org/women/docs/res_1325e.pdf. Accessed 13 November 2007.

URLs

Secretariat of the Pacific Community, Social Development Programme (SPC-SDP). http://www.spc.int/sdp/ Accessed 14 June 2018.

US Department of the Interior, 7 June 2006. 'Secretary Kempthorne Announces Intent to Visit Pacific Islands, Thanks Islanders for Service to the United States'. www.doi.gov/sites/doi.gov/files/archive/news/archive/06_News_Releases/060706.htm. Accessed 27 December 2017.

9 Education, violence and schools

The human security of girls in Afghanistan

Chloe Breyer

Access to education as a hallmark of human security

According to the 10 July 2006, Human Rights Watch report entitled 'Lessons in Terror: Attacks on Education in Afghanistan', there were 204 attacks on teachers, students and schools in the 18 months from January 2005 to 21 June 2006 (Human Rights Watch 2006) and later, from March 2007 to October 2008, 254 students and teachers were killed by insurgents and 220 schools were attacked (Human Rights Watch 2009). The 2006 Human Rights Watch report describes schools in the southern and eastern part of Afghanistan as being 'on the front line' of a resurgence of violent internal conflict in that country led by a variety of former and recently recruited Taliban trained in Pakistan, local warlords and drug criminals. A key recommendation of the report was that the ability of children to attend school safely should be an important benchmark of the success of security forces in Afghanistan – whether they be NATO-led international forces or the Afghan National Army. The report states,

> As the responsibility for providing security in southern Afghanistan shifts from the U.S.-led coalition to NATO forces, Human Rights Watch believes that a key measure of their success or failure should be whether children are able to go to school. This will require a military and policing strategy that directly addresses how to provide the security necessary for the Afghan government and its international supporters to develop Afghanistan's most difficult and underserved areas.
> (Human Rights Watch 2006: 10–11)

In recognizing the basic right to education established in the Convention on the Rights of the Child (UNHCR),[1] the 2006 Human Rights

Watch report takes a step toward endorsing the gender-inclusive concept of 'human security' around which the contributions in the volume are constructed (Reardon 2003).[2] It stops short, however, of fully embracing the principals of human security. While deploring the short-sighted way militarized security has been measured in Afghanistan – through troop numbers rather than school attendance – the Human Rights Watch report assumes that adequate military protection – Afghan, NATO or US-led – is the key factor in ensuring access to basic education. The report adheres to a traditional realist view espousing a military approach to conflict prevention. Indeed, the report's recommendations are directed toward military leaders and policymakers in Afghanistan, the United States and Europe tasked with overseeing a transition of responsibility for militarized security in southern Afghanistan from US-led coalition forces to NATO in the summer of 2006. The report makes little reference to the gender-based discrimination at play in the situation.

This article will attempt to introduce a gender analysis of the epidemic of school attacks in Afghanistan described in the 2006 Human Rights Watch report. It will also examine examples of violent resistance to girls' education as a case illustrating the connections between violence and the *pashtunwali*, the code of traditional Pashtun society that, when taken to an extreme in the hands of the Taliban, served to limit girls' education in certain parts of the country between 1996 and 2001. This violent practice of school burnings now stands as a significant obstacle to the development of a just and democratic nation aspired to in the Afghan Constitution and one articulated goal of the foreign military presence. This article will question the adequacy of the traditional realist view of security. It will also suggest that by shifting to a human security framework described in this volume – a framework that includes a role for legitimate force as a last resort in preserving human rights – certain development and justice goals in Afghanistan are more likely to be met.

In supporting this inquiry, I will draw from the work of leading conflict theorists whose work supports a central assertion of the human security approach. Among them are Johan Galtung, Ann Tickner, Cynthia Enloe and Betty A. Reardon. I will also draw on my own experience and ongoing involvement with a girls' school that was attacked in 2006 in a small village in Wardak Province, Afghanistan, as a prototypical case illustrating the connections linking patriarchal attitudes and practices to gender repression and violence. I will explore the possibility that a deeper gender analysis incorporating the broader requirements of human security – or at least a more reality-based understanding of the potential of patriarchal resistance – might have, in retrospect, mitigated the violence that took place in early 2006 at the Ismael Mayar Primary School in Wardak and could offer practical insight moving forward.

Schools and women as targets of repression in Afghanistan

Attacks on education are not new phenomena in Afghanistan. In 1996, within three months of the capture of Kabul, the Taliban closed 63 schools in the city, affecting 103,000 girls, 148,000 boys and 11,200 teachers of whom 7,800 were women (cited in Rashid 2001: 108). By December 1998, nine in ten girls and two out of three boys were not in school (ibid.). The breakdown of the Russian occupation of Afghanistan from 1979 until 1989, followed by six years of drought and civil war, provided the sort of political, economic and social chaos that prompted many residents of Kabul to welcome the Taliban in 1996 as a source of law and order. An ultra-sectarian version of Islam related to Wahhabism and combined with the cultural code of the Pashtuns (pashtunwali) provided the destructive ideology that justified infamous human rights abuses like the stoning of women in the UN Development Programme-funded soccer stadium in Kabul in the late 1990s. While the press focused on the particular human rights abuses that affected women under the Taliban, traditional practices like child marriage, polygamy and the giving of women as 'bad blood price' for restitution between warring families have contributed to making Afghanistan one of the most challenging places in the world for women to live – measured in terms of the 43-year life expectancy for women – after the Sudan.

To be sure, the protections and opportunities offered women by law in Afghanistan have varied over time. The 1977 Constitution of Afghanistan that stipulated that 'all the people of Afghanistan both women and men, without discrimination and privilege before the law, have equal rights and obligations' did not name the Hanifi school of Sharia interpretation as the official religious law of the country. Consequently, according to Helena Malikyar, the civil law of the same year adopted the more liberal Maliki school's interpretation of Sharia, making divorce proceedings easier for women, bringing the majority age for women from nine to 16 and giving adult females the right to enter a marriage contract without their guardian's permission (Malikyar 2004: 3). Under the Marxist regime that followed President Daud, marriage of girls under the age of 16 became illegal and punishable by imprisonment of six months to three years. With the civil war, a uniform family law disintegrated and judicial institutions disintegrated, with religious leaders, or *quadis*, settling disputes informally based on their own interpretations of the Sharia.

Today gender roles vary according to ethnic, tribal and religious customs as well. Hazara women, for example, mostly Shiite, are unlikely to be fully covered and are not banned from entering their local mosques at puberty like their Sunni Pashtun counterparts. Since 2002, the international non-governmental organization (NGO) Future Generations Afghanistan has run hundreds of mosque-based women's literacy programmes – primarily in Hazara communities – in the central provinces of Bamiyan, Ghazni, Nangarhar, Zabul and Uruzgan (Future Generations 2009).

Despite Afghanistan's patchworked legal history in the area of family law, along with its ethnic diversity and varying views about the education of girls, some of the greatest challenges for women in Afghanistan relate directly to narrow practices of the customary code of pashtunwali, a pre-Islamic patriarchal tribal code valuing hospitality and allowing for blood revenge. The use of women as peace offerings between warring families and arranged and child marriage is still prevalent in many parts of Afghan society and is arguably heightened during times of violent conflict. Today over 60 per cent of Afghan girls are married before the age of 16 (Human Rights Watch 2009), nearly 80 per cent of Afghan women are illiterate (UNESCO 2003) and, although it has improved for the first time in decades, Afghan women suffer from one of the world's highest rates of maternal mortality. In 2000, there were 1,600 deaths per 100,000 live births (UNICEF 2005) in Afghanistan, making the country's maternal mortality rate second only to Sierra Leone. Within any of the currently contested definitions of the concept, the human security of Afghan women has long been in jeopardy from centuries of cultural traditions and religiously justified repression.

An extreme form of repressive patriarchy cloaked in religious language became the very source of Taliban identity. In the 1990s, Taliban recruits grew up in environments that were physically removed from women – the madrassas and a war culture – so that the exclusion of women itself became 'a symbol of manhood and a reaffirmation of the student's commitment to Jihad' (Rashid 2001, 111). Later, with the Taliban's successive territorial conquests from Kandahar into Herat, Bamiyan and Kabul, harsh edicts on the role of women continued to be justified as a means of keeping troop morale high. Compromise on this issue came to be seen as defeat and defiance of Western – or Soviet – norms, victory.

Cynthia Enloe argues that when the United States began supporting the mujahideen in a proxy war against the Soviet Union, 'male privilege gained a foreign ally' (Enloe 1989: 56). While the Afghan military leaders were supported with billions of dollars from the West and heralded as freedom fighters, 'the cause for which the insurgent Muhjahidin fought was a traditional rural clan way of life that is unambiguously patriarchal', (ibid.). Even then, before the rise of the Taliban, life in the refugee camps of Pakistan was radically different for men and for women. In a passage that was not only descriptive of the then present reality but eerily prescient about what the future would hold for Afghan women, Enloe wrote,

> The militarization of Afghanistan has proved disastrous for women in the rural clan communities waging war . . . The women's husbands and fathers enforced the seclusion of their women far more strictly in the camps than they did in Afghanistan itself. Here they believed the risk was greater that their women would be seen by men outside the safe boundaries of the family. Whereas back in their villages women had field work, cooking and housework to do, in the camps they have no legitimate reason to leave their mud huts. Girls are kept out of the UN schools by protective fathers. In March 1988 the total enrollment in UN schools stood at 104,600 boys and 7,800 girls . . . This civil war has been fought in a way that has militarized purdah. It has threatened men's control over women and so intensified men's determination to police the behavior of women.
>
> (Enloe 1989: 57)

When the Soviet occupation of Afghanistan ended in 1989, the same mujahideen leaders who had fought the Soviets turned their mostly US-supplied weapons on one another. The period of civil war in the early 1990s heightened the instability that had led to increased policing of women in the refugee camps, bringing the violence to a whole new level. Many Afghans were impressed by the Taliban's initial claim that they were establishing law and order, 'only to hand over power to a government which was made up of "good Muslims"' (Rashid 2001: 95). The Taliban's first prohibitions on women's travel outside the home were justified as necessary for the protection of women who, during the civil war period particularly, were victims of rape and abduction (interview with Najibullah Mojadidi 2003).[3] As the Taliban increased its restrictions on the lives of women, banning any outdoor travel without a male escort, forbidding work or education of women and shutting down women's health facilities, the 'protective' logic quickly disappeared, revealing the misogynistic underpinnings of the Taliban regime. With the American-led military intervention of coalition forces and the subsequent installation of the Transitional Government of the Islamic Republic of Afghanistan in early 2002, written goals of the new government – later enshrined in the Afghan Constitution – included recognizing and abiding by the UN Charter and the UN Declaration on Human Rights as well as recognizing the equality of men and women before the law (Afghanistan 2004).

The wave of 2006 school attacks in southern Afghanistan and around the country, however, signaled that what existed on paper, four years later, was still not reflected in reality. Many of the same radicalized perpetrators of violence who had fought the US-led invasion in October and November 2001 were reasserting themselves through the school burnings and attacks on teachers. In parts of the country, schools sponsored by the Afghan central government and those sponsored by local and national NGOs were identified as evidence of compromise with un-Islamic forces. (This seemed to be true even of schools that were run out of mosques.) Primary schools and the education of children were not neutral indicators of 'shared values'. Rather, the very existence of educational institutions threatened the self-understanding of a generation of fighters.

The July 2006 Human Rights Watch report provided critical information and analysis on the rise of school attacks in Afghanistan. First, it addressed the question of who was actually committing attacks on schools – important information whether one is a policymaker considering sending armed troops or an aid worker assessing development of a new school. The report stated,

> Three different (and at times overlapping) groups are broadly responsible for causing insecurity in Afghanistan: (1) opposition armed forces, primarily the Taliban and forces allied with the Taliban movement or with veteran Pashtun warlord Gulbuddin Hekmatyar, (2) regional warlords and militia commanders, ostensibly loyal to the central government, now entrenched as powerbrokers after the flawed parliamentary elections of October 2005, and (3) criminal groups, mostly involved in Afghanistan's booming narcotics trade – a trade which is believed to provide much of the financing for the warlords and opposition forces.
> (Human Rights Watch 2006)

This assessment was confirmed by Elizabeth Rubin in her cover story for the *New York Times*, 'The Undefeated: Why the Taliban Have Returned' (22 October 2006), which claimed that the insurgency had three different fronts: Mullah Omar's Council in Quetta, Afghanistan; Jalaludin Haqqani, a mujahideen hero based in Wazirstan and orchestrating attacks in Paktia and Zabul provinces; and Gulbuddin Hekmatyar, the person whom the most arms were funnelled to, by the US and Pakistani intelligence forces during the Soviet occupation (Rubin 2006). Although the Human Rights Watch report did not ask the deeper question about the resurgence of the insurgency or the patriarchal ideology supporting it, still it recognized that the label 'Taliban' did not refer to exactly the same constellation of people who were active in Afghanistan before 2001.

Along with this important understanding of the different actors involved, the Human Rights Watch report provided an analysis of the mixed motivations for the attacks.

> The motives behind the attacks differ. In some instances, it appears that the attacks are motivated by ideological opposition to education generally or to girls' education specifically. In other instances schools and teachers may be attacked as symbols of the government (often the only government presence in an area) or, if run by international nongovernmental organizations, as the work of foreigners. In a few cases, the attacks seem to reflect local grievances and rivalries.
>
> (Rubin 2006)

Although the motives are complex, it is likely that in all cases the purpose is to destroy what are perceived as foreign threats to the perceived traditional culture and social order through influencing the minds of young people (Esfandiari 2006).

In the section 'Nation Building on the Cheap: the US-led Coalition, ISAF and Provincial Reconstruction Teams (PRTS)', the report clearly identifies Afghanistan's disintegration as a result of a lack of US commitments to reconstruction. It quotes the British Department of International Development, saying,

> Whatever assessment criteria one uses . . . there have been significant shortcomings in international efforts to consolidate peace. There has been a major mismatch between the ambitions of the international community and their willingness to commit the requisite military, political and financial resources. It has been . . . a 'bargain basement' model . . . Security assistance to Afghanistan has consistently lagged far below that of recent post-conflict situations, such as East Timor, the Balkans, and, of course, Iraq.

Security assistance to Afghanistan has also consistently lagged behind the obvious and tangible needs of the country.
(Human Rights Watch 2006)

If ever there were a compelling argument for the just use of force in providing protection from avoidable harm – the fourth of four pillars of human security as defined in this volume – securing access for schoolchildren to education and protecting their teachers from violent attack would seem to warrant such force. The report's focus on school attacks and intimidation makes a strong case for increasing the number of foreign militarized peacekeeping troops in Afghanistan. In proposing that the measure of successful security in Afghanistan must be the safety of children to attend school rather than the number of insurgents killed or members of Al-Qaeda captured, the report performs an important service in both identifying a problem that is overlooked by the international community and press and expanding the definition of human security to prioritize education and development. Although proposing new measures for success, the Human Rights Watch report, however, still locates the responsibility for peace entirely in the hands of armed security forces – Afghan and international.

The traditional realist perspective toward international conflict that underpins this report lacks a comprehensive gender lens, even while it advocates for universal access to education for girls as well as boys. Although the report does an adequate job of stressing the ongoing and increasing need for military presence in parts of Afghanistan where schools are targets of violence, its assumptions that a militarized solution is the primary means of providing access to girls schools is in opposition to the conflict resolution theorists like Johan Galtung and certain feminist scholars who would argue that reliance on armed peacekeepers comprises only one part of successful conflict prevention (Galtung 1996: 72, 103).[4] If, as Robin Burns suggests, peace and development are linked, then 'peace is defined not as the absence of war, but the achievement of positive social and cultural goals' (Burns 1982).

The report does not address how attitudinal change can happen – something critical to the overall peace in Afghanistan if the very presence of peacekeepers themselves is not to become an added incentive for more violence. Nor does it speak to the issue of gender equality that is an essential element of a human rights approach to human security. Like most NGOs and governments, the authors of 'Lessons in Terror . . .' tend to see gender as a distinct issue rather than as one that is integral to human security. My discussion of the school burning in Afghanistan is intended to view the issue as one that can illuminate the need for an integral and comprehensive gender perspective.

Viewing Afghan girls' access to schools through a gender lens

Because the analysis and conclusions of this article are intended to extend the previous work of feminist scholars, selected writings on gender and security will be the foundation for developing an integral gender perspective on this Afghan case. Using the work of Cynthia Enloe, Ann Tickner and Betty A. Reardon, I will critique the realist position of conflict prevention adopted by the Human Rights Watch report by applying a gender lens. I will suggest that without incorporating a gender critique, the report may not anticipate the continuum of violence against women within the public and private spheres in Afghanistan. Indeed, 'Lessons in Terror' lacks appreciation for the way that a militarized solution to assuring universal primary education for girls may be effective in the short-term, but it may also serve to reinforce gender roles that are detrimental to peace and development in the long run. Further, based on my own experience with an NGO in Afghanistan committed to building schools for girls in the southern, largely Pashtun, province of Wardak, I will also assert that an incomplete gender analysis may have contributed to setbacks in our work. This assertion is grounded in feminist critiques of realist international relations theory summarized next.

Kenneth Waltz, in his book *Man, the State, and War*, uses 18th-century philosopher Jean-Jacques Rousseau's metaphor of a stag hunt to describe the security-seeking behaviours of states in a traditional realist approach to international relations theory. Five hungry men agree to trap and share a stag, but when a hare runs by, one man grabs it, thereby letting the stag escape. By defecting from the common goal, this hunter sacrifices the long-term cooperative interests of the group, his own included, for his immediate short-term interest (Waltz 2001). Ann Tickner, author of *Gender in International Relations*, disagrees with this view. For realists, writes Tickner, the story of the stag and the hare illustrates the problematic nature of national security:

> Since men are self-seeking, politically ambitious, and not always rational, [realists] must assume that some states and some men will not be cooperative and will start wars. Given the lack of an international government with powers of enforcement, states must

therefore depend on themselves for their own security needs even if this is not in the best interests of the system as a whole.

(Tickner 1992)

She goes on to summarize the views of another author of the realist perspective, Hans Morgenthau, who she reports would say that the security of the state is attained and preserved through the maximization of power, particularly military power. Conflict resolution theorists like Richard Betts ascribe to this view as well. Betts argues that only through armed conflict can states understand how power is distributed and that this understanding is necessary for a lasting peace. In other words, like other realists, Betts argues that the threat of war is what most effectively preserves the peace.

In contrast to adherents of the realist approach to international affairs, Tickner herself believes that the view of human nature espoused by realism is not objective, universal or scientific, as its proponents argue, but rather represent an understanding of human nature based on the experience of a limited number of men. In this sense, traditional realism has a gendered quality to it that calls into question some of its conclusions about the role of force in international affairs.

Tickner suggests that realism relies heavily on a dichotomy between a safe domestic order and an anarchistic and violence-filled world beyond national boundaries. The resources and sacrifices societies give to the creation of a military requires, she suggests, a notion of violence and disorder existing beyond the boundaries of the state. This, she points out, has never been the case for women when, as a 1997 UNICEF publication reported, between one-quarter and one-half of women around the world have suffered violence at the hands of an intimate partner (Bunch 1997). Like Reardon, Tickner suggests that military violence is often connected to other sorts of violence, so, for example, the families of soldiers and veterans experience a high level of domestic violence (Enloe 1989). Cynthia Enloe observed that the US government's vast military support of the mujahideen in their armed struggle against the USSR had the additional consequence of arming an internal socially conservative movement opposed to the rights of Afghan women. Her analysis suggests that there may be a long-term cost to an exclusively militarized approach to promoting peace and development in the form of assuring universal access to education in Afghanistan.

In addition, Tickner draws attention to the masculine notion of the ideal citizen-warrior in realist theory, in which the highest ideal of citizenship is expressed in the sacrifice of one's life for the nation. This is in contrast, she writes, to such activities as caring for the elderly or educating the youth – work often done by women proscribed to the sphere of family and not often classified as civic virtues. Because of the polarization of gender roles during wartimes, Tickner suggest the perception is that women have few roles to play other than as victims in armed conflicts.

> Little material can be found on women's roles in wars; generally they are seen as victims, rarely as agents. While war can be a time of advancement for women as they step in to do men's jobs, the battlefront takes precedence, so the hierarchy remains and women are urged to step aside once peace is restored.
>
> (Tickner 1992)

Even in the military, she writes, women's position is ambiguous; men do not want women fighting alongside them, and the public perceives the role of wife and mother as less compatible with being a soldier than that of husband and father (Tickner 1992). She goes on to quote Judith Stiehm, suggesting that American military leaders think of the armed services as 'belonging' to men, whereas in reality they belong to citizens, more than half of whom are women.

Without a multidimensional approach to peacemaking, an entirely militarized solution to the restrictions on school access for girls in parts of Afghanistan may fall into the trap of reinscribing a narrow gender role for girls as victims only and depart from the comprehensive approach to human security advocated in this volume. Rather than highlighting the courage of girls and teachers who continue to seek out education in an environment where hostility can turn violent at any moment, a call for increased troop levels to protect these girls without simultaneous community-based action and education for peace runs the risk of being counter-productive in the long-term. Indeed, the presence of foreign troops in Afghanistan has been a motivating force for violent conflict and has helped forge a national identity among diverse factions for years (Clifford 1989) – something that speaks to the respect-for-identity component of the feminist human security framework. In a country that has been most united when fighting off foreign invaders, the involvement of foreign troops serving as peacemakers – even ones with credible track records – may be problematic. An 8 March 2009, statement from a group of women in Kandahar stated, 'We believe that only Afghans themselves can stop the use of violence against other Afghans'. Ingeborg Breins, in her statement 'Obama, Ask Afghan Women', interprets this statement as meaning that the strong military presence seems to have 'reinforced hegemonic masculine ideals' (Breines 2009).

The peacebuilding and peacemaking components of conflict prevention in the southern provinces of Afghanistan as it relates to schools are not addressed in the Human Rights Watch report. There is little room for an assessment of the contribution of non-armed interveners as contributors to peace and no place for an examination of an effective peacemaking process – what William Ury would call thirdsiders, individuals who have a direct relationship to the conflict but who also stand outside it. In this report, military peacemakers are the only arbiters of security. Government officials, religious leaders, foreign aid workers and the students and teachers themselves must be protected by these forces in order to be able to do their work. There is little attention given to the fact that these individuals, Afghan and non-Afghan, have a role to play as well. Such an approach would be far more in accord with the comprehensive concept of human security advocated by several feminist scholars.

Constructing and destructing the Ismael Mayar Primary School in Wardak Province, Afghanistan: assessing a comprehensive approach to human security

The Human Rights Watch report mentioned 204 cases of school attacks in the 18-month period from January 2005 to June 2006. Three of these attacks were on a school called the Ismael Mayar Primary School in Wardak Province. As a board member of Afghans4Tomorrow, an NGO registered in Afghanistan and the United States that raised money, constructed and oversaw the function of the school, I will review the history of the school – its construction in 2004, its opening for girls in 2005, its closing as a result of three attacks five months later and its negotiated reopening the following fall for boys. In addition, I will examine the steps we took as an organization that describes itself as a 'non-political, humanitarian organization dedicated to the reconstruction and development of Afghanistan' focusing on sustainable education, agriculture and health projects, to respond to the attacks on the school. Using this experience as a case study, I will offer a gender analysis of the situation that might inform the way we move forward in the future.

According to Wahid Omar, then director of education for A4T and a member of the board of directors, the idea for the construction of a school in the small, remote village of Sheik Yassin, Wardak Province, came about at a social occasion. Wahid Omar, an Afghan-American who left Afghanistan at the age of 19 when his father, the former minister of health, was imprisoned by the Marxist government of Noor Mohammad Taraki, heard on the radio that the regime was beginning to conscript young Afghan men. In a note delivered to Wahid through a prison guard in 1979, Omar instructed his son to leave the country immediately. Wahid and his younger brother travelled to France, where they spent the next two years. Eventually, they settled in Colorado, where Wahid became an adjunct professor of French.

After 2001, like many educated ex-patriots, Wahid returned to his country for months at a time – splitting time between his family in Colorado and work opportunities as they came up in Kabul. He was first hired as a country director for Global Exchange, then as a consultant in education and finally full-time in 2007 to be Afghan Masters Manager for the Higher Education Project run as a collaboration among the University of Massachusetts, Amherst, AED, Indiana University and the Ministry of Higher Education in the Afghan Government and USAID. During this time, Wahid worked in a volunteer capacity for the NGO Afghans4Tomorrow that he and four other returning Afghans professionals had helped found with the vision of inspiring others to return and rebuild their country. As of January 2009, the organization has founded three schools – two catch-up schools for girls in Kabul and one in Wardak; started a health clinic and raised money for the salaries of male and female doctors; transported multiple containers of humanitarian supplies from the United States to Kabul; planted thousands of trees; and assisted with wells and other agricultural projects around the country. In addition, beginning in 2008, with the assistance of the founders of Engineers Without Boarders, A4T embarked on an income-generation project for its schools, producing briquettes made of paper waste and collected from piles of refuse around the city that can be used and sold for fuel.

Like Wahid's father, Eshan Mayar had been a successful and influential person in Afghanistan in the 1960s and 1970s. Founder of the major utility company in Kabul that supplied power to the city as well as to many of Afghanistan's 32 provinces, Mayar discovered while on a business trip to Switzerland that the Marxist government of President Nur Muhammad Tarki had taken over his company, and like other members of Afghanistan's traditional elite, members of the religious establishment and the intelligentsia, was targeted for arrest, imprisonment and execution. Without returning to Afghanistan, Mayar travelled to the United States and settled in Texas. He had also founded the first Rotary Club of Afghanistan.

Wahid Omar and Ehsan Mayar met at the Springhar Hotel in Kabul in March 2002, during the period of possibility and excitement following the routing of the Taliban. Wahid recounted how he had been explaining the work of Afghans4Tomorrow and how Mayar had offered to donate land near his family home in Sheik Yassine village in Wardak Province, where his son, Masude Mayar, lived and his niece, Dr Roshanak Wardak, ran a weekly clinic.[5] Part of a prominent, landowning family in Wardak Province whose members included parliamentary representatives, Mayar agreed with Wahid Omar that it was important to have development in the Pashtun south as well as in the north and west of the country – places that were already receiving the majority of reconstruction aid and projects. Mayar would donate the land and on behalf of A4T, and Wahid committed himself to raising money and constructing a school on the ruins of an old existing building.

I first saw the planned site for the Ismael Mayar Primary School on a trip to Afghanistan in 2003 on behalf of the Episcopal Diocese of New York. I had gone over to assist with the final stages in the construction of a mosque that had been, according to the villagers living in the Shamali plan near it, destroyed by US bombs. The Episcopal Diocese of New York and the Hazrat-I-Abu-Bakr Mosque in Flushing, New York, had raised money to rebuild the mosque in Shamali as a gesture of interfaith good will. As a member of a Global Exchange Delegation led by Wahid Omar, who was the then country director, we had visited Sheik Yassine, seen the site of the school and met Masude Mayar and his cousin Dr Roshanak Wardak, who was running a clinic in the same village.

Like representatives from other US donor agencies and communities of support, including the Rebuilding Afghanistan Foundation, United Nations Association of Colorado, and Engineers Without Borders, I was impressed by the construction of the school – already under way with the assistance of a member of Engineers Without Borders – as well as the remoteness of the village and the fact that there had never been a girls school before. Dr Roshanak, whose clinic we attended while in Sheik Yassine village, was adamant that with a 14 per cent literacy rate for women in Afghanistan, girls needed education more than anything else. Dr Roshanak herself, a cousin in the Mayar family whose grandfather and uncle had served as leaders in the former Afghan National Assembly during the reign of King Nadir Zahir Shah, had wanted to be a politician when she was a young girl, but her family had convinced her that teaching or medicine were more suitable careers for women.[6] She left the country during the Soviet occupation to take care of Afghan refugees in Pakistan and returned to start her own clinic in Wardak during the time of the civil war. She continued treating patients under the Taliban and refused to wear a burqa. 'I told them, if you can show me where the Qu'ran says I should wear the burqa, I will wear seven burqas' (Witte 2005). Dr Roshanak ran for and won a seat in the Afghan National Parliament in 2005 and continues to see patients and commute to her home province once a week. At the time of my first visit in 2003, she was adamant that the school should be for girls.

Inspired by my conversations with Dr Roshanak and Wahid Omar and impressed by the need for girls' education, I returned home from Afghanistan to raise money for the final phase of construction for the Ismael Mayar Primary School from the Episcopal Diocese in New York. I later connected Afghans4Tomorrow to the Episcopal Church's relief and development agency, Episcopal Relief and Development (ERD had raised money for Afghanistan after 9/11 and was looking for a project to support). ERD has also funded two other Afghan4Tomorrow girls' schools in Kabul that had their first graduating class in 2006.

On 12 October 2005, the Wardak School opened classes for girls. This was due primarily to the efforts of Dr Roshanak, who met with community leaders that fall and urged them to make the school for girls who had had little or no education. By the second week of classes, 120 girls ages six to 14 were enrolled in the first, second and third grades. The Afghan Deputy Minister of Education and President of Primary Education were both present at the opening, along with A4T volunteers, local Pashtun leaders, students and teachers. There were nine teachers, a principal and two guards.

Shortly after this opening ceremony, however, the school came under attack. In December 2005, a mine was discovered by the school guard and deactivated. On 2 February 2006, about 60 chairs were set on fire in an attempt to destroy the whole building. The one guard who had been hired was not present when the attack happened. Following this incident, the school director hired two more guards for the school and wrote to the governor of Wardak Province, requesting arms for the guards. His request was denied. Finally, in April 2006, the school was attacked at night by a group of 10 men who tied up the guards, threatened them and their families and started another fire in the school, burning a large section down. In the same month, three other girls' schools in Wardak were attacked, bringing the total to 12 in the province. A4T officials who oversaw the school met with the governor and police chief, both of whom said they could not help. Shortly after the meeting, the governor's office was attacked, along with the main police station in Wardak's capital. By September 2006, there was only one girls' school left open in the entire province.

At Wahid's encouragement, Ehsan Mayar for the first time held a meeting with members of the community, the local shura, to discuss the school and what had happened. Following the meetings, Mayar agreed to turn over the deed of the land to the community, something he had not done earlier.

In June 2006, I returned to Afghanistan, this time on behalf of Episcopal Relief and Development, and joined Wahid Omar to meet with a delegation of six representatives from Wardak Province. Three members of the delegation came to Kabul to discuss the future of the school and clinic in Sheik Yassine village, and two had signed a letter requesting rebuilding of the school. The delegation members assured us of the community's ongoing commitment to education, saying that from the point of view of Islam, girls as well as boys should be educated.[7] They told us that there was no problem with the Mayar family and that there were a total of 18 schools in the Chak District. (Our suspicion was that there was some resentment against Mayar as a large landowner.) They also said that Mayar had agreed to turn over the deed of the land when he had spoken with them the previous month.

The delegation told us that other schools had been burned, that security was a big problem and that schools had been targeted throughout the province. They wanted to reopen the school for boys and girls – girls having classes in the morning and boys in the afternoon. I asked the delegation why they thought local people were collaborating with the attackers. One of the delegation members replied with a story about how, during the wars, the Wardak commanders brought notebooks and not guns and that under the Taliban they persuaded them to let children go to school. One representative said that A4T should have gathered the people together before building the school (A4T had done that) so that they could choose teachers and staff. He assured us that from here on they would pay more attention to the school.

> We will tell you what our plan is from the community. The area is in need of education and schooling. It is important that A4T and the Moyar [sic] family are present at the Shurah of the people and we should ask that everyone sign the letter. We will impose our conditions: that the guards be from Sheik Yassine [sic] and that we should again ask the entire village if they need a school they should protect it. If not they should not waste our time. In my village, the guard is a volunteer.[8]

Wahid proposed that the first thing to do was to have a village-wide 'shura' that a member of A4T would attend. We also suggested that the village pay for rudimentary repairs to the building as an interim measure and that A4T would then reinstate the operational funding for the teachers and staff. After six months of classes running smoothly, A4T would consider requesting funds to rebuild completely. Wahid also concluded that the Mayar family needed to share power in the village of Sheik Yassin and that in the future Afghans4Tomorrow would operate through the shura's structure – a structure based on local mutual consultation among respected men – rather than through the family.

In late August 2006, I learnt through emails from A4T staff in Kabul that the school had been partially rebuilt as the delegation had promised. Members of the delegation wanted the operating funds to be released but said they wanted to open the school for boys only for the first month for security reasons. Apparently, violent conflict had increased, and there had been fighting 10 miles from the school (Afghans4Tomorrow 2010). In emails back and forth with the A4T staff, it became clear that the community was afraid to open the school for girls, unlike what they had said at the meeting. The school director did not respond to the calls from the A4T staff in Kabul. The question was raised as to whether they should release the operating funds and open the school just for boys or to keep the school closed. Although initially I was in favour of the latter, I changed my mind after the board of A4T, members of the Episcopal Relief and Development staff and Wahid himself reluctantly thought it was better to open the school just for boys. In 2007, 55 girls were allowed to be educated not at the school but in home schools in the village.

In retrospect, a deeper understanding of the connections between patriarchy and violence might have assisted Afghans4Tomorrow in several ways. A comprehensive gender analysis might have caused us to look beyond the immediate and glaring problem of lack of equality between girls and boys in terms of education access in Wardak Province and ask questions about power relations more generally that included class, economics, role stereotypes and unequal inheritance laws. In her book *Bananas, Beaches, and Bases: Making Feminist Sense of International Politics*, Cynthia Enloe discusses the way that power relations within the US military, for example, put military wives, local prostitutes and female military personnel at odds with one another – augmenting existing differences of class and educations – as a threat to their immediate interests. 'It is the very division between these women that provide military bases their security', she writes, postulating that when women in different countries and from different classes begin networking to resist the expansion of US military bases around the world, they are more likely to be successful (Enloe 1989).

If A4T had paid more attention to class distinctions within the village of Sheik Yassin, perhaps questioning at the start the landowner Eshan Mayar's ability to speak on behalf of the community for whom the school was being built, we might have been able to anticipate some of the resentment at work when a tiny village miles from the Pakistan boarder stood by as 'outsiders' attacked the school. We might not have assumed that Dr Roshanak's passion for building a school for girls would be shared by all the families who lived in that area. There were large differences between the Mayar family – a landowning, educationally elite family, some members of which had gone abroad to the United States decades previously – and the non-landowning, largely uneducated group of villagers whose children the school would serve. Many of these villagers had remained in Afghanistan throughout the Soviet occupation, civil wars and Taliban time. When Mayar first offered his land for a girls' school to be built, A4T assumed that the villagers were behind it. This assumption may have been misplaced. Although a local shura was called to discuss the proposed school in 2003, at which time many of the village elders appeared to be enthusiastic, by the opening of the school in late 2005, very few of the villagers were present. Interest on their part seemed to have dwindled. Had A4T considered that the patronage system within Afghanistan might have changed in 25 years of war and drought and that resentment between expatriate Afghans and those who had remained in country would be high, we might have made some different decisions. The director of Afghan4Tomorrow, himself a returning educated expatriot, might not have assigned a project director function to Mayar's nephew.

A gender analysis sheds light on Mayar's decision not turn the deed of the land over to the villagers immediately. The transaction of property in that part of the country required signatures of all the male relatives of the family – a logistically difficult and time-consuming task in a diaspora community and one that no doubt would have daunted Mayar, even if his intentions in turning the land over to the community had been straightforward.

A gender analysis might have helped decode words like 'jealousy' and 'resentment' when they were used to explain how local people allowed the school attacks to happen. In an interview with Dr Roshanak Wardak about the possible causes of the Sheik Yassin school attacks in 2006, in addition to mentioning the negative influence of a former warlord in the area, she added resentment about employment and social status to the list of possible causes for the school burning.

> Imagine you are an old retired jihadi and you fought in all of the wars and you don't know how to read and you don't have a job and now a young woman in your village – someone who previously had no status – is hired to teach as a teacher in the school. This causes much jealousy and anger.[9]

In taking on the task of providing access to education, introducing a basic awareness of the challenges for both men and women of narrowly defined gender roles might help bring about lasting reform.

In addition to showing the added difficulties of working in a patriarchal system – ones that ran much deeper than the discrete problem of lack of access to education for girl children, however, a more thorough gender analysis would have also given our organization other benchmarks for measuring success. For example, the fourth-quarter report on the Ismael Mayar School in 2009 painstakingly showed the number of students attending, the number of grades, the numbers who passed the government exams, and so on – and with it the great disparity between the number of girl and boy students. Although the attacks have been reported and recorded on the A4T website, there is no mention of a 2008 attempt to burn down the door of one of the home schools, and there is nothing on the bravery of the teachers and girls who continued to teach classes in the face of such attacks. Without at least anecdotal evidence of the proactive and courageous role that girls and women teachers are playing in securing their own education, outsiders would be left with a picture in which girls and women continue to be victims only in the face of gender violence. The request and focus for armed guards should not overshadow the work girls are doing on their own behalf to define their own 'security'. They have demonstrated that without education there is no peace – simply by showing up to learn in the face of danger.

In the case of school attacks in this part of southern Afghanistan, one question for further exploration regards the role of force as a means of providing 'protection from avoidable harm'. In *Sexism and the War System*, Betty A. Reardon writes,

> There is a strong possibility that [the] connection between violence against women and the war system will gain greater significance in the women's movement's current emphasis on equality. The

presence of the threat of force always prevents authentic equality in any relationship.

(1996)

In the case of southern Afghanistan, where it is now clear that fewer than half of all children are attending school as a result of direct intimidation, equality between girls and boys is already under siege. Although it is clear that a gender analysis is key to understanding the destructive depths of violence and its role in perpetuating inequality, what might the human security framework say about whether the outside military intervention on behalf of girls' human rights – the suggestion and premise of the Human Rights Watch report – further entrenches these inequalities or provides protection from them? In what extreme cases may the threat of force – call it legitimate – actually serve to preserve equality?

Recently, the lack of militarized security on the part of the Pakistan government forces in Swat Valley, where the government's controversial 'truce' with the Taliban has led to the closing of girls schools on a massive scale, the imposition of a regressive form of the Sharia and even public floggings of women who go outside alone, appears to take gender concerns less seriously than, for example, a government-sponsored armed attack on Taliban forces. A *New York Times* editorial on 27 April stated,

> If the Indian Army advanced within 60 miles of Islamabad, you can bet Pakistan's army would be fully mobilized and defending the country in pitched battles. Yet when the Taliban got that close to the capital on Friday, pushing into the key district of Buner, Pakistani authorities sent only several hundred poorly equipped and underpaid constabulary forces.

(2009)

The editorial questions the Pakistan government's definition of a national security threat. It poses the question of why the denial of girls' education and threat to women's human rights does not, it seems, rise to the level of threat that military movements on the Indian-Pakistan border do. In this case, if pressure from members of the US government mobilizes military confrontation by the Pakistan army against the Taliban's occupation, the overall effect on the wellbeing of women and girls in Swat and Bruner may be positive.

The framework of human security, with its focus on providing for basic needs like education, health and sustainable environments; its respect for the identity and dignity of persons and groups; and its focus on protection from avoidable harm, sheds light on the entrenched violent conflict and gender discrimination that is commonplace in Afghanistan.

In the case of Wardak Province, it is possible that additional security forces might have prevented the school attacks on the Ismael Mayar Primary School and others in the area. For example, had the road from Kabul to Kandahar been less threatening for drivers, Afghan4Tomorrow staff members might have felt more able to have made regular visits to check on their development projects. Assigning an exclusively military solution to this security problem, however, seems short-sighted. John Paul Lederach provides great examples of key turning points in situations of entrenched conflict where the courage and creativity of key individuals did more to break a cycle of conflict than political, economic or military power.[10] Thus, moving forward, these theorists provide motivation and rationale for a variety of participants in the process of peacemaking and nation building to keep at their work and to continue to learn ways of being effective.

Notes

1 Article 28.1 of the 'Convention on the Rights of the Child', ratified by 192 countries, states that 'Parties recognize the right of the child to education, and with a view to achieving this right progressively and on the basis of equal opportunity, they shall, in particular: (a) Make primary education compulsory and available free to all'. 'Convention on the Rights of the Child', 20 November 1989. Adopted and opened for signature, ratification and accession by General Assembly Resolution 44/25. Accessed 5 April 2009 (UNHCR).

2 Women activities and educators at The Hague Appeal for Peace Civil Society Conference in 1999 in The Netherlands sought to contrast the concept of 'national security' which, they argued, was not gender-inclusive and did not adequately capture the daily threat to women of domestic violence, environmental hazards and poverty with the idea of 'human security'. Human security argues that people and communities are secure when (1) the environment in which they live can sustain human life; (2) their basic physical survival needs for food, clothing, shelter, healthcare and education are fulfilled; (3) their personal and cultural identities are respected; and (4) they are protected from avoidable harm (Reardon 2003: 3).

3 Sympathy for the 'protective' function that the Taliban served when they first arrived in the ruins of Kabul in 1997 was evident in the account I heard from more than one Afghans when I visited Kabul in 2003 of what happened when the Taliban arrived in a Hazara-held part of Kabul called Wazir Akbar-Khan. In this Kabul neighbourhood, Hazara military leaders were reportedly holding women of other ethnic groups. According to the story, when the Taliban began their assault of this neighbourhood, the

women ran out of the houses naked. The Taliban fighters then reportedly took off their turbans and threw them to the women so they would be able to cover themselves. This incident was described as having preceded a massacre of Hazara in the Wazir Akbar-Khan neighbourhood by the Taliban during their contest for power in Kabul. Najibullah Mojadidi. 2003. Interview in Kabul, Afghanistan. 17 June.
4 Johan Galtung's 'conflict triangle' is helpful in pointing out the relationship among peacekeeping (control of destructive behaviour), peacemaking (changing attitudes and assumptions about the other) and peacebuilding (overcoming the contradiction or incompatibility at the root of the conflict. In a successful conflict intervention, Galtung argues that a peacekeeping function that controls the destructive functioning of actors in a conflict while not making demands that prohibit communication between the parties must take place at the same time that changing attitudes toward peace are being developed. Both these processes must be contemporaneous with a third one: addressing the way that a basic contradiction at the root of the conflict, 'incompatible goal states in a goal seeking system', may be overcome (Johan Galtung, *Peace by Peaceful Means: Peace and Conflict, Development and Civilization*, London: Sage, 1996, pp. 72, 103.
5 Examples of successful Afghan campaigns against foreign invaders since the beginning of modern Afghanistan with Ahmed Shah Durrani in 1747 include the first Afghan War (1834–47), which ended in the retreat and massacre of British forces, the third Afghan War (1919–21), which resulted in independence for Afghanistan, and the Soviet occupation (1979–89), which ended with the withdrawal of Soviet troops and arguably contributed to the collapse of the Soviet Union (Mary Louise Clifford, *Afghanistan*, New York: J. B. Lippencott, 1989, pp. 70–85).
6 Interview with Wahid Omar in Kabul, Afghanistan, 24 June 2004.
7 Interview with Dr Roshanak Wardak in Sheik Yassin, Wardak Province, Afghanistan, 14 June 2003.
8 Interview with local shura/community delegation representing the Ismael Mayar School and local community of Sheik Yassin village in Chak Province, Wardak, 15 June 2006.
9 Interview with local shura/community delegation representing the Ismael Mayar School and local community of Sheik Yassin village in Chak Province, Wardak, 15 June 2006.
10 Interview with Dr Roshanak Wardak in Kabul, Afghanistan, 19 July 2006.

References

Afghanistan. 2004. 'The Constitution of The Islamic Republic of Afghanistan' (ratified). 26 January. www.afghanembassy.com.pl/afg/images/pliki/The Constitution.pdf. Accessed 15 December 2017.
Afghans4Tomorrow. 2010. Video. www.youtube.com/watch?v=l-041cFSZLY. Accessed December 15, 2017.
Breines, I. 2009. 'Obama, Ask Afghan Women'. Association for Conflict Resolution, Unpublished.
Bunch, C. 1997. 'The Intolerable Status Quo: Violence against Women and Girls'. UNICEF Report.

Burns, R. 1982. 'Development, Disarmament, and Women: Some New Connections', paper presented at the Victorian Association for Peace Studies. Melbourne, Australia. Quoted in Betty A. Reardon, *Sexism and the War System*, Syracuse: Syracuse University Press, 1996, p. 60.
Clifford, M. L. 1989. *Afghanistan*. New York: J. B. Lippencott.
Enloe, C. 1989. *Bananas, Beaches, and Bases: Making Feminist Sense of International Politics*. Los Angeles: University of California Press.
Esfandiari, G. 2006. 'Afghanistan: Militants Are Targeting Schools'. *Radio Free Europe*. 22 February. www.rferl.org/a/1066060.html. Accessed 26 January 2009.
Future Generations. 2009. 'Future Generations Afghanistan: An Overview'. www.future.org/afghanistan. Accessed 4 May 2009.
Galtung, J. 1996. *Peace by Peaceful Means: Peace and Conflict, Development and Civilization*. London: Sage Publications.
Human Rights Watch. 2006. 'Lessons in Terror: Attacks on Education in Afghanistan', *Human Rights Watch*, vol. 18 (6 [C]). www.hrw.org/reports/2006/afghanistan0706/index.htm. Accessed 10 September 2006.
———. 2009. 'Human Rights Watch Letter to President Barak Obama on Afghanistan'. 26 March. www.hrw.org/en/news/2009/03/26/human-rights-watch-letter-president-barack-obama-afghanistan. Accessed 2 April 2009.
Lederach, J. P. 2005. *The Moral Imagination: The Art and Soul of Building Peace*. London: Oxford University Press.
Malikyar, H. 2004. 'Modern Family Law, 1800–2000: Afghanistan', in *The Encyclopaedia of Women, Gender and Family Law*. The Netherlands: Brill Publishers.
New York Times. 2009. '60 Miles from Islamabad', editorial, A22. 27 April.
Rashid, A. 2001. *The Taliban*. London: I. B. Taurus Publishers.
Reardon, B. A. 1996. *Sexism and the War System*. Syracuse: Syracuse University Press.
———. 2003. 'Toward Human Security: A Gender Approach to Demilitarization' (Ningen no anzenhosho wo mezashite: jenda no shitenkara kangaeru datsugunjika), *Women's Asia*, vol. 33: 7–13.
Rubin, E. 2006. 'The Undefeated: Why the Taliban have Returned', *New York Times Magazine*, no. 95.
Tickner, A. 1992. *Gender in International Relations*. New York: Columbia University Press.
UNESCO. 2003. 'UNESCO and the Government of Afghanistan Launched Nationwide Literacy Project'. http://portal.unesco.org/en/ev.php-URL_ID=9031&URL_DO=DO_PRINTPAGE&URL_SECTION=201.html. Accessed 3 April 2009.
UNICEF. 2005. 'Information by Country: Afghanistan: Statistics: Women'. 1 May 2009. www.unicef.org/infobycountry/afghanistan_statistics.html?p=printme.
Waltz, K. 2001. *Man, the State, and War*. New York: Columbia University Press.
Witte, G. 2005. 'Afghanistan's Chance to Heal: Diverse New Parliament Will Bring Together Former Adversaries', *The Washington Post*, A22. 18 December. Accessed 5 April 2009.

Interviews

Najibullah Mojadidi in Kabul, Afghanistan. 17 June 2003.
Wahid Omar in Kabul, Afghanistan, 24 June 2004.
Dr Roshanak Wardak in Sheik Yassin, Wardak Province, Afghanistan, 14 June 2003.
Local shura/community delegation representing the Ismael Mayar School and local community of Sheik Yassin village in Chak Province, Wardak, 15 June 2006.
Dr Roshanak Wardak in Kabul, Afghanistan, 19 July 2006.

10 The Soldiers' Mothers, human security and the Russian-Chechen Wars

Valerie Zawilski

Introduction

In Chechnya the peace process has been endorsed by the elections in 2016, in which reportedly the majority of Chechens voted for United Russia. Did they vote 'freely', did they vote for this political party or did they vote at all? Is this the price that must be paid for peace? On the one hand, most Chechens would agree that, after living through a decade of brutal warfare, this is a minor price to pay if it means they are guaranteed peace and security. On the other, residual resentments will lay dormant as Chechens wonder – Is this what thousands of Chechens and Russians died for? How long will this peace last? How long will it be before another insurrection will develop? Perhaps the most important question of all is: Will the government be able to provide them with human security?

Peacebuilding is a people-centred approach to conflict resolution, which has developed in parallel in the 1990s to the concept of human security. Definitions of the concept of human security attempt to broaden security thinking from the 'national security' and the military defence of political boundaries orientation to a people-centred non-militarized approach of anticipating and coping with multiple threats against ordinary people in an increasingly globalized world (Chen et al. 2003: 3). In 2001, the United Nations established the independent International Commission on Human Security, which has been mandated to clarify what is meant by the concept of human security and how it may be translated into global policies and action. Three major trends have contributed to the new way of thinking about human security. These trends include (1) the end of the Cold War; (2) a better understanding of the depth of social inequality and the growth of global poverty; and (3) the impact of globalization on all sectors of society. In 2005, Kofi Annan addressed the General Assembly of the United Nations. He spoke about the number of wars and the high levels of violence in the New World Order. He said,

> All of us have been shocked, over the last fifteen years, by the spectacle of countries apparently emerging from a bitter, destructive conflict, only to slip back again because the international community lost interest too soon and moved on to other crises. One reason for this has been the lack of any international institution specifically devoted to peace building, as opposed to peacemaking or peacekeeping. And therefore I think one of the most encouraging results was the decision to fill this institutional void by establishing a Peace Building Commission, backed by a small Peace Building Support office within the Secretariat, and a voluntary Peace Building Fund.
>
> (Annan 2005: 1)

This chapter will address the serious social concern that surrounds the dilemma of how state sovereignty limits international intervention in cases where the human security of civilians is at risk. The Treaty of Westphalia, in the year 1648, established an internationally recognized policy of non-intervention of foreign powers into the domestic politics of a nation state. This concept was endorsed by the League of Nations and later by the United Nations in the 20th century. Thus, each internationally recognized nation state that is represented in the United Nations is considered to be a sovereign state. Stephen D. Krasner proposes that domestic sovereignty refers to the 'organization of public authority within a state and to the level of effective control exercised by those holding authority' (Krasner 2001: 6–7). Today, the security of people living in a particular nation state lies within the jurisdiction of the nation state's government. It is understood, therefore, that each internationally recognized nation state should develop its own system of law and order which is to be used to control its citizenry with prudence and respect. It is also understood that other nation states do not have the right to interfere in this internal process, regardless of the internal political struggles, civil wars or human rights violations that may take place.

The UN's non-interventionist sovereignty policy is essentially beneficial for political elites. Krasner points out that leaders of nation states 'make decisions that are determined by rulers whose violation of, or adherence to, international principles and rules is based on calculations of material or ideational interests, not taken-for granted practices' (1999: 9). Unfortunately, the concept of domestic sovereignty has been used to justify the lack of international social concern and non-interventionist policies held by the world community, where the violations of human rights and the security of communities in nation states have been violated. The Union of Soldiers' Mothers of Russia challenges this assumption and proposes that Russia should not be permitted to hide behind the concept of domestic sovereignty, shirking its responsibility to prevent human rights abuses, and should be held accountable for war crimes that have been committed in the region of Chechnya during the Russian-Chechen Wars of 1994 to 1996 and 1999 to 2006.

Although the Committee of Soldiers' Mothers (CSM or the Soldiers' Mothers) plays an important political role in contemporary Russian civil society, a collective male dominance generally limits the voice of women in the formal political arenas of power. The social status of women in Russia has drastically declined since the end of the Soviet period. From 1980 to 1985, women comprised 35 per cent of the deputies elected to the Supreme Soviet. In 1990, due to the abolition of gender quotas, women made up only 5.3 per cent of the People's Deputies and only 8.9 per cent of the members of the People's Deputies of the Russian Soviet Federated Socialist Republic (Kanapianova 2008). Subsequently, women in the post-Soviet era are oppressed by the patriarchal power structures of Russian society. Similar to the Mothers of the Plaza de Mayo of Argentina and the Mothers Front of Sri Lanka, during periods of civil unrest, women who seek social justice for their families politicize their social roles as mothers, which in turn enables them to collectively enter the arena of political dissent.

The CSM was created in 1989 in Moscow, Russia, during the last days of the Soviet-Afghanistan War. Three hundred women formed this organization, which lobbied the Soviet government to free their sons from compulsory military service. The organization contested the human rights violations that Russian soldiers had inflicted on junior conscription soldiers. In 1995, during the First Russian-Chechen War of 1994–1996, the Soldiers' Mothers organized a peace march in Chechnya which opposed the violence, social injustices and lack of concern for the safety of civilians. They were nominated for the Nobel Peace Prize and received the Sean McBride Peace Prize (Germany) and the Professor Rafto Prize (Norway) in 1995 for their political activism, which included reporting on and contesting the Russian and Chechen military tactics that violated the Geneva Convention's stance on protecting vulnerable and defenceless populations against human rights abuses and war crimes (Zawilski in Webber and Mathers 2005: 234).

The second section of this article will examine the agnatic capacity of the Russian Soldiers' Mothers, who have acted with agency in order to enable themselves. In addition to examining and critiquing the social constraints of Russian patriarchal society, the actions of the Soldiers' Mothers and how they have been shaped by cultural representations of motherhood and their social relations as women in Russian society will be the focus of this post-structural feminist analysis. The Soldiers' Mothers represent a form of 'embedded feminism' in which their actions of resistance have taken place 'within' the framework of a hegemonic, patriarchal, military-industrial nation state. In 2006, the Soldiers' Mothers were officially recognized as a legitimate organization by the Russian government. The Union of the Committees of the Soldiers' Mothers of Russia,[1] or the Party of Soldiers' Mothers, is now an official member of the Russian Democratic political party: Yabloko. Similar to Russian women who wrote about human rights abuses in the Soviet underground, the Soldiers' Mothers, in tandem with other human rights groups in Russia, such as Memorial, actively challenge social injustices carried out by the Russian military industrial complex and have publicized information about human rights violations during the 1994–1996 and the 1999–2006 Russian-Chechen Wars. The role that Russian women have played in addressing the issue of human security during the development of a nascent civil society in post-Soviet Russia will be the central theme of this chapter.

Sociopolitical origins of the First Chechen War, 1994–1996

Chechnya, or the Republic of Chechen-Ichkeria, borders the province of Stravropol Krai in Russia in the north-east, Daghestan to the northeast and east, Georgia to the south and Ingushetia and North Ossetia to the west. Chechnya is 17,000 square kilometres, or 6,000 square miles, in area (the size of the state of Connecticut in the United States). The northern part of the region is a fertile plain, and in the southern part of the state, there are wooded foothills, which rise to the northern slopes of the Caucasus mountain range. Chechens are an indigenous people who primarily herd animals and are farmers. They are the largest North Caucasian group, and after the Georgians, the second largest Caucasian group living in the world today.

In 1989, in the last census completed in the Soviet Union, the total population of Chechnya-Ingush was 1,270,000 people. After the peaceful partition of 1992 into the separate regions of Chechnya Ichkeria and Ingushetia, the population of Chechen-Ichkeria[2] was at the time 1,084,000 people. In 1989, 715,000, or 66 per cent of the population, were Chechen; 269,000, or 25 per cent, were Russian; and 25,000, or 2 per cent, were Ingush. By the 1990s, approximately 42.9 per cent of the population was urbanized. In the capital city Grozny, of the 397,000 people living there, 210,000, or 53 per cent of the inhabitants, were Russians, and 127,000, or 32 per cent, were Chechens.[3] By 1994, 100,000 mainly younger Chechen males had, due to high rates of poverty and unemployment, left Chechnya to live and work in other Central Asian republics and Russia. Today it is estimated that 58,000 Chechens are living in Daghestan, 50,000 in Kazakhstan, 19,000 in Ingushetia and approximately 2,000 in Moscow (Bhardwaj in Singh 2002: 351).

The Chechens and their ancestors have lived in the North Caucasus region for 6,000 years. Similar to Afghanistan, there are a multitude of ethnic and linguistic groups living in the North Caucasus. There is an old saying in the North Caucasus, 'When God was sprinkling the people like salt over the earth, he clumsily spilt his shaker on the Caucasus Mountains'. Within the radius of a few kilometres, language dialects may be distinctly different due to periods of cultural and geographical isolation.[4] The inhabitants of the Republic of Chechnya speak distinct Caucasic languages, which are non-Slavic, non-Turkic and non-Persian languages. Most Chechens can speak and understand between one to six different Chechen dialects, and their language is closely related to the neighbouring Ingush languages. Chechens were converted to Christianity in the fourth century and later to Islam in the eighth century AD. The Muslim religion has played an important role in shaping the ancient kinship structure, which is called a *teip*. A teip is a cluster of families who live in the same territory and share the same ancestors. Today in Chechnya there are 170 teips[5] (Bazarya 2006). Political life is decentralized and organized around the local politics of the nine *tykxum* (family – territorial *gars* or unions between teips). A teip may act as a sole unit; however; individuals will try to maintain their own authority and status within the teip. Leaving the teip is strongly discouraged by the family, and although women play an important role in community life as caregivers and kin keepers, they are considered subordinate to men.

During the late 1980s, an economic crisis developed in Chechnya as 60 per cent of the oil and gas fields which had been active for almost 100 years were now depleted. Chechen industries started to downsize as the oil refineries were not being fully utilized. Mechanical engineering plants, where many Chechens and Russians worked, creating products from rolled ferrous metal goods, were also being closed down. Until 1993, the North Caucasus region exported 80 per cent of all Russia's grain, 25 per cent of its vegetables and melons and 35 per cent of Russian meat. Due to a breakdown in the agricultural sphere from 1989 to 1993, there was a mass exodus of 8,600 farmers from Chechnya to find work in other regions of Central Asia. In other regions, such as Daghestan, 60 per cent of unemployed workers received unemployment allowances, while only 6 per cent of unemployed workers in Chechnya did. Thus, from 1989 to 1991 alone, 9,400 people left Chechnya to find employment elsewhere. As a result of this agricultural crisis, an economic depression developed in which Chechen food prices rose in parallel with the rising expectations of the Confederation of Caucasus Peoples. Chechens made such claims as 'Without Russia we will turn our region into another Switzerland' or 'We shall achieve prosperity in the North Caucasus only outside of the Russian Federation'. If Chechnya was an independent nation, they said, 'then Turkey, Iran and Saudi Arabia would come to our aid as trading partners and investors' (Ruban 1994).

These economic factors, coupled with rising ethnic tensions and Russophobia throughout the former Soviet Union, made travelling and transporting goods safely across the region difficult. The inflow of Chechen migrants to neighbouring Central Asian republics upset the national hierarchies of the Astrakhan region, where local inhabitants were feeling threatened by Caucasus traders. For example, in 1991, clashes occurred in collective markets where Tartars expelled Caucasus traders from the area. In the autumn of 1992, Chechens and Kazakhs living in the Baskunchyak region rioted over the production and sale of beer, and in October, the cooperative shop Prazdnik was looted for two days. In May 1993, conflicts between Chechens and local inhabitants were frequent, but the defiant behaviour of young Chechen men intimidated the local population. The conflict escalated, and Larissa Ruban describes it not as a struggle between local people and Chechen traders 'but as a battle between local and outside criminal groups who were involved in turf wars' (Ruban 1994).

In 1992, local populations complained that Chechens were antagonistic bandits, murderers and swindlers, and they disliked them because they considered them to be impudent, loutish and cruel. The monopolization of collective farms and goods, along with the corruption of governmental hearings and other violations of law and order, resulted in massive mobilization and pogroms against Chechen immigrants in July 1993 (Ruban 1994). Essentially, the massive migration of civilians from Chechnya was the result of a drastic loss in production in the agricultural sector and the diminished use of local labour power. The forced migration pattern of Chechens to other republics and the unprecedented rise in criminal activities in the North Caucasus was due to deep absolute poverty, which forced Chechens and other citizens in the North Caucasus republics to compete for scarce resources and to work in the underground economy during the unstable political climate of the early to mid-1990s.

In the 1990s, while Chechens were struggling to find work in other republics, several important political changes had taken place. On 27 October 2001, a prominent Chechen, the former Soviet Air Force General Dzhokhor Dudayev,[6] was elected as the president of Chechnya. President Dudayev received 412,671, or 90 per cent, of the 458,144 votes that were cast. In November 1990, in cooperation with Chechen and Ingush leaders, President Dudayev declared Chechnya to be an independent state from the Soviet Union. During the following years, three failed attempts were made by President Boris Yeltsin's post-Soviet Russian government to convince President Dudayev to abandon the idea that Chechnya should become an independent nation from the Russia Federation. However, President Dudayev enjoyed popular support from his constituency who trusted him; thus, he was able to mobilize the Chechen population to accept his political position that Russia was a constant menace and that it was responsible for Chechnya's present (and past) trials and tribulations (Campana 2004). When President Yeltsin realized that President Dudayev would not be persuaded to remain within the Russian Federation, President Dudayev and the Chechen Congress were declared to be 'criminals' and false leaders who did not have the popular support of Chechen citizens. President Yeltsin's government suggested that President Dudayev's anti-Russian attitudes and nationalist aspirations for Chechnya were unreasonable and unacceptable (Baydeyev in Singh 2002: 362–63).

Throughout the summer of 1994, there were daily reports in the Russian media about the souring Russian-Chechen relations, which was tempered by numerous accounts of the Chechen mafia's criminal activities throughout Russia, especially in Moscow.[7] In the autumn, an intense period of media stigmatization and negative reporting about Chechens developed in tandem with the bombing of several Moscow apartment buildings. The bombs killed several hundred Russian civilians, and the bombings were blamed on Chechen terrorists. The strategic shift from diplomatic negotiations to the 'open military option' was then pursued in November 1994.The Russian public was incensed, and at the time of the military invasion of Chechnya, public opinion polls showed that 75 per cent of Russians supported the invasion by the 40,000 Russian military forces, which were deployed to Chechnya on 11 December 1994.

The Russian Federal Security Forces entered Chechnya in December 1994 with the intent of capturing the breakaway southern republic. The military operation was disastrous, as tank contingents of poorly trained conscript soldiers were massacred in the streets of Grozny. According to estimates, more Russian soldiers were killed in the first three days of the war in Chechnya than in the entire 11 years of warfare in the Soviet-Afghanistan War from 1979 to 1990. The failed military campaign was highlighted by testimony given by US department official James Collins to the US Helsinki Commission on 27 January 2005. Collins reported that 455,000 persons were displaced by the war and 260,000 civilians fled to other regions of Chechnya, while 130,000 sought refuge in Ingushetia, 45,000 in Daghestan and 20,000 escaped to other regions. He also said that during 25 November 2004 to 25 January 2005, between 24,000 and 30,000 civilians had been killed (Collins in Kline 2005). Approximately 10 per cent of the population, or 100,000 of the one million civilians living in Chechnya before the war began, died between November 1994 and August 1996. During the war, the Russian air attacks had shifted from bombing not only military targets but also schools, hospitals and community centres as well as industrial centres and oil fields. On 27 February 1995, in a statement at the 44th UN Human Rights Commission, the commission condemned the military invasion of Chechnya.

> The Commission strongly deplores the high number of victims and the suffering inflicted on the civilian population who are subjected to the effects of armed confrontation on displaced persons. It also deplores the serious destruction of installations and infrastructure used by civilians. The Commission on Human Rights calls urgently for an immediate cessation of the fighting and of violations of human rights and for the holding of a dialogue without delay with the aim of achieving a peaceful solution to the crisis, with respect for the territorial integrity and the constitution of the Russian Federation, as well as a guarantee of human rights, the restoration of constitutional order and the organization of free and fair elections in the Republic of Chechnya.
> (United Nations High Commissioner of Human Rights 1997)

The mass killing of civilians in Chechnya was a strategy that was used by the Russian government to defeat the Chechen insurgents. In a study completed by Benjamin Valentino, Paul Huth and Dylan Balch-Lindsay, the incidence of mass killings of civilians in guerilla wars from 1945 to 2000 was examined. After analyzing data from 147 wars, the authors claim that there is strong evidence to support the hypothesis that

> mass killing is often a calculated military strategy used by regimes attempting to defeat major guerilla insurgencies. Unlike conventional military forces, guerilla armies often rely on the local civilian population for logistical support. Because guerilla forces are difficult to defeat directly, governments facing major guerilla insurgencies have strong incentives to target the guerillas' civilian base of support. Mass killing is significantly more likely during guerilla wars than during other kinds of wars. In addition, it was found that the likelihood of mass killing among guerilla conflicts is greatly increased when the guerillas receive high levels of active support from the local population or when the insurgency poses a major military threat to the regime.
>
> (Valentino et al. 2004)

After President Dudayev was murdered in 1996, an uneasy truce was declared between the Russian and Chechen leaders and the First Russian-Chechen War ended. In 1997, Aslan Maskadov[8] was elected by 60 per cent of all voting Chechens under what seemed to be free and fair elections (according to international observers). President Maskadov was the first internationally recognized Chechen president and was considered to be a moderate and diplomatic military leader. It was believed that his personal integrity, patience and social skills would be needed during the post-war period of reconstruction and rehabilitation. While Chechnya lay in ruins, Russians were appalled and horrified when they learnt that 100,000 civilians had died. They were also shocked by the official Russian statistics, which estimated that 5,500 Russian soldiers had died. Other estimates of Russian losses were even higher. The Committee of Soldiers' Mothers of Russia proposed that, according to their records, over 14,000 Russian soldiers died between 1994 and 1996 during the First Russian-Chechen War.

The Committee of Soldiers' Mothers and the First Russian-Chechen War, 1994–1996

The Committee of Soldiers' Mothers is an organization that was originally created to protest the human rights violations in the Soviet military forces. During the First Chechen War of 1994–1996, they evolved into an organization which would play an important role in informing the Russian public about human rights abuses in Chechnya. The Soldiers' Mothers movement developed in the Soviet Union during a period of time when political opportunities increased due to the introduction of *glasnost* (openness) during *perestroika* (era of reform) (1985–91) (Zdravomyslova 2005). The Committee of Soldiers' Mothers in Moscow, Russia, which was founded during this period of liberalization, is an organization of women which was led by Maria Kirbassova. In 1988, Kirbassova's son was attending university and was drafted into the Soviet Army. When Kirbassova requested that her son be transferred to a unit that was relevant to his education, the commander ridiculed her. When the Russian journal *Tretii Sektor* reported that Kirbassova's son was suicidal, the commander said, 'So what? If he hangs himself we'll look into the matter' (Caiazza 1998). The CSM lobbied the Soviet government for the return of 180,000 young men from the battlefront during the 1979–1989 Soviet-Afghanistan War. During the spring and summer of 1990, the newly organized CSM claimed that 15,000 peacetime or non-combat deaths had occurred in the Soviet armed forces during the preceding four-year period and that the military force was actively engaged in covering up these deaths. Julie Elkner reports that 'mass soldiers' mothers' demonstrations over this issue were held in Moscow and elsewhere in the early summer of 1990' (Elkner 2005).

The CSM was established in Moscow in 1989, and two years later, in 1991, the Soldiers' Mothers Organization (SMO) was registered as a public organization in St Petersburg. The SMO was established to educate draftees and their relatives about the conscription law[9] and to help mothers to save their sons from military service. Thus, if men are understood to be the soldiers and 'sons' of the Father State and women are seen to be the 'mothers' of the Fatherland's soldier-sons, then the 'meaningful world' of the Soldiers' Mothers is based upon kinship ties. Maja Hojer argues,

> Drawing on such metaphors of kinship and gender, the obligations felt towards the state are deeply embodied in the nation. It is the goal of The Soldiers' Mothers to change people's relation to the state into formal and legal instead of moral ties. Thereby they seek to establish new understandings of 'public' and 'private' and new ways of filling out the intermediate social space in between that is new ways to conceptualize and enact 'civil society'.
>
> (Hojer 2005)

The role of educating, informing, protecting and ultimately changing a person's perception about his or her relationship to the state was extended during the time of the First Chechen War in 1994–1996, when the SMO of St Petersburg, along with the CSM of Moscow, or as they are now collectively known as the Union of the Committees of the Soldiers' Mothers of Russia (or the Soldiers' Mothers), took a leading role against the use of Russian military aggression in the Chechen region. During the anti-military campaign, the activists were exposed to the inhumane conditions of the Soviet armed forces. Subsequently, the Soldiers' Mothers expanded their protest agenda to demanding reforms that would change the organization of the Russia military forces. These demands included reducing the length of military service and allowing recruits the right to alternative service and exemptions from conscription for students of higher education. Eventually, they argued that there should be an end to mandatory conscription which they claim is the foundation of problems with *dedovshchina* (a violent form of hazing or torturous initiation practices), which have resulted in the deaths and suicides of over 1,000 soldiers annually (Caiazza 1998; Lfgren 1996).

In December 1994, when the First Russian-Chechen War began, the focus of the Soldiers' Mothers both in Moscow and in St Petersburg shifted from writing petitions, educating conscripts about human rights issues and lobbying the Russian government to addressing military reform issues, organizing and staging regular demonstrations opposing the Russian-Chechen War and actively questioning Russia's use of military force to control the landlocked area of Chechnya. According to Valentina Melinkova, spokesperson for the CSM, in an interview in the *St. Petersburg Press* (7 February 1996), 'when the Russian-Chechen war erupted in 1994, the offices of the CSM received approximately one hundred telephone calls and two hundred letters per day from people seeking information about the war'.

The CSM is one of the few grassroots non-governmental organizations (NGOs) in Russia. The CSM (in Moscow) and the SMO (in St Petersburg) are both financially supported by donations from such countries as Norway, Switzerland, Germany and other international NGOs. In similar situations in other regions of the world, politicized mothers, such as the Madres of Argentina, embraced a philosophy of public non-violent protest as a method of resistance. Diana Taylor suggests that 'The Mothers of the Plaza de Mayo realized that only by being visible could they be politically effective. *Only by being visible could they stay alive*' (Jetter et al. 1997: 187). This commitment to non-violent protests enabled the Madres and other Motherist groups, such as The Mothers Against Silence of Israel or The Parents Against Silence of Israel[10] and the Mother's Front of Sri Lanka, to mobilize broad public support for their cause without having to directly confront the dominant male discourse or the military forces of the government in power.

In Sri Lanka, where the civil war had led to thousands of deaths and to the abduction of approximately 60,000 young and middle-aged men, 1,500 women formed the Mothers Front on 15 July 1990, in the southern district of Matara. Even though the Mothers Front received bomb threats and was harassed by the authorities, they were able to publicly protest the disappearance of their sons and husbands through rallies and petitions to the government. By 1999, 25,000 women were members of the Mothers' Front (De Alwis in Jeffery and Basu 1999). The women of the Sri Lankan Mothers' Front and the Russian Union of Committees of Soldiers' Mothers have been excluded from the political realms of power precisely because of their subordinate status as women and mothers which now, due to the politicization and mobilization of their Motherist identity, has enabled them to enter areas of conflict that civilian men could not enter without being at risk of being incarcerated or killed.

Following the example of the Argentinean Madres and the Sri Lankan Mother's Front, the Russian Soldiers' Mothers also entered dangerous conflict zones. During the height of Russia's bombing campaign of Chechnya in 1995, Russian television showed images of the Soldiers' Mothers braving bombs and artillery fire around Grozny, Chechnya's capital city, to pull their sons out of what they believed to be a pointless war. The CSM was evicted from their offices in Moscow, and women from both the CSM and the SMO were thrown off trains, lied to, harassed and confronted by both Russian and Chechen soldiers. Yet they continued to campaign for the end of the war. The Soldiers' Mothers marched to the frontlines of Grozny in Chechnya, where they demanded entrance into prisons and scoured the countryside in search of their sons. Some Soldiers' Mothers freed their sons from prison, some found their sons already dead, and some found nothing[11] (Caiazza 2002; Zawilski in Webber and Mathers 2005).

The Soldiers' Mothers received tremendous public support for organizing the Mothers' March for Life and Compassion in March 1995, which was covered extensively by the International and Russian media. Wherever they went in Chechnya, 'they [the Soldier's Mothers] were given emotional welcomes in war-devastated towns and villages, and bore witness to the horrific abuses of war' (Lfgren 1996). In September 1995, the CSM was awarded the Sean McBride Peace Prize and the Right Livelihood Prize (also called the Alternative Nobel Prize). According to an article in the *St. Petersburg Press* (1 February

1996), the CSM's campaign was actively supported in Germany, where 50,000 signatures in favour of their nomination by the International Peace Bureau (IPB)[12] and female German Parliamentarians was collected in 1996.

Similar to the mother activism during the beginning stages of the *infitada*, Rena Hammami explains,

> In direct confrontations with soldiers, mother activism was in many ways more successful than women's activism. Soldiers were in shock when these old traditional mothers in peasant dress physically grabbed them and struggled with them . . . It became very clear, at least in the beginning stages of the infitada, that older women were much less likely to be beaten and were more successful in getting a person out of harm's way then were young women.
> (Hammami in Jetter et al. 1997: 167)

Russian Soldiers' Mothers received similar reactions from Russian and Chechen soldiers, who were perplexed by the role that the Mothers were playing. The Russian soldiers did not regard the middle-aged 'mothers' as politically threatening, as younger female political activists might have been. Subsequently, the Soldiers' Mothers who, acting with agency as 'mothers', hold some moral authority in Russian and Chechen society, entered the war zone and actively mourned with Russian and Chechen women and their families, buried the dead and searched for their sons.

When the Soldiers' Mothers entered the Russian-Chechen war zone in 1995, this act of courage captured the collective sympathy not only of the international community but also of the Russian people themselves. Subsequently, it was largely public opinion that influenced the Russian government to end its military campaign in Chechnya in 1996. It is difficult to assess the degree of influence that the Soldiers' Mothers had on the outcome of the First Russian-Chechen War; however, it is impossible to conceive of this military conflict without taking into account the civic action and the critical role that the Soldiers' Mothers played in bringing this war to an end. Thus, this grassroots social movement led by women succeeded in the dissemination of a pacifist ideology and encouraged the development of the human rights movement in Russia. After the official end of the Russian-Chechen War on 31 August 1996, the active mobilization of the Soldiers' Mothers declined. However, during the inter-war period from 1996 to 1999, the Soldiers' Mothers continued their anti-military activities which included

1 collecting statements from Russians opposed to war and military aggression;
2 searching for missing or disappeared soldiers and civilians from the Russian-Chechen War of 1994–1996;
3 establishing physical and psychological rehabilitation centres for soldiers, civilians and their families;
4 providing legal counselling for soldiers and their families; and
5 organizing conferences and demonstrations against military aggression.

Although the demonstrations and protests that the Soldiers' Mothers have staged since the 1994–1996 Russian-Chechen War have had less public support, in November 1997, the CSM and the Novocherkassk NGO Women of the Rostov Region organized the Women for Life Without War and Violence International Conference. Five hundred participants from all the former Soviet republics attended and discussed the common human security issues that women experience as victims and refugees of war. At the conference, a Chechen woman, Khadijad Gateva, was named Woman/Mother of the Year because she had adopted 47 children who were orphaned due to the Russian-Chechen War. Families had rejected some of the orphaned children because their mothers had been victims of war rape. Some of the mothers of the children had, for various social and psychological reasons, committed suicide, and it is suspected that other Chechen women died as victims of honour killings by their husband's families.

In August 1996, the five-year Peace Accord left Chechnya's status as an independent nation undetermined: Chechens considered themselves to be an independent nation, and Russians listed Chechnya as part of the Russian Federation. In the August agreement in the city of Khassaviurt, provisions for the withdrawal of Russian troops from Chechnya and the rebuilding of the republic were made, but the agreement did not suggest that a referendum should be held about Chechnya's status. On 3 October 1996, a commission which was the result of the Khassaviurt Agreement stressed that economic measures were needed to restore and to reconstruct Chechnya and that that was their first priority. Chechen leaders referred to this provision repeatedly until the end of February 1997, but their requests were not answered.

Due to a lack of economic and humanitarian aid to the region from Russia and from the world community at large, Chechens were, during the inter-war period of 1996 to 1999, living in a lawless society which was fraught with political corruption and violent confrontations between Russians and Chechens and between Chechens themselves.

260 *Valerie Zawilski*

Daily reports from the region spoke of kidnappings and murders, escalated incidences of intimate violence against women and food and housing shortages among the refugees of war. A lucrative business had developed in kidnapping and holding people for ransom. According to Andrew Jack,

> No one seemed safe in Chechnya. Contractors hired to rebuild Chechnya, aid workers helping the sick and the hungry, Chechnya's displaced and homeless refugees, journalists, businessmen, academics and missionaries were all targets of kidnapping, torture and in some cases some people were sold into slavery. Between 1997 and 1999 . . . approximately 1,000 hostages were taken for ransom.
>
> (Jack 2004: 96)

Although the follow-up agreements dealing with the Chechen oil fields (April 1998) and law enforcement (May 1998) were enforced, the level of human security in Chechnya had descended into an internal chaos of civil war between Chechen teips, in which drug, oil and human trafficking became serious issues (Francis 2006). President Yeltsin and his government did not resolve this issue, nor was Chechnya's political status clarified. Subsequently, the future of Chechnya was to be determined by Vladimir Putin, the new president of Russia.

Islamization of Chechen nationalism: the Second Russian-Chechen War, 1999–2006

Before President Putin became the head of the Russian state, leaders of a radical Islamic movement in Chechnya and Daghestan in 1999 convened a council at which they decided that Chechen President Aslan Maskhadov should declare that Chechnya was now an Islamic state – he did this, apparently with some reluctance. The Russian-Chechen situation had become dire as the economic resources to rebuild the Chechen Republic were not forthcoming from the Russian government. In addition, the state of lawlessness that had emerged between vying warlords in Chechnya (a situation which President Maskhadov had difficulty controlling), created a human security vacuum in the region. Thus, Chechen separatists turned to Islamic organizations for financial and moral support and began to establish a form of Sharia law in an effort to regain law and order in the region (Tishkov 2004). At this point, the nature of the Russian-Chechen conflict changed. Russian authorities were convinced that an Islamization of the Russian-Chechen conflict was taking place. This social movement was believed to be similar to the rise of the Taliban's neofundamentalist movement during the politically unstable period of civil war from 1989 to 1992 in Afghanistan (Behr 2005). Although certain Islamic terms, such as 'jihad' (holy war), were now being used, the discourse in the Chechen daily media was generally specific to the cultural context of the Chechen's quest for national autonomy and not a pronounced form of religious fundamentalism known as Wahhabism[13] (Radnitz 2006).

The Islamic shift of the Chechen national movement and several other important factors set the stage for the Second Russian-Chechen War which began in 1999. Several villages in Daghestan made declarations that they also wished to be part of an independent Islamic republic, which gravely concerned the Russian government. Fighting broke out between military forces in various Daghestani villages, where separatists were able to repel the Russian forces. Thus, Russian authorities began to pursue Chechen separatists living on the borders of Daghestan in order to subdue what they believed was the beginning of an Islamic neofundamentalist movement.[14] These actions set off a wave of violence in Daghestan and throughout the region. Once again, due to the renewal of violent conflict, 259,000 Chechen civilians fled to Ingushetia, and 12,000 persons arrived in North Ossetia, where they lived as refugees (Barayedeve in Singh 2002: 363).

In Moscow, a series of bombs, which were ignited on 8, 13 and 16 September 1999, killed 235 Russian civilians and injured over 500 others. The Russian government was incensed, and although apparently the bombs may have been the work of the Daghestan Liberation Army, Russian authorities blamed Chechen leaders, and the internationally known terrorist Osama bin Laden was also accused of being responsible for these bombings (Politkovskaya 2001; Jack 2004). The targeting of military enemies with suicide bombings, the attacks on civilians and the raids made by the Chechen military leader Shamil Basayev and his followers on several villages in Daghestan led to the renewal of the Russian-Chechen conflict in 1999. According to Georgi Derlugian, Basayev was not motivated by religious fundamentalism; instead, he suggests that he was 'more interested in overthrowing the corrupt pro-Russian leadership in Daghestan than creating an Islamic state' (Derlugian 1999). Meanwhile, in Moscow, Operation Foreigner took effect as 15,000 'undesirables' were expelled from Moscow, and 70,000 racialized minorities were ordered to register with the police.

On 1 October 1999, the Second Russian-Chechen War officially began when Russian ground forces re-entered Chechnya, and the Russian Air Force bombed Grozny with ground-to-ground air missiles.

Eventually, Grozny fell under the control of the Russian military on 1 February 2000. By mid-January 2000, the CSM reported that 3,000 Russian soldiers had died and another 5,000 had been wounded (Politkovskaya 2001: 327). Conversely, the Russian Ministry of Defence reported, on 10 August 2005, that roughly 3,450 Russian army soldiers were killed in action between 1999 and 2005 and an additional 8,000 soldiers had been wounded. The CSM of Russia estimates are higher, and they report that 12,000 to 13,000 servicemen were killed, with another 25,000 wounded since 1999 (Vaknin 2005).

Although the number of causalities among the Russian military forces was undeniably grim, the world community was shocked to learn that 250,000 Chechen civilians died during the two Russian-Chechen Wars between 1994 and 2006. Unlike the First Russian-Chechen War, international non-governmental agencies, such as the International Red Cross, Human Rights Watch, Amnesty International, Doctors Without Borders, journalists, reporters, human rights and aid workers and other organizations, were not allowed into the region. Thus, there is limited information about what actually took place during this war. According to a statement submitted to the United Nations in February 2006 by the Society for Threatened Peoples, an NGO based in Germany, 'The second war in the Chechen Republic of the Russian Federation has played an integral role in the rollback of human rights in President Vladimir Putin's Russia and has affected its political trajectory, helping to strengthen those in favour of authoritarianism'. The Society for Threatened Peoples states that the war had led to a rise in terrorism not only in Chechnya but also in the neighbouring republics of Ingushetia and Daghestan. The organization has documented examples of human rights abuses, including masked security forces kidnapping fathers and sons as well as stripping a young man to his underwear, beating him and throwing him onto flames (Society for Threatened Peoples 2006). During the inter-war period of 1996 to 1999, kidnappings by Chechens were frequent in Chechnya. During the Second Russian-Chechen War, Russian *krontrakniki* (mercenary soldiers) not only were kidnapping civilians for ransom but also were paid by the number of searches and roadblocks they completed. These searches were a convenient method of concealing their actions as they took 'blood money' that supplemented their official pay, as they were no longer paid by the length of their military contract (Steele 2001). In 2006, a Human Rights Watch report stated, 'The civilian population of Chechnya lives in constant fear', and it added that 'today Chechnya has become one of the most dangerous places in the world for civilians to live' (Rotstein 2006).

In March 2004, over 100,000 Chechens who were living as internally displaced persons in refugee tent camps in the neighbouring republic of Ingushetia did not want to return to Chechnya. In an attempt to normalize the situation, the Kremlin ordered the refugees to return to Chechnya, and if they did, they would benefit from President Putin's 2004 Peace Plan. The Peace Plan included (1) amnesty for rebels who returned to live in Chechnya; (2) the possibility for Chechens to elect a new Chechen president; and (3) $20,000 USD would be given to each returning family. The deadline for the plan was 1 March 2004. Some refugees accepted the offer and did return to their homes, but thousands of displaced persons were afraid to return to their homeland due to the ongoing lack of human security. In a letter to President Putin in 2004, Chechen citizens voiced their concerns about the lack of protection for civilians returning to live in the wartorn region.

> Dear Mr. President: Over a period of four years, unknown people in camouflage have kidnapped 255 persons. One hundred and ninety-seven of them have disappeared, 39 were returned to their villages bearing signs of torture, and in 18 cases corpses were found bearing signs of a violent death. One can say this data is not the whole truth, because there are many more victims and this happened in a very small territory with only 13 villages so you can understand how enormous our tragedy and pain is. In most cases the kidnappings were carried out with the help of military equipment such as APCs [armoured personnel carriers] and military cars. Some of these same cars were found on the territory of the military command's office or in the police headquarters. These facts make it evident that, in most cases, these crimes were committed by representatives of federal law enforcement.
> (Families of Chechens 2004)

Even though the Chechen government set up temporary accommodation for returning refugees, people who did return said that they had very little support from the Russian government. 'It would have been better to stay in Ingushetia', said Rumisa Chokayeva, a 47-year-old German language teacher who returned to Grozny in October 2004, after living for four years in a tent camp, because 'there are no international organizations to aid us here' (Chokayeva in Page 2004).

Even refugee camps, such as the camp called *Bart* (a word in North Caucasus language meaning 'concord' or 'harmony') in Ingushetia, 3,200 refugees were provided with only the bare necessities of life in terms of food, medicine, shelter and sanitation. In an effort to close the camps and to convince Chechens to return home, the Chechen Resettlement Committee, who represented the pro-Kremlin administration in Chechnya, came to the camp promising that the refugees would be compensated for their homes that were destroyed in the war and that they should immediately return to Chechnya. Many refugees were concerned about the reports of people disappearing and the ongoing torture and killing of civilians in the region. According to Lora Guenther, a camp refugee, the promise of compensation was not enough for the war-weary and Kremlin-wary refugees. Thus, the authorities used intimidation tactics, such as switching off the refugees' gas and electricity. When this form of coercion did not work and the refugees refused to leave, they then began to receive threats from a government representative who said that 'if you do not leave the camp by 10 March 2004, President Kadyrov's militias will show up' (Guenther in Hodge 2004). Thus, the human rights codes of the Universal Declaration of Human Rights Articles 13 and 14 were violated by the local authorities. Article 13, the right to free movement in and out of the country, and Article 14, the right to asylum in other countries where the individual will be free from persecution, were violated (Universal Declaration of Human Rights, Articles 13 and 14, 1948).

By 1 March 2004, approximately 65,000 refugees did return to Chechnya, but a substantial number of them did not. Instead, they fled to various countries in Europe where they applied for political asylum. According to a UN report, there was a drop in the overall number of people in the world applying for asylum in 2004. However, the highest number of political asylum seekers in Europe in 2004 was Chechens from the Russian Federation. The largest Chechen community in Europe today can be found in Austria, where the Chechen diaspora includes approximately 17,000 people. France and Germany report that there are approximately 10,000 refugees living in their respective countries. There are also several thousand Chechen refugees living in Belgium, Norway, Sweden and Poland. These countries are considered to be only temporary residences by Chechen refugees. Canada and the Middle East also have Chechen communities, which include several hundred people (Partos 2005). In 2000, European Union leaders allocated $286 million to the European Refugee Fund (ERF). This fund was replenished and extended to 2013, and 628 million euro was divided among different states in the European Union, based on objective criteria which depended on the number of asylum seekers. In addition to the ERF, The Hague Program, which was adopted in November 2004, was put into place to give 10 million euro in aid, in the form of emergency funds, to house, feed and offer medical assistance to Chechen refugees. These funds are allocated to EU member states which, due to their geographical location, face a disproportionately high influx of asylum seekers. These funds are especially important to newer EU member states, such as Cyprus, Malta, Poland and Slovakia, which have seen a 4 per cent increase in asylum seekers (ibid.).

The price of peace in Chechnya

Even though there are many Chechens living in Europe, the largest community of Chechens who live outside of Chechnya live in the Russian Federation. Moscow reports indicate that close to 100,000 Chechens live in Moscow[15] and several thousand live in outlying areas and in smaller cities in the region (Vatchagaev 2008a). In the last few years, there has been a rise in hate speeches and beatings of racialized minorities, especially Chechens and other minorities from the North Caucasus by youth groups, such as *Nashi* (Our Guys), and neo-Nazi groups in major urban centres in Russia. One of the goals of the youth group Nashi is to combat racism. Nashi has enjoyed some support from the Kremlin. The organization's strong patriotic message attempts to exploit xenophobic feelings in the country, a charge that its leaders' deny. Critics of the group have suggested that Nashi's anti-racist rhetoric is far too selective and that it is directed primarily at the Russian government's opponents. Despite Nashi's political actions, most opinion polls in Russia have found that 62 per cent of the general population, especially middle-aged and older women, strongly opposed the Second Russian-Chechen War. This is a reversal of opinion polls carried out in November 1999, in which 62 per cent of the Russian public supported the military operations and only 27 per cent thought that open peace talks should be held. Initially, the Russian population supported the new military intervention in Chechnya in 1999. The Putin administration, after the 11 September 2001, terrorist attacks on the United States, shifted the 'framing' of the Second Russian-Chechen War from a nationalist secessionist war to a global war on terrorism, which was similar to the global War on Terror that the West was facing (O'Loughlin et al. 2002) After the Beslan school hostage crisis in 2004, Chechen separatists lost some of their Russian and international support. However, in March 2004, after five years of war, this trend was reversed, as only 23 per cent of the Russian population thought that the military campaign should continue and 65 per cent of the population thought that the Russian and Chechen leaders should engage in open peace talks (Le Huerou 2004).

Today, Russians believe that the only solution to the Russian-Chechen conflict is through open peace negotiations between the Russian and Chechen governments. At one time this seemed like a possibility when the country was led by President Maskhadov, who was elected by the Chechens in 1997. President Maskhadov repeatedly claimed that his government did not sanction the Beslan school hostage crisis, that he did not engage in terrorist tactics and that this was the work of his rival, Shamil Basayev (Dlugy 2005). Even before the world community became focused on the Chechen question due to the Beslan school hostage crisis in 2004, Russia was asked by international human rights observers and diplomats to find a political resolution to the Chechen problem[16] (Graney in Bahchelli, Bartmann and Srebrnik 2004). President-in-exile Maskhadov requested a three-week cease-fire in February 2005 and agreed to have open, 'unconditional' peace talks with President Putin during the second week of March 2005 in Strasbourg, Germany.[17] These peace talks were to be mediated by Valentina Melinkova, chair of the Union of Soldiers' Mothers. Unfortunately, the peace negotiations never took place as Maskhadov was murdered by Russian special operations military forces in his home on 8 March 2005.

After the death of Maskhadov in 2005, interim leader President Sergey Abramov resigned in 2006. The de facto emissary in Chechnya, Ramzan Kadyrov, took over as the interim leader of Chechnya. The Russian government then imposed a top-down political solution, and Chechen citizens were asked once again to return to their homes in Chechnya. In addition to the promise of money to rebuild their homes, amnesty was to be granted to parties who shot and killed people during the First and Second Russian-Chechen Wars[18] (Cherkazov 2008). The elections that were promised by the Russian government were held. According to official reports, on 2 December 2007, 99.6 per cent of the Chechen population voted for President Putin and the United Russia Party in the Russian State Duma elections. Subsequently, Ramzan Kadyrov became the president of Chechnya.

In 2008, Dukuvakha Abdurakhmanov, speaker of the Chechen Parliament, said that in Chechnya 'There is peace. People are coming back. They are getting married and they are working. We have a new airport. We have schools. People are satisfied. Credit for this transformation comes down to one man. Grozny is completely different from three years ago. The victory is due to President Kadyrov' (Abdurakhmanov in Harding 2008). In its return to peace, Chechnya has been transformed into what Luke Harding describes as a 'totalitarian fiefdom with a flourishing personality cult of the 31-year-old President

Kadyrov'. He continues, saying that 'Kadyrov's distinctive features can been seen at bus stops, along boulevards and at the airport' (ibid.).

During the Second Russian-Chechen War from 2004 to 2006, Grozny had the dubious distinction of being named the most destroyed city in the world, according to UN reports. The rapid reconstruction of the war-ravaged region has, however, come at a price. While Chechnya's unemployment rate is 80 per cent and although there are new apartment blocks being built in central Grozny, there is an acute accommodation shortage for returning refugees. Many Chechens have decided not to stay in Chechnya and instead plan to immigrate to Europe. The main obstacle faced by Chechens who wish to leave Chechnya and Russia is the daunting challenge of obtaining a passport for travel abroad, which costs over $300 USD, or two to three months' salary. A second barrier for immigrants is the frequent refusal of European and US embassies to consider visa applications submitted by Chechens. This in turn forces people to seek contact with numerous mafia groups specializing in the illegal trafficking of Chechens from Ukraine into Poland.

In December 2007, more than 1,200 Chechen refugees were registered at the Paris airport, the largest number of Chechen refugees to leave Russia since the beginning of the Second Russian-Chechen War in 1999. Chechen travellers usually purchase tickets to countries that do not require a visa, and they then choose a route with a stopover in Paris instead of flying directly to their destination. Upon arriving at the Paris airport, they immediately apply for refugee status instead of moving on to the transit hall. Although Chechens have now flooded into European countries requesting immigrant status, Maribek Vatchagaev explains that regardless of where Chechens live, it is a common practice among Chechens to request that, if they die while they are living in the diaspora, that their bodies should be buried in Chechnya. During the Soviet period, burying a Chechen outside of Chechnya was considered to be an insult to the family; thus, this tradition continues today (Vatchagaev 2008a). In the past 15 years, Chechen civilians and their families have fled from the violence of two Russian-Chechen wars. Currently they are forced to live as impoverished refugees in European and Central Asian countries, but they will, as their ancestors before them did, return, one way or another, to their beloved homeland – Chechnya.

Notes

1 The Union of the Committees of Soldiers' Mothers of Russia (Союз Комитетов Солдатских Матерей *Soyuz Komitetov Soldatskikh Materey*

Rossiy) works to expose human rights violations within the Russian military. The organization was founded in 1989. Before 1998, it was known as the Committee of Soldiers' Mothers of Russia.

2 Although the correct name of the region is Chechnya-Ichkeria, it is most often referred to as Chechnya. Ichkeria is the northern mountainous area of the Republic; sometimes the media refer to Chechnya as the Republic of Ichkeria. From this point on, I will refer to the region by the less formal and more commonly used name: Chechnya.

3 Conversely, in 1959, the ratio of Russians to Chechens was higher in Chechnya. At that time the total population was 710,424 people, of which 49 per cent of the population was Russian and only 34 per cent was Chechen. This was due to the fact that in 1944 massive numbers of Chechens had been deported from the region and only began to return in 1957–1958 to Chechnya.

4 Daghestan is the republic, which is the farthest east of the seven republics that make up the North Caucasus; 1.8 million people live there, and they speak 34 distinct languages. The largest ethnic group in the region is the Avars, who are estimated to be about 500,000 to 600,000 people. The other people living in the region may be divided into 14 linguistic groups which have their own names and dialects.

5 The most influential teip is the *Benoy* teip, which has 70,000 to 80,000 members. The Chechen military leaders Basayev and Kadyrov are from this clan (Bazarya 2006).

6 General Dzhokhor Dudayev was a Chechen Muslim who was born in 1944 and grew up as a deportee in Kazakhastan. He eventually rose to the rank of general in the Soviet Air Force, graduating from the Gagarin Air Force Academy in 1974. He did not disclose his ethnicity to anyone while he was in the military forces. In 1987, he was the commander of the air base in Tartu, Estonia. He refused to violently suppress the Estonian Singing Revolution by shutting down the Estonian Parliament and television stations in Tartu, Estonia, where an independence movement had developed. In 1990, his unit withdrew from Estonia, and he resigned from the air force and returned to Chechnya. He earned the love and respect of the Baltic peoples. Female Baltic snipers were among his military units who fought against the Russian forces in the First Russian-Chechen War. President Dudayev was killed in 1996.

7 In Moscow in June and July 1994, many examples of discrimination toward Chechens were taking place. Russians had been warned by the media and local authorities to be cautious and leery of Chechen men (and women) who were considered to be dangerous and unpredictably violent. Riots and other forms of racial violence occurred in marketplaces in Moscow. On 3 July 1994, for example, a car bomb went off in downtown Moscow. Russians immediately blamed the Chechen mafia for the bomb. On a daily basis Chechen men were routinely singled out, detained and harassed by police officers (Zawilski 1994).

8 Aslan Maskhadov was born in Kazakhstan in 1951 to a family who had been deported there by Stalin in 1944. At the age of six, he returned to his homeland. Trained as an artillery officer in the Red Army, he became chief of staff of the Chechen rebel forces during the first war of independence, between 1994 and 1996. He outmanoeuvred numerically superior

Russian forces and finally drove the Kremlin to the bargaining table. In January 1997, he defeated hard-line opponent Shamil Basayev to become elected as the first internationally recognized president of Chechnya. He was killed by Russian forces on 8 March 2005 (Dlugy 2005).

9 The Russian constitution provides a section that discusses conscription (Article 59). Under the Law on Military Duty and Military Service, as amended, boys must register for the draft before the end of March in the year in which they reach 17. Those aged between 18 and 27 are subject to the draft, which lasts 24 months or 12 months for university graduates. Candidates for voluntary military service must be 18, and conscripts may transfer from compulsory to voluntary service after six months (Article 34). The 1997 Law on Mobilization Preparations and Mobilization, which sets out liabilities for call-up and military service, states that only those subject to federal conscription laws – that is, 18-year-olds – are eligible to be called for service. There were no reports of under-18s being called up for military service (Constitution, www. constitution.ru. and Russian Federation Legal Acts on Civil Military Relations, Collection of Documents, Moscow, 2003).

10 Simona Sharoni claims that despite the insistence of members of the group explaining this, Parents Against Silence was a group that included men. However, the media and public insisted on calling the group Mothers Against Silence (Sharoni in Jetter et al. 1997: 153).

11 In the case of Private Vladimir from Bashkir, Chris Hunter recounts, 'Vladimir, a 21-year-old soldier from Bashkir in the Urals, told me that he had been doing military service for six months before being sent to the North Caucasus at the beginning of December. He had used a gun twice before in his life when he and other young men were put into a tank and told to drive from the military base in Dagestan into Grozny. They were stopped at a blockade of Chechen civilians on the Chechen border where they gave themselves up. From 11 December to 13 January, Vladimir was kept as prisoner in the basement of the presidential palace. He describes the conditions as being satisfactory, the attitude of the Chechens towards him and his 130 colleagues decent. Vladimir was released to return home because his mother came to Grozny to find him. Galina Sevruk of the Soldier's Mothers Committee was told by the Chechens guarding the palace, that if the mothers of Russian soldiers came to Grozny to collect their sons they would be allowed to take them home with them. However, soldiers that were set free were warned, that if they were caught a second time, they would be shot – as happened recently with one group of former prisoners' (Hunter 2007).

12 The International Peace Bureau is the world's oldest and most comprehensive peace network, comprising 19 internationals, plus 140 national/local member organizations of all types in over 40 countries. It was established in 1892 in Bern, and it was awarded the Peace Prize in 1910 (thus earning the right to make nominations). Thirteen of its officers have been awarded the Peace Prize individually over the years. The current bureau president is Dr Maj-Britt Theorin, MEP, former Swedish Ambassador for Disarmament.

13 Wahhabism is an austere, uncompromising version of Islam that harkens back to an early Muslim era. Mohammed Ibn Abd-al Wahhab, an

Arab Bedouin born in 1703, who became an important religious teacher, preached it. He believed that the Islam of his time had become weak and corrupt because Muslims had fallen away from their original faith. He advocated the strictest interpretation of the Koran, total adherence to Sharia law and absolute rejection of all foreign influences. He converted the ruling family of the Nedj region to his creed, and their tribal forces captured Mecca in 1803 and Medina in 1805. The Wahhabis, in keeping with Islam's policy against idolatry, destroyed all shrines in these cities. The heart of the Wahhabi movement was the *Ikhwan* (warrior-preachers), who were modeled after the *Ansar* (devoted warriors) and who accompanied the prophet Mohammed in his early struggle to bring Islam to Arabia. The Ikhwan continued to spread Wahhabism across Arabia and Central Asia until the 20th century.

14 During the latter part of the 1990s, the Chechens gave some mixed public messages using some Islamic terms that were attributed to the Islamization of the movement. Basayev, who was considered to be the new spiritual leader of the movement and a Wahhabi Muslim, used Islamic messages to justify the war. Maskhadov also made more references to Islam in his public speeches than he had done in the past (Radnitz 2006).

15 The intellectual core of the Chechen diaspora is concentrated in Moscow and St Petersburg. There are some foundations that claim to represent Chechens, but they are not well supported by the Chechen community. The community is divided between supporters of Kadyrov and those who are separatists. The younger members of the community are generally more radical and more likely to support a version of Islam taught by Sheikh Fathi, a Chechen Salafi leader who died in 1997. He is viewed as a true *mujahid* and young Chechens support his goal of creating a Chechen state and propagating Salfi ideas among all Chechens (Vatchagaev 2008b).

16 For example, Kate Graney points out that editorials in the *New York Times* (28 October 2002) and the *Wall Street Journal* (28 October 2002) called on Russia to find a political solution to the crisis in Chechnya. Even before the hostage drama took place, high-profile figures, such as former US national security advisor Zbigniew Brzezinski, had called on Russia to find a political solution. The Council of Europe Chechen Committee also continued to press Russia to find a political solution. See the *Washington Post*, 21 June 2002 (Graney in Bahchelli 2004).

17 The memorandum for the peace talks included more detailed proposals by the Chechen side, which stated that the main elements of a political solution to the conflict are (1) a ceasefire and demilitarization, with the participation of peacekeeping forces formed by both sides; and (2) a political settlement between the Russian Federation and the Chechen Republic of Ichkeria based on the 'Peace Treaty and Principles of Interrelation between Russian Federation and Chechen Republic of Ichkeria' signed by then Russian President Boris Yeltsin and then Chechen President Aslan Maskhadov on 12 May 1997.

18 Alexander Cherkasov, a representative of the internationally acclaimed Memorial Human Rights Centre in Russia which specializes in monitoring the human rights situation in the North Caucasus, has reservations about the amnesty agreement which he says 'should not cover those who held hostages and committed crimes against civilians' (Cherkazov 2008).

References

Annan, K. 2005. *Report of the Secretary-General: In Larger Freedom: Towards Security, Development and Human Rights for All.* New York: United Nations. Doc. A/59/2005.

Bahchelli, T, B. Bartmann and H. Srebrnik (eds.). 2004. *De Facto States: The Quest for Sovereignty.* London: Routledge.

Bazarya, I. 2006. 'The Phenomenon of Chechen "Black Widows": Becoming a Suicide Terrorist', Conference paper. Columbia University, New York: Association for the Studies in Nationalism. 23–25 March.

Behr, R. 2005. 'Chechnya Loses Its Yasser Arafat', *The Guardian.* 8 March.

Caiazza, A. 1998. 'Russia Meets Its Matriarchs', *Transitions*, vol. 5 (1).

Campana, A. 2004. 'Construction of National Identity and Resentments: A Comparative Study of the Crimean Tatar and Chechen Case', Conference paper. Columbia University, New York: Association for the Studies in Nationalism. 15–17 April.

Chen, L., J. Leaning and V. Narsimhan. 2003. 'A Human Security Agenda for Global Health', in L. Chen, J. Leaning and V. Narsimhan (eds.), *Global Health Challenges for Human Security.* Cambridge: Harvard University Press.

Cherkazov, A. 2008. 'Russian Human Rights Activists Approve of Kadyrov's Amnesty Initiative', *Interfax: Moscow.* 21 February.

Constitution and Russian Federation Legal Acts on Civil Military Relations. 2003. Collection of Documents. Moscow. www.constitution.ru.

Derlugian, G. M. 1999. 'Che Guevaras in Turbans', *New Left Review*, vol. 27 (3). September.

Dlugy, Y. 2005. 'Maskhadov: Chechnya's Moderate Rebel Leader', *Associated Federal Press.* 8 March.

Elkner, J. 2005. 'Dedovshchina and the Committee of Soldiers' Mothers under Gorbachev', *The Journal of Power Institutions in Post-Soviet Societies.* Pipss.org 2.

Families of Chechens. 2004. 'Letter to Vladimir Putin'. *The Guardian* International Edition, February 19, 2004.

Francis, C. 2006. 'Russian Conflict Management during the Chechen Conflict: Conflict Resolution Initiatives in Chechnya from 1995 Till 2005', Conference paper. Columbia University, New York: Association for the Studies in Nationalism. 23–25 March.

Harding, L. 2008. 'There Is Peace: We Have a New Airport: People Are Satisfied: The Once War-Torn Country Has Been Transformed But Change Has Come at a Price', *The Guardian.* 22 February. www.guardian.co.uk.

Hodge, N. 2004. 'Chechens Go Home!', *Election Week in Russia*, vol. 11: 22 AMPT, 9 March. www.slate.com.

Hojer M. 2005. 'Reforming Habitus, Reordering Meaningful Worlds: Soldiers' Mothers and Social Change in Post-Socialist Russia', thesis submitted for the Candidate of Science. Copenhagen, Denmark: Institute of Anthropology, University of Copenhagen.

Hunter, C. 2007. 'The Soldiers' Stories', *Peace News Ltd.* webmaster@peacenews.info.

Jack, A. 2004. *Inside Putin's Russia: Can There Be Reform without Democracy*. New York: Oxford University Press.

Jeffery, P. and A. Basu (eds.). 1999. *Resisting the Sacred and the Secular: Women's Activism and Politicized Religion in South East Asia*. New Delhi: Kali Women.

Jetter, A., A. Orleck and D. Tayor (eds.). 1997. *The Politics of Motherhood: Activist Voices from the Left to Right*. Lebanon, IN: University Press of New England.

Kanapianova, R. M. 2008. 'Women in Structures of Authority', *Sociological Research*, vol. 47 (4): 61–73.

Kline, E. 2005. *Chechen History*. Moscow: Andrei Sakharov Foundation. www.newsbee.net. Accessed 1 June 2009.

Krasner, S. D. 1999. *Sovereignty: Organized Hypocrisy*. Princeton: Princeton University Press.

———. 2001. 'Problematic Sovereignty', in S. D. Krasner (ed.), *Problematic Sovereignty*. New York: Columbia University Press.

Le Huerou, A. 2004. 'Nation, Identity, and Conflict', Conference paper. Columbia University, New York: Association for the Studies in Nationalism. 15–17 April.

Lfgren, M. 1996. 'Russian Mothers for Peace, Oppose Sons in War', *Inter-Press Service Journal*. 7 March. www.ips.org.

O'Loughlin, J., G. Tuathail and V. Kolossov. 2002. 'A Risky Westward Turn? Putin's 9–11 Script and Ordinary Russians', *Europe-Asia Studies*, vol. 65 (1).

Page, J. 2004. 'Kremlin Orders Refugees to Return to "Peaceful" Chechnya', *The Times*. 21 February.

Partos, G. 2005. 'Analysis: Europe's Asylum Trends', *BBC News*, vol. 16: 55 GMT, 1 March.

Politkovskaya, A. 2001. *A Dirty War: A Russian Reporter in Chechnya*. London: Harvill Press.

Radnitz, S. 2006. 'Look Who's Talking! Islamic Discourse in the Chechen Wars', *Nationalities Papers*, vol. 34 (2): 237–56.

Rotstein, N. 2006. 'Chechen Immigration Here and There', *Medill News Service*. 28 June.

Ruban, L. S. 1994. 'Developments of Conflict in a Multi-Ethnic Region', Paper for the Institute of Socio-Political Research, Russian Academy of Sciences. Moscow.

Singh, G. (ed.). 2002. *Ethno-Nationalism and Emerging World (Dis)Order*. New Delhi: Kanishka Publishers.

Speckhard, A. and K. Akhmedova. Steele, J. 2001. 'No One Knows What the War Is about, or When It Will End', *The Guardian*. United Kingdom. 27 July.

Tishkov, V. 2004. *Chechnya: Life in a War-Torn Society*. Berkeley: University of California Press.

United Nations High Commissioner of Human Rights. 1997. 'Situation of Human Rights in Chechnya: Statement of the 44th Human Rights Meeting', Geneva. 27 February 1995.

Universal Declaration of Human Rights. 1948. 'Article 13 and Article 14', *Global Importune*. Minneapolis, MN. www.globalimportune.org.
Vaknin, S. 2005. 'Chechnya War: Economic Cost to Russia', *Global Politician*. 10 March. www.globalpolitician.com.
Valentino, B, P. Huth and D. Balch-Lindsay. 2004. 'Mass Killing and Guerilla Warfare', *International Organization*, vol. 58 (2): 375–407.
Vatchagaev, M. 2008a. 'Chechnya's Exodus to Europe', *Chechnya Weekly*, vol. 9 (3): 24.
———. 2008b. 'The Chechen Diaspora in Russia', *Jamestown Foundation Weekly*. 27 March.
Webber, S. L. and J. G. Mathers (eds.). 2005. *Military and Society in Post-Soviet Russia*. Manchester: Manchester University Press.
Zawilski, V. 2004. 'Constructing Images of the Other', Unpublished field notes. Moscow.
Zdravomyslova, E. 2005. 'Peaceful Initiatives Soldiers' Mothers Movements in Russia'. www.ips.org.

Part IV
Alternative and transitional approaches to human security

11 Security Council Resolution 1325

Toward gender equality in peace and security policymaking

Soumita Basu

Introduction

There appears to be an inherent contradiction between UN Security Council Resolution 1325 (SCR 1325) on women, peace and security and the UN Security Council (SC), which adopted the resolution in October 2000. The (normative) international policy instrument is at odds with the SC, an institution often criticized for its implicit support to the sustenance of a militarized interstate system (Väyrynen 2004; Whitworth 2004). As demonstrated in the extensive literature on women, war and peace, many challenges to the security and wellbeing of women lie in this international arena (Enloe 1990; Lorentzen and Turpin 1998; Rehn and Sirleaf 2002). The primary aim of this chapter is to explore the manifestation of such contradictions between SCR 1325 and the SC, following the passage of the resolution in October 2000. To do so, I examine the ways in which the council mobilized the human security elements of SCR 1325 into its subsequent resolutions up until the passage of SCR 1820, the second SCR on women, peace and security in June 2008.

SCR 1325 is the first international policy instrument of its kind that explicitly recognizes the gendered nature of both war and peace processes. It includes recommendations for the protection of women in conflict situations and their participation in peace negotiations, post-conflict reconstruction and conflict prevention. A glance at the issues for which SCR 1325 has been used in the text of subsequent Security Council resolutions (SCRs), however, indicates that the council has focused more on 'protection' compared to other components of the resolution. This trend is cemented with the passage of SCR 1820, which is primarily directed toward addressing the challenges of sexual and gender-based violence against women during armed conflict. Thus, elements more compatible with the traditional thinking of the SC (e.g. seeing women in need of protection) are adapted into the proceedings over others that recognize, for instance, the agency of women in both exacerbation and alleviation of armed conflict. This stifling of the potential of SCR 1325 may well illustrate the editors' contention that 'human security [which, as discussed next, implies more than protection of human beings] cannot exist within a militarized security system'. Through a close examination of my primary data, the 494 SCRs bookmarked between SCRs 1325 and 1820, I seek to highlight the inherent contradictions between the SC and SCR 1325.

Further, the interface here is not between a monolithic institution, the UNSC, and a static piece of international policy mechanism, SCR 1325. A network of actors, including UN member states, civil society organizations and other UN entities, such as UN Women (earlier UNIFEM), have been involved in driving the 'women, peace and security' (WPS) agenda at the SC. The diversity among these actors with regard to their interpretation of the resolution and its implementation makes it possible to envisage multiple future pathways, including some which may be more inclined toward human security aspects. Staying within the precincts of the SC and the text of SCRs in particular, I focus on these multiple interpretations and the contestations therein as a promising sign for future policymaking on such issues. A major proportion of the work of the SC may be dominated by militaristic, state-centric considerations. However, by playing host to the SCRs on 'women, peace and security', and by providing the political context for the policy questions that these resolutions generate, the SC offers useful mechanisms for human security advocates.

The chapter is divided into three sections. First, I present a critical overview of the mandate and work of the SC and contrast it with the concept of human security proposed by the editors. The evolution of the human security discourse at the United Nations and the passage of SCR 1325 are also discussed here. This is followed, in the second section, by an analysis of the use of SCR 1325 in subsequent SCRs. The continued use of the resolution, resulting also in the passage of SCR 1820, implies that the SC has adapted some human security standards relating to gender, albeit in particular ways. I seek to explore the articulations and implications of these interpretations. In the third and final section, I discuss SCR 1820 with respect to two aspects of its origins. These also demonstrate the key argument in this article regarding contestations in and around the SC. Although the 'protection' component of SCR 1325, developed further in SCR 1820, appears to be most compatible with the engagement of the SC with the WPS agenda, debates preceding its passage in 2008 highlight the vibrancy of the politics around this agenda.

This chapter, in the second edition of the volume, maintains its focus on the evolution of the WPS agenda until the passage of SCR 1820 in 2008. Since 2009, six additional WPS resolutions have been adopted by the council. Three of these, SCRs 1888 (2009a), 1960 (2010) and 2106 (2013a), are centred on 'protection'. The remaining, SCRs 1889 (2009b), 2122 (2013b) and 2242 (2015), have sought to highlight and promote women's roles in peacebuilding and conflict prevention, and to strengthen institutional mechanisms for the implementation of the WPS agenda. It is notable that this study was undertaken prior to the passage of the third resolution, but it echoes the trajectory of the WPS resolutions and their subsequent implementation by the SC in more recent years (see PeaceWomen 2017a).

Gender, human security and the Security Council

The concept of human security has been widely interpreted both in the realm of international policymaking and in scholarly work (see Burgess 2004). I align my research here with the position taken by Asha Hans and Betty A. Reardon in this volume. They write that human security derives from 'the experience and expectation of wellbeing'. The human security framework presented by the editors resonates with the 'non-traditional' and 'critical' approaches to security that have grown in strength since the 1990s (for overviews, see inter alia, Collins 2007; Smih 2000). The emphasis on human wellbeing, as present also in the writings of Hans and Reardon in this volume, is different from the traditional, state-centric, militaristic notion of security. Moreover, the editors identify patriarchal violence as both underlying and being symptomatic of human insecurities in global politics.

As I understand it, patriarchal violence here refers to the violence – structural and personal/physical – perpetrated through the societal institution of patriarchy that systematically treats women as inferior to men in human society. The concept of gender is particularly useful in understanding this framing of patriarchal violence. Gender may be defined as a relational notion that is articulated in a 'set of variable but socially and culturally constructed characteristics' (Tickner 1997: 614). It embodies relationships marked by inequalities in power wherein perceived masculine values, such as power, autonomy and rationality, are linked to perceived feminine ones, such as weakness, dependence and emotions, in a manner that gives precedence to masculine characteristics over the feminine in all political practices.

Using the lens of gender and drawing on experiences of women, feminist scholars have uncovered the patriarchal underpinnings of the security discourse that dominates international politics (Cockburn 2007; Reardon 1996). They/we are particularly concerned with the ways in which militarization of societies – through armed conflicts as well as anticipatory preparations – tend to strengthen forces of patriarchy. 'When people develop the attitude that differences can be settled through violent means, then we perpetuate a mentality that brings violence into all human relations, and right into the home, where women and children are the primary victims' (Women for Mutual Security 1991 cited in Reardon 1996: 226). Thus, theorizing on the basis of women's experiences of violence, feminist scholars point to the dangers of armed conflict and the zero-sum power dynamics that drive these.

Women's insecurities in armed conflict emerge primarily from the dual forces of patriarchy and militarization, and from the violence against women and human relations that they respectively denote. However, as many scholars have demonstrated, insecurities for women do not relate solely to armed conflicts (Cockburn and Zarkov 2002: 10; Enloe 1990). Attempts to secure women must thus address not only the points at which patriarchy and militarization intersect during armed conflicts but also in contexts where they appear independent of each other. The concept of human security – with its focus on human beings – provides a compatible framework within which to think about addressing concerns regarding women's security. As suggested in the contributions to this volume, many resources for realizing human security have been identified in this political realm. My focus in this chapter is on the first two SCRs on women, peace and security. In this section, I present a brief outline of the relevant work of the SC and introduce the first resolution – SCR 1325.

Potential of the Security Council

The SC may well appear to be a curious choice in view of concerns relating to human security. Of all the UN bodies, it has been the most steadfast in clinging to the political goals and alignments which characterized the international arena following World War II. Consisting of 15 member state representatives at a time, the SC is nevertheless driven significantly by the interests of its five permanent members – China, France, Russia (formerly the Union of Soviet Socialist Republics or USSR), the United Kingdom and the United States. These victorious nations of WWII hold the veto power that allows them decisive stay in all SC decisions. The council mandate is governed by Chapters VI and

VII of the UN Charter and relates to the 'maintenance of international peace and security'. Toward this overarching goal, however, respect for the sovereignty of member states has been one of the key guiding principles.

The council has traditionally tended to rely on diplomacy and economic sanctions as tools to implement its resolutions. The use of armed force only gained significance in later years, particularly since the late 1980s, as the United Nations expanded its role through peace operations (see inter alia Krasno 2004; Thakur 2006). In view of its state-centric nature, control by a handful of powerful member states and tacit acceptance of a militaristic international status quo, the SC appears to be at odds with human security aspirations. This chapter argues, however, that there is both scope and need for reappropriating the work of the SC in this regard. Transformations inside and outside the United Nations following the end of the Cold War encourage such an engagement.

The 1990s heralded a new era for the council, as the international context within which the SC carried out its functions was markedly different from the one in which the United Nations was created (Malone 2004; Mingst and Karns 2000). As the United Nations gained visibility as an international actor in its own right – and not merely as a convenient platform for interstate power politics – it began paying greater attention to issues that went beyond the narrow interests of its member states. Former Secretary-General (SG) Pérez de Cuellar, for instance, wrote that his office [the UN Secretariat] had to serve two constituencies: 'the governments of the member states and the people from whom the governments act' (de Cuellar 1993 cited in Cronin 2002: 57). The SC was now working as part of an organization that was beginning to take direct responsibility for the welfare and protection of human populations. Corresponding to these changes, the understanding of security at the United Nations also became more human oriented (MacFarlane and Khong 2006; Thakur 2006).

Boutros Boutros-Ghali, the Secretary-General who succeeded de Cuellar, submitted one of the first and most influential reports – entitled 'An Agenda for Peace: Preventive Diplomacy, Peacemaking and Peacekeeping' (1992) – on expanding the understanding of the security sector for the United Nations and the SC. More broadly, the 'Human Development Report' (1994) of the UN Development Programme (UNDP) brought the discourse of 'human security' – that sought to privilege human referents in UN policymaking on security and development – into the UN lexicon (see also MacFarlane and Khong 2006). The report identified seven areas of concerns for global security policymaking: economic, food, health, environmental, personal, community and political

(UNDP 1994). The agenda was soon reinterpreted into two broad categories: 'freedom from fear' (directed to address violent conflicts) and 'freedom from want' (holistic approach taking into account such concerns as poverty and health).[1]

In this dynamic international environment, the council members became open to reinterpreting the mandate of the SC and to broaden the scope of Chapters VI and VII in its work (Wallensteen and Johansson 2004: 24; Naraghi-Anderlini 2007: 12). One of the results was the passage of several thematic resolutions that reflected the human element in matters of international peace and security. Indeed, in some recent literature, these have been identified as 'human security resolutions' (True-Frost 2007). The first set of themes addressed in SCRs – adopted during the period between 1999 and 2001 – relate to children and armed conflict, protection of civilians in armed conflict, HIV/AIDS and women, peace and security.[2]

The council's interests took another turn after the attacks on the World Trade Centre in New York on 11 September 2001. Since then the SC deliberations have been frequently interspersed by the threat of international terrorism, conflicts in Afghanistan and Iraq and concerns regarding humanitarian crises in places like Sudan and Chad. Once again, the council focused its attention on immediate crisis alleviation. Indeed, as will be discussed in the following sections, it lost many opportunities to effectively integrate the human security-oriented elements of the thematic resolutions into this subsequent work (see inter alia Cohn 2004: 134). However, it is because of the existence of resolutions such as SCR 1325 that the council and its member states can be normatively, if not always legally, held accountable for discrepancies in meeting their commitments to such 'thematic' concerns.

Security Council Resolution 1325

The passage of the first SCR on women, peace and security – SCR 1325 – is considered to be a historic feminist moment in the realm of international security. Unanimously adopted in October 2000, SCR 1325 includes provisions to address a range of concerns relating to women and armed conflict. Such issues as women's participation in peace processes and conflict, and sexual and gender-based violence against women during armed conflict, are clearly recognized for the first time by the SC in this resolution. The '3 Ps' that appear often in the text of SCR 1325, and were later widely adapted in the advocacy literature, are participation, protection and prevention. The focus is on the humanitarian aspect of armed conflict and the formal and informal processes associated with conflict resolution.

The provisions of the resolution, as noted by Jennifer Klot, senior governance advisor at UNIFEM at the time of the drafting of SCR 1325, are 'as specific and narrow as the Security Council's mandate . . . it represents a hugely significant, though very narrow and restricted part of a political and military agenda' (2002: 18–19). These are directed toward UN peacekeeping operations, peace negotiations, demining operations, as well as decisions relating to repatriation and resettlement, rehabilitation, reintegration and post-conflict reconstruction (including nation building), and disarmament, demobilization and reintegration (DDR). The potential role of the United Nations and its agencies in this context is highlighted even as the council calls on a range of actors in the international arena, including all parties to armed conflict and 'all actors involved'.

In view of its importance, SCR 1325 has been scrutinized closely in academic literature and by activists who seek to use it as a tool for making international security practices gender-sensitive and, in particular, responsive to issue of women's security. I will briefly summarize the critique here. First, it has been argued that SCR 1325 is a co-option of the WPS agenda into existent security practices of the SC and the United Nations, and it may well be used to lend credence to the militarized international system (see Väyrynen 2004; Whitworth 2004). Second, member states – who individually and through the United Nations are key agents for the implementation – perceive SCR 1325 to be a cost-free resolution (see Carey 2001; Cohn 2004). This is reflected in the ambiguity of some actors in their political commitment to the resolution and evidenced in the low levels of resource mobilization. Third, there are concerns that women's experiences of conflict that do not fit into the language of SCR 1325 are likely to be sidelined and silenced.

On the other side of the spectrum, scholars and practitioners, including gender-friendly 'insiders' in formal policymaking bodies, have sought to use SCR 1325 as a credible tool for action and advocacy. As a SC resolution, its passage is a step forward in developing a shared vocabulary for the international community about matters relating to women and armed conflict. SCR 1325 is used strategically in several ways. For instance, it can be directed to claim budget allocations by and from UN agencies, to demand spaces for women's voices in policymaking and to inject gender programmes into mandates and policies that would otherwise not take into account these issues (MacFarlane and Khong 2006: 219).

Even the staunchest advocates of SCR 1325 would admit, however, that it is not a panacea for all insecurities of women vis-à-vis armed conflict. It comes with the baggage of an intergovernmental agreement, and its scope is limited like other UN policies. At the same time,

284 Soumita Basu

its passage has made a difference to the traditional SC discourse on armed conflict. As noted earlier, in this chapter I focus on its use in subsequent SCRs (until the passage of SCR 1820, the second WPS resolution). The patterns in this usage can provide insights into the nature of manifestations of the tensions between, on the one hand, the SC agenda underpinned by an understanding of militarized peace and security, and, on the other, a human security-oriented SCR 1325.

The analysis is an illustration of the editors' contention regarding the incompatibility of human security with prevailing military security arrangements. The problems with the implementation of SCR 1325 at the United Nations, and particularly in the SC, echo the experiences of earlier proponents of the WPS agenda at the international policymaking level. Indeed, this may well be traced to the peace plans proposed by international women's organizations during the run-up to World War I. Their manifesto, which included a 'proposal for a permanent institution of arbitration', was rejected by the national delegations engaged in, or preparing for, war (Brock-Utne 1994: 207–208; Galey 1995: 3). The following discussions demonstrate diversity within recent responses to SCR 1325, and I seek to highlight the instances of successes of the WPS agenda that are apparent in the subsequent use of the resolution by the SC.

Women and gender in Security Council Resolutions (2001–2008)

The terrain of SCRs reflects the outcome of the intense behind-the-scenes negotiations between the council members. More recently, and particularly in the case of 'thematic' resolutions – wherein the SC engages with a broad theme pertaining to international peace and security instead of the more prevalent practice of focusing on a geographic location – this has also included the active involvement of UN agencies and non-governmental organizations (NGOs) (in the context of SCR 1325 see Adrian-Paul 2004; Cockburn 2007; Cohn 2004; Cohn et al., 2004; Hill et al. 2003). Strongly influenced by the five permanent member states, and the differences between them, the SCRs often represent the lowest common denominator of different positions on any given topic. The aim of this section is to examine this shared SC vision for SCR 1325 and to identify the elements of the WPS agenda at the United Nations that emerged from the negotiations in this forum to find place in subsequent SCRs.

I examine the 494 SCRs bookmarked between SCR 1325 (October 2000) and SCR 1820 (June 2008). This research was organized in two steps. In the first instance, I searched for four keywords in each of the SCRs – 1325, gender, women and girls – and identified the sentences/paragraphs in which the keywords appeared. The keywords were selected on the basis of their relevance for the research: 1325 as the pivotal SCR, gender as the key analytical category and women and girls as the subjects.

In the second stage of the research, I combed through each identified reference for the following details: whether the appearance is in an operational or preambular paragraph, whether Chapter VII is invoked and which element of SCR 1325 it corresponds to – protection, prevention, participation and/or UN reporting. I also noted the country, region or theme that the resolution focused on and, where relevant, the actors addressed in the resolution. In addition, I sought to identify any other particularities of the specific paragraph. For instance, if the reference corresponded to the protection mandate, I looked at which particular element it focused on – sexual and gender-based violence, sexual exploitation and abuse, protection of human rights and/or another issue.

The data analysis is presented here in two parts. First, I discuss the general patterns that are identifiable in the engagement of the SC with SCR 1325 in its subsequent resolutions. I present some statistical observations in this respect, looking at, for instance, the frequency with which the different components of the resolution are used by the council. In the second part, I focus on the ways in which the presence of women and the relevance of the concept of gender are adapted into the SC thinking on security through references to SCR 1325. These insights also feed into the subsequent discussions in the third section on the links between the use of SCR 1325 by the SC and the eventual passage of SCR 1820.[3]

Patterns and rhetoric

During the period between the passage of the two WPS resolutions, SCR 1325 and SCR 1820 on October 2000 and June 2008 respectively, the keywords – SCR 1325, women, girls and gender – appear in approximately 18.4 per cent of the resolutions adopted by the SC. Of the 494 SCRs examined for this chapter, 56 resolutions make references to SCR 1325. Thirty-five additional resolutions – wherein SCR 1325 is not invoked – include references to gender, women and/or girls in the text.[4] Admittedly, some of the 494 resolutions relate to procedural decisions, such as admission of new members, but this overall record is not encouraging. It is a significant leap, however, when compared

286 Soumita Basu

to the earlier record wherein women, girls and gender were explicitly mentioned/considered in 2 per cent and 4 per cent of the resolutions adopted by the SC during the periods between 1994 to 1998 and January 1994 to October 2000, respectively (True-Frost 2007: 209).

There are four further statistical observations that are relevant to the discussion here. First, of the 92 resolutions that include the keywords, 71 refer to specific countries and/or regions, nine can be broadly classified under the rubric of thematic resolutions and 12 are reports of the Secretary-General to the SC. As noted earlier, SCR 1325 itself falls into the category of thematic resolutions wherein the SC addresses an issue which does not directly correspond to any particular country or region. Prior to the year 1999, when the trend of 'human security' resolutions in the SC began, the thematic resolutions had a very narrow focus and were primarily either about non-proliferation and disarmament or terrorism.

A survey of the thematic resolutions makes it evident that the 'old' and 'new' sets of concerns for the SC have yet to find a common ground, even though they speak to the same world. The thematic resolutions in which the keywords come up relate to protection of civilians in armed conflict, post-conflict peacebuilding and UN peace operations, conflict prevention, and children and armed conflict.[5] The WPS agenda fits well with the humanitarian aspect of the aforementioned themes. However, it is clear that the divide between the pre- and post-1999 themes has not been resolved, at least in relation to issues of gender.

Second, in an analysis which examines the relative value attached by the SC to SCR 1325 in its resolutions, it is important to note whether the keywords – women, gender, girls, SCR 1325 – appear in the preamble of a particular resolution or in its operational paragraphs. The former usually provides the introduction and background to the subject matter of the resolution, while the latter lays out the actions recommended or authorized by the SC. Out of the 91 resolutions in which the keywords appeared, 39.5 per cent had them only in the preamble to the resolution. In these instances, thus, the SC noted the relevance of gender for the subject matter but did not prescribe any actions directed toward addressing the specific concerns in that context.

Third, it is encouraging to note that approximately 45 per cent (41 out of 91) of the examined resolutions include a Chapter VII mandate. As mentioned in the previous section, the mandate of the SC is governed by Chapters VI and VII of the UN Charter that are related to maintenance of international peace and security. Because Chapter VII implies the sanction to use force by the international community, it is taken more seriously by member states (MacFarlane and Khong 2006: 229). Not all references to the keywords in these Chapter VII resolutions are, however, made in operational paragraphs. Thus, the strength of being part of the Chapter VII mandate is undercut by the absence of any specific directions given to the actors involved.

Finally, a striking feature of the SCR 1325-related references is the repetitions that mark the usage of some of the language in the latter period (2006–2008). Prior to 2006, one of the illustrations appears in the 2000–2001 period wherein the SC expresses '[deep concern] at the increased rate of HIV/AIDS infection, in particular amongst women and girls in the Democratic Republic of the Congo' in three resolutions.[6] After this, the issue disappears from the agenda.[7] But, in general, there are few such repetitions in the early phase.

That the council is still coming to grips with the implications of SCR 1325 is also evident in a curious sentence in SCR 1333 (2000h) on the situation in Afghanistan in which the SC reiterates 'its deep concern over the continuing violations of international humanitarian law and of human rights, particularly discrimination against women and girls, and *over the significant rise in the illicit production of opium*' (emphasis added). The links between the two distinct parts of the sentence are not explained. It would appear that the council sought piecemeal to include these 'new' themes but without seriously considering the implications.

In the latter period, there are increasing repetitions in the language on such issues as disarmament, demobilization, reintegration; protection of human rights; sexual and gender-based violence; and sexual exploitation and abuse. One such turn of phrase that appears several times is as follows: '[UN mission] to fully take into account gender considerations as set out in Security Council resolution 1325 as a cross-cutting issue throughout its mandate'.[8] The phrase is used in UN missions to places as diverse as Timor Leste, the Democratic Republic of Congo, Burundi, Haiti and Côte d'Ivoire and at different points in the conflict. In this context, the council appears to have identified suitable language to acknowledge SCR 1325 without making specific recommendations.

It is only in few cases – the UN Operation in Côte d'Ivoire (UNOCI) being one – that the sentence used as an illustration here has any specific suggestion or prescribes a desired outcome. The need to consult 'local and international women's groups' is highlighted in the resolutions. Indeed, Chapter VII is invoked in relation to the relevant paragraph in SCR 1721 (2006e) on 'The Situation in Côte d'Ivoire'. However, this is a rare example of the council exploring the implications of identified gender concerns and treating it as a matter of significance.

At the end of this part of the discussion, it is important to note that the SC does not seem to have ignored SCR 1325. Even though there are periods of time during which gender concerns are completely missing from the SCRs, there has been an attempt to include language on SCR 1325, gender, women and girls in multiple contexts. In some cases, newer challenges, such as an increasing number of reported cases of sexual exploitation and abuse by UN mission staff and members of peacekeeping operations, have been integrated into the agenda (Kent 2005). However, repetitions of the kind noted earlier appear to lend support to the criticisms that the council has assimilated the potential of SCR 1325 to suit its essentially narrow understanding of security.

Implications of the use of gender in SCRs

Next I examine the specific ways in which the SC has chosen to construct 'women' and to understand gender in the resolutions. Seventy-six of the 91 resolutions narrowed down for this article make direct references to women. The references are made in several contexts that take into account the complex (and multiple) experiences of women during periods of armed conflict. Women are primarily seen as victims of armed conflict, refugees, ex-combatants, peacemakers, potential electoral candidates and UN mission staff. However, not all the concerns related to each of these aspects is specifically explored, addressed or indeed given equal weight.

The need for gender perspective appears several times.[9] But just as in SCR 1325 itself, no definition of the term 'gender' is offered, and ways to find/apply 'gender perspective', for instance, are not detailed. There are a few exceptions. As noted earlier, at least two of the resolutions (SCR 1721 [2006e] and SCR 1739 [2007a]) on the UNOCI mission recommend consultation with 'local and international women's groups'. In general, though, the repetitions and ambiguity in language relating to gender are in keeping with the lowest common denominator approach of the SC. Valerie Oosterveld writes that gender is used in two ways at the United Nations: 'the minimalist approach taken at the multilateral (state-negotiated) level', which tends to associate gender with sex, and the approach followed by the United Nations and its agencies that emphasizes gender as a social construct (2005: 67). The language in the resolutions clearly corresponds to the former rather than to the latter approach. The disagreements on understanding women and gender within the council – an intergovernmental forum – are reflected in the ambiguity regarding gender in the language. There are two further implications of the SC understanding of gender.

First, men are mentioned only twice in relation to the keywords identified for this research. In SCRs 1806 (2008c) and 1746 (2007d) on the UN Assistance Mission in Afghanistan (UNAMA), the role of women and men of UNAMA is acknowledged. The SC appears to bring parity to the contributions made by both sexes in this regard. However, there is no other mention of men in the excerpts identified for analysis. As Dianne Otto (2006–2007) notes in the context of the text of SCR 1325, which does not refer to men at all, this absence of men 'avoids recognizing that there will also be 'implications for "men" if the Resolution is to be fully implemented' (p. 160). In such cases, the burden of realizing the 'gender component' falls on women, while the societal contexts within which the gendered relations are practiced are left unproblematized.

Consequentially, leaving out references to men when addressing the human aspect of conflict may well be taken to imply that peace and security issues are the natural domain of men to which women are added. Indeed, it would appear that women are merely factored into the violence that exemplifies armed conflict (Charlesworth 2005: 15). Combined together, the understandings of security and gender espoused in the SCRs create a picture of international security that does not depart significantly from the way in which conflict is understood in SC deliberations and in the related work of the United Nations.

Second, many welcomed the passage of SCR 1325 in the year 2000 as breaking away from the 'women and children' (Enloe 1993: 166) syndrome of international policymaking, particularly in the context of armed conflicts. The resolution made references to the role of women in conflict prevention, encouraged their participation in negotiations and also recognized the specificities in the lives of women combatants. In its use in the subsequent resolutions, however, the focus is primarily on protection. Of course, the different mandates – protection, prevention and participation – are not exclusive to one another, and it is necessary to address the violation of human rights of women, sexual and gender-based violence against them and indeed other ways in which women are affected. However, in the resolutions examined, there is an overall tendency to lump women and children together as if their needs are the same. Indeed, it is not clear why a resolution on children and armed conflict (SCR 1460, 2003a) 'notes with concern all the cases of sexual exploitation and abuse of *women* and children, especially girls, in humanitarian crisis' (emphasis added). These may well be the more vulnerable populations, but to constantly refer to them together harks back to the earlier (arguably continuing) practices of equating women with children, thereby infantalizing them (Shepherd 2006: 394–5).

Further, about one-third of the 91 resolutions closely examined in the chapter address only the protection aspect of SCR 1325, referring to such issues as sexual and gender-based violence, sexual exploitation and abuse and protection of human rights. The paternalistic stand of the SC toward women is, thus, clearly evident.

Based on the previous discussions, there is a strong case for challenging at least two aspects of the SC's treatment of SCR 1325: first, the growing comfort with paying 'lip service' to the components of the resolution, and second, the narrow perception of women's experiences of, and engagement with, armed conflict. There are, however, some exceptions to these patterns. In some instances, the SC adopts the language of SCR 1325 in ways that are compatible with the idea of human security:

1. increasing women's participation in political processes,[10] including references to participation in electoral processes and recognition given to 'women and men' of UN peace missions; and
2. making policies inclusive and gender-sensitive[11] through consultation with women's groups and strengthening gender expertise.

Although only the Mano River Women's Peace Network is mentioned by name,[12] the SC encourages UN missions and, in some cases, newly formed governments to consult women's organizations and other civil society organizations. The role of these actors toward mitigating conflicts and their potential for conflict prevention is highlighted. In the case of Afghanistan, Burundi and Haiti, the resolutions also encourage full participation of women in the new parliamentary processes of the country. The agency of women is also recognized with respect to deployment of women as military observers.[13]

Inclusion of gender-related information from conflict regions in the reports of the Secretary-General to the SC, and in the work of the council itself, has the potential to contribute to a greater number of specific recommendations in relation to women and armed conflict, possibly toward realizing aspirations of human security. In the penultimate paragraph of the SCR 1325, the council 'requests the Secretary-General, where appropriate to include in his reporting to the Security Council progress on gender mainstreaming throughout peacekeeping missions and all other aspects relating to women and girls' (UNSC 2000e). The information thus obtained can be used to generate context-specific directives in the use of SCR 1325. However, this aspect of the resolution does not make an appearance until much later in the period examined in this article, the first reference being in SCR 1719 (2006d) directing the UN Integrated Office in Burundi in relation to 'the situation in Burundi'. Since then, this component has been included in nine other SCRs.

To summarize, it would not come as a surprise to feminist scholars that the patriarchal biases of the SC did not go away with the passage of SCR 1325. The use of the resolution in subsequent SCRs is a manifestation of the lack of self-reflection regarding the UN's role in reproducing militarized peace and the dominance of the self-interests of powerful nations. The predominance of male delegates in SC proceedings is also a trend that has neither been contained nor reversed. This is not to claim that women delegates would necessarily have a better record of implementing gender-sensitive policies. However, the disproportionate sex ratio in the council reflects the challenges regarding participation of women in the larger political arena.

In this respect, I appreciate the critique of some scholars that the use of SCR 1325 would never meet the expectations generated by its adoption because the resolution's text is inherently flawed (Charlesworth 2005; Shepherd 2008a, 2008b). Such criticisms notwithstanding, my examination of the references to SCR 1325 in the subsequent SCRs here should have served two purposes: (1) further qualified criticisms in the feminist International Relations literature regarding the commitment, or lack thereof, of the council to SCR 1325 and (2) brought clarity to the specific points of engagement between a women-oriented SCR and an intergovernmental institution driven by interests of powerful states. At the same time, the SC's references to women's agency – discussed earlier – cannot and must not be ignored. As unsatisfactory as the implementation of SCR 1325 may be, it does strike at the symptoms, if not the roots (in the short-term), of the militaristic, patriarchal modus operandi of the SC.

SCR 1820: the way forward?

In view of the implementation record of SCR 1325, part of which was previously discussed, the passage of SCR 1820 on women, peace and security by the SC in June 2008, approximately eight years after the adoption of SCR 1325, evoked mixed reactions from women's rights groups and gender activists. The cautious response was also due to the narrowed focus of SCR 1820, through which the SC primarily demanded the 'immediate and complete cessation by all parties to armed conflict of all acts of sexual violence against civilians' (UNSC 2008e). The emphasis on protecting women from sexual and gender-based violence during armed conflict is a much-needed policy development (see Kent 2005). The challenge, however, is to ensure that the remaining dimensions of SCR 1325 are not ignored due to this. In this final section, I assess the value of SCR 1820 and its implications for the broader WPS agenda at the SC and the United Nations, specifically as represented in SCR 1325. The role of civil society in this context is specifically noted toward highlighting the vibrant nature of the politics of the two resolutions.

The two resolutions

There are two (not mutually exclusive) ways of looking at SCR 1820: it can be perceived of as advancing a component, or indeed, narrowing the focus, of SCR 1325 and/or it can be perceived as part of the overall protection mandate of the SC, focusing specifically on gender. As noted earlier, the SC has adopted several resolutions on protection of civilians in armed conflict. SCR 1820 can well be considered key in highlighting the gendered nature of this thematic concern of the council. It also has implications for the WPS agenda; this is discussed next.

Reflecting the debate within the civil society in this regard, Sam Cook writes, 'some believed that this focus [of SCR 1820 on 'protection'] would take away from the powerful breadth and depth of Resolution 1325 . . . they argued that it would diminish the importance of Resolution 1325 by reducing the women, peace and security agenda to issues of sexual violence and victimhood again' (2009: 127). In response, Cook makes a strong case for the emphasis on protection of women from sexual and gender-based violence on two grounds: first, violence affects the participation of women in political processes and thus needs to be addressed, and second, SCR 1820 strengthens one aspect of SCR 1325 and takes the WPS agenda forward on this particular theme (see Cook 2009). She places her contentions within the larger context of efforts to 'end militarism and conflict and bring peace' (Cook 2009: 139).

To this strong case presented by Cook (2009) in favour of the advocates for the passage of 1820, I would add another pragmatic argument. Given the past record of the council's use of SCR 1325, the 'protection' dimension of the WPS agenda was best placed to be carried forward by the SC. It is evident from the previous section that 'protection' was most readily adapted into SC policies, at least at the level of rhetoric. This, along with the tendency to marginalize those provisions of the WPS agenda that give agency to women – for instance, recognition of their participation in conflict processes and supporting their role in conflict prevention and mitigation – would be compatible with the patriarchal underpinnings of the SC. As the earlier analysis also suggests, SCR 1325 has not posed any substantive challenges to the traditional state-centric interests and militaristic mechanisms of the council. And SCR 1820 may well represent the path that the SC has taken on issues relating to women and armed conflict.

That said, SCR 1820 is encouraging to the extent that it builds on UN policies against sexual and gender-based violence, a serious threat faced by women during armed conflict. Its passage also injected some dynamism into the work of the council on gender issues just as it was settling into routine references to SCR 1325. At least two concerns are of vital importance, however, if the WPS agenda is to survive the strong militaristic and patriarchal embrace of the SC: first, the need to monitor and contest, where necessary, the SC policies on gender and armed conflict – within and from outside the council, and second, the responsibility of other UN agencies, member states and civil society actors to implement the more 'radical' elements of SCR 1325, such as prevention of armed conflict and increasing the participation of women in higher echelons of policymaking.

Many actors, multiple interpretations

As has been noted earlier, SCRs are often the lowest common denominator agreements that come out of intense negotiations among relevant actors. It is government delegations that are the key players within the council, and the contentions among them demonstrate the variations in their commitments (Basu 2016). In the context of the origins of SCR 1325, some individuals (ambassadors) and delegations stand out. With his presidential statement 'Peace inextricably linked with equality between women and men' on 8 March 2000, Ambassador Anwarul K. Chowdhury of Bangladesh introduced the WPS agenda into the SC (UNSC 2000a). The missions of Namibia and the United States to the United Nations hosted the passage of SCRs 1325 and 1820 respectively. The governments of the United Kingdom, Jamaica, the Netherlands and Canada have also been associated with the WPS agenda in the council. Their participation in these processes is a response both to the demands of their national constituencies and to the international community.

Outside the council, member states have adopted national action plans (NAPs) that are intended to provide them guidelines in relation to their roles as contributors of troops to UN peace operations, as donors for UN and civil society projects and for resource mobilization at the country level. Importantly, some countries have also adopted NAPs as part of their national post-conflict reconstruction processes. As of December 2017, 74 countries have adopted WPS NAPs (PeaceWomen 2017b; also see Miller et al. 2014).

With respect to government policies and statements in the council, Carol Cohn (2004) has argued that these proclamations vis-à-vis the WPS agenda often clash with direct or tacit participation of these same governments in escalation of armed conflicts. State institutions and interests of political elites considered play a key role in the construction of patriarchal, militaristic international systems in which SCR 1325 can be articulated only in particular ways, as discussed in the previous section. Sandra Whitworth writes, 'the UN context is one that privileges the idea of liberal internationalism as an always benign and humanitarian endeavour, while at the same time ascribing to the realpolitik principles of state sovereignty and power politics' (2004: 120). Although the council may have inched closer to human security aspirations, it is yet to recognize its own complicity in creating human insecurities – for instance through militarized peacekeeping (see inter alia Väyrynen 2004). Specific individuals and delegations from within this establishment, however, have also argued for alternative formulations, and it is important to remain cognizant of such differences.

In this respect, the efforts to make states accountable – for instance by linking the SCRs on women and armed conflict with the Convention on the Elimination of All Forms of Discrimination against Women (CEDAW), which is legally binding on most (arguably all) states, and country reports at the periodic meetings of the Commission on the Status of Women (CSW) – are encouraging developments. This reference to CEDAW and CSW is also aimed to highlight another crucial aspect of SCRs 1325 and 1820. Niamh Reilly rightly points out that 'the transformative potential of SCR 1325 relies upon it being understood as an interlocking piece in a growing body of international commitments to women's human rights, gender equality and gender mainstreaming' (2007: 167–8). This is relevant also in the case of SCR 1820.

Both resolutions recall several related international mechanisms, including CEDAW, the Beijing Declaration and Platform for Action and the Rome Statute of the International Criminal Court, and agencies inside and outside the United Nations have sought to highlight the synergy between these policy instruments. Linkages have also been made with issues relating to nuclear disarmament (see inter alia Hill 2004–2005). It is this diversity of the WPS agenda in and around the SC that needs to be preserved to ensure that SCR 1325 can be imagined in creative ways that have not been considered yet, particularly by the SC.

Conclusion

In their book on human security and the United Nations, S. Neil MacFarlane and Yuen Foong Khong write, 'the UN, its central agencies, and its associated agencies have played a central role in the interplay of forces that produced considerable change in the way in which international society views the human security needs of women' (2006: 217). The discussions in this chapter focused on exploring a particular element of this role: the perceptions and responses of the SC toward women's experiences of armed conflict, as evidenced in the use of SCR 1325 in the subsequent resolutions, and the diversity in understanding the gendered nature of armed conflict, within and outside the SC. It is clear that the theme of 'protection' stands out in references to SCR 1325, and this is confirmed with the passage of SCR 1820. As such, using the dominant vocabulary on human security, there is greater emphasis on 'freedom from fear'.

Asha Hans and Betty A. Reardon, however, have a more expansive definition of human security in this volume, one that would arguably demand further attention toward those elements of SCR 1325 that focus on conflict prevention and greater participation of women in political processes. They further contend that 'human security cannot exist within a militarized security system'. It is to explore this contention that I closely examine the ways in which the SC, which gives implicit support to forces of patriarchy and militarism, engages with the aspirations of SCR 1325, which do not – at the very least – sit comfortably with these ideological forces. This analysis in the second section is textual as I study references to some keywords – SCR 1325, gender, women and girls – in the SC resolutions in the period between the passage of SCRs 1325 and 1820. It is important to take note that the very mention of gender and women in the SC is a far cry from the traditional state-centric proceedings and that the provisions do challenge business-as-usual at the council. These include, for instance, clear recognition of reported cases of complicity of UN officials and peacekeeping forces in sexual exploitation and abuse; encouraging consultation with local and international civil society groups, including women's organizations; supporting participation of women in electoral processes and UN missions; and recognizing the role of conflict prevention. And yet such challenges incorporated into the texts of the resolutions are few and far between.

The discussion in the third section on the debates around the passage of SCR 1820, and acknowledgement of the differences among the actors involved (this argument is developed in Basu 2016), further highlight the contestations – some favourable to human security aspirations – that exist at this level of international policymaking. The role of civil society in this respect is particularly noteworthy and has been discussed by Cynthia Cockburn (2007), Laura J. Shepherd (2008b) and Felicity Hill et al. (2003), among others. Although the structures of the militarized international state system have a strong grip on the workings of the SC, I also demonstrate the contentions within the WPS agenda. Certain aspects of the implementation of SCR 1325, and the role played by a varying set of actors, suggest that there is some commitment to realizing the human security aims laid out in this volume, even if in a piecemeal manner.

In conclusion, challenges in the implementation of SCR 1325 and around the passage of SCR 1820, discussed here, lend support to views regarding the incompatibility of human security and intergovernmental institutions such as the SC. However, treating the SC as a monolithic institution and the resolutions discussed here as inherently flawed is to lose sight not only of the opportunities for transformation – short-term and long-term – within the council but also the work of 'gender-friendly' actors within and outside who are actively engaged in this politics. As much as the human security language is always in danger of being co-opted into the militaristic, patriarchal tendencies of the SC, it would be counter-productive to ignore the instances of resistance and change that coexist. The close examination of the texts of the SC resolutions in this chapter demonstrates these complexities, and the contestations between those involved hold the potential for better responses to the challenges of patriarchy in relations to issues of women and armed conflict.

Acknowledgements

I am grateful to João Reis Nunes, Asha Hans and Laura Routley for their comments on earlier drafts of this article.

Notes

1 *In Larger Freedom: Towards Development, Security and Human Rights for All*, the 2005 report of the UN Secretary-General, adds 'Freedom to live in Dignity' to the framework, thus also putting emphasis on human rights (Annan 2005).
2 These SCRs are children and armed conflict (SCR 1261 [1999a]; SCR 1314 [2000d]; SCR 1379 [2001e]); protection of civilians in armed conflict (SCR 1265 [1999b]; SCR 1296 [2000b]); HIV/AIDS (SCR 1308 [2000c]); and women, peace and security (SCR 1325 [2000e]).
3 Three corresponding studies on SCR 1325 are compatible with this analysis. The first two are scholarly publications by True-Frost (2007) and Black (2009). The third is an ongoing web initiate by the PeaceWomen project of the Women's International League for Peace and Freedom that 'tracks and analyses gender-specific language in country-specific United Nations Security council peacekeeping resolutions through a Women, Peace and Security Lens' (PeaceWomen 2017a). As a research assistant at the PeaceWomen

project in 2007, I took part in the compilation of these data for the web resource. The data for this article, however, draw on original research (unless otherwise noted).
4 This includes a reference to 'gender' – presumably referring to biological differences between women and men – in a form included in SCR 1735 (UNSC 2006g).
5 These are protection of civilians in armed conflict (SCR 1674, 2006a); post-conflict peacebuilding and UN peace operations (SCR 1645, 2005f; SCR 1327, 2000f); conflict prevention (SCR 1625, 2005e; SCR 1366, 2001c); and children and armed conflict (SCR 1539, 2004b; SCR 1460, 2003a; SCR 1379, 2001e).
6 These are SCR 1332 (2000g); SCR 1341 (2001a); and SCR 1355 (2001b).
7 The only other time that HIV/AIDS and gender comes together is in SCR 1410 (2002c), in which a special representative of the Secretary-General with focal points for gender and HIV/AIDS is appointed for the UN Mission of Support in East Timor (UNMISET).
8 The relevant SCRs are SCR 1719 (2006d); SCR 1721 (2006e); SCR 1739 (2007a); SCR 1743 (2007b); SCR 1745 (2007c); SCR 1756 (2007e); SCR 1791 (2007g); SCR 1794 (2007i); and SCR 1802 (2008b).
9 References are also made to gender 'mainstreaming' 'component' and 'considerations'.
10 'Participation in electoral processes' is referred to in SCR 1536 (2004a) and SCR 1542 (2004c). Recognition is given to the 'women and men of UNAMA' in SCR 1746 (2007d) and SCR 1806 (2008c).
11 Reference to 'consultation with women's groups' is made in SCR 1625 (2005e); SCR 1645 (2005f); SCR 1719 (2006d); SCR 1721 (2006e); SCR 1739 (2007a); SCR 1772 (2007f); and SCR 1801 (2008a). The need to 'strengthen gender expertise' is noted in SCR 1327 (2000f); SCR 1590 (2005a); SCR 1603 (2005b); SCR 1608 (2005c); SCR 1609 (2005d); SCR 1702 (2006b); SCR 1706 (2006c); SCR 1734 (2006f); and SCR 1793 (2007h).
12 The relevant SCRs are SCR 1370 (2001d); SCR 1400 (2002a); SCR 1408 (2002b); and SCR 1478 (2003b).
13 The relevant SCRs are SCR 1370 (2001d) and SCR 1493 (2003c).

References

Adrian-Paul, Ancil. 2004. 'Legitimising the Role of Women in Peace-Building in the United Nations: A Campaign Approach', in Mari Fitzduff and Cheyanne Church (eds.), *NGOs at the Table: Strategies for Influencing Policy in Areas of Conflict*. Lanham, MD: Rowman & Littlefield for INCORE, Belfast.

Annan, Kofi. 2005. 'In Larger Freedom: Towards Development, Security and Human Rights for All', Report of the UN Secretary General. New York: United Nations.

Basu, Soumita. 2016. 'Gender as National Interest at the UN Security Council', *International Affairs*, vol. 92 (2): 255–73.

Black, Renee. 2009. 'Mainstreaming Resolution 1325? Evaluating the Impact on Security Council Resolution 1325 on Country-Specific UN Resolutions', *Journal of Military and Strategic Studies*, vol. 11 (4): 1–30.

Boutros-Ghali, Boutros. 1992. 'An Agenda for Peace: Preventive Diplomacy, Peacemaking and Peacekeeping', Report of the Secretary-General Pursuant to the Statement Adopted by the Summit Meeting of the Security Council. New York: United Nations. 31 January.

Brock-Utne, Birgit. 1994. 'Listen to Women, for a Change', in Robert Elias and Jennifer Turpin (eds.), *Rethinking Peace*, pp. 205–209. Boulder, CO: Lynne Rienner.

Burgess, J. Peter (ed.). 2004. *Security Dialogue*, vol. 35 (3).

Carey, Henry F. 2001. '"Women and Peace and Security": The Politics of Implementing Gender Sensitivity Norms in Peacekeeping', *International Peacekeeping*, vol. 8 (2): 49–68.

Charlesworth, Hilary. 2005. 'Not Waving But Drowning: Gender Mainstreaming and Human Rights in the United Nations', *Harvard Human Rights Journal*, vol. 18 (1): 1–18.

Cockburn, Cynthia. 2007. *From Where We Stand: War, Women's Activism and Feminist Analysis*. London: Zed Books.

Cockburn, Cynthia and Dubravka Zarkov. 2002. 'Introduction', in Cynthia Cockburn and Dubravka Zarkov (eds.), *The Postwar Moment: Militaries, Masculinites and International Peacekeeping*, pp. 9–21. London: Lawrence and Wishart.

Cohn, Carol. 2004. 'Mainstreaming Gender in UN Security Policy: A Path to Political Transformation?', Boston Consortium on Gender, Security and Human Rights Working Paper No. 204. www.amherst.edu/media/view/92331/original/mainstreaming+gender+in+UN+security+policy.pdf. Accessed 29 November 2017.

Cohn, Carol, Helen Kinsella and Sherri Gibbings. 2004. 'Women, Peace and Security: Resolution 1325', *International Feminist Journal of Politics*, vol. 6 (1): 130–40.

Collins, Alan (ed.). 2007. *Contemporary Security Studies*. Oxford: Oxford University Press.

Cook, Sam. 2009. 'Security Council Resolution 1820: On Militarism, Flashlights, Raincoats, and Rooms with Doors: A Political Perspective on Where It Came From and What It Adds', *Emory International Law Review*, vol. 23 (1): 125–39.

Cronin, Bruce. 2002. 'The Two Faces of the United Nations: The Tensions between Intergovernmentalism and Transnationalism', *Global Governance*, vol. 8 (1): 53–72.

Enloe, Cynthia. 1990. *Bananas, Beaches and Bases: Making Feminist Sense of International Politics*. London: Pandora.

———. 1993. *The Morning after: Sexual Politics at the End of the Cold War*. London: University of California Press.

Galey, Margaret E. 1995. 'Forerunners in Women's Quest for Partnership', in Anne Winslow (ed.), *Women, Politics, and the United Nations*, pp. 1–10. Santa Barbara, CA: Greenwood Press.

———. 2004–2005. 'How and When has Security Council 1325 (2000) on Women, Peace and Security Impacted Negotiations Outside the Security Council',

Master's thesis. Uppsala University, Sweden: Programme of International Studies. http://www.peacewomen.org/sites/default/files/1325_1325scnegotiations_hill_2005_0.pdf. Accessed 25 May 2017.

Hill, Felicity, Mikele Aboitiz and Sara Poehlman-Doumbouya. 2003. 'Non-governmental Organizations' Role in the Buildup and Implementation of Security Council Resolution 1325', *Signs: Journal of Women in Culture and Society*, vol. 28 (4): 1255–69.

Kent, Vanessa L. 2005. 'Examining the UN's Plans to Eliminate and Address Cases of Sexual Exploitation and Abuse in Peacekeeping Operations', *Africa Security Review*, vol. 14 (2): 85–92.

Klot, Jennifer. 2002. 'Women and Peace Processes – An Impossible Match?', in Louise Olsson (ed.), *Gender Processes – An Impossible Match?*, pp. 17–23, Uppsala: Collegium of Development Studies.

Krasno, Jean E. 2004. 'To End the Scourge of War: The Story of UN Peace-keeping', in Jean E. Krasno (ed.), *The United Nations: Confronting the Challenges of a Global Society*, pp. 225–68. Boulder, CO: Lynne Rienner.

Lorentzen, Lois Ann and Jennifer Turpin (eds.). 1998. *The Women and War Reader*. New York: New York University Press.

MacFarlane, S. Neil and Yuen Foong Khong. 2006. *Human Security and the UN: A Critical History*. Bloomington: Indiana University Press.

Miller, Barbara, Milad Pournik and Aisling Swaine. 2014. *Women in Peace and Security through United Nations Security Resolution 1325: Literature Review, Content Analysis of National Action Plans, and Implementation*. www.peacewomen.org/assets/file/NationalActionPlans/miladpournikanalysisdocs/igis_womeninpeaceandsecuritythroughunsr1325_millerpournikswaine_2014.pdf. Accessed 30 December 2017.

Mingst, Karen and Margaret Karns. 2000. *The United Nations in the Post-Cold War Era*, 2nd edn. Oxford: Westview.

Naraghi-Anderlini, Sanam B. 2007. *Women Building Peace: What They Do, Why It Matters*. Boulder, CO: Lynne Rienner.

Oosterveld, Valerie. 2005. 'The Definition of "Gender" in the Rome Statute of the International Criminal Court: A Step Forward or Back for International Criminal Justice?', *Harvard Human Rights Journal*, vol. 18: 55–84. Spring.

Otto, Dianne. 2004 and 2006–2007. 'A Sign of "Weakness"? Disrupting Gender Certainties in the Implementation of Security Council Resolution 1325', *Michigan Journal of Gender and Law*, vol. 13 (1): 113–76.

PeaceWomen. 2017a. 'Resolution Watch'. www.peacewomen.org/security-council/resolution-watch. Accessed 30 December 2017.

———. 2017b. 'Member States'. www.peacewomen.org/member-states. Accessed 30 December 2017.

Reardon, Betty A. 1996. *Sexism and the War System*. New York: Syracuse University Press.

Rehn, Elizabeth and Ellen Sirleaf. 2002. *Women, War and Peace: The Independent Experts' Assessment on the Impact of Armed Conflict on Women and Women's Role in Peace-Building*. New York, NY: UNIFEM.

Reilly, Niamh. 2007. 'Seeking Gender Justice in Post-Conflict Transitions: Towards a Transformative Women's Human Rights Approach', *International Journal of Law in Context*, vol. 3 (2): 155–72.

Shepherd, Laura J. 2006. 'Loud Voices Behind the Wall: Gender Violence and the Violence Reproduction of the International', *Millennium: Journal of International Studies*, vol. 34 (2): 377–401.

———. 2008a. 'Power and Authority in the Production of United Nations Security Council Resolution 1325', *International Studies Quarterly*, vol. 52 (2): 383–404.

———. 2008b. *Gender, Violence and Security: Discourse as Practice*. London: Zed Books.

Smih, Steve. 2000. 'The Increasing Insecurity of Security Studies: Conceptualizing Security in the Last Twenty Years', in Stuart Croft and Terry Terriff (eds.), *Critical Reflections on Security and Change*. London: Frank Cass.

Thakur, Ramesh. 2006. *The United Nations, Peace and Security*. Cambridge: Cambridge University Press.

Tickner, J. Ann. 1997. 'You Just Don't Understand: Troubled Engagements between Feminists and IR Theorists', *International Studies Quarterly*, vol. 41 (4): 611–32.

True-Frost, Cora. 2007. 'The Security Council and Norm Consumption', *NYU Journal of International Law and Politics*, vol. 40 (1): 115–76.

United Nations Development Programme (UNDP). 1994. *Human Development Report 1994*. New York: Oxford University Press.

United Nations Security Council (UNSC). 1999a. *SCR 1261 on Children and Armed Conflict*, UN Doc No. S/Res/1261.

———. 1999b. *SCR 1265 on Protection of Civilians in Armed Conflict*, UN Doc No. S/Res/1265.

———. 2000a. 'Peace Inextricably Linked with Equality between Women and Men Says Security Council, in International Women's Day Statement', Press Release SC/6816, March 8.

———. 2000b. *SCR 1296 on Protection of Civilians in Armed Conflict*, UN Doc No. S/Res/1296.

———. 2000c. *SCR 1308 on HIV/AIDS and International Peacekeeping Operations*, UN Doc No. S/Res/1308.

———. 2000d. *SCR 1314 on Children and Armed Conflict*, UN Doc No. S/Res/1314.

———. 2000e. *SCR 1325 on Women and Peace and Security*, UN Doc No. S/Res/1325.

———. 2000f. *SCR 1327 on Implementation of the Report of the Panel on United Nations Peace Operations (S/2000/809)*, UN Doc No. S/Res/1327.

———. 2000g. *SCR 1332 on Democratic Republic of the Congo*, UN Doc No. S/Res/1332.

———. 2000h. *SCR 1333 on Afghanistan*, UN Doc No. S/Res/1333.

———. 2001a. *SCR 1341 on Democratic Republic of the Congo*, UN Doc No. S/Res/1341.

———. 2001b. *SCR 1355 on the Democratic Republic of the Congo*, UN Doc No. S/Res/1355.

———. 2001c. *SCR 1366 on Role of the Security Council in the Prevention of Armed Conflicts*, UN Doc No. S/Res/1366.
———. 2001d. *SCR 1370 on Sierra Leone*, UN Doc No. S/Res/1370.
———. 2001e. *SCR 1379 on Children and Armed Conflict*, UN Doc No. S/Res/1379.
———. 2002a. *SCR 1400 on Sierra Leone*, UN Doc No. S/Res/1400.
———. 2002b. *SCR 1408 on Liberia*, UN Doc No. S/Res/1408.
———. 2002c. *SCR 1410 on East Timor*, UN Doc No. S/Res/1410.
———. 2003a. *SCR 1460 on Children and Armed Conflict*, UN Doc No. S/Res/1460.
———. 2003b. *SCR 1478 on Liberia*, UN Doc No. S/Res/1478.
———. 2003c. *SCR 1493 on Democratic Republic of the Congo*, UN Doc No. S/Res/1493.
———. 2004a. *SCR 1536 on Afghanistan*, UN Doc No. S/Res/1536.
———. 2004b. *SCR 1539 on Children and Armed Conflict*, UN Doc No. S/Res/1539.
———. 2004c. *SCR 1542 on Haiti*, UN Doc No. S/Res/1542.
———. 2005a. *SCR 1590 on Sudan*, UN Doc No. S/Res/1590.
———. 2005b. *SCR 1603 on Côte d'Ivoire*, UN Doc No. S/Res/1603.
———. 2005c. *SCR 1608 on Haiti*, UN Doc No. S/Res/1608.
———. 2005d. *SCR 1609 on Côte d'Ivoire*, UN Doc No. S/Res/1609.
———. 2005e. *SCR 1625 on Threats to International Peace and Security (Security Council Summit 2005)*, UN Doc No. S/Res/1625.
———. 2005f. *SCR 1645 on Post-Conflict Peacebuilding*, UN Doc No. S/Res/1645.
———. 2006a. *SCR 1674 on Protection of Civilians in Armed Conflict*, UN Doc No. S/Res/1674.
———. 2006b. *SCR 1702 on Haiti*, UN Doc No. S/Res/1702.
———. 2006c. *SCR 1706 on Sudan*, UN Doc No. S/Res/1706.
———. 2006d. *SCR 1719 on Burundi*, UN Doc No. S/Res/1719.
———. 2006e. *SCR 1721 on Côte d'Ivoire*, UN Doc No. S/Res/1721.
———. 2006f. *SCR 1734 on Sierra Leone*, UN Doc No. S/Res/1734.
———. 2006g. *SCR 1735 on Threats to International Peace and Security Caused by Terrorist Acts*, UN Doc No. S/Res/1735.
———. 2007a. *SCR 1739 on Côte d'Ivoire*, UN Doc No. S/Res/1739.
———. 2007b. *SCR 1743 on Haiti*, UN Doc No. S/Res/1743.
———. 2007c. *SCR 1745 on Timor-Leste*, UN Doc No. S/Res/1745.
———. 2007d. *SCR 1746 on Afghanistan*, UN Doc No. S/Res/1746.
———. 2007e. *SCR 1756 on Democratic Republic of the Congo*, UN Doc No. S/Res/1756.
———. 2007f. *SCR 1772 on Middle East*, UN Doc No. S/Res/1772.
———. 2007g. *SCR 1791 on Burundi*, UN Doc No. S/Res/1791.
———. 2007h. *SCR 1793 on Sierra Leone*, UN Doc No. S/Res/1793.
———. 2007i. *SCR 1794 on Democratic Republic of the Congo*, UN Doc No. S/Res/1794.
———. 2008a. *SCR 1801 on Somalia*, UN Doc No. S/Res/1801.
———. 2008b. *SCR 1802 on Timor-Leste*, UN Doc No. S/Res/1802.

———. 2008c. *SCR 1806 on Afghanistan*, UN Doc No. S/Res/1806.
———. 2008d. *SCR 1820 on Women and Peace and Security*, UN Doc No. S/Res/1820.
———. 2008e. 'Security Council Demands Immediate and Complete Halt to Acts of Sexual Violence against Civilians in Conflict Zones, Unanimously Adopting Resolution 1820 (2008)', Press Release SC/9364, June19.
———. 2009a. *SCR 1888 on Women and Peace and Security*, UN Doc No. S/Res/1888.
———. 2009b. *SCR 1889 on Women and Peace and Security*, UN Doc No. S/Res/1889.
———. 2010. *SCR 1960 on Women and Peace and Security*, UN Doc No. S/Res/1960.
———. 2013a. *SCR 2106 on Women and Peace and Security*, UN Doc No. S/Res/2106.
———. 2013b. *SCR 2122 on Women and Peace and Security*, UN Doc No. S/Res/2122.
———. 2015. *SCR 2242 on Women and Peace and Security*, UN Doc No. S/Res/2242.
Väyrynen, Tarja. 2004. 'Gender and UN Peace Operations: The Confines of Modernity', *International Peacekeeping*, vol. 11 (1): 125–42.
Wallensteen, Peter and Patrik Johansson. 2004. 'Security Council Decisions in Perspective', in David Malone (ed.), *The UN Security Council: From the Cold War to the 21st Century*, pp. 17–33. Boulder, CO: Lynne Rienner.
Whitworth, Sandra. 2004. *Men, Militarism and UN Peacekeeping: A Gendered Analysis*. Boulder, CO: Lynne Rienner.

12 Jordanian women define security

A feminist approach to an age-old problem

Norma Nemeh

This article is abstracted from a dissertation based on field research conducted in Jordan from September 2001 through May 2002. It presents perspectives of human security held by a sample group of Jordanian women. The sample for the study consisted of women from various regional, social, economic and ethnic groups that reflect the cultural mosaic of Jordan.

Introduction

Throughout history, when it comes to addressing issues of national, state or even economic security, women have been effectively marginalized and, until fairly recently, completely excluded from participating in the discussion. The mainstream parameters that warrant a secure state have been defined and conditioned by militaristic ideals of power and aggression and do not allow for alternative visions or interpretations of security to be included in the equation. The assertion of this article is that current security systems are extremely sexist and militarist in their scope; they are not addressing the survival needs of societies in general and the security needs of women in particular.

The principle goals of this article, therefore, are to offer a culturally gendered perspective on the terms and conditions that would warrant a state of security to be identified and to allow Jordanian women a chance to express their ideals and visions for a peaceful and secure state. The first section of this article will present an analysis of the various dimensions that militarism and sexism play in marginalizing and silencing the security needs of Jordanian women. The second part will present the findings of a study in which Jordanian women were asked to define and prioritize the conditions of security based on a gender-specific categorization of human security.

Militarism and sexism: a Jordanian woman's perspective

A social and cultural transformation has been taking place in Jordan that in many ways contradicts the traditional norms and values of Jordanian society regarding the normal perceptions of security. It should be noted that prior to its formation as a state, the region which composes the state of Jordan was primarily a tribal and nomadic society whose conflict and security issues were maintained within the boundaries of the survival and security of the tribal group. The establishment of the Arab Legion under British command (1916–18) was the preliminary step toward the formal militarization of the Arab tribes and the first step toward transforming the segmented, tribal form of security toward a modern and highly centralized version of state security. The phenomenon that is further transforming the traditional perceptions of security today is driven in part by the political and economic demands that the modernization paradigm is imposing on Jordanian cultural and social systems.

The focus on economic growth as a process toward modernization is functioning to further promote the militarization of traditional Jordanian society, as the primary objective of the process is an economically and militarily secure state. Majid Rahnema (2001) attributes the militarization/modernization[1] phenomenon in Arab states to the priority given to economic growth as the primary model pursued toward development. The focus on military and economic interests has shifted the security priorities from the traditional expectations, which concentrated on protecting the interests, safety and survival of the tribe, the community or the land, toward a militaristic approach where national sovereignty, territorial, economic and regime security take precedence.

It is precisely within this highly militarized and sexist construct of state sovereignty and security that women are further marginalized, their sense of security is increasingly threatened and their subjugated status as silent and controlled members of society disqualifies them from their full rights as citizens and members of the community. When one considers that women in Jordan have been marginalized from positions of power and authority and are allowed only to participate in issues that are solely in the private and cultural spheres of society, state security, then, would not allow consideration of the needs and interests of women in the public or the political sphere. The current model of state sovereignty and security in Jordan is contributing to the violence and injustice experienced by women in several ways. The foremost is how the terms and conditions of security are being categorized and defined in highly militaristic and sexist terms that concentrate on the security of the state (i.e. masculine authority as portrayed in the public/political arena) rather than the security of the people (i.e. feminine qualities as portrayed in private/cultural arena).

It is important to discuss how the militarization of Jordanian society is intimately related to the male/female dynamics of dominance and subjugation found in patriarchal structures and systems of power. The symbiotic relationship between militarism, sexism and patriarchy needs to be clarified in order to analyze the effects each has had on traditional Jordanian society and how each has affected the security of women in Jordan.

Patriarchal systems emphasize the sexist approach toward gender constructs by stressing the dominance of men over women in social, political, economic and cultural settings. The structures of patriarchy privilege men with positions of power and authority by allowing them greater (if not exclusive) access to resources and information. Patriarchy also rewards men with absolute rights to the structures and systems of power publicly and privately. Militarism, on the other hand, functions as a mechanism geared toward the social and cultural formation of individuals to believe military ideals, needs and beliefs to be normal and valuable, involving institutional, ideological and economic transformations as well. Militarism focuses on instilling and normalizing such concepts as sexism, patriotism, nationalism, violence, the excessive use of force and control to maintain its legitimacy. Finally, 'sexism', a term coined in the 20th century, refers to the belief or attitude that one gender or sex is inferior to or less valuable than the other. Historically, sexism is a social and cultural mechanism used to subordinate and subjugate women.

The power over attitude inherent in militarism and sexism can be found in almost all realms of Jordanian society – social, political, cultural and economic – and is reflected in the excessive use of violence and force that has become the accepted norm both in the public/political arena and in the private/cultural arena. The excessive use of violence to deal with social and political issues is evident throughout the Middle East, where the dynamic duo – the constant threat of war and the abuse of Islam as a spiritual ideology – has created sexually segregated societies that reinforce the principles of sexism and militarism as the primary means of defining security as well as national and individual honour.

Honour within Jordanian society, both at the national and individual levels, is an integral part of any individual's social standing and is used to justify any and all forms of violence, particularly violence against women. Sexism and militarism are strongly reflected in the Jordanian perception of honour and function to further marginalize women by reducing honour down to a woman's biological and physiological capacities while at the same time placing control over her honour in the hands of her male relatives. A woman's integrity as a human being and as a member of the community is therefore condensed to nothing more than her virginity and her moral standing. It is through this sexually constructed lens that the subjugation of women is enhanced and a woman's security is threatened, as the use of excessive violence, even to the point of murder, is considered an appropriate measure for men to take in order to regain 'their honor'.

Within such a construct, a feminist perspective on security would bring forth the shared experiences that Jordanian women would be able to relate to. In *Teaching to Transgress: Education as the Practice of Freedom* (1994), bell hooks (1994) defines feminist opposition to patriarchal attitudes by describing how feminist theory is most significant when it invites readers to engage in critical reflection and to actively engage in the practice of feminism. She explains how

> this theory emerges from the concrete, from my efforts to make sense of my everyday life experiences, and from my efforts to intervene critically in my life and the lives of others . . . Personal testimony, personal experience is such fertile ground for the production of liberatory feminist theory.
>
> (p. 70)

Setting the context

The intent of my research was to elicit the conditions and terms that Jordanian women defined as significant to them, based on their lived experiences. Efforts were made to incorporate women from diverse regions and backgrounds in order to present a balanced and accurate perception. The geographic setting of the study was restricted to the boundaries of the Hashemite Kingdom of Jordan. Half of the participants in the study were elicited from the capital city of Amman. As the largest urban centre in the country where close to one-third of the nation's population lives, Amman offered the perfect environment in which to solicit a broad range of participants. The other half of the participant pool represents four non-urban and geographically diverse areas which reflect the diverse collectivity of the Jordanian population, from the *Badia* (Bedouin areas) to the *Qiryia il Asha'ereeyeh* (tribal village), from the *Qiryia il Fellah'een* (farming village) to the *Mu'khayam il Laag'een* (refugee camps). The communities included in the study are as follows: Al Karak, a tribal[2] community in the south; Al Safa'wy, a Bedouin community in the East; Deir All'aa, a rural farming village west of Amman; and Al Baqaa, a Palestinian refugee camp north of Amman. Each community offers a unique perspective into the national and cultural characteristics of Jordan through the varied communal lifestyles, environment and cultural representations of their national identity.

It should be noted that the women who participated in the study represented two significant categories and qualifications. The urban women from Amman were all politically active and were involved with nongovernmental organizations (NGOs). The non-urban women had no organizational affiliation and were not politically active. The decision to incorporate these two groups was to reflect the diverse lifestyles and attitudes of Jordanian women based on their regional and political socialization experiences with the intent to bring forth a culturally relevant and regionally specific conceptualization of security.

A feminist framework for defining human security: WINGHS

The feminist concept of human security elaborated in this volume, as it was presented at The Hague Appeal for Peace Conference in 1999 by the Women's International Network on Gender and Human Security (WINGHS), is the theory utilized in this study for addressing the inadequacies of the highly militarized and state-centred approaches to security. The women who comprised WINGHS came together to introduce a gender approach to security represented over 12 countries from all geographic regions of the world. They were activists, scholars, students, researchers and politically active women representing NGOs. Many of the women had experienced the horrors of war directly and had struggled to ensure that the rights of women, children and unarmed civilians in times of armed conflict are recognized and preserved. According to the WINGHS manifesto, their conceptualization of human security is primarily defined as the 'expectation of well-being', which resides in the following:

1   that the environment in which we live can sustain human life;
2   that our basic, physical needs for food, clothing and shelter will be met;
3   that our fundamental human dignity, personal and cultural identities will be respected;
4   that we will be protected from avoidable harm.[3]

For the purpose of this study, these four conditions were categorized for the participants as:

1 environmental security;
2 economic security;
3 social and cultural security; and
4 national security.

First priority: economic security

The characteristic of security chosen as the first priority is the most interesting from an analytic point of view. If one were to rely solely on the statistical data, one would be wary of claiming that economic security truly is the primary concern for the participants when only 35 per cent ranked it as their first priority. What made this prioritization interesting was the way that national and social and cultural security were equally ranked in this category, both receiving 27.5 per cent of the responses, which weakened the position of economic security as the first priority in the selection process.

Focusing primarily on the participants' responses, particularly the segment of the interview where women are first asked to identify the conditions of security in their own terms, 96 per cent clearly identified financial and economic factors as indicators of security that were relevant to their lives. When consideration is given to the verbal responses identifying the terms of security, economic security is strongly supported as the first priority of security identified by the participants. Or, to use the words of one respondent, Maha, when the first question regarding security was posed to her, 'Security for woman in our part of the world is basically economic security'.[4]

While coding and analyzing the data, the following general concepts[5] were used to qualify the properties of economic security: poverty, education, housing and employment. These generalized terms were selected because of their direct relationship to income and expenditure capabilities and financial resources. Education and employment were repeatedly identified as the two most important factors contributing to women's sense of economic security. As Suha, a 25-year-old unmarried woman from Amman states, 'Education and employment are the two major factors that make me feel secure. Education and certificates[6] secures work and a respectable life for women. They are required for people to develop their own sense of security'.[7]

Suha's comment suggests that education and employment offer women more than just a reliable source of income. One could infer that a sense of respectability and personal confidence is also obtainable through these two factors. Her comment 'a respectable life for women' and their ability to 'develop their own sense of security' also suggests elements of self-actualization and independence, the line of reasoning being that women who are employed and are generating their own income are less likely to be dependent on anyone for financial assistance; the lack of dependency indicates a level of personal confidence and independence. In this example, education and employment offer more than just financial stability; to Suha they are projected as liberating and empowering agents. This embodiment of education as an empowering agent is not unique among the participants; a majority of the participants hold Suha's perspective that education is not only a means for financial independence but also a way to empower women.

Throughout the course of the interviews, women repeatedly emphasized the relevance that economic and financial security had to their lives, and all directly linked education and employment as the most significant factors in obtaining economic security. The priority given to education may account for the fact that Jordan has the highest rate of adult literacy in the Arab region. According to the Arab Human Development Report (2007–2008), 91.1 per cent of the adult population in Jordan is literate. A possible factor contributing to the emphasis on education as a form of security can perhaps be found within a historical context. Given the lack of natural resources and material wealth, Jordan's largest export and income generator throughout the latter part of the last century was a highly educated and trained workforce. Nihal from Amman explains how.

> The Jordanians learned their lessons from the Palestinians, they felt that if they educated their children they secured them. This is the true security – to give them the opportunity to study. For this reason you'll find they won't eat, but they'll study, they probably won't enjoy life, but they will study. They will sell their land to educate their children. This attitude you won't find among the Syrians for example, because they never experienced the tragic migration of Palestinians that the Jordanian people have ... That's why in Jordan there is much attention given to education, especially for children. The reason of which we were the country most affected by the Palestinian refugees after the catastrophes of 1948 and 1967, these people left their land, their homes, their money and everything, those that came with a degree or a certificate had opportunities available that would allow them to work in the Gulf – if they were educated.[8]

It was a well-known fact that Jordanians, as well as Arabs from other neighbouring states, helped to fill the massive labour needs in the Gulf states during the oil boom of the 1970s and 1980s with a trained and skilled workforce. Those who were fortunate enough to obtain employment in the Gulf states were able to secure positions that offered them generous salaries, which in turn they sent back home and reinvested in the local economy. The Jordanian economy came to rely on the remittance income flowing back from the Gulf states as the income required to generate and sustain the local economy. Educating the citizenry of Jordan, therefore, became the capital that the state invested in and utilized in order to maintain its local economy while at the same time allowing opportunities for people to improve their living conditions (that were not readily available at home).

It is not surprising, then, to find that education is such a high priority on the individual level and is directly linked to economic security. It represented the means of obtaining employment opportunities that would secure their livelihood, offering them a sense of respectability, confidence and prosperity. Innam aptly describes the connection between education, poverty and disempowerment when she claims that 'people need to study, need to work, if I am not economically secure, I will be subjugated and under the mercy of the person who supports me'.[9]

A prominent theme identifying economic security as the first priority can be examined through the lens of meeting the basic physical needs for survival. As detailed in the definition given to economic security, it is a form of security that requires that the most basic of physical needs will be obtainable. A psychological theory that supports this concept as significant to human development and growth can be found in Abraham Maslow's (1943) hierarchy of needs.

In Jordan, the responsibilities of maintaining, sustaining and managing the affairs of the private sphere (the home and family) have and still are the primary responsibility of women. A great deal of that responsibility includes what Maslow refers to as the more basic needs in the hierarchy, the *physiological* welfare and needs of the family, as well as a number of the higher needs, the *safety and care* of family members, and, finally, instilling a sense of *belongingness and love* to members of the family in general.

With the cost of living continually on the rise and national unemployment figures reaching unprecedented levels, women are the first to feel the impact and confront the budgetary realities of an economic crisis. The daily challenge of meeting the financial requirements for food, clothing and shelter may be one of the factors that influenced women's responses about why education and employment were important characteristics of economic security – education was seen as the means (acquiring credentials to qualify for employment) to an end (employment which meant income for meeting basic survival needs of the family and home). The following passage offers some insight as to the motives for women's prioritization of economic security. Luma emphasizes that

> you would see that people would want shelter, food and a good education, basic necessities of life – food drink, shelter and education. Economic stability is necessary because poverty leads to deviations within society, like drugs, abuse, sexual, mental, all of it. The effects of poverty on people are tremendous, it's not just that people don't have enough to eat or drink, they start doing things that are harmful to themselves and to others.[10]

Luma correlates the belief that basic needs relate not only to satisfying physical needs but also that they have implications on the integrity and nature of social interactions, the social fabric or moral character of a society. Einad from Deir All'aa explains how.

> If my husband is pleasant and my children are good that gives me more security. When the economic situation is good, we are comfortable. And for education, I exert all my efforts to make my sons educated because certification is a weapon for facing all of life's problems . . . In spite of a difficult financial situation we are trying to offer everything to our children in order to study.[11]

Einad's metaphor of education as 'a weapon for facing all of life's problems' is a powerful example of how, for those living in the Middle East, education is perceived as a force that strengthens the carrier with the knowledge and skills necessary to survive. Einad's statement is all the more meaningful considering that she is the mother of ten children – six sons and four daughters – and despite the reference to educating her 'sons', Einad was just as determined about educating her daughters to ensure that their future husbands would not abuse and disrespect them. She explained how educating her daughters will ensure that the husband would respect his wife as an intelligent and honourable woman and never consider marrying a second or third wife if his first wife was educated.[12]

Shareen from Amman introduces three new categories in her definition of economic security:

> Financial independence I would say of course also the psychological and emotional satisfaction is just as important. To have

our needs satisfied, it's mainly financial, then psychological, then emotional, then social.[13]

Ghada from Al Karak expands the term even further.

Respectability of the individual is important for my family's security, freedom of their opinions, to pursue their own happiness, to have *opportunities* available to them.[14]

Najriyeh, from the Al Baqaa refugee camp, presented the most politicized approach to the concept of 'basic needs' and economic security when she explained how 'the subject is not just food or drink, but it is to see the Palestinian people in a comfortable situation without killing or torment'.[15] Meanwhile, Hala in Amman insists that meeting basic needs has to be extended to include

all Arabs, I envision it would be difficult for me to be secure when I see how the people in Iraq are living . . . I'm not the type of person who could be comfortable knowing that my neighbors were hungry while I am eating. I can't! Knowing my health is fine and my neighbor is ill is very difficult for me to cope with . . . of course to be in security they will be comfortable, living without fears or major concerns, having freedom to express their opinion, to have opportunities for employment, not to fear the future, to have health insurance and to be financially secure. I cannot be comfortable unless there is a standard of security that encompasses all of the Arab world.[16]

It should be noted that these narratives were all taken from the segment of the interview transcripts where the participants were asked to identify the generic conditions of security in their own words. Therefore, the preceding selection of quotes offers a unique insight into Jordanian women's conceptualization of economic security based on their lived experiences and cultural realities. References to such terms as poverty reduction, psychological and emotional security, social respectability, justice, collective security and stability suggest that Jordanian women are concerned with needs that extend beyond basic survival needs. In addition to addressing the basic survival needs that economic security suggests, the preceding narratives demonstrate other concerns like the cognitive needs that contend with the emotional as well as the psychological needs of people. Malsow maintains that such conditions as 'the freedom to investigate and learn fairness, honesty and orderliness in interpersonal relationships are critical because their absence makes satisfaction of the five basic needs impossible'.[17]

Another characteristic that emerged from the participants' responses while defining the conditions for economic security was that they regularly referred to the concept in temporal terms. The participants always related economic security to the future and rarely spoke about it in the present tense, in a sense suggesting that economic security is something that still needs to be obtained. There are two possible reasons why economic security was placed in temporal and futuristic terms. The first may be anchored in the day-to-day economic difficulties for many in Jordan. The facts may be that their economic insecurity was the basis of their concern and their thoughts were on finding ways to protect the limited resources they possibly had or were trying to acquire. The second may be related to the possibilities or 'opportunities' that may be available for their children's future, hence the emphasis on projecting education as a means to an end.

These variations offer an interesting example of how women understand and address the economic conditions in their lives and how they choose to address the problems of survival and meeting the basic needs of the home and family. The emphasis on education and employment as means of addressing the threat or challenge to economic security suggests that women tend to seek out long-term rather than short-term solutions to economic problems.

This outlook was confirmed by the emphasis placed on the future orientation of economic security. The participants' ideals of what would ensure economic security were based on practical and sustainable conditions. Women's concerns toward economic security tend to focus more on meeting the basic survival needs of others – their family, their children, even the needs of their fellow nationals, as Nihal from Al Baqaa and Hala from Amman demonstrated. Or as Nuha explains; 'Jordanian women in general think collectively rather than individually. There are exceptions, but generally speaking, she sacrifices always for her family.'[18] So far, the perspectives on the conditions that define security and how economic concerns are identified and resolved by the participants in this study offer us the first gendered variation on how the conditions of security are perceived differently by Jordanian women and how education is equated with economic security.

Second priority: social and cultural security

Upon initial examination, at first it appeared that economic security held a much stronger ranking in the second position than it did in the first, with 52.5 per cent of the participants selecting it as the second priority in the security ranking. What is also of interest is how social and cultural security maintained its position second to economic security with 27 per cent – the same percentage and position it held in the first arrangement along with national security.

Based on the quantitative data, one could presume then that economic and social and cultural security are the two most dominant characteristics in women's prioritization of security in Jordan. The focus of social and cultural security as the second prioritization is also reinforced by the qualitative data presented which clearly indicates that the characteristics of social and cultural security were the second most significant concern identified by the women in the study. What was interesting to discover was how economic security and social and cultural security were perceived to share several characteristics by the participants. The question this raises then is why these two categories are so closely related. What are the factors that influence the interconnections between the two?

There may be many factors contributing to the cause that both economic and social and cultural security were ranked so high and were viewed to share common traits. The first and perhaps most significant may be in how the terms describing the characteristics of security were translated into Arabic, particularly through the use of the term *taqafa*, meaning culture. The meaning implied in taqafa carries many of the same characteristics of the term 'culture' in Arabic as it does in English – for one minor detail: in Arabic, taqafa is associated more with educational references and connotations than with the social and behavioural connotations that it carries in English. The Hans-Wehr Arabic-English dictionary defines taqafa as 'to be trained; be educated; educational and intellectual; cultivation of the mind; training; education; instruction'. Of the six major functions of the term in English, only one deals directly with education, 'the act of developing the intellectual and moral facilities esp. by education',[19] while the other five address the various functions of the word that relate directly to behaviours and are not directly linked to education.

Given the significant role that education was given in the economic security category, the fact that social and cultural security can also be attributed to education may be one of the reasons that it was in such close competition to economic security in the first and second ranking. As Nancy states,

> I'll tell you something, the issue of culture and the religious cultural aspects are very important because without their presence

you won't have basic needs. Any issue, religious or secular diminishes the security of the state ... The society will be healthy when you insure individual rights, respect and responsibility.[20]

Maysoon, on the other hand, has a different perspective on social and cultural security and suggests the following in relation to culture: 'The second thing I want is justice here I wish for my children to complete their studies without any hindrance ... I want justice for our sons to study what they want according to their qualifications, not according to *wasta*'.[21]

Maysoon and Nancy both reference the term *haq* in their narratives. Haq in Arabic is a complex term that is used to express a variety of meanings ranging from justice, truth, rights, entitlement, punishment, research and to investigate. The concept of haq was a recurring theme in many of the participant's responses as to why they selected social and cultural security as the second priority. A possible factor may be the language used to define the conditions of social and cultural security on the card: 'the expectations that our fundamental human dignity and personal and cultural identities will be respected'.

While coding and analyzing the data, the following general concepts were used to qualify the properties of social and cultural security: honour, tribal and regional affiliations and religious identity.[22] These generalized terms were selected because of their ability to reflect the traditional characteristics of how personal and cultural identities are represented and respected in Jordan and how they also contribute to individual perceptions of the self and the 'other'.

Based on the data generated, it was surprising to find how much emphasis participants from both communities – urban and non-urban – placed on the cultural concepts of security. Collective issues, such as honour, religion and the tribe, suggest a strong attachment to traditional as well as cultural conceptualizations of security which are still relevant to Jordanian society. When these figures are juxtaposed against the definition presented to the participants, identifying traditional and collective means of security as highly significant would suggest some kind of contained struggle in how the participants view social and cultural issues.

When one considers that the interpretation of social and cultural security in a sense challenges traditional interpretations, the emphasis placed on traditional concepts of security by the participants suggests an ethical dilemma among the participants to, on the one hand, maintain their Arabic values with that which is traditional, while at the same time trying to incorporate Western ideals and standards into their lives. Amal describes the ethical dilemma in the following passage:

My surroundings and my whole existence within the society that I am in, society is important because the woman is afraid of people. The men destroy the woman's honor but he is not afraid . . . the woman does not have the basics to be strong even if she works. There is a psychological difference between them. All of this is because of society.[23]

This role of society is attributed to the cultural boundaries of what the participants referred to as the 'culture of shame' prevalent in Jordanian society. The culture of shame was a recurring theme identified in the study and was identified as the primary obstacle preventing women from achieving their full capacity as citizens.

The ideological struggle between Western versus Eastern that defined values of the rights and responsibilities of women within Jordanian society was a significant concern for a majority of the women in the study and was reflected in several intriguing ways that will be discussed. These social and cultural aspects of security were significant for women in that they reflected many societal concerns of identity formation, the most prominent being what Buzan (1998) describes as the 'high degree of identification with a mostly religiously, pan-Islamic and in part pan-Arabic (thus meta-nationalist) defined defence against Western dominance, cultural imperialism, and the imposition of Western standards of international society' (p. 133). In other words, questions of ethnicity and cultural identity constitute a serious issue for the participants, with conscious attempts being made to distinguish and maintain their cultural and traditional identity while simultaneously trying to incorporate the Arab 'meta-nationalist' aspects as well.

The culture of shame dilemma

Asma, a highly respected and active attorney in Amman, presented a thought-provoking example of the East-West strain in cultural expectations of security. Asma offers us a legal example of how the contentions between cultural and social factors are at odds within the Jordanian legal system and how it is affecting women's sense of security in Jordan.

Yes, the laws[24] are there, but social pressure and cultural values favor the interests of men over women. In many situations women have no choice but to give up their rights in order to appease the male members of their family. If it's regarding inheritance, many times a woman will give up her inheritance to her brother. Not because she has to, legally she has a right to inherit from her father, but social and cultural norms 'shame' women into giving up their own rights so that men can reach their full rights. The same holds true in divorce settlements, many times women get nothing out of the marriage, and the legal system makes no attempts to insure justice – according to the law – is served for women. These are just some of the characteristics of insecurity for women here.[25]

Asma's narrative offers us an insight into how the discord between constitutional law, based on Western models, conflict with Sharia laws (Islamic codes of jurisprudence) and traditional Jordanian tribal law, which interestingly enough holds precedence over both constitutional and Sharia laws on certain cases in Jordan. Asma suggests that in many ways the constitutional laws based on Western models, along with the changing cultural expectations of women and their roles in Jordanian society, are preventing women from acquiring what is referred to in Arabic as haq – justice.

The traditional concept that a person's actions and behaviours are a direct reflection on their family and tribe has become feminized in the sense that today only the actions and behaviours of women are considered to have any bearing on a family or tribe's honour. Women have become the responsible bearers of honour, while men have been exonerated of much of the responsibility. Hence the social and cultural pressure on women to give up what is rightfully theirs by 'shaming' them.

Asma even goes so far as to suggest that the whole issue of 'honor' killing in Jordan is not rooted in traditional Arab culture but is linked to French laws regarding crimes committed in the 'heat of passion'. Asma claims that in order to conceal the real reason for their crimes, men rely on the 'heat of passion' clause in the constitutional laws to basically get away with murder. Asma insists that the traditional Sharia and tribal laws have specific conditions that need to be in place before any accusation, much less action, can be taken against a woman in cases of honour.

The uncertainty created by current modifications in the customs of Jordanian society, particularly those regarding the traditional roles and responsibilities of women and men, were a recurring theme throughout the study. Women were constantly referring to the concept of 'the culture of shame', which was identified as the prominent theme contributing to much of the injustice and lack of progress in the women's movement in Jordan. As Maysoon, a mother of five daughters and a school supervisor in Amman, explains,

> Our problem is that the women are afraid to tell people about the violence. This is shameful and as a result the sword falls on

the woman's neck. The American woman is separated from this because of the law. Here if the woman goes back to her family her father will take her back to her husband. Our problem is this *culture of shame*. Not just for women but also for men. Many young men refuse to do some jobs because of shame. Also this prohibits the man from helping the woman.[26]

Maysoon's reference to 'the traditions' and the 'culture of shame' which are meant to apply to men as well as to women is important in that it reflects the Bedouin or traditional mores of Jordanian society which are still valued in Jordan and which recognize that the honour and integrity of women was just as significant as that of men. The following reference by Asma allows us an opportunity to note the gendered variation to the concept of shame by linking it to the concept of sacrifice:

> Women need to feel that they are free human beings and that others are not looking to them as minors or dependents but as individuals to respect their differences, their points of views, their special needs which are not necessarily the needs of their children or their families. Women need to be recognized as independent human beings who have *haq* – rights and justice, which would not necessarily be compatible with others. They need to stop being the person who is asked to sacrifice. Everyone is expecting from a woman to be ready to sacrifice herself, so she feels ashamed if she has a specific need for herself.[27]

In this passage, Asma was challenging the gendered and biassed expectation that women would naturally be willing to sacrifice what was rightfully theirs in order to appease others. She shows us in a sense how women are shamed into accepting positions of inferiority based solely on the constructed characteristics of their gender. Asma also highlights the significance that women in Jordan place on respecting the integrity, opinion, independence and humanity of women as members of society who deserve to be recognized and afforded haq – justice.

The concept of '*ayb*' (shame) was continuously identified as a prominent social deterrent in keeping women in positions of inferiority and subjugation to men and is somehow almost always linked to women's sexuality. The method of 'shaming' or challenging the integrity and honour of an individual is the traditional Bedouin means of maintaining social order and establishing standards of behaviour. Fardos from Amman offers a solution to the problem of *ayb* that may be helpful to women.

> Women need to trust their intellectual abilities more and for that they need to have access to education. Some of the reasons why women are not achieving their capabilities are because of the culture of shame that is so prominent in our society. Women are afraid of other people's gossip. They are ashamed if they are accused of anything, even if they have done nothing to be ashamed of. Fear of gossip and false accusations make them passive and less motivated.[28]

It should be noted that the tactics of 'shaming' women to conform to certain standards of behaviour described by Fardos are not necessarily being applied to men the way they normally would be, which supports the argument on the feminization of honour. Fatima from Deir All'aa gives us insight into how honour has become feminized in Jordan by describing how men have come to be exonerated, in a sense, from the culture of shame by the lack of consideration given to the traditional responsibilities of men.

> It is seldom to find a woman who trusts her husband. Perhaps 50 per cent of the women trust their husbands. Some women work and their husbands stay in the house. They do not care about this. They are jobless and the women work. They do not consider this shameful for them. Many houses the women take the responsibility for everything. It is seldom to find a man to take the responsibility for the family. Many husbands do not know their house except in the night. When the woman finds that the man does not take care of the children she has to leave her house to get money for the children. That is not what the Islamic system says.[29]

Fatima's narrative exemplifies how honour and shame have become feminized in Jordan. The lack of trust afforded to men, their inability or their disinterest in obtaining employment to meet their families' needs are characteristics that in the past would have dishonored and shamed men considerably. Her emphasis on the fact that men 'do not consider this shameful to them' clearly was an aspect that upset Fatima. Her stress on the fact that now women have to seek employment to support their families and the direct link she makes to the 'Islamic system'[30] suggests that she is disappointed with the social changes that she is witnessing and that she resents the injustice that the changes are forcing on women. After meeting Fatima and getting to know her personally, I would have to say that her attitude is in line with both – she is gravely disappointed and resents the position the women currently find themselves in.

The second aspect of significance in the social and cultural security configuration – tribal association/affiliation – was perhaps the most fascinating discovery in the study, with 82.5 per cent indicating that tribal affiliation was an important aspect and contributed to their sense of security. This was an unexpected finding, particularly from the standpoint of the urban and Palestinian participants in the study. It was naturally expected that the Bedouin and rural villages would still value and adhere to the traditional identifying markers, but in the large urban capital, it was assumed that tribal affiliation would not be as meaningful or as significant an aspect of social life, which was not the case at all.

Tribal affiliation was just as significant a characteristic to the Palestinians and the urban city dwellers as it was in the Jordanian *Badia* and the *Reef*. Participants were quick not only to identify the name of the tribal group from which they originate but also to always linked the tribal name to a specific region or village where their families originated. A significant detail that may be of interest is the fact that of the several participants who did not place any emphasis on tribal affiliation, all were from Amman except for one Iraqi refugee from Al Safawy. The expectation was that the participants who were Christian Arabs or of Palestinian decent would not identify tribal affiliation as an important identifying marker in their lives because the tribal system was not the normal standard among their regional or religious groups.

What was surprising to note was how prominent tribal links were among the Palestinian women in the Al Baqaa refugee camp. Two-thirds of the women from Al Baqaa identified from the same tribe or familial clan, while the remaining identified different tribal groups. Again, with the Palestinian women in Al Baqaa, reference to the town, village or area that they originated from in Palestine was also immediately identified.

A possible cause for this incongruity may stem from the fact that the women interviewed from Al Baqaa all came from communities that were part of the Kingdom of Jordan prior to British withdrawal from Palestine and the subsequent occupation of Palestinian lands by Israeli forces. The historical bonds between Jordan and Palestine may explain why tribal and regional affiliations among the Palestinian refugees were similar to the Jordanian system in that identity was directly linked to the region and the land. Their insistence on referring to familial and regional ties, despite over 50 years of displacement, may be rooted in the Palestinian vision of returning to Palestine. Yussra explains, 'I want my sons to be educated and go back to Palestine with good houses to live in. This is my dream. I want a good life for all Palestinians'.[31]

Jordanian women define security 321

Tribal links and affiliation had both positive and negative implications for women in Jordan. For example, May directly attributed her loss in the previous parliamentary elections to her tribe.

> Now we have to consider that we have a system here, society looks at women as unequal to men. I wish as a woman that society looked at me as a man. The tribal system doesn't give the woman a chance. Even if the woman has qualifications for example, I had a desire to run for election. I had support from women, but the society hindered me and the people changed my father's opinion of me. In spite of the fact that I belonged to a big tribe, my tribe did not support me, just my husband and some of his relatives. Society refused to support me because they said, 'do you think we will give our votes for a woman?' Even educated people and people who have authority fight the women.[32]

May's argument was a recurring theme at numerous conferences and meetings[33] and was recognized as one of the main deterrents preventing women from running in elections and from becoming actively involved in political parties and events.

On the other hand, the participants from Al Karak, a community in the south of Jordan with strong and historically significant tribal associations, highlighted some of the positive characteristics attributed to tribal affiliation. It should be noted that Al Karak is the home of two very old, historically prominent and respected tribes in Jordan – the Majalys and the Tarawnehs. Ghada explains how living in Al Karak and her relations to the tribe offer her a sense of security.

> For example women have their full rights and we are working like the men these days. We are free to move about as we please. We have a very secure family like community, which gives us independence that is security. We have security internally and externally – at the level of the individual and family and as members of the community. All these things offer us a sense of confidence and security.[34]

The positive and equitable attributes of tribal life were highlighted even by contemporary urban women in Amman. For example, Lena fondly describes memories of her childhood experiences.

> Originally we're from Irbid, farming rural area. I grew up there as a child. I remember wheat fields surrounded our house, they no longer exist. I am influenced by the traditions of the *Fellaheen* (farmers).

The – family is very *Fellaha* in the sense of the word. The real *Fellaheen* I experienced it as a child, I know what it is. Its people who are very open minded, very liberal, girls and boys dance together in weddings We had a tradition in Jordan, it doesn't exist anymore, unfortunately, but there was something called a *Ta'leeyeh*.[35]

Again, we are exposed to two varying perspectives or approaches on traditional systems of social and cultural interactions in Jordan. For a significant portion of the participants (82.5 per cent), the tribal system in Jordan offers women a sense of amn – security – and in some instances haq – equity and justice – based on the traditional interpretations and perspectives of women within the system. But the same tribal ways that offered women a sense of identity, security and equity can be perverted to place women in positions of inferiority, insecurity and injustice. Herein lies the paradox Arab women must confront in their lives and is perhaps why social and cultural security was so important an aspect in their lives. Social and cultural traditions afford them the opportunity to create a unique cultural identity which links them to the rest of the Arab world (meta-nationalism) on a cultural level and establishes links with the international community on a social level.

Third priority: environmental security

The third priority selected by the participants – environmental security – is supported by the quantitative data more so than the qualitative. The difference between environmental security and the other categorizations is that unlike economic and social and cultural security, environmental security enjoys a secure position as the third priority based on the quantitative data. This position is not supported by the qualitative data (narratives) as much, but the quantitative data offers some interesting qualities that would not have been revealed by examining the qualitative data alone.

One example that immediately drew attention was the emphasis placed on environmental concerns among the various regions in Jordan while prioritizing the categories of security. For example, in the large urban centre of Amman, 40 per cent of the 20 participants from Amman, 22.5 per cent of the overall group, ranked environmental security as the third priority. In the non-urban areas, it was expected that environmental security would take a much more prominent position which surprisingly enough was not the case. With the exception of Al Safawy, the Bedouin community in the east, and Al Baq'aa, the refugee community in the north, environmental security was considered a relatively insignificant priority in the non-urban communities.

What makes these figures interesting is the fact that in Al Safawy, the environment is incredibly barren and hostile given that the geography in Al Safawy consists of primarily rocky desert. The atmosphere is very dry and incredibly hot for most of the year. There is very little, if any, precipitation, and for miles you will see nothing but sand and large black stones scattered about. Jamila explains why environmental concerns are so important to the Bedouin of Al Safawy.

> The current environment has nothing to make one secure . . . for example the natural environment in the village is different from the Badia. The village has green land and the children there are much more self-confident. The Badia on the other hand has extremely high temperatures in the summer and the children have no way to feel comfortable and play. There are many difficulties in the Badia, it is a remote area, with high temperatures, high price for sheep and water bills are very expensive.[36]

It was interesting to note how Jamila equated environmental health with the physical and psychological health of children in Al Safawy. Another interesting issue that was brought up later in the interview was Jamila's response when she was asked whether the concept of clean air and water were important or had any relation to security. Her immediate reaction was, 'This is the freedom that everyone dreams about. All of us dream about green land and grass that gives us comfort'.

The refugee camp in Al Baq'aa did not share the same geographic characteristics of Al Safawy. The land surrounding the refugee community was converted into an agricultural zone, producing crops for the local markets and for the population living in Al Baq'aa. For the inhabitants of Al Baq'aa, their environmental concerns were also related to health conditions but in a very different way. Because of the cramped living conditions, environmental concerns were directly related to the problems associated with living in a densely populated area where the formal infrastructures that are meant to maintain the sanitary requirements of a community were inconsistent and unreliable. Many of the residents living in the area did not have access to clean water on a regular basis; garbage and waste disposal was not consistent either. The residents were living in unhealthy conditions that were extremely cramped and polluted. Broken sewer lines polluted the air and the streets, and refuse and debris were scattered throughout the area.[37] Yussra states why the environment was her first priority.

> You saw when you came in how the street was outside. My youngest daughter gets very sick and cannot leave the house. When she smells the dust and dirt outside the house her breath is captured and she can't breathe. Everything here is not healthy and, nobody cares.[38]

It turns out that Yussra's 15-year-old daughter suffers from an asthmatic condition and has an extremely negative reaction to strong scents. Her condition worsens whenever she leaves the home because of the polluted environment which causes her to experience asthma attacks – 'her breath is captured'.

Comments by both Yussra and Jamila focused on and defined environmental security as a natural setting that would offer them a healthy and comfortable environment to live in. For Yussra, Jamila and others, environmental security meant something that would sustain and foster healthy living conditions. These two characteristics represented the properties of environmental security and demonstrated how a majority of the participants felt that health, along with clean air and water, had strong relationship to their sense of security.

In contrast to Al Safawy and Al Baq'aa, for the participants from Al Karak and Deir All'aa, environmental security did not even rank second in significance despite the shared environmental concerns these communities had in common. For example, Deir All'aa in the Jordan Valley is one of the most fertile regions in the country and like Al Baq'aa produces much of the crops that supply the local markets. Al Karak shares some of Al Safawy's characteristics in that it is normally a very dry area that is subject to severe drought conditions. The communities of Al Karak and Deir All'aa, which also require a healthy and sustainable environment to ensure their livelihood, were less supportive of environmental security than the other regions in Jordan. One possible reason for the lack of consideration is probably because the natural environment these communities were experiencing at the time this study was conducted was what Jamila would describe as 'the freedom that everyone dreams about . . . green land and grass that gives us comfort'. The interviews in Deir All'aa and Al Karak were conducted in March, at the end of the rainy season, and the participants were enjoying the positive and life-sustaining qualities that a healthy, green and bountiful environment offers.

Equating environmental security with health security

The prominent theme or pattern that emerged from analysis of the participants' responses is the way that environmental security was automatically equated with health security. Once again, it was assumed that perhaps the language translation may have been a factor in influencing their understanding and their correlating environmental issues to health issues.

Upon closer examination of the meaning and possible connotations of the Arabic word used to define environmental, which in Arabic is *il Bee'a*, the original translation was accurate, and il bee'a carries the same meaning and connotation in Arabic as it does in English without any significant variation. The only other possibility that may explain how the term il bee'a suggests health may be in the fact that the root of the word in Arabic is the same root used to define 'nature', which in Arabic is *il Tabee'a*. The postulation being that all things that are related to nature are also healthy.

Both in Amman and in the rural communities, the participants directly correlated environmental security with health concerns and issues. For instance, Suzanne from Amman identified environmental security as the first priority in her categorization and explained how she felt that 'environmental security is necessary for health'.[39] Reem, also from Amman, stated that 'the environment means health'.[40]

Nancy offered a different correlate to environmental security and health. In the following dialogue, I had initially asked Nancy to identify whether certain concepts had any relation to security; when the term 'health' was presented, this is how Nancy (here identified as 'R') responded:

R: Do you know in our religion of Islam, poverty is considered sacrilegious '*Kufur*' and the highest offence? Omar Khattab once said that if poverty were a man, I'd slay him.
N: I repeated 'health'.
R: Look, if poverty is a collective in a society, then health would be the individual. What do you want me to say, something for each word?
N: If you feel it has any impact on security – if this is present or not will it affect security?
R: I'd say that people's low sense of security or insecurity contributes to their lack of health and disease because it depletes their immune system, their positive perspective, their motivation to live. I feel that if a society is not healthy and comfortable, this will increase the amount of disease in a society. For example, if you're not feeling well one day and decide to turn on the TV to watch the news. You hear about this one being killed here another explosion over there, increase in crime and so on, of course people will remain unhealthy.

If their whole society is unhealthy, with poverty, corruption, crime and violence – these are diseases that affect people just as much as they do a society.[41]

Nancy's response was totally unexpected at this point but was also surprisingly imaginative. Her metaphor comparing a healthy environment, which encompasses our physiological ills as well as our social, cultural and economic ills, was an incredibly unique approach to viewing the connectivity within the environment and our human condition. I was impressed with how Nancy attributes such factors as physical health, poverty and corruption with a healthy environment. She cleverly highlighted the connectivity between the 'social illnesses' that affect the human condition as well as the physical impact it has on the social and physical environment.

Shareen, also from Amman, discussed the impact of environmental 'illnesses' on human health in the following narrative:

> It's really important to have healthy surroundings, atmosphere, air, especially, I have in mind our agricultural products, which are extremely polluted. Hardly anyone is aware of what is being used in our food. Insecticides and many unknown chemicals have been used on our food and we are all eating them. So many kinds of chemicals that we are not supposed to have in our bodies. We are always getting sick and no one understands why. People are starting to question, why there are so many cases of cancer all over. When they look back, they realize that they were not restricting the types of chemicals used in our agricultural products for the past 20 years. Now we're seeing the effect of it. It's very important the effects on public health and now we are seeing the results. Look around – the percentage of people who have cancer in Jordan is really serious for such a small country.[42]

Shareen's direct linkage between cancer and the unmonitored use of chemicals and insecticides in the food supply follows the pattern of correlating a healthy environment to personal health. Later it was discovered that Shareen's concerns about the safety and health effects of chemicals in the food supply stem from her personal experiences and knowledge on the matter. A very close relative of hers suffers from kidney cancer, which has impacted her greatly, to the extent that she dedicates a portion of her time each week volunteering at the *Medina il Tib'eeyeh* – the medical centre in Amman – caring for cancer patients.

May, on the other hand, offered a political twist to the environmental question by describing it as

> a world demand. If we do not care about this now, the next generation will have many problems. There is no awareness about this. I think sustainable development is necessary in this country. Water is vital and in Jordan, water for one person is the least in the world. Many people steal water to live. That creates problems and insecurity. Water is behind every one of Jordan's problems. Why does Israel fight us – she wants control of the water.[43]

Given that the geographic environment in Jordan is primarily desert, with very limited natural resources or fertile farming land,[44] it was disturbing to find that the issue of water was not a primary concern that the participants felt needed to be addressed. Along with the issue of water, other environmental concerns that were not addressed by the participants include recycling, deforestation, overgrazing, overmining of mineral resources, soil erosion, desertification, water pollution caused by the large tanker ships that crowd the port of Al Aqaba and the drying up of the Dead Sea. None of these environmental issues were addressed at all by the participants.

I found it odd that only May in Amman brought up the question of the water shortage or the drought conditions that have affected the region for so many years. The only other time the issue of water came up was with Fatima from Deir All'aa who briefly referred to the topic of water by criticizing the Peace Accords that were signed between Jordan and Israel in Wadi Araba in 1995. According to Fatima, one of the terms of the agreement was that Israel would stop diverting the natural flow of the River Jordan as it passes through Israeli territory and allow water that would normally flow through Jordan from Lake Tiberius to reach the River Jordan.

Water scarcity was a security concern that was expected to draw much more attention as a security threat to the participants than it actually did. A possible reason for the lack of attention given to the water issue is perhaps based on the fact that the population has been living under restricted water usage conditions and scarcity for such a long time that the scarcity of water has been normalized as the standard and is no longer perceived as a social or environmental problem. Another probable cause may be that the population is so clearly aware of the situation and also recognizes how little can be done to remedy the situation that they have come to accept the fact that they cannot complain about something they know they do not have.

Fourth priority: national security

Focusing primarily on the quantitative data, national security is given a stable ranking as the fourth priority, with 42.5 per cent of the participants ranking it at the fourth position. An interesting discrepancy was found when examining the qualitative data for national security that must be mentioned. In comparison to environmental security, national security has a considerable bit of leverage over environmental security, as will be demonstrated in the narratives offered by the participants. This discrepancy is attributed to the properties that structured the terms of national security which were also perceived as political security, as the term for national in Arabic is *mu'watan*, which automatically connotes loyalty to the monarchy. This may explain the participants' reference to the governing body in Jordan and its responsibilities to the general public when national security was mentioned.

From a regional perspective, national security received the highest ranking in two extremely diverse communities – Amman and Al Safawy. What was interesting about the ranking process was to see how certain communities prioritized national security. For example, it was expected that Al Baq'aa would not rank national security as the priority because the population is composed almost entirely of Palestinian refugees, which turned out not to be the case. Of the participants in Al Baq'aa, none selected national security as the first or second priority. What was surprising to find was that in Al Safawy, national security did not receive first or second ranking at all. In Amman, the selection was much more consistent.

What makes these figures interesting is the fact that historically the Bedouin and the *Qu'raa* (villagers) have always been the staunchest supporters of the monarchy in Jordan, with the majority of the population from these areas selecting military service as a career choice. The *Jeash il Badia* – Bedouin army – in Jordan is still considered the most prestigious branch of the Jordanian military and is mostly comprised of Bedouin and village recruits. Thus, it was expected that political security would hold a much stronger position in the rural and tribal villages because these communities have always played an integral part in the military, particularly during the reign of the late King Hussein.

The concepts identifying the properties of national security were intended to reflect the sociopolitical characteristics that offer a citizenry a sense of security and worth within a given society. The use of the term 'democracy' would qualify as a Western concept because it is neither the norm nor the customary standard of political leadership in Arab or Islamic societies. The terms 'equality' and 'rights' in relation to the concept of democracy were meant to deal with identity and gender issues as well as the sociopolitical realities that Jordan was experiencing in its transition toward democratization.

What was interesting to note was how the Western-defined notions of governance received a slightly higher ranking than the traditional and culturally specific characteristics. The discrepancy between the value placed on personal and familial honour (82.5 per cent), along with religious (87.5 per cent) and tribal affiliation (82.5 per cent), which are the historic and normal standards for the region in comparison to the characteristics of democracy (97.5 per cent), equality (92.5 per cent) and human rights (95 per cent), is an indicator of the social and political shift that the country is experiencing at the time this study was conducted.

The shift toward Western-defined values suggests that women in Jordan are much more politicized than originally thought and that they are expanding the parameters of the traditional and cultural values that offer women security to include Western values or, as Nancy states, when asked whether democracy has a role in security, 'Democracy and security? Definitely! Not to let dictators rule of course. To feel secure you need to make decisions collectively, that are studied, not just imposed by one person'.[45] This shift in political consciousness corresponds to the notion of the 'third space' defined by Shahnaz Khan (2002) and is evident in the comments presented by the participants as they redefine their roles within Jordanian society on the social and political front.

The expectation was that the participants from Amman who were politically socialized through their NGO activities would expect such concepts as democracy, equality and rights to be available and that the non-urban women would not find these concepts meaningful to their day-to-day experiences. But that was not the case. Najah, the youngest and poorest of the participants from Al Safawy, explains why democracy 'is important, so you can express your opinion and you feel freedom but with restrictions'.[46] The realization that along with the concept of rights there are responsibilities was even expressed by Jan'na, a primary school teacher at the girl's school in Al Safawy, when she explains that democracy 'gives you social security that makes you feel you are not alone ... but it doesn't mean freedom without restrictions'.[47] Along with a conscious awareness of the rights and responsibilities, the participants also displayed an awareness of the responsibilities that the government owed to the people. Jamila describes how

> government interests in this area make me feel more secure, so that now we are living on equal footing with the people from Amman ... my children here have more chances because of the

government interest in this area. I think the government's interest in this area is wise.[48]

Later Jamila explains how

> I came from a government that is different from here [Jamila is originally from Baghdad, Iraq] but I like this government in Jordan, that its decisions are calm and not revolutionary. Jordan's resources are limited and hinder its development. If Jordan had the same resources that Saudi Arabia has, it would be a pioneer in the Arab world. The mentality here is open.[49]

Nazieha from Al Baq'aa refugee camp claims that 'democracy leads to corruption' but at the same time holds that 'equality is necessary for justice . . . [and] that it is bad for anyone to lose their rights'.[50] Najriyeh was the first and only participant to refer to King Abdullah in the interviews, and her statement was actually to request that 'Abu Abdulla [incorrect title] deal gently with the Palestinian people'; she goes on to say that she wishes 'peace to all the Arab countries and I ask God to give Abu Hussein [correct title] good health'.[51]

Ghada from Al Karak explains,

> We have a democracy in Jordan, it is limited but it offers boundaries to how far people can go in transgressing against each other. This freedom allows security for all people in Jordan . . . because culture requires a sense of nationalism and religion these are required in today's world.[52]

Dallal gives a very tribal interpretation of national security when she explains how

> anyone that belongs to a large tribe feels more secure than someone who belongs to a minority. The tribal system is very important in our community . . . national security depends on this type of community, none of this will be of any benefit without national security . . . The tribal security is very important. There are many problems solved by the tribes in Jordan that affect everyone in the country.[53]

Dallal offers an excellent example of how non-urban women are combining modern and traditional characteristics of nationalism and citizenship to create their own unique interpretations which directly apply to their lives, in a sense creating their own (third) space within the mainstream culture.

Ajeebeh from Deir All'aa also demonstrates the merging of values and ideals when she defines national security as something related to

> Jordan as a whole, to live in peace and be secure in every day life. National security means that the country does not face any problems that are threatening its people. Democracy is very important and it is a natural right for us. Through democracy women can know their rights and can ask for their rights ... We need equality, but not about everything. Women need to assert themselves. For example, I have to respect my brother, my husband, my father and they have to respect me. We have to respect each others opinions. If anything takes my rights by force, I will not feel comfortable until I get my rights back.[54]

Fatima gives an example of how Jordanian nationalism was created when she explains how national security is understood in Jordan: 'We have a saying here in Jordan, '*All'a, il Malik, il Watan*' – God, King, the Nation[55] – these three things protect us from harm'. She then goes on to describe how Jordan

> is a democracy, everyone's opinion is different. Everyone has an opinion in a democracy. It gives us security because we can say anything we want, before we could not do that. Democracy means everyone can have an opinion based on his principles.

Conclusion

Amal, a college-educated and politically active grandmother from Amman, very eloquently captures the essence of what her vision of security would comprise by incorporating the ideals and aspects that many of the women from both the urban and the non-urban areas identified.

> Now this has a perspective that falls back on experience. In other words it's important for there to be a democracy in the state. This encourages me to emphasize my opinion in full freedom, full honesty without fear of any negative repercussions. Eliminating laws that are violent and oppressive that decrease the security and freedom of an individual that allows the security mechanisms to control the liberties and freedoms of people within their homes . . . I feel security when the opportunity for education, training and

the opportunities that allow me to pursue employment are made available to me. I feel security if the legal system is just and fair without biases between men and women, because any bias between men and women would expose me to such situations as hunger and poverty and these two factors, hunger and poverty are the most horrible factors violating the freedom of a human being. Which is the freedom to live with honour and respect and have his basic needs met. I feel security if the Palestinian crisis was resolved justly and according to international standards – for as long as the Palestinian situation is not resolved, the security of Jordan is threatened and therefore my security, individually, personally is threatened, every citizen then lives in insecurity. Security is most important for women by eliminating all types of violence against women. Respect for the humanity of women. Perhaps these points in general compose the fundamental conditions for insuring the security of the people – all of these are important.

In closing, Amal's statement eloquently summarizes the conditions of security the participants in this study identified as significant to their lives. By identifying such concepts as democracy, liberty, freedom, political stability and the just resolution of conflict, she has outlined the conditions of security from a Jordanian woman's perspective. Her intent in identifying structural violence as obstacles of justice and equality for people was directed primarily at the legal system in Jordan. Although her reference is clearly directed at the injustice people experience at the personal level, her conceptualization can be expanded to include the violence and injustice directed at the natural environment as well and would address the question of environmental security, which ties in with Nancy's analogy of how social ills affect individuals. Finally, Amal's claim that education and employment are the factors that prevent violent actions against individuals is reflective of all four dimensions of security addressed in this study and demonstrates how women tend to focus on constructive rather than destructive means of addressing violence in Jordan.

Notes

1 Rahnema (2001: 117–18) defines modernization for developing countries as the following: 'firstly, the needs regulated to the power of the state – i.e. the army, the police and security forces, the administration, transport and communication services and the mass media; secondly, the infrastructural requirements of modernization and economic development; and finally, at

Jordanian women define security 333

the very bottom of the list, the social and cultural needs of the population most seriously hit by the first two categories of needs'.
2 The term 'tribal' used herein is based on the Arabic use of the term *asheera*. According to the Hans-Wehr Dictionary of Modern Written Arabic, the term is defined as 'clan, kinsfolk, closest relatives; tribe'. In Jordan, the term does not carry the pejorative connotations that it does in English. A person's tribal affiliation is a significant factor in the personal representation of an individual and is justified as a culturally relevant form of social identity.
3 The following parameters of human security are taken from a WINGHS manifesto, distributed at the International Hague Appeal for Peace Conference in Den Hague, The Netherlands, May 1999.
4 Interview transcript: MK_02_10_21.
5 Within these concepts the following properties were also used in coding: work, job, financial, basic needs, needs, wealth, expenditures, salary, home, income, bills and opportunities.
6 The term 'Sha'hayid' in Arabic translates into 'certificates' which implies some form of diploma or official accreditation.
7 Interview transcript: SB_01_10_16.
8 Interview transcript: NB_02_02_15.
9 Interview transcript: AA_02_10_23.
10 Interview transcript: LT_02_02_15.
11 Interview transcript: ER_02_03_16.
12 Interview transcript: ER_02_03_1.
13 Interview transcript: SN_02_02_1.
14 Interview transcript: GST_02_03_0.
15 Interview transcript: NZ_02_03.
16 Interview transcript: HK_02_03_12.
17 Biehler and Snowman (1993: 516–17).
18 Interview transcript: NB_02_02.
19 *Merriam-Webster Dictionary*, 9th ed. (1991: 314).
20 Interview transcript: NB_02_02_15.
21 Interview transcript: MAS_02_01_29.
22 Within these concepts the following properties were also used in coding: justice, human rights, equality and citizenship.
23 Interview transcript: SN_02_02_17.
24 The reference here is to religious Sharia laws – Islamic codes of jurisprudence – not constitutional law.
25 Interview transcript: AK_01_11_18.
26 Interview transcript: MAS_02_01_29.
27 Interview transcript: AK_01_11_18.
28 Interview transcript: FM_01_10_14.
29 Interview transcript: FS_02_03_16.
30 Reference to the term 'Islamic system' in this passage is intended to mean the traditional or tribal ways of interpreting honourable and shameful behaviour.
31 Interview transcript: YAK_02_03_08.
32 Interview transcript: MAS_02_01_29.
33 17 September 2001, House and Garden's Club, Marriott Hotel, 'Discourse on the Participation of Women in Public Life'. 24 September 2001, General Federation of Jordanian Women, 'Organizational Plenary Meeting'.

12–15 March 2002, Jordan Institute for Diplomacy, SAS Radisson, 'Gender & Democratic Transformation in the Arab World'.
34 Interview transcript: GST_02_03_02.
35 Interview transcript: LT_02_02_15.
36 Interview transcript: JN_02_02_05.
37 Field notes, 8 March 2002.
38 Interview transcript: YAK_02_03_08.
39 Interview transcript: SB_01_10_16.
40 Interview transcript: RZ_01_12_21.
41 Interview transcript: NB_02_02_15.
42 Interview transcript: SN_02_02_17.
43 Interview transcript: MAS_02_01_29.
44 According to the CIA World Fact Book 2002, the percentage of arable land in Jordan is only 2.87 per cent, and the percentage that produces permanent crops in only 1.52 per cent. The natural resources are limited to potash, phosphates and shale oil, all products that are mined.
45 Interview transcript: NB_02_02_15.
46 Interview transcript: NE_02_02_05.
47 Interview transcript: JS_02_02_05.
48 Interview transcript: JN_02_02_05.
49 Interview transcript: JN_02_02_05.
50 Interview transcript: NaZ_02_03_08.
51 Interview transcript: NZ_02_03_08.
52 Interview transcript: GST_02_03_02.
53 Interview transcript: DT_02_03_02.
54 Interview transcript: AH_02_03_16.
55 The meaning of the term *il watan* in Arabic literally means 'the land' but has developed to incorporate nationalistic/political values or, in this case, loyalty to God and King.

References

Buzan, B., Waever, O., and de Wilde, J. (Eds.). 1998. *Security: A New Framework for Analysis*. London: Lynne Rienner.

Hans Wehr: A Dictionary of Modern Written Arabic. New York: Spoken Languages Services, Inc.

hooks, bell. 1994. *Teaching to Transgress: Education as the Practice of Freedom*. New York: Routledge.

Khan, Shahnaz. 2002. 'Muslim Women: Negotiations in the Third Space', in Therese Saliba, Carolyn Allen and Judith A. Howard (eds.), *Gender, Politics and Islam*, pp. 305–36. Chicago: University of Chicago Press.

Maslow, Abraham. 1943. 'A Theory of Human Motivation', *Psychological Review*, vol. 50 (4): 370–96.

Rahnema, Majid. 2001. 'Participation', in W. Sachs (ed.), *The Development Dictionary: A Guide to Knowledge as Power*, pp. 116–31. London: Zed Books.

UNDP. 2002. *The Arab Human Development Report 2002: Creating opportunities for future generations*. New York: UNDP/RBAS.

13 Public health and patriarchy

Militarism and gender as determinants of health insecurity

Albie Sharpe

> What, for example, is the 'cause' of death of a starving person, caught in a civil war, who ends up in a refugee camp, and then dies of measles?
> – W. P. Falcon and R. L. Naylor (2005: 1114)

Introduction

Health is fundamental to the human experience. It is a precondition for most of the activities that we define as human: our culture, economy, child-raising, laughter, sex, work, freedom of choice, the affirmation of our rights – all are in some way dependent on the health of the individual and their community. Health is also an outcome of the human experience: humans work to create and use resources that result in health and wellbeing, such as food, education or leisure. Positive endeavours lead to greater social capital, success and even positions of social dominance. This then increases overall wellbeing and life expectancy for both individuals and communities. However, this same principle also leads to poor health outcomes. In situations where freedoms are denied, education not provided, work not done or environments in which violence, inequity and exclusion are common, there are often significant negative effects on health. The health status of populations can, therefore, serve as an indicator of the levels of equality, trust and wellbeing in a community, just as it can provide evidence of the levels of direct and indirect violence, inequity and the abuse of the environment. Using this approach means that health becomes a lot more than just a product of medicine – it becomes an outcome of the effects of these social and environmental 'determinants' of health. For health and development workers, this represents a paradigm shift in thinking: to improve health, we need to challenge the underlying injustices and social conditions which lead to poor health outcomes. It also means that health extends far beyond the responsibility of the professional health worker – it requires active and critical citizenship.

In establishing a connection among poverty, inequality, exclusion and violence, health can be analyzed not as a medical problem but as a human security issue. Human security is a paradigm in which human beings replace the state as the central focus of security analysis. It provides a systematizing and multi-sectoral framework around which development and peacebuilding can be organized, implemented and evaluated. The 1994 Human Development Report (UNDP 1994), with its dual focus on freedom from fear and freedom from want, established a connection between human deprivation and manifestations of violence. It focused on ways in which people could be protected from insecurities caused by such factors as disease, unemployment, crime and political upheaval – all of which may contribute to the outbreak of violence. According to the Commission on Human Security (hereafter CHS), human security means protecting 'the vital core of all human lives in ways that enhance freedoms and human fulfillment . . . it means protecting people from critical (severe) and pervasive threats and situations' (CHS 2003: 4). It entails that the range of actors in working toward the realization of human security is broadened beyond the government and that empowerment of people to achieve their own aspirations is a key goal.

However, there are key underlying questions in human security approaches that often remain unexplored, particularly in terms of the complex and discursive ways in which power is constructed and utilized by a state and its citizens. States monopolize power in patriarchal forms that exclude and marginalize more vulnerable sections of the community. Empowerment of citizens may be considered contrary to the goal of preserving state-based institutions, particularly the military, deemed necessary for the perpetuation of the state. Consequently, it would be expected that states are more likely to adopt approaches based around protection rather than around genuine empowerment of citizens. 'Empowerment' becomes little more than a 'buzzword' to 'pepper the discourse with positive flavor' (Gibson and Reardon 2007: 54). Likewise, the CHS (2003) calls for the creation of 'political, social, environmental, economic, military and cultural systems that together give people the building blocks of survival, livelihood and dignity' (ibid.: 4). If states define these processes, then there is a chance that the same hegemonic structures will be maintained, and human security, rather than being complementary or an alternative to state security, will be subsumed into state security discourses.

The aim of this article is to explore the connections between militarism and gender as determinants of health insecurity. It will argue that state security structures are fundamentally patriarchal and that these are manifested both in militarism and in the Western medical system. It will examine how health security approaches in the literature attempt to alleviate negative health outcomes for both women and men, primarily by replicating state security mechanisms through protectionist approaches. However, the literature also points in several other less paternalistic, more horizontal directions, such as the redistribution of resources, human rights, primary healthcare and empowerment. The article will argue that only these strategies used in combination, based on principles of social justice and gender equity, will be effective in developing a non-patriarchal approach to health and security. Although this article does focus specifically on health security, this does not mean that health is here defined as a separate or parallel problematic but rather that the development of a health perspective on insecurity has potential implications for human security as a whole. In particular, this article draws from the theoretical approaches and practices of New Public Health. These approaches have been underutilized within health security and could do much to inform a broader human security framework (Feldbaum and Lee 2004: 21).

Health and security: a determinants' approach

Health is much more than the absence of disease. It is defined by the World Health Organization (WHO; 1946) as 'complete physical, mental and social well-being, and not merely the absence of disease or infirmity'. This highly aspirational definition, subsequently adopted by the CHS (2003: 96), recognizes that health is not just an individual state which is passed down through genes or a result of individual decision-making. Health is a product of a large range of biological, environmental and social determinants, such as wealth, gender, ethnicity and education (see Reidpath 2004). 'Gender' as a social determinant of health, for example, leads to poor health outcomes for both men and women. It creates 'different risks and protections for physical illnesses, produces different behaviour when ill, elicits different responses in healthcare personnel, affects the social worth of patients, and influences priorities of treatment, research and financing' (Lorber and Moore 2002: 3). In many countries, girls are perceived as a financial burden and are less likely to receive medical treatment. When they do they receive care, it is often at a later stage in an illness in comparison to boys. Girls are also likely to receive less food, making them much more vulnerable to disease. Maternal illness and mortality is also less a result of biological determinants than social ones, with enormous disparities between those with access to care and those without (CSDH 2008: 154). Men's health is also affected by socially defined gender roles. Higher rates of suicide and substance abuse (partly as a result of men failing to live up to the culturally defined expectations of their gender) are a result. Men often refuse to accept illness, putting off health-seeking behaviours, such as visiting doctors, refusing HIV tests or changing their lifestyle, until the illness has become significantly worse (see Lorber and Moore 2002: 14).

A determinants' analysis allows health to be connected to many other interrelated and mutually supportive aspects of human security. Health is central to human security, as it is not just a component but a precondition and outcome of other aspects of human security. According to Chen (2004),

> good health is 'intrinsic' to human security, since human survival and good health are at the core of 'security'. Health is also 'instrumental' to human security because good health enables the full range of human functioning. Health permits human choice, freedom and development . . . the attainment of health is not possible without peace and equitable development.
>
> (2004: 2)

A determinants' approach to human security allows movement beyond state-based medical systems, which reflect state security structures and are significantly overrated as a means of providing basic health. Societies revert to the old model of a 'war on disease' without recognizing that infectious disease is, for the most part, opportunistic, taking advantage of poverty, inequality and hunger. The WHO is currently renewing its focus on health determinants. The report by the WHO Commission on the Social Determinants of Health (CSDH 2008) noted that social inequalities are 'killing people on a grand scale', with social inequity manifesting itself 'across various intersecting social categories such as class, education, gender, age, ethnicity, disability, and geography'. This occurs, according to the report, not simply as a result of difference but hierarchy, 'and reflects deep inequities in the wealth, power and prestige of different people and communities' (CSDH 2008: 18).

Gender, militarism and patriarchy: defining the connections

Gender in this article is defined as the culturally constructed attitudes, behaviours and roles that are based on sex and sexual identity.

Gendered behaviours and attitudes are a result of a process of negotiation between individuals and the society in which they live, meaning that multiple genders and multiple behaviours are possible and that these can change according to time and place. In most societies, there are socially constructed limits on opportunities for individual exploration of gender identity, particularly as a result of patriarchal beliefs. The concepts of sex (the biological differences between men and women) and gender often become conflated, with assumptions about the roles of men and women becoming essentialized: for example, that males are predisposed toward violence and that women are natural carers. In patriarchal societies, institutions, values and beliefs define the relations between women and men in socially prescriptive ways (Elster 1981: 15). In this respect, both men and women are oppressed by patriarchy: it is a denial of the freedom of choice to define one's own gender roles and therefore a denial of human dignity.

The gender approach taken in this article does not mean denying the reality that women in most, if not all, societies are more vulnerable to the effects of militarism. Militarism is, according to Betty A. Reardon, 'the belief system that upholds the legitimacy of military control of the state' (1996: 14). The more militaristic a society, Reardon argues, the greater the sexism in its institutions and values. The military is 'the distilled embodiment of patriarchy; the militarization of society is the unchecked manifestation of patriarchy as the *overt* and *explicit* mode of governance' (1996: 15). The significant effects of militarism and war on the health of women have already been addressed elsewhere (see, for example, Ashford and Huet-Vaughn 2000). However, victim-perpetrator discourses may ultimately perpetuate rather than reduce gender inequalities by reasserting the value of 'protection' for those that society has deemed 'vulnerable' (something this article will explore further). Instead, a gender-based approach, which considers the effects of militarism on the health security of both women and men, can focus on the ways in which gender-restrictive behaviours and beliefs act through institutions (such as the health system and militarism) to produce negative social outcomes. Hence, it could be argued that a broader social definition of gender, in which men and women are encouraged to negotiate their own gender identities, may benefit health significantly by reducing the potential for stress and violence. There is some evidence to show that health outcomes are worse in societies where male-female gender structures are more restrictive. Peacock and Weston (2008) showed that social restrictions on males as health carers limited their ability to care for sick partners. However, more work needs be done to show that the inverse – greater gender freedom leads to better health outcomes – is also true (Snow 2007).

Violence as a public health issue

Public health deals with health at the level of populations rather than individuals. The focus of New Public Health approaches has shifted in recent years to dealing not only with water and sanitation or alcohol and tobacco but also with much broader threats to health. The consequences of violence – injuries, preventable deaths, torture, effects on the environment, food and water, livelihoods and social exclusion – have profound effects on the health of communities. In this sense, militarism and war are both significant public health issues. Medicine-based approaches mitigate the effects of situations of violence on individuals (Krug et al. 2002: 215). A determinants' approach, on the other hand, would need to challenge the underlying political, social and gendered structures that cause violence. In the *Human Security Now* report, the CHS argued that 'all forms of violence – collective, interpersonal and self-directed – are public health problems. Indeed, the growing social crises of violence all have strong health dimensions' (CHS 2003: 98). Similarly, the World Report on Health and Violence (Krug et al. 2002) specifically examined violence as a public health issue. The report used the WHO (1996) definition, which referred to violence as 'the intentional use of physical force or power, threatened or actual, against oneself, another person, or against a group or community, that either results in or has a high likelihood of resulting in injury, death, psychological harm, maldevelopment or deprivation' (ibid.: 5). The report also discussed the range of forms that violence can take – physical, sexual, psychological and deprivation or neglect. Most importantly, it challenged the assumption that violence can be thought of as a natural part of the human condition. However, the definition frames violence only in terms of the intentionality of the actor or perpetrator. This means that many forms of social injustice, particularly those caused by exploitation and environmental destruction (as unintentional), are excluded from consideration as acts of violence. Furthermore, it focuses on the effects of militarism, such as sexual violence, prostitution, disease, poverty and its opportunity costs, rather than on its underlying determinants. Even though the report explores both gender-based domestic violence and violence committed as a result of military action and expenditure, it fails to make any connection between the two. Militarism, as an outcome of a gendered system of state security, is not examined; only its effects.

Mann (1998) took a somewhat different approach by establishing that violations of dignity should also be considered forms of violence. He referred to violations of human dignity as 'pervasive events with potentially severe and sustained negative effects on physical, mental and social wellbeing', thereby moving beyond the limitations imposed by the need for 'intentionality' in defining violence. 'Future generations', he wrote,

> may look back at the current limited and narrow understanding of health and wonder how we could have missed seeing violations of dignity as sources of injury to well-being . . . Dignity's meaning in the universe of human suffering may be as evident in the future as the role of HIV in causing AIDS is today.
>
> (1998: 37)

Public health is an evidence-based practice. Consequently, a necessary step for public health workers in defining issues related to violence and humiliation as health issues would be to develop an epidemiology of the causes and effects. Recognizing this need, Mann called for a new process of 'naming' violations of human dignity as public health issues. The identification of violations of human dignity as health issues involves a process of discovery: lifting the veil of silence and developing a descriptive epidemiology which makes an analysis of the problem possible, leading ultimately to 'an understanding sufficiently broad for developing public health policies and programmes geared towards prevention and amelioration of the newly-identified public health problem' (1998: 35). By identifying violence as an issue that is important to the improvement of public health, there are new opportunities for not only addressing the consequences of violence but also the causes of it. Health security becomes an issue of fundamental human dignity that can be addressed by health workers through the determinants of health, the application of rights-based approaches to health and community empowerment and democratization. The next step would therefore be to begin the epidemiological process by looking at the effects of militarism and gender on health and dignity.

An epidemiology of gender and militarism

Militarism and gender are significant determinants of poor health that have corresponding and interrelated effects on other health determinants. War and militarism are obviously detrimental to health. One of the effects, if not the goals, of war is damage to the health of the other, the enemy – whether the individual or state. Until the WHO began the World Health Report in 2001, there were few consistent attempts to quantitatively analyze the number of people who lost their lives as an indirect result of conflict (Murray et al. 2002: 349). According to Geiger (2000: 40), of the 20 million people killed and 60 million people injured in declared conflicts over the past 60 years, more than 80 per cent have been civilians, of which 60 per cent have been children. This atrocity comes about through direct attacks on civilians, attacks with indiscriminate weapons, ethnic cleansing and indirect attacks on civilian infrastructure. With most recent wars being intrastate conflicts, one of the goals of conflict has been ethnic cleansing, as opposed to control, over enemy populations. Health (or its lack) becomes a major weapon in ensuring that populations flee rather than stay. There are several ways in which this is done – through direct military means, more indirect weapons, such as landmines, and destruction of livelihoods and property, along with attacks on hospitals and state institutions. There are also profound effects on mental health as a result of the psychological pressures caused by constant stress and deliberate, politically motivated sexual violence.

In many ways, militarism can be shown to disrupt the ways in which the physical and human environment supports health – intentional or not. The use of chemical defoliants in Vietnam, nuclear no-go zones in the former USSR, poisoned water supplies and depleted uranium dust from weapons used in Iraq are all examples of environmental consequences that have continued, and will continue, for long after the short-term political goals of conflict. In particular, nuclear, biological or chemical weapons' use (or even accidents) may be potentially devastating, causing interrelated health and environmental problems for communities or ultimately the entire planetary population. Furthermore, the resources and environmental waste from the use of weapons, as well as their manufacture, have both immediate and long-term consequences. Attacks during the Gulf Wars and sanctions between them on systems designed to protect public health – sewerage (see MacQueen et al. 2004), water, food distribution, power, hospitals and communications – are deliberate attempts to disrupt the health of the other and, by doing so, intimidate or 'shock and awe' the local population into surrender. This has disproportionate effects on society's most vulnerable members. Food production and transport is disrupted, resulting in increased malnutrition, poverty and disease. The poor have little resistance to external shocks, such as war, and may be forced to sell whatever physical resources they have in order to survive. Ashford and Huet-Vaughn (2000) describe this as a new strategy that 'appears to be making war on public health . . . a ruthless assault on the survival needs of the population' (2000: 187). Geiger (2000) concludes that targeting of infrastructure is part of a military policy of 'bomb now, die later', in which the major powers breach the Geneva Conventions without the 'stigma of direct attack on the bodies and habitats of non-combatants' (2000: 46).

The extent to which a society is militarized and the way in which that militarism is practiced is a significant determinant of health, and it can be shown to undermine health security. War is a form of gendered violence. It impacts on the health and wellbeing of all genders, but not equally, and in different ways. Militarism increases vulnerability in societies through its assertion of patriarchal values: men as dominant; women as passive and in need of protection. In wartime, gender roles often become more proscribed, with fewer options for alternative expressions of gender identity or sexual orientation. This has consequences in terms of both human dignity and health security. Men who refuse to join the armed forces, for whatever reason – conscientious objection, religious beliefs or lack of 'national fervour' – are often feminized and taunted, even subjected to violence. Male recruits to armed forces are usually defeminized, encouraged to take risks and behave in a more aggressive manner, with a corresponding increase in sexually risky, aggressive behaviours. According to UNAIDS (1998), social constraints on the behaviour of young soldiers are removed, as are the social support mechanisms that would exist were the soldiers based near their local communities. The remote location of army bases and the relatively high income of the security forces attracts sex workers. In many countries, this is an illegal (and therefore unregulated) profession, exposing sex workers, soldiers, their families and ultimately their communities to risks, such as HIV and other sexually transmitted diseases (STDs). Even in peacetime, the prevalence of STDs amongst armed forces personnel is two to five times that of the general population. During war, the rate can be as much as 50 times as high (UNAIDS 1998: 3). According to some reports, the prevalence of HIV in the Zimbabwean military at one point topped 70 per cent of personnel in some areas (Machipisa 1996), meaning that the diversion of resources away from healthcare, HIV prevention and education undermined the state's ability to provide national security.

Women also suffer as a result of greater confinement and stricter gender roles. Ashford and Huet-Vaughn (2000) highlight the increased burden on women in Iraq, as men's roles did not change or were diminished as a result of their inability to work. At the same time, the conflict increased women's workloads, expanded them 'to include securing water and firewood for their families on a day-to-day basis' (2000: 187), a fact which would expose them to the risk of further violence.

Furthermore, they reported that for the most vulnerable sections of the community, the lack of social welfare services, along with loss of employment and financial security, has driven many women into dangerous occupations, such as prostitution or begging. In situations of violent conflict, men often leave – to fight, to escape the fighting and political persecution or to travel in search of employment. Women who remain behind are much more likely to be drawn into the conflict as refugees, sex workers or victims of sexual violence. Women and children are reported to make up approximately 80 per cent of all refugees and internally displaced people (ibid.: 188). Conditions in refugee camps and the highly vulnerable state of people on the move create situations where women are much more likely to become victims of sexual violence and trafficking. The effects of violence on health also do not disappear at the end of a conflict – through disease and loss of infrastructure – with women and children again suffering disproportionately. The greater effects on women after the cessation of conflict occur regardless of which gender suffered most of the casualties in the wars (ibid.: 199).

Sexual violence, such as that seen in Bosnia and Darfur, becomes a weapon with profound physical, psychological and social implications. Although sexual violence has also been directed at men, it is primarily directed toward women. Rape is used as a weapon of war, symbolizing the ultimate failure of the 'enemy' men in their duty to protect 'their' women. Seifert (2002) refers to the symbolic act of rape, in which the female body comes to represent strategic territory (ibid.: 291). Although it would be easy to suggest that rape constitutes an individual act of violence, state structures and policies can go a long way toward creating an environment where such violence is condoned.

> Certain individual acts, such as rape, have not been a traditional concern of human rights law, except when resulting from systematic state policy (as alleged in Bosnia). However, it is increasingly evident that state policies impacting on the status and role of women may contribute importantly, even if indirectly, to a societal context that increases women's vulnerability to rape, even though the actual act may be individual, not state sponsored.
> (Mann et al. 1999: 10)

For women who have been raped, there are direct health consequences – psychological trauma, depression, the chance of sexually transmitted diseases and other physical consequences of the assault (Isaksson

2002). In many societies, women who experience sexual violence are blamed for their behaviour rather than the perpetrators. Women who become pregnant as a result of rape are often ostracized from their families or communities or have difficulty in accepting their own children born as a result of rape (Ashford and Huet-Vaughn 2000: 190).

These examples point to underlying patriarchal values that perpetuate the military system and deny both women and men of choices. Even within the military system, women who participate are confronted by the assertion of patriarchal values, with higher levels of sexual harassment and assault in the armed forces (see Nelson 2002: 67). This means that the potential for the development of new, alternative possibilities for freedom of expression and alternatives to violence is severely curtailed by gender and militarism. Militarism, in that it embodies a particular set of beliefs about the way in which the state should maintain its power, is a 'norm' that can be challenged on the grounds that it represents a distortion of the real security needs of people – to have the resources, abilities and political power to protect themselves and their communities from threats to their physical, mental and social wellbeing. As Cook (1999) points out, 'it is a notorious fact that states invoking poverty to justify non-observance of duties to defend women's health often provide disproportionately large military budgets. This is consistent with male-gendered perceptions of a population's needs' (1999: 262).

Patriarchal structures, whether manifested in government, education, healthcare or the exploitation of the environment, rely on the use of hierarchies and, where necessary, militarism and systemic violence to maintain themselves. Human security should provide a holistic means of identifying the complex interrelationships between factors – such as poor health status, violence and inequality – that undermine human dignity. Health security literature has attempted to deal with this in several ways, through protection from threats, redistribution of resources away from military spending toward social development, advocacy of health rights and empowerment. The following section will critically examine each of these approaches in greater detail. Many of these current approaches, rather than reducing inequality, actually perpetuate use of the same 'protectionist' and hierarchical forms of state power. There is a danger that human security, rather than providing a coherent alternative to state-military conceptions of security, may revert to old security discourses of dominance, control and oppression. The very institutions that are given the task of providing health are subject to the same gendered, exclusionary and hierarchical structures that embody militarism, with the result being that many people – especially those most vulnerable – are excluded from access to basic healthcare.

Health security approaches

Protection from threats

Much of the literature on health security focuses on the role of the state in protecting people from threats (Price-Smith 2002; Heymann 2003; Chen and Narasimhan 2003). According to CHS (2003), the goal of health security is to protect 'the vital core of human lives' from 'critical and pervasive threats while promoting long-term human flourishing'. In order to do this, 'protective strategies would promote the three institutional pillars of society: to prevent, monitor and anticipate health threats' (ibid.: 103). Price-Smith (2002) focuses on the necessity of ensuring state capacity to protect the health of citizens, as well as the environment, as a means of enhancing security. The emergence of new pathogens has the potential to create public fears which bear little relation to the risks of the actual disease itself. New diseases tend to 'generate paranoia, hysteria and xenophobia that may affect the foreign policy of a state by impairing decision making' (ibid.: 16). Price-Smith notes that the ability of states to respond to increasing morbidity and mortality caused by infectious disease could be economically and socially undermined by a corresponding increase in the demands of the people on the state for medical resources. The state therefore needs to play a central role in the protection of its citizens, primarily through the use of state security and medical institutions. This promotes human security as 'the mastery of high morbidity and mortality rates in a population has been a driver of state prosperity and economic strength throughout recorded history' (ibid.: 78).

Protectionist approaches also attempt to reduce the possibility and probable aftereffects of biological and chemical weapons as well as the health-related implications of environmental change. Heymann (2003) advocates technical solutions, such as the development of strong government-centred policies, better international cooperation and global surveillance. He calls for more 'dual-use' facilities, including additional hospitals that can address prevailing health problems, while ensuring there is sufficient emergency capacity to mitigate the effects of terrorism or natural disasters. According to this model, financial and technical support for health systems need to be provided by wealthy industrialized nations on the basis of self-interest – globalized health threats can easily cross borders and be transmitted around the world in a matter of hours, thereby undermining national and global security. The spread of HIV/ AIDS, malaria and emerging and re-emerging infectious diseases can be impeded through surveillance and massive campaigns against specific diseases, going beyond health 'to include national security, defense and international development aid' (ibid.: 208).

In protectionist approaches, disease and health-related threats are the challenges to health security that must be managed. While not negating the efforts of those working to help people facing such health threats, there is little in this approach that enables people to develop their own capacity to deal with threats to their security. Dual-use health facilities may have some benefits in improving health, but again, they may also result in misallocation of resources. The anthrax scares in the United States following the September 11 terrorist attacks did not result in increased opportunities for health but, as Petchesky (2003) put it, 'expanded stockpiles of vaccines and antibiotics, construction of containment laboratories, research into new drugs and biodetectors – in other words, a new bioterrorism industry, not more public hospitals, clinics or sexual and reproductive health or primary healthcare services for the poor' (ibid.: 251). The self-interest of states to provide protection for themselves becomes the driving argument for any intervention. This means that even though the definition of security has expanded to encompass a greater range of potential and actual threats to security, the fundamental goal of protectionist approaches is still the perpetuation of the state and only by this ensuring its ability to protect its citizens. The state is the main actor and beneficiary, preserving a paternalistic, top-down role as protector.

Many of the health security measures suggested in this 'protection from threats' approach deal with protecting people who are already living in situations of violence, yet there is very little exploration of the upstream causes of that violence. Current research on health security has largely focused on only a couple of issues – primarily infectious disease and biological weapons – yet, according to Lee and McInnes (2003), these may not comprise the major threats to global health (ibid.: 47). The determinants of violence, in particular the state's paternalistic role in sustaining gendered and potentially violent structures, need to be examined. Furthermore, by ignoring the determinants of poor health, 'patients' are 'patched up' and sent back out to face the same unclean water and lack of opportunities and threats to their physical and mental wellbeing. Few would argue that all forms of protection are completely unnecessary. The problem is more that in much of the human security literature, in particular that related to health, this has become the dominant discourse, with little discussion of alternative approaches.

Redistribution of resources from military spending toward greater social spending

Military spending diverts capital and resources away from the provision of healthcare and preventive health services into unproductive, capital-intensive areas. If it can be shown that military spending represents a misapplication of resources needed to protect the real security needs of people, then an argument could be made that those resources should be redistributed to such areas as health and education which would directly meet their needs, thereby increasing human security. Political will could then be garnered in order to 'enact the required redistribution of fiscal resources, ingenuity and technology to stem the rising tide of disease and to promote global prosperity and stability' (Price-Smith 2002: 179). According to SIPRI (2008), military spending has increased in real terms since the early 1990s, with total global military expenditures reaching $1,339 billion at the end of 2007. In many countries, after post–Cold War reductions, military budgets have increased rapidly in the past decade. In both Africa and Asia – areas of the world which can least afford it – there has been an increase of 51 per cent in overall military expenditures since 1998 (ibid.: 10).

There have been several reports tying military spending to negative social and health outcomes and increased violence. In 1994, the World Development Report (UNDP 1994: 50) found that the internal security of developing nations was much more likely to be harmed than helped by a country's own military. The report also highlighted that the chance of dying from some form of social neglect (such as an infectious disease or malnutrition) in a developing country was 33 times greater than the chances of being killed in a war of aggression. Hyatt (2006: 320–1) reported a statistical correlation between higher levels of military spending and child mortality, concluding that for every 1 per cent reduction in military expenditures, the infant mortality rate would decline by 2.5 deaths per 1,000 births each year. There is also some evidence that violence can be related to the failures of governments to provide equitable access to healthcare and educational opportunities. Azam (2001: 442) showed that governments in Africa that failed to deliver the services that people wanted, as a form of wealth redistribution, were much more likely to face violent upheavals and rebellions, while spending on defence caused an increase in the incidence rate of armed rebellion. Conversely, the redistributive effects of public health and education spending worked to reduce outbreaks of violence.

However, there is a question as to whether redistribution of state resources to health and education will inevitably result in improved health. There is a distinct possibility that even if there were the political will to enact such a proposition, the additional resources would be transferred to protectionist/state-centred models that may do little to address the determinants of poor health. Globally, there are gross inequalities in health spending. Until quite recently, more than 90 per cent of the planet's health resources were spent on the 10 per cent of the world's population who least needed it (Global Forum for Health Research 2004). The vertical models used within most Western healthcare practice are hierarchically organized, with the elite, usually male specialists at the top, and the patients situated much lower on the scale. It comes almost as a surprise to learn that the majority of the world's health workers are women (WHO 1993: 32; WHO 2006: xxiii), given that many important medical decisions, research and resource allocations are made (or ignored) by men on women's behalf. The vertical health system does more than materially and socially privilege those at the top of the system – it also disempowers patients. In terms of understanding the societal conditions from which their patients derive, there may be little connection between professional health workers and their patients (see Querubin and Tan 1986). The patient is often treated as a passive receiver of healthcare. This points to the need not only for a redistribution of resources but also of power – a system based on a horizontal rather than on a vertical system.

In 1978, in the Declaration of Alma Ata (WHO 1978), the WHO developed a more horizontal approach to health. A determinants' approach to health works on the basis that better health can be provided if illness is prevented rather than cured. The Declaration of Alma Ata articulated a multi-sectoral approach to health, which included agriculture, food, industry, education, housing, public works, communications and demilitarization as essential components for improving health. Most importantly, the declaration recognized inequalities in health status as a major concern and noted that failure to address those was 'political, socially and economically unacceptable' (WHO 1978). It called for the introduction of Primary Health Care (PHC), in which basic healthcare and prevention would be provided by a system of community health workers at the local level. It also drew attention to the world's misplaced security priorities, requiring governments to redistribute resources that were being spent on arms with the goal of 'health for all by the year 2000'. Horizontal health systems, such as PHC, open up new opportunities for community participation in health services, particularly by women and other marginalized population groups. They offer possibilities for women to challenge established hierarchies, improve status by becoming health providers, enhance their own health and the health of their communities and participate in peacebuilding and human rights-related work within their communities. Although the declaration itself predates the development of the concepts of human security by more than a decade, it does represent a theoretical strand of the health security literature and is referred to in both the Human Development Report (UNDP 1994: 92) and *Human Security Now* (CHS 2003: 107).

There are already several clear cases where the PHC approach has been tried and proven effective (see Werner and Sanders 1997). In Kerala and Sri Lanka, despite tiny budgets and limited resources, life expectancy and morbidity improved through public health and education programmes. The barefoot doctors' programme in China in the 1970s is touted as a major success that underlies the country's current development. Costa Rica now has better health indicators than many areas of the United States. However, Alma Ata's underlying message of social liberation as a means of improving health also proved to be its downfall. The CHS (2003: 107) noted the failure of the international community to meet the goals of Alma Ata, ranging 'from weak political will to economic incapacity'. The result was that 'public systems have not been adequately developed, and private markets in healthcare have catered only to those with the money to pay for care'. However, this is only part of the explanation. The idea of PHC was, according to Werner and Sanders (1997), 'disembowelled' by those committed to maintaining the system as it was – the medical-industrial establishment. Werner and Sanders argued that governments were uncomfortable with the broad messages of participation, empowerment and social action. In several countries that had introduced successful PHC programmes, such as Nicaragua and Mozambique, health workers were deliberately targeted for elimination. Governments also misused the opportunities presented by PHC to dismantle programmes designed to promote a truly grassroots-based health movement (1997: 20).

Another example of the redistribution discourse can be seen in the attempts to contrast global military spending priorities with the failure of the world's governments to meet their obligations in achieving the Millennium Development Goals (MDGs). Of the eight MDGs, three are directly related to health, and all eight have relationships as determinants of better health. All have some connection to the effects that gender has on social development. The Global Forum for Health Research (2004) reports that the goals will not be reached 'without an explicit, coordinated and systematic focus on the gender dimension of all MDGs' (2004: 145). The total amount of spending required for the nations of the world to meet their MDG obligations is put at approximately $135 billion per year, just over 10 per cent of the annual global military spending. However, as Mack and Furlong (2004) note, 'the MDGs call for a halving of world poverty by 2002 – yet there has been no call for halving the numbers of wars or refugees' (2004: 72). In other words, the pathological system that leads to insecurity remains unchallenged and underlying injustices are ignored. All the while, the symptoms are partially addressed through technical solutions.

Health as a human rights issue

Human rights are based around the concept of dignity: humans are entitled to life, liberty and security of person and to be free from all forms of discrimination. Human rights documents define the responsibility of the state toward individual citizens in that citizens can use rights to demand that certain freedoms are protected and that governments provide services on an equitable basis. The CHS (2003) describes the relationship between human rights and human security as complementary in that they can inform each other 'by identifying the importance of freedom from basic insecurities – new and old'. Human security can provide a rationale – or 'reasoned substantiation' – for human rights actions. Similarly, human rights can provide an underlying ethical basis and political recognition for human security (ibid.: 9). Human rights do not have to be legitimized through legal systems in order to create motivation for advocacy or to provide a framework for monitoring abuses. Freedman (1999) argues that 'human rights is not just an exercise of legal formalism for lawyers and judges to undertake; it is also the legitimate territory of those who make political demands about basic justice' (ibid.: 147). This applies very strongly to health, with Brundtland (2005) noting that

> health and human rights should inform and inspire each other. Both health and human rights recognize the ultimate responsibility of governments to create the enabling conditions necessary for people to make and effectuate choices, cope with changing patterns of vulnerability and keep themselves and their families healthy.
> (2005: 61)

Petchesky (2003) argues that viewing human rights as either a fixed body of principles or as normative tools for use by the oppressed is inadequate. Rather, she says, human rights are 'a discursive field of power relations that operate within the domain of racialized, gendered global capital ... relations that are constantly in a process of realignment and change' (2003: 22). Taking a socially constructivist approach such as this creates the possibility of seeing human rights as something that progressively transforms and conditions the discourse of human rights from within the very language and structures used to realize them.

The importance of a rights-based approach is less that it offers immediate recourse to those who do not have access to health than it creates a framework by which those rights can be progressively realized. These rights are laid out in the International Covenant on Economic Social and Cultural Rights General Comment No. 14 (Committee on Economic, Social and Cultural Rights 2000), which explicitly recognizes the role of socio-economic factors as underlying determinants of health, such as 'food, nutrition, housing, access to safe and potable water and adequate sanitation, safe and healthy working conditions, and a healthy environment'. Many states do not have the resources to provide access to healthcare for all, but a rights-based approach to health means that at least some levels of equity are ensured. Healthy populations can then more actively pursue the further development of rights, providing a basis for advocacy, as citizens and civil society groups can challenge their governments to provide necessary services, particularly when marginalized groups are not receiving care to which they are entitled. Rights approaches can challenge the legitimacy of inequitable systems, limit arms sales, end military destruction of the natural environment, prevent torture, ensure disarmament and demobilization after a conflict and create the possibility of new normative principles for behaviour. They also provide a means of creating international comparative standards that can be used to direct resources to those most in need.

If rights are addressed, according to rights-based approaches, then health status should improve. Fundamental to the principle of human dignity is the right to control one's own body, including the right to engage in (and to refuse) sexual activity, to have children and not to be subjected to violence or threats of violence. Unequal rights for women enhance the spread of diseases and increase risks of child and maternal mortality. Lack of sexual and reproductive rights, which means that safe sex cannot be negotiated, lead to higher birthrates, increased child and maternal mortality and the spread of HIV and other diseases, resulting in insecurity. Legal systems provide some measures to protect women, including laws against deliberate HIV infection, along with stricter penalties for marital rape and sexual violence. The Rome Statute redefined rape, sexual slavery, forced prostitution, forced pregnancy, enforced sterilization or any other form of sexual violence as crimes against humanity 'when committed as part of a widespread or systematic attack directed against any civilian population' (ICC 1998).

Poor health status also results in a lack of rights by denying people access to opportunities that a more equitable society might otherwise offer. Unfortunately, laws against sexual minorities and prostitution also deny many people access to education and protection and make seeking help much more difficult (see Zungu-Dirwayi et al. 2004: 59). Even in countries which have laws designed to protect minorities, mechanisms may not be in place to ensure that laws are enforced adequately.

On the other hand, rights-centred approaches can further humiliate and marginalize those with no access to the resources to make use of their rights. Petchesky (2003) notes that reproductive rights for women may be of little use if they have no money to travel to procure services, cannot find information in their own language or will be beaten by a relative for using birth control. The 'means to do so', according to Petchesky, contains 'a universe of freedoms and capabilities out of reach for many women and girls' (2003: 18–19). Rights can promote an overly legalistic and confrontationalist approach to problems that may be solved instead through negotiation. Governments are also always likely to be constrained by the moral implications of failing to implement international laws. As in the case of Sudan, arguments over sovereignty and allegations of external forces interfering in a nation's domestic policy may result in an inverse reaction to the issue that is being advocated. In countries where treaties are signed but not implemented, this represents a major potential barrier to those seeking to use the legal system as a means of ensuring their right to health. With health rapidly globalizing, the development of better mechanisms of public health may be an important means of ensuring that many of the most aspirational features of international law are not abandoned.

Patriarchal systems can be challenged on human rights grounds in that governments and providers of healthcare fail to serve their populations equitably. Felice (1998) argues that 'high levels of military spending in less developed and developed countries prevent all of these from fulfilling the basic economic and social rights articulated in the International Bill of Human Rights' (1998: 27). Militarism is incompatible with these rights in that it results in direct harm to the human and natural environment from which our economic, environmental and social health derives. It deprives resources from programmes that would enhance rights and undermines people's ability to pursue behaviours that would enhance their own wellbeing. Militarism can therefore be described as a challenge to the principles underlying a human right to health in that it furthers inequality, increases situations in which violence is likely to occur, creates narrower, more proscribed gender roles and denies resources to the most vulnerable, leading to worsening health status. International laws on armaments can also have profound effects on health, with the WHO questioning the legality of nuclear weapons in 1994 by putting the case to the International Court of Justice that signatories to the WHO Constitution may have been in breach of their obligations to world health by maintaining a nuclear weapons arsenal. The court rejected the arguments on the grounds that it was not within its jurisdiction (Matheson 1997: 418). More successful was the recent 'Ottawa' Convention on the Prohibition on the Use, Stockpiling, Production and Transfer of Anti-Personnel Mines and on Their Destruction (1997). Even with some major powers refusing to sign the treaty, the legitimacy of the use of such weapons is gradually being undermined, a fact which strengthens Petchesky's aforementioned notion of human rights as discursive and progressive.

Empowerment and the democratization of health

The final and least explored approach of health security literature calls for people to work toward a radical reorientation of health services to make them more accountable to citizens. A central feature of this approach lies in the empowerment of people to take charge of their own health and security. Empowerment embodies elements of improved capacity, action for change and political and social awakening. It must, necessarily, involve a change in a person's or group's power status within a community. Empowerment is defined by the WHO as the 'process of enabling people to increase control over, and to improve their health' (Rissel 1994: 40). Laverack (2005) argues that empowerment provides a means for both individuals and communities to attain power. He points out, however, that there is often a superficial understanding of power by those working to empower communities (ibid.: 112). It involves much more than the simple transfer of knowledge or resources to a community. It is a process of critical awareness, community mobilization, and development of decision-making capacity (see Laverack's nine domains of community empowerment, 2005: Chapter 5). Empowerment has become a central feature of new approaches in public health (Baum 2008: 484); however, it has been largely ignored in health security. An example of how little emphasis has been placed on empowerment for health in the literature can be seen in the way that the UN Trust Fund for Human Security (UN-OHCA 2008) has ignored its health potential. Although empowerment of communities has an equally important role to protection in many key goals of the trust fund, health is consigned to merely protective approaches, through access to government provision of healthcare services. This points again to the primacy of protectionist models in health security and to a significant deficiency in health security literature.

Although empowerment of individuals is, as noted earlier, a popular buzzword within human security, a close look at how empowerment has been framed within human security literature seems to indicate that the state is still the main actor. The CHS (2003) report argued that protection and empowerment should be seen as complementary activities to develop human security. Activities for human security should be based on the question 'How does this activity build on the efforts and capabilities of those directly affected?' (2003: 11–12). Empowerment of people and societies, according to the CHS, means that 'people can contribute directly to identifying and implementing solutions to the quagmire of insecurity. In post-conflict situations, for example, bringing diverse constituents together to rebuild their communities can solve security problems' (2003: 6). The goal is less empowerment, along the lines of Laverack, than participation, with those in charge of its implementation – potentially the state – acting as a guide in bringing people together. People are not actually encouraged to take power from the state but to become participants in the state-defined processes. Furthermore, the aim of empowerment in its true form would mean working toward ending all forms of gender oppression – a goal which is inconsistent with the needs of a militarized state. The more militarized a state, the less likely it is to encourage any form of empowerment, as such an approach will undermine the basis of the security systems on which the state depends. Therefore, protection and empowerment should not be considered only complementary but also competing approaches. True empowerment will necessarily reduce the need and capacity for the state to continue as the sole provider of protection.

Empowerment is connected to the application of rights; however, it extends far beyond this as a legalistic framework to the critical awareness of the need for social change and working toward the achievement of social justice. The act of empowerment itself builds social capital and therefore health. Workers in health promotion have been aware for some time that the provision of information and resources – through 'behaviour-change' models (see Baum 2008: 456–75) – was not enough to get people to develop health-seeking behaviours. Instead, it was noted that the social, economic and physical environment played a major role in developing healthier lifestyles. This was defined as an approach in the Ottawa Charter on Health Promotion (WHO 1986). In order to achieve a state of complete physical, mental and social wellbeing,

individual or groups must be able to identify and to realize aspirations, to satisfy needs, and to change or cope with the environment. Health is, therefore, seen as a resource for everyday life, not the objective of living. Health is a positive concept emphasizing social and personal resources, as well as physical capacities. Therefore, health promotion is not just the responsibility of the health sector, but goes beyond healthy life-styles to well-being.
(WHO 1986)

When we compare this to the approach in CHS (2003) just noted, the focus is much less on others developing people's capacities than on people developing their own capacities. In the Ottawa Charter, health is the responsibility of everyone, and all parts of society need to work together to promote health. The fundamental conditions and resources necessary to achieve health are peace, shelter, education, food, income, a stable ecosystem, sustainable resources, social justice and equity. Education is more than a means of ensuring behaviour change – it is part of a political process designed to allow people to take greater control over their lives, to prepare for health challenges and to promote community actions for better health.

Taking this approach still further, the People's Health Movement has also called for a greater democratization of health. The People's Charter for Health declared that

> inequality, poverty, exploitation, violence and injustice are at the root of ill-health and the deaths of poor and marginalized people. Health For All means that powerful interests have to be challenged, that globalization has to be opposed, and that political and economic priorities have to be drastically changed.
> (People's Health Movement 2001: 1)

In other words, health and security will come about through reframing global systems of power, with the goal of 'prevention and reduction of aggressive and violent behaviour, especially in men, and the fostering of peaceful coexistence' (2001: 10). The People's Health Charter also places a lot of importance on the necessity of demilitarization and disarmament, urging support for campaigns for peace and disarmament as well as campaigns against the development, testing and use of weapons. It demands an end to sexual slavery, the recruitment of child soldiers and the use of rape and torture. At the international level, it recognizes that sanctions often hurt civilian populations and calls for a radical democratic transformation of the United Nations. It focuses on peace not only at the national level but also at the local level, encouraging the development of local peace initiatives and weapons-free zones. The importance of the report is that it represents a civil society action rather than a government initiative – an important step toward the democratization of health.

A focus on empowerment has the potential not only to benefit women, who may achieve a much greater control over their own, their community's and their society's health, but also men. For women, it means that there can be stronger recognition of the right to control their own sexuality, reproduction and physical and emotional safety and dignity. It also means a much greater role in ensuring access for women to the policy-making processes of the health system and a greater focus on issues relating to women's health, particularly in the developing world. For men, greater freedom from the strictures of proscribed gender roles means that men may be able to act in ways that diminish the possibility of violence, allow the exploration of opportunities for community reconciliation and undermine a societal belief in militarism. It means that men will have more opportunities to develop alternative masculine values that promote peaceful societies rather than undermining them. However, approaches to gender planning need to proceed with empowerment carefully – programmes that address only the needs of one group may result in very limited outcomes or violent backlash. For example, education programmes in South Africa have been aimed at empowering women to take greater control of their lives through employment, education and awareness of sexual rights (Epstein 2007: 234). Yet as Epstein points out, women who are most likely to be subjected to violence or rape in South African society are those whom are deemed to threaten the patriarchal values of men (ibid.: 235). Gender is so deeply rooted in our social and cultural concepts that intervention is an extremely difficult thing to do, particularly when it is imposed from the outside. One way of dealing with this is to ensure that gender is dealt with from within the cultural and social context of the community. When gender mainstreaming or other interventions seem to be an *outside* concept, it becomes something that is forced on a community and may result in a backlash.

Conclusions

Militarism is a logical outgrowth of a patriarchal society – through the use of force as a means of regulating social hierarchies and ensuring that those at the top of the structure receive a disproportionate share of resources. The construction of gender, as part of a negotiation with society, is not in itself a problem. The problem occurs when gender roles are proscribed by society, resulting in oppression, discrimination, fear and violence, with adverse effects on the health of both men and women. Both gender and militarism are significant determinants of health and insecurity. Combined, they create structures which disproportionately affect women through exclusion, violence and misapplication of resources. A determinants analysis allows the development of alternatives to only simply focus on women as victims of militarism but also to look at the role that gendered behaviours, structures and institutions play in generating insecurity. When we define violence as a public health issue, as has been done earlier in this article, it means we need to challenge the social, political and cultural beliefs that support violence and lead to inequality, discrimination and exclusion. Based primarily on protectionist models, current human security discourse perpetuates patriarchy rather than addressing it.

A non-patriarchal human security, based around principles of social justice, the dignity and worth of the person and environmental and social sustainability, offers much greater possibilities for reducing the causes and effects of threats. This would need to be built around four mutually supporting strategies.

- Redistribution not only of resources but also of power. Redistribution for human security needs to be framed around the goals of undermining hierarchies, reducing the threats that militarism poses to human security and environmental sustainability and generating more equitable systems. This means empowering people not only to take resources from military spending in all its forms but also to ensure that people's basic needs are met through the equitable distribution of resources in such areas as food, healthcare, education, housing and employment opportunities. Fundamental to this is the need for gender equity – access for women to all levels of the decision-making process. It involves recognizing the major role that women already play in healthcare, education and all other aspects of social development.
- Human rights based on fundamental human dignity and a progressive recognition of values toward the development of positive rights. Rights approaches are one of the principle means by which individuals and communities can negotiate with the state about the equitable use of power and resources. Successful application of human rights enhances the development of new social values and increases empowerment.
- Empowerment occurs as a result of the raising of critical consciousness, a process that needs to be nurtured and reinforced by

civil society. Empowerment is an essential precondition for community use of power, the acquisition and utilization of rights and for redefining the power of the state. It is also an outcome of claiming human rights and of the successful use of power.
- Sufficient protection provided by the state through healthcare and other state-based services to ensure that people have access to protective services where required. This needs to be mandated by people through use of human rights mechanisms, and where necessary, civil action to demand the redistribution of resources and power.

A human security based solely around the state-based reduction of threats – through protection from harm – may succeed; however, it may also replicate those threats by reinforcing the very structures that lead to those threats in the first place. When we talk about the idea of abandoning policies, beliefs and behaviours that support militarism, the introduction of a rights framework will not by itself have an effect unless we can change the underlying sociopolitical beliefs and structures that support militarism and generate new values which can be transformed into rights. The realization of rights cannot be done without some form of critical consciousness-raising and community empowerment. In other words, we need individuals and communities – both women and men – to change their own environments to support alternatives to militarism. A human security framework that incorporates a gender perspective (through protection, redistribution, human rights, primary healthcare and empowerment) and that tackles the patriarchal foundations of militarism and the health system would provide beneficial outcomes for human dignity. It would allow people to make a greater economic and social contribution to their own societies, thereby reducing some of the determinants of insecurity and violence. By redirecting a larger portion of the massive resources spent on the world's militaries into social development, there is a chance for a real improvement in global health. This needs to be done systematically and in such a way that new insecurities are not generated in both the state through the military and in health systems through hierarchical and exclusionary healthcare.

This article began with an assertion that public health, and particularly New Public Health approaches, have a lot to offer human security. Health security interventions by health workers can function not only as a means of improving health but also in implementing broader human security objectives. These include new infectious disease threats, such as SARS and avian influenza, which require greater international cooperation if the diseases are to be dealt with effectively (Takemi et al. 2008: 6). They also include 'Health as a Bridge for Peace' approaches that began almost a century ago by focusing on education, reconciliation through health and humanitarian ceasefires, or days of peace, in which different parties in conflict agreed to suspend fighting to ensure that children in conflict zones were vaccinated. Other approaches include campaigns against armaments which are detrimental to human health (e.g. widely publicized campaigns against nuclear weapons, landmines and cluster bombs) and support for human rights (see Gutlove and Thompson 2003; Grove and Zwi 2008: 69; CHS 2003: 96–7). Mori et al. (2004) suggest that health workers can contribute to the strengthening of communities by broadening altruism and countering dehumanization between enemy populations. They also argue that health problems are more visible, with clear connections to other security priorities, and subsequently can be used as a means of rallying international support (2004: 187). Lee and McInnes (2003) note that health has major potential as an instrument of foreign policy in that it is a universally accepted value. They conclude that health is not a major consideration in international policy thinking and is therefore not always a focus of health security analysis. However, with many countries still non-interventionist in their approach to foreign policy, health programmes can be seen as 'less controversial and threatening' in comparison to other security challenges (Takemi et al. 2008: 6). Therefore, it could be argued that health interventions offer ways of promoting many other aspects of human security.

On the other hand, health workers are only a small part of what generates health in a society. Health, as Caballero-Anthony (2002) argues, is much too important to be left to the medical establishment. 'One could argue', she points out, 'that human security makes health everybody's business. This is an important part of the human securitization process' (2002: 38). Public health approaches, through the Ottawa Declaration and the People's Health Movement, have implications for the human security goals of peacebuilding and violence prevention. There is a great need for further research into health security, particularly in relation to contemporary public health research. Bunde-Birouste and Ritchie suggest that positive health outcomes are an effective way to build peace: 'in the sense of reciprocal determinism, health then becomes a determinant for peacebuilding or, in other words, peace ultimately becomes an outcome of health promotion action' (2007: 247). They conclude, however, that the 'extent to which health initiatives consistently include the necessary elements which facilitate a potential contribution to preventing violent conflict or promoting peacebuilding in post-conflict settings, remained elusive' (ibid.: 249).

Although the literature postulates the overall potential benefits of health security, there is little current evidence of effectiveness (Grove and Zwi 2008: 69). There needs to be more research and education on the experiences of women and men in the health system and how to deal with the health needs of different genders in ways that support better health outcomes. Finally, there are the possibilities entailed by Mann's (1998) assertion that human dignity and human rights violations should be treated, like violence, as public health problems that can be addressed through rights-based approaches. We are, he stated,

> creating, participating in and witnessing an extraordinary moment in social history – the emergence of a health and human rights movement – at the intersection and at the time of two enormous paradigm shifts. The possibilities for improving health through this momentous change cannot be overestimated, but will depend very much on an engaged civil society working to ensure the right to health becomes a reality.
>
> (Mann 2006: 1940)

Empowerment is both the key to the realization of Mann's transformative vision and an outcome of its successful implementation. However, if states are allowed to define this process, it is likely that the same forces which derailed Alma Ata and the message of 'health for all' 30 years ago may once again emerge.

References

Ashford, M. and Y. Huet-Vaughn. 2000. 'The Impact of War on Women', in B. Levy and V. Sidel (eds.), *War and Public Health*, pp. 186–96. Washington: APHA.

Azam, J. P. 2001. 'The Redistributive State and Conflicts in Africa', *Journal of Peace Research*, vol. 38 (4): 429–44.

Baum, F. 2008. *The New Public Health*, 3rd edn. South Melbourne, Vic.: Oxford University Press.

Brundtland, G. H. 2005. 'The UDHR', in S. Gruskin, M. A. Grodin, G. J. Annas and S. Marks (eds.), *Perspectives on Health and Human Rights*, pp. 59–62. New York: Routledge.

Bunde-Birouste, A. W. and J. Ritchie. 2007. 'Strengthening Peace-building Through Health Promotion: Development of a Framework', in D. V. McQueen and C. M. Jones (eds.), *Global Perspectives on Health Promotion Effectiveness*, pp. 247–58. Berlin: Springer.

Caballero-Anthony, M. 2002. 'Overview of Health and Human Security Case Studies', Health and Human Security: Moving from Concept to Action– Fourth Intellectual Dialogue on Building Asia's Tomorrow. www.jcie.org/researchpdfs/HealthHumSec/health_overview.pdf. Accessed 29 January 2008.

Chen, L. 2004. 'Health as a Human Security Priority for the 21st Century', paper for Human Security Track III, Helsinki Process, 7 December. www.eldis.org/document/A18905. Accessed 22 May 2018.

Chen, L. and V. Narasimhan. 2003. 'Global Health and Human Security', in L. Chen, S. Fukuda-Parr and E. Seidensticker (eds.), *Human Insecurity in Global World*, pp. 183–93. Cambridge: Harvard University Press.

CHS. 2003. *Human Security Now*. Final Report of the Commission on Human Security, chairs Sedako Ogata and Amartya Sen. New York: United Nations.

Commission on Social Determinants of Health (CSDH). 2008. 'Closing the Gap in a Generation: Health Equity through Action on the Social Determinants of Health', *Final Report of the Commission on Social Determinants of Health*. Geneva: World Health Organization.

Committee on Economic, Social and Cultural Rights. 2000. 'General Comment No. 14: The Right to the Highest Attainable Standard of Health', Article 12 of the International Covenant on Economic, Social and Cultural Rights, adopted by the Committee on Economic, Social and Cultural Rights on 11 May 2000. UN Document No. E/C.12/2000.4, 11 August 2000. Convention on the Prohibition on the Use Stockpiling, Production and Transfer of Anti-Personnel Mines and on their Destruction. 1997. Ratified on 3 December 1997 and entered into force on 1 March 1999.

Cook, R. 1999. 'Gender, Health and Human Rights', in J. M. Mann, S. Gruskin, M. Grodin and G. Annas (eds.), *Health and Human Rights: A Reader*, pp. 7–20. New York: Routledge.

Elster, E. 1981. 'Patriarchy', in W. Chapkis (ed.), *Loaded Questions*, pp. 14–15. Washington, DC: Georgetown University Press.

Epstein, H. 2007. *The Invisible Cure: Africa, the West and the Fight against AIDS*. New York: Farrar, Strauss and Giroux.

Falcon, W. P. and R. L. Naylor. 2005. 'Rethinking Food Security for the Twenty-First Century', *American Journal of Agricultural Economics*, vol. 87 (5): 1113–28.

Feldbaum, H. and K. Lee. 2004. 'Public Health and Security', in A. Ingram (ed.), *Health, Foreign Policy & Security: Towards a Conceptual Framework for Research and Policy*, pp. 19–28. UK Global Health Programme Working Paper No. 2. London: Nuffield Trust.

Felice, W. 1998. 'Militarism and Human Rights', *International Affairs*, vol. 74 (1): 25–40.

Freedman, L. 1999. 'Censorship and Manipulation of Family Planning Information: An Issue of Human Rights and Women's Health', in J. M. Mann, S. Gruskin, M. Grodin and G. Annas (eds.), *Health and Human Rights: A Reader*, pp. 145–78. New York: Routledge.

Geiger, H. J. 2000. 'The Impact of War on Human Rights', in B. Levy and V. Sidel (eds.), *War and Public Health*, pp. 39–50. Washington: APHA.

Gibson, I. and B. A. Reardon. 2007. 'Human Security: Toward Gender Inclusion', in G. Shani, M. Sato and M. K. Pasha (eds.), *Protecting Human Security in a Post 9/11 World: Critical and Global Insights*, pp. 50–63. London: Palgrave Macmillan.

Global Forum for Health Research. 2004. 'The 10/90 Report on Health Research 2003/4'. www.globalforumhealth.org. Accessed 8 March 2007.
Grove, N. J. and A. B. Zwi. 2008. 'Beyond the Log Frame: A New Tool for Examining Health and Peacebuilding Initiatives', *Development in Practice*, vol. 18 (1): 66–81.
Gutlove, P. and G. Thompson. 2003. 'Human Security: Expanding the Scope of Public Health', *Medicine, Conflict & Survival*, vol. 19 (1): 17–34.
Heymann, D. 2003. 'Infectious Disease Threats to National and Global Security', in L. Chen, S. Fukuda-Parr and E. Seidensticker (eds.), *Human Insecurity in Global World*, pp. 194–213. Cambridge: Harvard University Press.
Hyatt, R. 2006. 'Military Spending: Global Health Threat or Public Good?', in I. Kawachi and S. Wamala (eds.), *Globalization and Health*, pp. 311–29. New York: Oxford University Press.
International Criminal Court (ICC). 1998. 'Rome Statute of the International Criminal Court'. http://untreaty.un.org/cod/icc/statute/99_corr/cstatute.htm. Accessed 2 January 2009.
Isaksson, E. 2002. 'Women as Victims', in I. Taipale, Helena Mäkelä, Kati Juva, Vappu Taipale, Sergei Kolesnikov, Raj Mutalik and Michael Christ (eds.), *War or Health: A Reader*, pp. 267–73. London: Zed Books.
Krug, E. G., L. L. Dahlberg, J. A. Mercy, A. B. Zwi and R. Lozano (eds.). 2002. *World Report on Violence and Health*. Geneva: World Health Organization.
Laverack, G. 2005. *Public Health: Power, Empowerment and Professional Practice*. Basingstoke: Palgrave Macmillan.
Lee, K. and C. McInnes. 2003. 'Health, Foreign Policy & Security: A Discussion Paper', UK Global Health Programme Working Paper No. 1. London: Nuffield Trust.
Lorber, J. and L. J. Moore. 2002. *Gender and the Social Construction of Illness*. Oxford: AltaMira Press.
Machipisa, L. 1996. 'Zimbabwe-AIDS: Army Battles Random Testing', *InterPress News Service (IPS)*, March 26. www.aegis.com/news/ips/1996/IP960306.html. Accessed 6 April 2007.
Mack, A. and K. Furlong. 2004. 'When Aspiration Exceeds Capability: The UN and Conflict Prevention', in R. M. Price and M. W. Zacher (eds.), *The United Nations and Global Security*, pp. 59–74. New York: Palgrave Macmillan.
MacQueen, G., T. Nagy, J. Santa Barbara and C. Raichle. 2004. 'Iraq Water Treatment Vulnerabilities: A Challenge to Public Health Ethics', *Medicine, Conflict and Survival*, vol. 20 (2): 109–19.
Mann, J. M. 1998. 'Dignity and Health: The UDHR's Revolutionary First Article', *Health and Human Rights*, 3 (2): 30–8.
———. 2006. 'Health and Human Rights: If Not Now, When?', *American Journal of Public Health*, vol. 96 (11): 1940–3.
Mann, J. M., L. Gostin, S. Gruskin, T. Brennan, Z. Lazzarini and H. Fineburg. 1999. 'Human Rights and Public Health', in J. M. Mann, S. Gruskin, M. Grodin and G. Annas (eds.), *Health and Human Rights: A Reader*, pp. 7–20. New York: Routledge.

Matheson, M. J. 1997. 'The Opinions of the International Court on the Threat or Use of Nuclear Weapons', *American Journal of International Law*, vol. 91: 417–35.

Mori, L., D. R. Meddings and D. W. Bettcher. 2004. 'Health, Human Security and the Peacebuilding Process', in H. Sinoda and H. W. Jeong (eds.), *Conflict and Human Security: A Search for New Approaches of Peace-building*, pp. 176–96. IPSHU English Report Series 19. http://ir.lib.hiroshima-u.ac.jp/00015522. Accessed 10 June 2008.

Murray, C. J. L., G. King, A. D. Lopez, N. Tomijima and E. G. Krug. 2002. 'Armed Conflict as a Public Health Problem', *BMJ*, vol. 324: 346–9.

Nelson, T. S. 2002. *For Love of Country: Confronting Rape and Sexual Harassment in the US Military*. Binghamton, NY: Haworth Press.

Peacock, D. and M. Weston. 2008. 'Men and Care in the Context of HIV and AIDS: Structure, Political Will and Greater Male Involvement', United Nations Division for the Advancement of Women Expert Group Meeting on Equal Sharing of Responsibilities Between Women and Men, Including Care-Giving in the Context of HIV/AIDS. Geneva: United Nations Office. 6–9 October 2008. EGM/ESOR/2008/EP.9.

People's Health Movement. 2001. 'People's Health Charter'. http://phmovement.org/the-peoples-charter-for-health/. Accessed 7 June 2008.

Petchesky, R. P. 2003. *Global Prescriptions: Gendering Health and Human Rights*. London: Zed Books.

Price-Smith, A. 2002. *The Health of Nations: Infectious Disease, Environmental Change, and Their Effects on National Security and Development*. Cambridge, MA: MIT Press.

Querubin, M. P. and M. Tan. 1986. 'Old Roles, New Roles: Women, Primary Health Care, and Pharmaceuticals in the Philippines', in K. McDonnell (ed.), *Adverse Effects: Women and the Pharmaceutical Industry*, pp. 175–86. Toronto: The Women's Press.

Reardon, B. A. 1996. *Sexism and the War System*. New York: Syracuse University Press.

Reidpath, D. D. 2004. 'Social Determinants of Health', in H. Keleher and B. Murphy (eds.), *Understanding Health: A Determinants Approach*, pp. 9–22. Melbourne: Oxford University Press.

Rissel, C. 1994. 'Empowerment: The Holy Grail of Health Promotion?', *Health Promotion International*, vol. 9 (1): 39–47.

Seifert, T. 2002. 'The Female Body as a Symbol and a Sign: Gender-Specific Violence and the Cultural Construction of War', in I. Taipale, H. Mäkelä, K. Juva, V. Taipale, S. Kolesnikov, R. Mutalik and M. Christ (eds.), *War or Health: A Reader*, pp. 267–73. London: Zed Books.

Snow, R. 2007. 'Sex, Gender and Vulnerability', background paper prepared for the Women and Gender Equity Knowledge Network of the WHO Commission on Social Determinants of Health. www.who.int/entity/social_determinants/resources/sex_gender_vulnerability_wgkn_2007.pdf. Accessed 2 January 2007.

Stockholm International Peace Reseach Institute (SIPRI). 2008. 'SIPRI Yearbook 2008 Armaments, Disarmament and International Security', Stockholm

International Peace Research Institute Online. https://www.sipri.org/year book/2008.. Accessed 22 January 2009.

Takemi, K., J. Masamine, S. Ishii, Y. Katsuma and Y. Nakamura. 2008. 'Global Health, Human Security, and Japan's Contributions', paper presented at the FGFJ international symposium on 'From Okinawa to Toyako: Dealing with Communicable Diseases as Global Human Security Threats'. www.jcie.or.jp/thinknet/takemi_project/final_paper.pdf. Accessed 25 June 2008.

UNAIDS. 1998. 'HIV/AIDS and the Military'. http://data.unaids.org/Publications/IRC-pub05/militarypv_en.pdf. Accessed 7 April 2007.

UNDP. 1994. 'Human Development Report', United Nations Development Programme. http://hdr.undp.org/en/reports/global/hdr1994/chapters/. Accessed 10 June 2008.

UN-OHCA. 2008. 'Guidelines for the United Nations Trust Fund for Human Security', 4th revision, United Nations Trust Fund for Human Security. http://www.mofa.go.jp/policy/human_secu/guideline.pdf. Accessed 28 June 2008.

Werner, D. and D. Sanders. 1997. *Questioning the Solution: The Politics of Primary Health Care and Child Survival*. Palo Alto, CA: Healthwrights.

World Health Organization (WHO). 1946. 'Constitution of the World Health Organization', adopted by the International Health Conference held in New York, 19 June–22 July 1946, signed on 22 July 1946 by the representatives of 61 States (Off. Rec. Wld Hlth Org., 2, 100), and entered into force on 7 April 1948.

———. 1978. 'Declaration of Alma-Ata', adopted by the International Conference on Primary Health Care. Alma Ata, 6–12September 1978. http://www.who.int/publications/almaata_declaration_en.pdf?ua=1. Accessed 30 January 2007.

———. 1986. 'The Ottawa Charter on Health Promotion', International Conference on Health Promotion. Geneva: World Health Organization.

———. 1993. 'Implementation of the Global Strategy of Health for all by the Year 2000', Second Evaluation–Eighth Report on the World Health Situation, *Global Review*, vol. 1. Geneva: WHO. http://whqlibdoc.who.int/publications/1993/9241602813_eng.pdf. Accessed 2 April 2008.

———. 1996. *Global Consultation on Violence and Health: Violence: A Public Health Priority*. Geneva: World Health Organization, Document No.: WHO/EHA/SPI.POA.2.

———. 2006. *Working Together for Health: World Health Report, 2006*. Geneva: World Health Organization.

Zungu-Dirwayi, N., O. Shisana, E. Udjo, T. Mosala and J. Seager (eds.). 2004. *An Audit of HIV/AIDS Policies in Botswana, Lesotho, Mozambique, South Africa and Zimbabwe*. Cape Town: Human Sciences Research Council. http://apps.who.int/medicinedocs/documents/s17836en/s17836en.pdf. Accessed 4 April 2007.

14 Human security
The militarized perception and space for gender

Asha Hans

Introduction

In the last two decades, feminist writers and activists have been trying to draw attention to problems associated with the national security paradigm. Built on unifying and centralizing norms of nationalism and state power, the rhetoric and practice of national security constructs globally an explicit militarized nationalism. This militarization meant to protect citizens has become a source of extreme threat to them. In a globalized economy, as arms productions increase and weapons are easily available, many states find themselves vulnerable and consequently increase their own arsenals. The result of this inane arms race has been the excessive violence used against civilians, especially on borders which become only cartographic spaces signifying no difference between one's own citizen and the enemy.

The national security system has been found to be hazardous to the marginalized and excluded, especially women. We, therefore, need to deconstruct the national security paradigm so that we can draw attention to the violence perpetuated against women in these territorial spaces. This dominant culture of force has already been challenged by feminists as being patriarchal in nature and based on masculinity. Feminist scholars have rejected this paradigm and, in an effort to transform the militarized state to a peaceful space, have created new discourses on alternatives security. The deconstruction of national security would facilitate the introduction of human security as an alternative paradigm which would provide an enabling environment of peace.

Human security has emerged as a significant theme in feminist and other writings to replace the national security paradigm. This security system based on the quotidian principles (see Betty A. Reardon's article) provides people as the nucleus of its objectives. It is people's wellbeing and not that of the territory that is central to this alternative suggestion. Its core principle is non-violence and is aimed at removing militarized patriarchy in the state.

Some feminist writers on states (see Mesfin G. Ayele's article) as well as the United Nations (see Lisa S. Price's and Soumita Basu's articles) have adopted human security as an alternative to national security. As the canvas of acceptance enlarges, the concept and framework changes, producing a new standard very different than the one produced by feminist writers. This article analyzes one such attempt made by the military in India.

The concept of human security has been adopted by the army for implementation in the border region between India and Pakistan – a high-conflict zone. This raises questions about its legitimacy and usage. We need to interrogate the participation of citizens, specifically women, in the army's programme related to human security. We need to ask whether human security promoted by the army has provided the four requirements of human security on which his book is based – meeting basic needs, protection of the environment, protection of women from physical harm and whether women have been able to keep intact their dignity and self-esteem (see Reardon's article as well as Bernedette Muthien's article). There are also the extended issues of respect of religious and cultural diversity.

In this promise of a human security paradigm in coexistence with national security, we need to inquire into the functionality of the system to highlight women's insecurities under a national security system dependent on armaments and to see how the system constraints women's autonomy. This article will attempt to analyze the concept of the human security paradigm as developed by the armed forces called Operation Good will (*Sadbhavana*) within the context of the national security paradigm.[1] While answering the questions presented earlier, we need to know whether it is a new alternative designed for person-based security or a co-opting of a theme which does not spell change in the lives of those who live on the borders. This is especially of concern to women who face multiple levels of violence and are deprived of the core components of a feminist human security paradigm.

Women on the line of control

The Line of Control (LOC) between India and Pakistan in the state of Jammu and Kashmir has emerged as one of the most rapidly militarized spaces in the world. Militarization has increased since 1947, leaving civilians to bear its undesirable consequences. The price of militarization, needless to say, is met at the cost of other basic needs and has subsequently given rise to increased violence against women.

I have tried to listen to women's experiences of the conflict zone on the LOC, an Indo-Pakistan border, where the army is implementing its programme of 'human security'. The region selected for study on the border is 100 kilometres long and covers the Kargil, Drass and Batalik sectors in Jammu and Kashmir. The area has experienced low-intensity conflict since partition underwent border changes in the wars of 1948, 1965, 1972 and 1999. After the conflict of 1999, I documented women's voices, and this article communicates these women's concerns and desires for change.[2] Among these narrations on the LOC emerged the term of 'human security' used by the armed forces as a strategy of peace on the borders. Authored by a commanding officer of the Indian army, General Arjun Ray, it has turned into a full-fledged programme of the Indian Army.

To analyze the emerging perspective of a human security paradigm with in a militarized environment, the discourse that has emerged is documented here. The high level of violence against women in this zone is not created alone by killings due to incessant shelling but goes beyond it, to physical harm, such as rape, and domestic and psychological violence.

The rape of millions of women in historical and geographical perspectives has been documented globally in the gendered narrative of wars. In that narrative, dominant notions of masculinity merge with the ethnic element. Although we cannot rule out rape as an individual act carried out as a prize of war, it is also used as part of a tactic to defeat the ethnic or religious adversary. The documentation of the mass rapes in the South Asian subcontinent is part of the history of the subcontinent. These are narratives of 'dishonor' and abductions based on religious grounds, by both the Hindus and the Muslims. The rape of women of 'our' community by 'their' men figured prominently in the debates and discussions that took place in parliamentary circles (as expected mainly among men). The honour of the community and of the nation was seen to be the trajectories written across the bodies of women and the violation of their bodies and was therefore tantamount to a violation of the body of the nation, of Mother India (Butalia 1998; Menon and Bhasin 1998). During partition, although women should have been central in the writing of history, they found little space, and it is therefore not surprising that rape, as an instrument, finds no reference in the history of the LOC. With no public visibility and no impunity, the abuse is continued and maintained in different forms.

Militarized rape is viewed as a distinctive act perpetrated in the context of an institution – the military that is part of the state machinery. Post-partition, the new border that is the Line of Control was drawn in 1972 as a result of the Indo-Pakistani War. In that drawing of the temporary border, portions of land changed hands from India to Pakistan and vice versa.[3] In this fluid territorial situation, the armed forces perpetuated rape on an extensive scale, silenced forever due to the shame the community felt.[4] The children of the rapes are now grown up. There is silence over the fate of these 'wronged' children fathered by soldiers. It was a personal and a community humiliation. The memories are kept behind a shadow of silence. Their trauma cannot be overlooked, as two whole generations have suffered. For the women, the shame and dishonor of rape will always remain, even though they are in their 40s and 50s now. For the village at large, it was a community humiliation by a state meant to protect them. For them, independence as understood by the rest of India did not take place.[5]

Rape exacerbates women's vulnerability because of patriarchal definitions of women's purity (DeAlwis 2004).[6] A purity mapped on their bodies. This purity is not confined to conflict but is carried over from their daily lives. Concepts of virtue and family honour are part of the private, which during conflicts comes in to the public through rape. In the social milieu, being raped brings stigma to both mother and child. In this context, surviving rape and bearing a rapist's child means loss of family, community and livelihood. Women thus have strong incentives to mask or hide their experiences of sexual assault.

Sexual abuse continues to occur in the border region of Kargil, but due to the stigma associated with this issue, it is difficult for the community to discuss it openly. Gendered duties, it is seen, also bring gendered consequences. Women and girls are particularly vulnerable to attack when collecting and searching for firewood, as this may take them along distance from their homes and expose them not only to the danger of anti-personnel mines and unexploded shells but also to the risk of sexual.[7]

The collectivity of women's bodies in the eyes of the perpetuator, as representation of the community, cannot be perceived by women themselves, because for them, loss of self-esteem is a personal tragedy and loss of self-esteem and dignity comprise an important component of human security. The protection from violation of human dignity forms the core principle of human security. Rape has the most long-lasting effect on women's psyches and is the most difficult to heal. Any alternative security system that does not address these concerns of women violates their human rights. Unfortunately, the existing national security system provides no protection to women on this ground.

Fear and domestic violence

The connection between highly militarized societies and domestic violence has been well established. Besides rape, there are other types of violence perpetuated against women's bodies. During shelling, when tension increases and women show fear, men assault them physically. In Drass, the wife of a police man related that her husband regularly beats her up as she screams whenever the shells fall. When there are problem in accessing basic necessities, it also leads to domestic violence. The women and girls of Kargil feel that their inferior status in society, dependence on men and the discrimination that they face are causes for violence. 'We cannot work nor sit quietly at home. We cannot do anything. Whatever we do is not right, there is always tension at home. It is brought in by our husbands, frustrated with the *awam* (nation) . . . can we do anything to stop this violence?' Unemployed husbands losing dominant positions at home, discussions of war in public spaces frequented by men and humiliation by outsiders have resulted in aggressive masculinity.[8] Zorica Mrscevic analyzes a similar situation in former Yugoslavia, where domestic violence is 'caught in a vicious circle of mutual consequences and causation along with patriarchy and war' (2001: 42). The community shrinks during war as travel is limited, and in nuclear families there, is no one to act as a barrier to the domestic violence faced by women. In a situation where the military plays decisive roles, violence is a way of life, and women and children live in fear of violence from within and outside the home.

Violence against women in the private has been kept outside the legal framework of most countries, thus providing legitimacy to the acts. Such states as India have now started to recognize it as a crime by introducing a law. However, territory under conflict is kept outside the state laws under the mantle of patriotism and national security. During conflict no conceptual distinction emerges between public and private, and violence becomes a continuing threat against women in both spheres. This normalization of violence against women, as observed in the cases of Okinawa and the women of Jordan (see the articles by Kozue Akibayashi and Suzuyo Takazato and Norma Nemeh), must be avoided, as in long-term military presence it remains a constant threat to women's human security. Violence cannot be considered only as a crime but also as a human rights abuse, as the women of Okinawa demonstrated.

Violence and masculinity in conflict situations

In any conflict situation, national chauvinism exalts both militarism and masculinity. In this situation, violence becomes the normal expression of masculine identity. Heroes, patriots and martyrs are projected in terms of power and honour. Each nation state at war adds on to these two structures on which masculinity is endorsed. In this environment, patriarchy emerges as a significant marker of militarist nationalism, where men hold power and control over women.

This culture of power is part of the masculine discourse and mainstreamed into the 'natural', not viewed as an aberration of human nature. All countries at war produce their own version of them as culinist approach. In the South Asian subcontinent, on the borders of India and Pakistan, local versions of masculinity emerge during conflict to be used by leaders and supporters of war. In October 2001, for instance, after the loss of the Kargil War, President Musharraf of Pakistan was still sending messages to the Indian counterparts through the media of continuing the war, declaring, 'We in Pakistan have not worn bangles' (as noted in the *Tribune of Chandigarh* dated October 23, 2001). Bangles are worn by women and denote femininity and weakness. Prime Minister Vajpayee replied in a public address, 'In Punjab men also wear 'kada' [steel bracelet]', worn by the Sikhs, a martial race (as noted in the Tribune Chandigarh dated November 1, 2001). The *kada* is the religious epitome of Sikh valor.

Masculinity is not an overarching homogeneous attribute. It has its own complexities which the war system makes use of to sustain it. As methods of war change, the masculine determinants modify. The new wars enclose within themselves new methods, such as increased use of intelligence agencies or terrorism – war then becomes 'good' and can be used for protecting civilians from both external and internal elements, which are intermingled. The internal security becomes closely linked to the external, as it did in the United States after September 11. It happened in many countries, such as in Sri Lanka and India (both in Jammu and Kashmir and in the north-east), where security forces play an important role in protecting national security. This removal of lines between war and peace affect women's daily lives.

Women and issues of human needs in conflict situations

The daily needs of women found dominance in women's narratives during the field interviews. Their concerns were related to health, food and physical security. Shelling affects women physically and psychologically.

In Kargil, Nida Fatima's young daughter-in-law was affected psychologically after two miscarriages. Both were a casualty of war, the first when it started to shell and she fell and lost her child, and the second the unavailability of a doctor during birth, a common phenomenon in a war situation (visit to Kargil, 2002). Meeting a second woman on 6 June 2004 (Zabiain Batalik) who also had two miscarriages bears out the authenticity of the fact that women's health, especially reproductive health, is affected severely by conflict.

Their clergy does not approve abortions, but still many women resort to it, and most use other methods, usually Copper T. Nargis Bannoo, the nurse at the hospital, mentioned that both men and women come in for sterilization, which is different from the case in the rest of India. Khatiza Begum sitting nearby mentioned that many women do not go in for sterilization, as they are never sure about being given *talaq* (divorce). In case of a talaq, if they remarry they would not be able to have children. Due to the tremendous psychological pressure on them, women are sometimes allowed abortion so that their lives could be saved. Dr Hadol, who oversees the reproductive and child health care (RCH) programme, did not speak of RCH but of family planning. Reproductive health care is still a distant dream, even though a national policy exists.[9] Women are worshipped as reproducers of the nation, but the reproductive rights still remain with the men, who have control over women's bodies. During conflict, there is usually (as noted during my visit to Kargil in 2002) an added pressure on women to produce more children to replace the dead and maintain an ethnic balance.

The number of diseases which are related to the conflict increases. Shakira Banoo from Sankoo articulated her disgust at her young daughter-in-law who, instead of looking after her, was sitting in a corner either complaining or drowsy after taking anti-depressant pills. The husband escaped from home for days as he worked in Drass as a porter with the army and left them other to look after his wife. Heart disease and sleeplessness had increased among women. A chemist in Kargil town explained that the sale of anti-depressants always increased with the intensity of the war. Concern about their children in school, daughters in the field and husbands on the hills add to multiple worries. Women lose their appetite and thus always complain of weakness. With a globalized economy and implementation of health sector reforms, health services, especially medicines, are beyond the purchasing power of many people. The right to health is a human right and provides another reason why women would choose human security above national security.

In conflicts, health services are very important – there is greater need for them as a result of physical and psychological trauma and an inability to travel in dangerous situations to access health services. Usually, health infrastructure is destroyed and personnel usually leave for safer places. Malnutrition increases as shelling results in aches and pains, insomnia and lack of appetite. Consequently, the work output declines and food insecurity increases, creating a vicious circle. Meat, green leafy vegetables and barley (*sattu*) are some of the main sources of food for the people in Kargil. Because Kargil remains cut off from Srinagar due to the closure of Zojila Pass for nearly eight months in winter, the region faces shortages of food and other essential items. They have adopted a strategy to keep dried vegetables and meat so that during winter there is a food supply, but these do not meet their nutritional needs fully. Hunger is depressed by drinking large amounts of strong salted tea, which has resulted in an increase in gall bladder stones. The military stocks up food for itself which is not available to civilians, even for purchase. Food is not only a basic need but also a human right which the state is obliged to provide to its citizens. In conflict areas this right is either neglected or used as a weapon of war.

In traditional security studies, health or related issues of environment are not of concern, although wars damage the environment and create health problems. Early births and partial deafness are common among children. Hakima Banoo blames the loud shells for the early birth and deafness of her son Irfan. She lives near a military camp where shells are tested. The sound threatens the stability and tranquility of their lives. Hakima continued to point to the air around us and said,

> Can you smell the smoke of the guns . . . the smell . . . (*mushuk*) it never leaves our nostrils. The smoke of recurrent shelling in and around the house and the dust leads to breathlessness and asthma among many of us.

Because the army has come to the valley, said the Mushkoo resident, the level of pollution has increased. The army trucks and other vehicles emit heavy amounts of smoke and dust due to the rough terrain that ultimately takes a toll on the health of the people.

There has been drought for three to four years in the Garkone and Kharboo villages. 'The water in the rivers has reduced in quantity', explained Dolma from Garkone village, 'and affects women's daily lives'. For instance, in the village of Darchiks, continuous shelling, said the women, has resulted in increased poverty and loss of agricultural production. Because of shelling and the lack of an irrigation facility, drought has been a continuing occurrence atleast for the last three years in many parts of Kargil. As most of the cattle have also been killed in shelling, or they have been eaten due to lack of food, there is a lack of freely available organic fertilizer on which most farming depends. In some cases where farmers can buy pesticides, bio-friendly food has been replaced with food laced with pesticides and chemical fertilizers. Drinking water is also inaccessible in many parts of the LOC due to shelling. Food insecurity comes in many forms. The water brought down from the hills is limited. Men have to fetch water, which became a problem for those households where men had jobs. Men carrying water also brought shame to the village, as it was considered a woman's job. As risks increased the shame, combined with the fear of losing husbands to the shelling or detention by the army, it brought psychological stress. Visits to Kargil showed that this one concern in itself created societal cleavages and socio-psychological problems.

In conflict situations, women lose livelihoods or earn too little to lead a secure life. In Akchamal village overlooking Kargil, the women spend the day preparing cotton and wool to weave carpets. Each woman works from morning to evening to earn rupees 200 (US$4) per month. In Garkone, the girls had formed a SHG (Self Help – i.e. micro credit – Group) with the help of a non-governmental organization (NGO), KDP. They had been trained in another nearby state, but the men in the village did not let them form the SHG group. Our escort, Javed, said the villagers thought it would lead to disintegration and groupism within people and girls; the latter would start ignoring their households. Besides, he continued, they would only attract the attention of the army. Organized groups in any form are perceived as a threat to a nationstate in conflicts, be it even an economic activity, such as an SHG. Any empowerment is also a threat in a conflict situation.

Work, food, health and shelter are vital needs without which people's security is not realized. Any security system must fulfill these requirements. It has been observed that despite difficult situations and not withstanding a tyrannical security system, women do emerge with agency, both individual and collective.

Women's agency is related to the building of networks. Collectivity in networks during wars is invisible or unorganized as it deals with human issues. National security does not tolerate any kind of collective activity in conflict zones. Solidarity is a mark of empowerment which the state does not allow, its major motive being control which results in disempowerment and powerlessness of people on the borders.

There are few organized networks for peace on the border itself, but as one moves away, life gets more organized and normal, with sporadic intrusion of the conflict. One such place is Pushkum, not too far from the LOC, where women created networks rarely found even in non-conflict zones. Two *mohalla*s (villages), which used to leave their cattle to graze in the fields, were always in a state of conflict. The men refused to take any interest, as they were either working a sporters in the army or at other small vocations. Seeing the increasing violence and escalating food insecurity, as the cattle were consuming the food meant for the children, the women decided to act. As Zubeda Bano, the leader of the network, commented,

> Our children were starving, and we could not stand and do nothing. From Samar Mohalla emerged women's leadership and networking, solidarity so very important in women's lives during conflict. They grouped together five years ago to fight poverty induced by local conflict, and decided to keep the cattle out of each other's field. The grazing on the hills had also to be regulated to make available enough food for everyone's cattle. To do this, the women in groups of 5–10 members each, take charge of the cattle on a weekly basis. All women from the village have joined but if they do not carry out their share of the work they are forced to pay a fine.

Once the cattle problem was solved and conflict resolution strategies were in place, other issues emerged for discussion. The meetings became a place of activity for women – a place to negotiate marriages, celebrate births and discuss the gains of solidarity; to act together against domestic violence; and to provide the place for interacting so that the psychological pressures of war could be controlled. These women were not literate in the formal sense, and they had no support of their men and no NGOs to guide them. They knew no other language than their local one. It was not the young but the middle-aged and the older women who initiated this network and who remained part of this group. For them, although in the midst of war, it did not subsume their lives. More than the men, it was the women who had the grit and determination to provide quality and meaning to their lives during war. The stories of women's strength are common in this place. In nearby Locham, the *numberdar* (head of village), as per a local oral history, had been a woman, and when the enemy attacked, the men hid, but she mobilized the women to fightback.

The war-like situation continues in which both women's specific problems and agency play important roles. Within this environment, the army plays its traditional role of protectors of the border and not the population. In Kargil, a change has taken place as the army is projecting a space for 'human security' and a culture of peace. To understand the ground realities and to juxtapose them on feminist thought, this article goes onto analyze human security from a feminist viewpoint as applied to the Indo-Pakistan border.

Human security and its usage on the Indo-Pakistan border

While feminists are trying to use abroad-based concept of human security than the general human rights movement, the latter adopted by the state structures is being narrowed down, as in the context of Kargil. In India, the issue of Kashmir, a territory which both India and Pakistan have claimed, can be taken as a perfect example of being treated as within a national security paradigm. Since India's independence, the state of Jammu and Kashmir has been in the core of its conflict system.[10] It has fuelled an arms race, and wars have broken out at intervals with a continuous low-intensity conflict due to a dispute over territory. Under these violent conflict conditions, the concept of human security has found space in the ideology and working of the armed forces through Operation Goodwill.

General Arjun Ray, core commander of the 14th Division posted in Kargil, proposed human security as going beyond a theory and to an implementation strategy he called Operation Sadbhavana, or Operation Goodwill. It has, he argues, provided the armed forces with an instrument of nation building and peace building. It has projected human security as a core element of national security which is ensured through human development, its operational parameters being the army which functions as a 'facilitator' and the convergence of 'Goodwill' initiatives with the district administration, NGOs and people's representatives (personal interview, Bangalore, 2006; Parmar and Parmar 2002).

Arjun Ray has stated as part of his project that there cannot be a safe and secure border if one has human in securities, as 'National security does not mean defence. Gun and tanks do not give you security'. Operation Goodwill, in its implementation, laid the foundation of a new strategy for border development, making Ladakh (the larger area of the north Kashmir region which includes Kargil) a militant-free zone Bukhari 2001). Operation Goodwill would provide security through the provision of education, health, gender equality and community

Operation Goodwill and its ideology

Goodwill is an army operation started in Kargil just before the war in 1999. It is surprising that the Kargil region had not joined the Kashmir Valley in a full-fledged conflict situation starting in 1948. It was only in the 1990s that militancy from the valley started to slowly spread into Kargil, which now has a large number of displaced people. The increase in a sustained low-intensity conflict combined with the government's/army's insensitivity to local trauma has been a clear indicator of why they outh have resorted to militant activities. Militancy was easy to adopt, as the territory on the LOC between India and Pakistan is a divided territory, owing no allegiance to anyone nation, so there is no question of loyalty to the nation.

Operation Goodwill was introduced to counteract the militant activities in the Turtuk sector of the LOC. The four villages of Turtuk sector and the mountains around it had been part of Kashmir in Pakistan until the war of 1971. Turtuk continued to maintain its close links to Pakistan is across the border, which is not surprising as the area has been sometimes in Indian and sometimes in Pakistani occupation. It has a large Sunni and Balti (anethnic) population, in contrast to the local Shia majority of Kargil. During a visit to Turtuk before the Kargil War, Lieutenant General Arjun Ray, General Officer Commanding, was targeted by an explosion of the improvised explosive device (IED) set by the internationally known militant group the Laskhar-e-Toiba. Turtuk, 22 kilometres from the LOC, had innumerable divided families, as only a few villages were taken over by India in 1971. It could not be ignored because it was strategically a very important region for the Indian Army.[11]

Soon after, when war erupted in 1999, Turtuk became important again because of its close links to Pakistan. The intrusions by mercenaries and the Pakistani Army were not known to the Indian Army, and the civilians in Turtuk, unlike in other parts of Kargil, refused to provide any support to the Indian Army to fight the war. The challenge for the military was either to use the usual methods of questioning, search and imprisonment or to get the population to cooperate. General Ray chose the second course, and 'goodwill' was the instrument by which the distance between the army and local population was narrowed.

A year later, when former Deputy Prime Minister Advani visited Turtuk, he was to say that Turtuk was one border area in Kashmir where he could walk without any security. This change is attributed to a specially established core group, called Army Development Group (ADG), which was set up to carry out the new Operation Goodwill. Since the operation started, it has been pointed out, in a reversal of stance, that the Operation opened up new sites for debating patriotism and citizenship (Aggarwal and Bhan 2009:535).

What was it about Operation Goodwill that changed the situation so radically? The ideology and the implementation started on the basis of what Ray terms the bringing of a 'culture of peace' to be inculcated by the army (Ray to the author, August 2006). The culture of peace was interpreted as a multifaceted approach which would provide space for shared values of tolerance, solidarity, democracy and economic development. It is a non-violent, rights-based approach. It provides for disarmament and military security: 'A culture of peace should be elaborated within the process of sustainable, endogenous, equitable human development; it cannot be imposed from the outside'.

Ray's perception was that conflict prevention is better than conflict resolution because the role of the army in the 21st century is to prevent war (Sreenivas 2001). To this end, Operation Goodwill, Ray asserted, is a sociopolitical strategy for conflict prevention, a 'brand name for trust and restoring hope'. It is the promotion by the army of a nation-building activity by strengthening governance at the grassroots level and territorial consolidation, not geographic, but by winning the trust of the people. This nation-building activity is supposed to be carried out not byte army but by the people. The visibility of the projects would create goodwill and provide a positive image of the army and is projected as a new model of human defence, an ambitious project to build a functional community-army relationship.

Ray disagreed with the increasing public hatred against the Muslims and the concept that Islamic fundamentalism was emerging as an extreme danger to the nation. 'It is a myth. One who practices the fundamentals of his religion is not a fundamentalist', he said, adding, 'there is no Islamic fundamentalism in Ladakh and Kashmir. Muslims are being defamed'.

In this departure from traditional army methods, Ray mentioned that the role of the army now is to prevent conflicts.

> If we can be part of the UN peace keeping force, why can't we keep peace in India using the same method? Our approach to border management has to be reviewed. It comprises giving people quality life, the right to exercise options, and enough opportunities.

The best antidote to infiltration is border development. You cannot have a safe and secure border if you have human insecurities.
(Interview with Arjun Ray, August 2006)

The language of culture and peace and human security used by Ray seemed to have tremendous potential, unlike the human security projected by feminists which denies any place to armed national security. Ray does not disassociate human security from armed security but rather maintains the concept of national security in which human security becomes a part and a strategy. Conflict prevention and peace keeping is still part of national security through use of armed forces.

Implementing a human security paradigm: the beginning and spin-offs

As part of Operation Goodwill, the army setup schools, hospitals and vocational training centres for women and carried out community development work. Operation Goodwill runs 16 schools called the Goodwill Schools in 109 villages on the LOC to make education accessible to the children in a region where teachers are few and where outsiders, even from Jammu, do not want to work. Goodwill Schools, unlike government institutions, offer midday meals. Islam is one of the compulsory subjects being taught in all the schools run by the army. The schools also have maulvis and lamas as teachers where the population is Muslim and Buddhist, respectively. 'Religion is the best vehicle to teach values' was the motto of Operation Goodwill.

On asking about the operation, a local girl said, 'We got everything from the army and Arjun Ray. We have a school and we have a dispensary too'. There are an equal number of girls and boys. The Shia community has promoted girl child education which has been used by General Ray as a positive aspect of his school programme. The physical presence of the school contributed immensely to children's education; however, the militarization of minds cannot be overlooked. In an orphanage run by the army, I spoke with the children about a career in the army and about battles and fighting for the nation. They wanted to join the Air Force as airplanes most probably are visible and not as threatening as the soldiers. In another school, where shells had been falling, fear was written on the children's faces, and when I asked them to draw, their sketches showed schools and homes with bombs falling. Security can come only when war ends, but with children being surrounded by a militarized security system, peace seems a distant vision.

The teachers in the Goodwill Schools are also from outside the state and include many well-trained volunteers from Bangalore and Varanasi. Why do these people come? The answer from them was simple – it is patriotic, said a volunteer. With increasing global extremism, patriotism has taken on violent attributes, where freedom can be obtained only within a highly militarized system of national security.

There is no doubt that good schooling is required, and Ray's idea is what human security is about. Provision of education without any discrimination is a human right of children. As a universal right, it has to be for all children and not for a few Goodwill Schools. The aim should have been to provide an environment of security where all schools could function in peace. The setting up of Goodwill Schools provides high-quality and effective education but cannot be the answer unless the war situation is stopped and security is not undermined.

The war affects children in other ways. Many children are disabled by military activity. Targeted shelling and shell bursts are responsible for their disabilities. Although Operation Goodwill has Umeed (hope), are source centre for the whole of the LOC, it is obvious that it cannot meet the needs of all the children. Besides, the army is responsible for the children's disabilities, and providing services informs of wheelchairs and physiotherapy cannot compensate for the loss of a limb. National security based on militarization cannot provide security to the children. What is needed is an increased space for peace through the adoption of a culture of peace. A culture of peace can be created when children speak of peace and of friendship with children across the border and not of fear and continuing careers in the army.

Women's Empowerment Centres setup by Operation Goodwill are vocational training centres which provide training in carpet weaving and tailoring. Many women who joined the centres have travelled to other parts of the country, although only if their husbands have permitted it. Illiterate women are provided other training, such as 150 hours of functional literacy. These centres have not done so well Ray left. This is due to a low level of women's involvement and a lack of marketing for their goods. Ray had planned to bring in multi-national corporations to purchase carpets and other items, and the army had suggested it would purchase socks for its consumption. After Ray left, none of these promises were carried out.

The computer education centres for young women and men are doing well. It is a dream come true for the marginalized youth, as before the Kargil War young women had not anticipated the availability of cyberspace for them. It is Operation Goodwill that brought about these changes. Three years after they started and two years after Ray left

Kargil, the computer centres' popularity remained as high as in other parts of the country. The amazing thing about the computer centres is that they are being supported by the two Shia organizations in Kargil. While the Kargil centre is housed in the Islamia School, the other Shia organization, the Islamic Khomeini Memorial Trust, has been assisting in running it. Islam has not stood in the way of promoting women's education and of their joining professional jobs. There are two intersecting reasons for this. One is that Shia Kargil has always supported women's education because, according to them, their leader, Ayotollah Khomeini, had instructed them to do so.[12] It is also true that the army took an indiscriminatory view and opened the centres for both men and women. One has to also keep the broader picture of the Indian subcontinent in view, where computer skills are gaining the highest acceptability because of the high salaries and esteem associated with them.

For the women, therefore, what did this offer? The most visible is, as mentioned, computer education. It also provided them, through this education, equality with male students, and it helped them cross patriarchal barriers to some extent. It allowed them to go out of their homes and to search for professional jobs. But where were the jobs? Due to the conflict situation, except for the earlier graduates, the rest could not use their literacy. As regards other work, such as weaving, once General Ray, left time stood still for them. With no support system, they feel abandoned.

Community development initiatives have provided rural electrification, vocational training, village irrigation and cooperatives for poultry farming. A poultry cooperative at Turtuk provides the much needed economic independence. Tie-ups with agriculture universities in Srinagar and institutes help people learn to grow better crops and to winter vegetables as the region grows few vegetables, such as turnips and some greens. All this work is carried out by women. It is hard work in a region in which the climate is in hospitable and temperatures fall to 40° Celsius. Women during the agricultural season work from 4:00 a.m. to 9:00 p.m. The focus of the project is narrow – for instance, although there was drought in the region and farmers were struggling with it, there was no army focus on it. Above all, the army gets all its food from outside the region, so the absence of vegetables and other food does not affect it. The only food available during my trips was turnips and rice and, as an effect of globalization, packaged Maggie noodles (Nestlé) and Pepsi.

While applauding the army's human security programme for its gender-sensitivity, one has to look at it from a holistic viewpoint. The earlier part of the article depicted women's insecurities – of violence, health insecurity and physical harm. It also recognized the damage to the environment as an important insecurity faced by both men and women and food insecurity caused by the systemic violation of human rights by the same army that has introduced the concept of 'human security'.

What Operation Goodwill (Sadbhavana) could not do was bring down the level of militarization. One reason was that the war level and militarization was dependent on Pakistan and India, and unless they both change their mind-sets on what kind of security they want – whether based on the existing heavy militarization or human security – change is problematic. Under this broad parameter, Operation Goodwill is a new initiative, but the focus is still narrow and the vision limited. Change is necessary, but unless the right paradigm which caters to women's needs is not adopted, they will continue to suffer. There was no attempt of the Operation Goodwill strategy to engage with the military to end the violence against women or to reduce the armed forces.

People's response to state-sponsored 'human security'

Arjun Ray, an Indian soldier, projected a personality cult not seen in many years in the armed forces. In Kargil, posters were put up by the army under his command, showing his photograph and portraying his work. He became a household name. The people of Kargil made him an icon, a symbol of 'democracy, secularism and sympathetic support of the down trodden'. According to Maqbool, displaced from Kharboo village to Sankoo, 'Arjun Ray was a leader of leaders. He was like a brother. People were like wax in his hands as he had Goodwill and a humane perspective'.

He was not the only one to praise Ray. A shopkeeper in Drass, where the Kargil War was nearly lost, said, 'If he had not had this link with people India would have lost Drass. We are ready to fight for him'. It was the young and old alike who had made him into a hero. A 70-year-old man in Kargil said, 'If he wants to lead us as an army against Pakistan we are ready to follow him blindly' (visit to Drass, 29 May 2002).

The elite, especially from the education field, supported him fully. Amale teacher near Kargil said, 'Hemade Goodwill Schools. We willfight when he says so'. The principal of Muttahary Public School, a leading Shia leader of the town, supported Ray: 'The war had the worst torturous impact on Muslims. Social activist Arjun Ray was genuinely concerned for the Muslims'. His support to girls' education was not limited to computer education but also to other areas. The principal of the Kargil Girls High School, a woman, spoke with awe: 'Arjun Ray visited the school twice a month despite his busy schedule' (visit to Kargil, 20 May 2004).

According to Ray and the local people, the militant in filtration has come down, especially from Mushkoh Valley and Drass, which has always been a problematic area for the army and always under close scrutiny. It is sustainable as people contribute to it – for instance, in the form of labour. People have lost some fear of the army which had been overpowering (visit to Kargil and Drass, 15 May to 25 June 2002).

Limitation of Operation Goodwill

The army was not pleased with Ray, especially as he had already published a book – *Purple Primer: The Psychology of Militancy* (1997) – which was abou this experience in Kashmir from a human perspective. This book had created annoyance in military circles. Now he had come up with another unworkable scheme which would take them for what they considered a ride. The army was the first to respond that Operation Good will was for General Ray's own benefit and not of the community. 'He is a fraud', said my cousin, an army general, whom I spoke to. In 2002, two years after he started Operation Goodwill, Ray put in his papers of resignation.[13] About Operation Goodwill, Ray's view is different: 'It was discussed and endorsed by the upper echelons. Is cripted it myself'.

The operation, despite the army's acknowledgement, to some extent brought the army and the people closer. But did it build trust? Trust, we understand, provides justice and access to rights, which was not the case when implementing human security by the army. Ray was idolized, but the army still remained distanced from the people.

When my research associate fell severely sick due to the high altitude during our visit in June 2004, my cousin in the army requested the local army doctor to see what was wrong with her. A young girl – who was a neighbour and who was extremely friendly and who we shared the bunkers each night when the shelling started, visited her home for butter tea and apricots and she used to giggle a lot of the time, sharing her knowledge of the war with us – paled on seeing the soldier, and after that, she and her family distanced themselves from us. This did not show any trust in the army. In her case, it was also the fact that she was a beautiful young woman and must have been told to keep away from the army, but this was not all, as we were marked as being with the army. The vocal support for Ray and Operation Goodwill in most cases came from males.

On the one hand, the army, and specifically Ray, brought the empathy needed by the common person in a war-like situation which was very important to the people. At the same time, it also brought questions of the armed forces using peace as a strategy of war. In the case of Operation Goodwill/Sadbhavana, what was unusual was the personal involvement of Ray in creating these spaces of peace among the people. His regular contacts directly with the people, even in the villages, made him an icon of peace, the *Amanka Farishta* (Angel of Peace). As a man frustrated with the war told me, 'If General Ray asked us to join up and attack Pakistan, we will be there whenever the call comes'.

The armed forces personnel, who responded to my queries on Ray's strategy, said they preferred long-distance strategies, and for them, every individual is the enemy unless proved otherwise. They did not seem comfortable with this innovative process, although in Ray's strategy, while people lose their fear of the armed forces, they can also be easily made to approve the militarization process. This stand by the army has meant that Operation Goodwill lacks operational continuity. This might be acceptable with machines and tanks, but when dealing with the lives and sentiments of so many people in sensitive border areas, it is a thin line between sadhbhavana (goodwill) and *durbhavana* (ill-will) (*Ladags Melong* 2002:25–6). Ray's own response has been that everyone who matters is convinced that the Operation Goodwill approach is the desired way out. Where it faces problems is in the cultural realm. Indians, according to Ray, are by nature status quo-minded and do not like dramatic changes. In India, 'change is slow, a reality we must live with' (Ray 2003). The fact is that human security was introduced but left midway.

There are many others, especially a section of the media, who believe Operation Goodwill will not work. A media report argues that its success is limited, 'as it rests on the reductionist premise that development alone shapes history, to the exclusion of ideas and ideology' (Swami 2001). The media's insistence that religion-based terrorism cannot be controlled by developmental one is a regressive representation of their understanding because it assumes that all people following a certain religion, in this case Islam, are militants or potential militants. The women disagreed with this version and said the most important thing for them was fulfilling their daily needs.

It is obvious that Operation Good will had a mixed response from the people and the military. What we need to analyze is that if what we are speaking of interms of a new paradigm from the feminist perspective fits in with this.

National security and human security from a gendered perspective: historical background

The concept of human security has been at the core of feminist thinking of security. In order to understand the concept of human security in its totality, one should include the feminist perspective of the issue. As of today there have been very limited attempts at applying a feminist approach to theorizing on international relations in India. But at the same time, there is an increasing interest in dealing with the life and experiences of women in war and peace. These works focus on conflict and its repercussions on women in variety of settings, such as ethnic conflicts, military wars and religious strife (Butalia 2002; Chenoy 2004; Hans 2000, 2004; Menon and Bhasin 1998; Mangat 2000). The results are the emerging ideas about the concept of security, which strategically differs from a man to a woman.

From a feminist or human rights perspective, the narrow focus of the human security paradigm as we have observed in Kargil, which still aims at protection of territory by use of force, has many problems. In the context of the undefined borders, it ignores and negates everything people stand for – their lives, their concerns for their homes, their self-esteem. Environment and other related issues of social justice and poverty are marginalized. In this context, although their concern about security and rights becomes not only of critical but also of immediate concern, it is not achievable. We, therefore, need an alternative security paradigm which is humane and non-violent. To discuss an alternative would mean discussing a method and giving up the existing one. In an international system where, despite liberalization and globalization, states overeignty remains a significant factor, any change can only be a challenging process. An alternative must not only be powerful but also be adopted to provide a legitimacy through people's willingness to adopt it.

Although there is a felt need to address the root causes of insecurity, now here does Ray (or even the UN *Human Security Now* report) even mention the most important causes of women's in security – that is, patriarchy. It is important because women are neither decision makers where national security is concerned nor included in the general processes of war and peace. The violence women face is not only the violence of war and peace but also the violence in all other spaces they are connected with, such as domestic violence, health, education and other daily needs. The central positioning of power in the war national hierarchy, where the borders are more important than domestic sociopolitical needs, result in denial of women's rights at all levels of public and private spaces. This limits women's negotiations for more space and maneuverability within a patriarchal system. It is therefore not surprising that the feminist conception of human security is broader.

What is needed in our search for a new paradigm is a pragmatic non-violent approach to replace national security. The human security paradigm at this stage provides the alternative in our search for peace. It is therefore important that we look at a broader paradigm of human security to replace national security. Reardon's holistic conception of human security is thus broader than what is defined by Ogata and Senand needs serious consideration for adoption by the United Nations (Reardon 1993, 1998; Commission on Human Security 2003).

Conclusion

The security system globally is highly militarized, and national security, as we have seen, is placed at the core where the state, and not the people, come first. Boundaries have been more important than the humans living on them. It is therefore not surprising that in Kargil, from a military perspective, the protection of borders was of foremost importance, and people were marginalized. The animosity of the people became central in the state's relationships to its borders. When the system attempted change, the people's militarist response that they were willing to die/fight for Ray was not surprising. The aim of the article is not to be critical of the work done by the person who created the change but to analyze its importance and its relationship to the concept of human security, especially from a gendered perspective. The observation would help those who formulate good development policies in conflict situations to go further and include a policy of ending war itself.

Does Operation Goodwill fit into the feminist paradigm? If we take into account the four components most well-known feminist constituents of human security agree upon – physical security, environment security, daily needs and dignity – it will provide us with the guidelines to analyze Operation Goodwill. To begin with, the importance of the operation to the nationstate is that it controls militancy, so the security of its borders is achieved. Goodwill, Ray said, created trust between the armed forces and civilians on the border and brought the two civilians on both sides of the border closer. The Operation Goodwill strategy was a good beginning, especially the use of the vocabulary of a culture of peace and its linkage to human security, but when it stipulates that human security is a core element of national security, it goes against the principle of human security as projected by feminist writers. Although Operation Goodwill provides more developmental space to the citizens on the border, more equality to women, educational and health opportunities, the question that arises is does it fulfil women's human security needs?

Although it can be considered a commendable attempt in the context of understanding a development strategy paradigm, its human security understanding and sustainability is questionable, without which it becomes a half-hearted attempt by those who continue to use it. Although termed a sociopolitical strategy for conflict prevention, it stops short of attempting to do this. Using the terminology of culture of peace and human security is not enough, especially as the approach is narrow and the aim is basically only to stop the opposition. One of the advantages of this has been projected as the number of people from this region joining the armed forces. This is militarization, an opposing force in women's search for security. Militarization is not easily tackled because states deliberately use it not only through the armed forces but also as an ideology of power which influences the society and civilian life as a whole. In its process of implementation, patriarchy plays an important role. This ideological manifestation of power relations between state and citizen internalizes militarist values, including the use of force and reinforcement of patriarchal norms. A human security system would, unlike national security, not assume a confrontationist position and attempt to suppress it with armaments and do further harm. It would create space for non-violent protest and would not, in the process, wipe-out its own populations together with that of the opposition across the border.

Operation Goodwill speaks of a non-violent, rights-based approach of disarmament, of sustainable, endogenous, equitable human development, and in the same breath of military security. Although Operation Goodwill is based on the reasoning that guns and tanks do not provide security and is a brand name for trust and restoring hope and effective border management, Ray also speaks of security as being a 'human defense line that can serve as its "eyes and ears" on the border'. In this concept the villager turns out to be the central point of focus to manage the border areas and build a functional community-army relationship. The visibility of the projects would create goodwill and provide a positive image of the army – an important objective – but in reality, instead of demilitarization, it militarizes the mind. Nowhere does the Operation Goodwill strategy of a culture of peace speak of a peace strategy amongst people across the borders. Unless we speak of peace amongst people who are the 'enemy', of moving from the nation as territorial protection to a people living in peace and of open borders and including women in its peace strategy, the culture of peace will not achieve the goals of human security.

We recognize that with the conceptualization of human security challenges and the large expenditures on the armed forces in a market-oriented economy, it will be difficult to get states to agree to it, even to this limited version of security presented by Ray. Armaments are where the money lies. Above all justice is important, as the military expenditure is at the cost of other sectors, especially social sectors, such as education, health and gender inequality, the factors which influence the notion of justice. Any order which is not just has to be challenged and changed. Among this is the hegemonization of the state which has patriarchal tendencies and so marginalizes the weak and especially women. The other vulnerable sections are the minorities, especially religious and ethnic communities. For a human security paradigm to work, it must facilitate the creation of these changes. Can this alternative suggested by Ray create the space for change? It is obvious from women's concerns, even after human security was implemented by the army, that women's security was excluded. They still go without fulfillment of health and other needs, and their bodies are violated.

In this framework provided by Ray, human security is achieved through provisions of education, health, gender equality and community development programmes. The programmatic approach is not enough; if these are to be provided, it must be to all citizens in conflict zones, but it stops short of universalization in implementation. It goes without saying that the culture of peace and space for the shared values of tolerance, solidarity, democracy and economic development that Operation Goodwill wanted to achieve fits into the feminist human security paradigm. At the same time, in keeping with its links to armed national security, it falls short of visioning what it means to women.

What kind of a world of peace can we visualize? Can human security as a paradigm be adopted by states? A human security paradigm should aim for the wellbeing of the people and avoid the harmful effects of armed national security. At this point we need to remind the Indian state that soon after independence in the 1950s, sponsored policies of non-aggression and promoted policies of collective security displayed faith in the United Nations. As the power of the country increased, the United Nations became highly politicized the more radical its national security determinant became. About adoption of non-violence by states, Mahatma Gandhi said that it is blasphemy to say that non-violence can be practiced only by individuals and never by nations which are composed of individuals. Thus, he suggests the role of non-cooperation which he argues is an attempt to awaken the masses to a sense of their dignity and power. Women need to adopt these practices when state power threatens their rights.

Finally, what we require is disseminating the information on what a feminist perception of human security is. This should beat all levels, in general education and in civil society teachings. We need to include in our research the linkages that emerge among violence, masculinity, gender and human security to create a culture of peace that will replace the violence in our lives.

Notes

1 In the rest of the article, Operation Goodwill will be used.
2 The villages visited between 2002 and 2004 were Akchamal, Batalik, Bhimbet, Chiktan, Darchiks, Garkone, Gomoh Kargil, Goshan, Hardas, Holiyal, Hundurman, Kako Shilkchay, Kaksar, Karkitchu, Kharboo, Locham, Moradbagh, Mushkoo, Pandrass, Panikhar, Parkachik, Pashkum, Poyen, Tambiss, Shilikchay, Shergole, Trespone, Thasgam and Nurbakshi.
   Fieldwork was conducted from May 15 to June 25 in 2002; May 20 to 25 June 2004. I acknowledges the assistance provided by the University Grants Commission.
3 The territory had changed earlier, during the two wars of 1948 and 1965.
4 The name ofthe village isnot mentioned as there have been incidents in Kashmir where such incidents took place and media and other activism harmed the women as much as rape had done. Unless the women themselves do not come forward, it would be unethical to highlight the case. Visit on 5 June 2002.
5 The changes in the village after the rape are apparent. Men be at the women if work is not done. Men do the shopping and attend weddings if they are outside the village. 'We are not as scared of shells', said an old woman, 'as we are of the birth of girls as the army may take them away and bring further humiliation to the community'. The army post and the battalion were stationed opposite the village on a hill, standing as a reminder of what had happened.
6 In many countries, the concept of purity is linked to religion and in others to honour, where women who cohabit with the army or outsiders are termed of 'loose character' and are viewed as impure.
7 As per the United Nations Conference on women population and development in Cairo 1994 the policy of reproductive healthcare viewed women's development from abroad perspective of the provision of literacy, health and not reducing children through family planning measures which can be forced.
8 The older conflict is in the north-east of India, which has not been internationalized as much though people have suffered equally.

9 Under the United Nations, a meeting in Cairoin 1994 laid down the policy of reproductive healthcare which views women's development from abroad perspective of the provision of literacy, health andnot reducing children through family planning measures which can be forced.
10 The older conflict is in the north-east, which has not been internationalized, although it has suffered as much.
11 It is the world's highest battlefield, and each year thousands of soldiers suffer the devastating cold. Siachen was taken over by India from Pakistan in 1984. Turtuk provides the only road link to the Siachen base camp from where supplies are launched to Indian troops on the Siachen glacier. Losing Saichen is not as important strategically as the loss of agained territory and the consequent humiliation.
12 Although Khomeini is dead, all business centres, schools and so on, carry his photographs.
13 A plane carrying Air Vice Marshal V.K. Bhatia, trying to make an inaugural landing at Kargil Airport, ventured near Pakistani territory and was fired at (*The Tribune* 2002); General Ray in 2012 brought out another volume which gave details of 'Sadbhavna' but does not change the analysis in this article (Ray 2012).

References

Aggarwal, Ravina, and Mona Bhan. 2009. 'Disarming Violence Development, Democracy, and Security on the Borders of India'. *The Journal of Asian Studies*, vol. 68 (2): 519–542.

Bukhari, Shujaat. 2001. 'PM's Call: Winning People over in Ladakh', *The Hindu*, 31 July.

Butalia, Urvashi. 1998. *The Other Side of Silence: Voices from the Partition of India*. New Delhi: Viking.

———. (ed.). 2002. *Speaking Peace: Women's Voices from Kashmir*. New Delhi: Kalifor Women.

Chenoy, Anuradha M. 2004. 'Gender and International Politics: The Intersection of Patriarchy and Militarisation', *Indian Journal of Gender Studies*, vol. 32. New Delhi: Sage Publications.

Commissionon Human Security (Sadako Ogata Sadako and Amartya Sen, chairs). 2003. *Human Security Now*. New York: United Nations.

De Alwis, Malathi. 2004.'The "Purity" of Displacement and the Reterritorialization of Longing: Muslim IDP sin North western Sri Lanka', in Wenona Giles and Jennifer Hyndman (eds.), *Sites of Violence Gender and Conflict Zones*, pp. 213–31. Berkeley: California University Press.

Hans, Asha. 2000. 'Women across Borders in Kashmir, the Continuum of Violence', *Canadian Women's Studies*, vol. 19(4):77–87.

———. 2004. 'Escaping Conflict: Afghan Women in Transit', in Wenona Giles and Jennifer Hyndman (eds.), *Sites of Violence Gender and Conflict Zones*, pp. 232–48. Berkeley: California University Press.

Ladags Melong. 2002 'Sadbhavana: Army's Radical Approach', vol.1 (4):25–6.

Mangat, Rajwant. 2000.'Legislating Women's Lives: Women and the Partition of India', *Canadian Women's Studies*, vol. 19(4):61–4.
Menon, Rituand Kamla Bhasin. 1998. *Borders and Boundaries: Women in India's Partition*. New Delhi: Kali for Women.
Mrscevic, Zorica. 2001. 'The Opposite of War Is Not Peace-It Is Creativity', in Marguerite R. Waller and Jennifer Rycenga (eds.), *Front Line Feminisms: Women, War, and Resistance*, pp. 41–55. New York: Routledge.
Parmar, Leena and Major Dajlit Singh Parmar. 2002. 'Operation Sadbhavana: A Culture of Peace Process in Kashmir', unpublished, Inter-University Seminaron Armed Forces and Society, Canada. 25–27 October.
Ray, Arjun. 1997. *Kashmir Diary: Psychology of Militancy*. New Delhi: Manas Publications.
———. 2003. "Peace in South Asia: Is It Attainable? *the-south-asian* asks Lt. Gen. Arjun Ray (Retd.)." www.the-south-asian.com/Jan%202003/Peace%20in%20South%20Asia%20-%20Gen.%20Arjun%20Ray.htm accessed 20 June 2009.
———. 2012. *Peace Is Everybody's Business a Strategy for Conflict Prevention*. New Delhi, India: Sage.
Reardon, Betty A. 1993. *Women and Peace: Feminist Visions of Global Security*. New York: State University of New York Press.
———. 1998.'Gender and Global Security, a Feminist Challenge to the UN and Peace Research', *Journal of International Cooperation Studies*, vol. 6(1): 29–56.
Sreenivas, K.R. 2001. 'Infosys to Help Ladakhi Women Learn Computers', *Times of India*, 26 October. https://timesofindia.indiatimes.com/city/bengaluru/Infosys-to-help-Ladakhi-women-learn-computers/articleshow/1231787723.cms. Accessed 11 November 2017.
Swami, Praveen. 2001. The Week 2001. *Kargil Realities Frontline*, vol. 18 (16): 4–17. August.
The Tribune. 2002. General Puts in Papers February 28 Chandigarh Online edition. http://www.tribuneindia.com/2001/20010906/main3.htm. Accessed 19 May 2018.

15 Patriarchy and the bomb

Banning nuclear weapons against the opposition of militarist masculinities

Ray Acheson

Introduction

On 27 March, the first day of UN negotiations to ban nuclear weapons, the US ambassador to the United Nations, Nikki Haley, opened her press conference (Democracy Now 2017) opposing negotiation of a treaty prohibiting nuclear weapons, stating, 'First and foremost I'm a mom, I'm a wife, I'm a daughter'. And, 'as a mom, as a daughter, there's nothing I want more for my family than a world without nuclear weapons. *But we have to be realistic*' (emphasis added). 'Today when you see those walking into the General Assembly to create a nuclear weapons ban, you have to ask yourself, are they looking out for their people? Do they really understand the threats that we have?' she asked, talking to reporters outside the UN General Assembly Hall with what others have described as a 'ragtag band of about 20 diplomats' standing behind her (Mian 2017).

Ambassador Haley's statements are deeply rooted in patriarchy. She identifies the desire for disarmament with her womanhood but connects her desire to 'protect' her family to the 'necessity' of retaining nuclear weapons for the indefinite future. The objections to banning nuclear weapons are at their core patriarchal and racist. Several have observed the colonialism (Egeland 2016) and racism (Intondi 2017) of the opposition to the ban treaty. Less explored are its sexist underpinnings, rooted in patriarchal power structures and militarist masculinities.

There are several dimensions to the link between patriarchal power and militarist masculinities that contribute to the link's significance and complexity. There is the 'ubiquitous weight of gender' (Cohn 1987a) throughout the entire nuclear weapons discourse and the association of nuclear weapons with masculinity described by Carol Cohn in her groundbreaking work on gender in nuclear weapons discourse. The discourse denies women's lived experiences of the weapons cited by some who pursue nuclear abolition and asserts a monopoly on realism – that is, denial of others' perceptions of reality. Such denial is characteristic of patriarchy and psychologically abusive relationships. It attempts to justify and to link opposition to the ban to 'womanhood' or 'care-giving', as in Haley's protest press conference. All these complex dimensions are important to explore and expose in order to achieve the goal of prohibiting and eliminating nuclear weapons and to overcome the patriarchal norms currently opposing abolition.

Despite the entrenched opposition expressed by Haley and echoed by the other powerful nuclear-armed states, the conference adopted a treaty prohibiting nuclear weapons on 7 July 7 2017. This landmark in the long struggle to outlaw the weapons was achieved through a process involving the vast majority of the world's governments, international organizations and civil society – including women's peace organizations – after decades of effort. Over 130 governments (International Campaign to Abolish Nuclear Weapons 2017) participated in the conference, while the absence of the nuclear-armed states and their nuclear weapon-supportive allies demonstrated their opposition. The absent governments continue to espouse the 'security benefits' of nuclear weapons. In the face of overwhelming evidence of the catastrophic humanitarian and environmental consequences of the use of nuclear weapons (Fihn 2013), the destructive environmental effects of their testing and production and the growing risks of their accidental or intentional detonation, they still deny that human security is better served by the fact that most countries in the world have already rejected nuclear weapons entirely.

The adoption of this treaty is transformative. It is extremely rare, if not unheard of, for the United Nations to do anything if the five permanent members of the UN Security Council (all of which possess nuclear weapons) oppose it. States and civil society alike were told it was impossible to get traction on any issue if faced with a united front of opposition from the 'powers that be', yet there was not only traction but also momentum for this treaty. In this instance the minority of states' claims to control and dominance did not prevent the majority of countries from prohibiting nuclear weapons, a historic development that challenges colonialism, racism and the very structures of global patriarchy, politics writ large.

Gendered weapons, gendered discourse

To understand the power dynamics working against the treaty negotiations, it's useful to look at the role patriarchy and sexism has played throughout the nuclear era. Cohn's 'close encounter with nuclear strategic analysis' starting in 1984 led to illuminating (sometimes amusing) articles in *Signs* and the *Bulletin of Atomic Scientists* about the gendered coding of nuclear weapons. These articles – 'Sex and Death in the Rational World of Defense Intellectuals' (Cohn 1987a) and 'Slick 'ems, Glick 'ems, Christmas Trees, and Cookie Cutters: Nuclear Language and How We Learned to Pat the Bomb' (Cohn 1987b) – provided the foundations for a feminist analysis of nuclear war, nuclear strategy and nuclear weapons themselves.

The relevance of these articles, and their accuracy, persists to this day. It is impossible for any feminist to sit in a room full of men discussing nuclear weapons without thinking of the 'sanitized abstraction and sexual imagery' and the 'ubiquitous weight of gender' Cohn so vividly described in 1987. The intrinsic association between militarist masculinity and nuclear weapons runs deep. In later years Cohn, along with Felicity Hill and Sara Ruddick, expanded the inquiry into the sense of masculine strength afforded by nuclear weapons. They listened to a Hindu nationalist leader after India's 1998 nuclear weapon tests, who explained, 'we had to prove that we are not eunuchs'. They also look at mass media reactions to the 11 September 2001 attacks, which included appeals to the US government to 'bomb 'em back to the Stone Age, and then make the rubble bounce'. They argue these statements are meant to 'elicit admiration for the wrathful manliness of the speaker' and to imply that being willing to employ nuclear weapons is to 'have the balls' or to be 'man enough' to 'defend' your country (Cohn, Hill and Ruddick 2006).

This link between masculinity and the power of force persists today. Think of Trump 'becoming presidential' by launching missiles at Syria or by dropping the largest-ever conventional bomb on Afghanistan. Think of Kim Jong-un and his massive parades of missile hardware in a literal showcase of 'mine is bigger than yours'. Think of Theresa May giving a resolute yes to the question of whether she would be willing to 'personally authorize a nuclear strike that could kill 100,000 innocent men, women and children' (Mason, Asthana and Sayal 2016). Thus, it is the women leaders as well as the men who are conditioned to prove their capacity to lead by a 'manly' show of force.

The connection between masculinity and warfare creates and reinforces the widely observed gender stereotype, assuming men to be inherently violent and inclined to participate in violent acts. Men do constitute the majority of those committing violence and participating in armed conflict. But there is a distinct social history fostering this behaviour, perpetuated by assumptions about masculinity and femininity and by the institutions and social structures influenced by these assumptions. When gender differential treatment of men becomes integral to political or military policy, it is difficult to change. Like institutional racism, it becomes part of the social fabric, continuously reinforced through practice, and so conditions the environment in which all disarmament negotiations take place.

Within the context of nuclear weapons, the masculinity-warfare connection displays two key elements of gendered obstacles to denuclearizing security policy. First, the association of weapons and war as a symbol of masculine strength makes it harder to open up discussions about disarmament or collective security. Proponents of abolition are put down as unrealistic and irrational, as 'emotional' or 'effeminate'. Second, as a symbol of strength, nuclear weapons are seen as the platinum credit card of state security, admission to a very elite club of the powerful, making disarmament more difficult to achieve and proliferation more difficult to prevent.

In light of such perceptions, there was surprise and excitement when, from 2007 to 2011, it seemed there was a revival of a 'credible' disarmament discourse. Cold Warriors and members of the US male power elite, George Shultz, William Perry, Henry Kissinger and Sam Nunn (known apparently un-ironically as the 'four horsemen' in policy circles), argued that the long-standing policy of deterrence is no longer a legitimate justification for maintaining nuclear weapons. In the absence of a bipolar world order, they argued in a 2007 op-ed in the *Wall Street Journal*, nuclear deterrence 'is becoming increasingly hazardous and decreasingly effective' (Morgan 2007). To the detriment of world security, their warning came to naught.

Nuclear weapons continued to be held as the hallmark of powerful states. The momentum from this change of view proposed by the four policy elite, followed by US President Obama's much-lauded 'Prague speech', articulating an aspiration toward abolition could have moved the world closer to the elimination of nuclear weapons (Obama 2009). Instead, 10 years later, we face perhaps greater resistance to nuclear abolition from the nuclear powers than ever before, exemplified in the summer and fall of 2017 with a blood-chilling exchange of nuclear threats between the sitting president of the United States and the head of state of North Korea.

Many of the political and defence intellectual elites in nuclear-armed countries and their allies continue to valorize nuclear deterrence as a fundamental element of security. Those in the United States point to 'extended deterrence' as a primary rationale for retaining a considerable nuclear arsenal. They argue that US nuclear weapons in Europe, NATO nuclear strategy and extended deterrence covering Australia, South Korea and Japan prevent other states from 'going nuclear'. Developments in North Korea and Iran clearly contradict this argument.

Military strategists and politicians continue to emphasize the importance of maintaining a credible and effective nuclear deterrent until nuclear weapons are legally eliminated. The economic and political stronghold of the nuclear weapon laboratories in the United States remains a major impediment to nuclear disarmament. All nuclear-armed states keep their weapons because specific political constituents benefit from investment in their production and maintenance. The argument made to the public, however, is that the weapons are essential to national security.

Nuclear weapons are also part of a bigger picture of power projections. The work of the four horsemen, while ostensibly aiming for the elimination of nuclear weapons, in reality reflected a pragmatic strategy to maintain US military and economic dominance well into the 21st century, resulting in the formation of a foreign policy paradigm described as 'anti-nuclear imperialism' (Graham et al. 2010). This form of imperialism characterized the Obama administration. Illustrative of Cynthia Enloe's 'adaptive patriarchy', as defined further on, its proponents issue some verbal support for nuclear disarmament but do so in terms that prescribe restrictive measures on the rest of the world, such as extending the realms of applicability of non-proliferation and securing stronger commitments from those states that do not possess nuclear weapons to refrain from doing so, thus maintaining the current global power hierarchy – all for the stated purpose of making the world 'more secure' (Enloe 2014).

However, the delegations that gathered at the treaty negotiation conference in 2017 saw a world of insecurity, one in which none of the elements of human security were assured to the world's peoples. They saw nuclear weapons as the greatest threat to human security, putting the environment in extreme danger, diverting resources from meeting human needs, claiming national security interests to limit human rights and likely leading to the 'fire and fury' threatened by the US president within months of the adoption of the treaty. On this topic, the negotiators' concept of national security was in stark contrast to that of the patriarchal notion of state security that is used to rationalize maintaining nuclear arsenals.

On the other hand, there is much in common between the nuclear-armed states' gradualist approach to nuclear 'disarmament' embodied in non-proliferation policy and Cynthia Enloe's concept of 'adaptive patriarchy'. Enloe explains that one way the patriarchal system deals with changing landscapes that might upset its interests is by co-opting the movements or initiatives that oppose it (Enloe 2014). Applying this concept to the nuclear world, we can see a picture of 'adaptive disarmament', whereby the nuclear-armed states affirm their support for nuclear disarmament but seek to attain the 'ultimate' goal through immediate, strong-arm measures that do not actually involve getting rid of their own nuclear weapons so much as restricting other's access to such weapons as they do through the non-proliferation regime. As with adaptive patriarchy, adaptive disarmament folds the process into its own agenda, preserving the current order. Clearly the resisting nuclear-armed states see their respective national interests to be well served by a patriarchal interstate system assured by their nuclear arsenals.

The concept of 'adaptive patriarchy' illuminates both the tenacity of the patriarchal global gender order referenced in this book's introduction and the need to face and overcome the fundamental obstacle that patriarchy poses to disarmament that this collection of essays argues to be the truly realistic approach to global human security.

Monopoly on realism

'No one believes more firmly than Comrade Napoleon that all animals are equal', says the character Squealer in George Orwell's *Animal Farm*. 'He would be only too happy to let you make your decisions for yourselves. But sometimes you might make the wrong decisions, comrades, and then where should we be?'

In order to uphold the current order, the 'nuclear powers' and some of their allies have tried to establish themselves as authorities on legitimacy and realism. They have berated the vast majority of states for supporting the negotiation of a legally binding treaty to prohibit nuclear weapons, ridiculing their perspectives on peace and security and accusing them of threatening the world order, risking total chaos. They have sought, in an increasingly belligerent way, to stake their claim to truth *and* power rather than allowing truth to be spoken to power. They perpetuate the dominant 'realist' worldview, long challenged by critical, alternative worldviews; among them feminist views such as that of Sweden Foreign Minister Margot Wallström, who supported the ban treaty as consistent with her 'feminist foreign policy' (Barry 2017).

Prohibiting and eliminating nuclear weapons is neither practical nor feasible, these governments assert. Those who support the prohibition of nuclear weapons are delusional. They are 'radical dreamers' who have 'shot off to some other planet or outer space' (Acheson, 2015). They do not understand how to protect their people. Their security interests do not matter – or do not exist at all (Acheson 2016a: 3). Initiatives toward abolition are illegitimate, naive, 'terminally unserious' (Harries, 2017) and destabilizing. *Banning nuclear weapons might undermine international security so much it could even result in the use of nuclear weapons* (Acheson, 2015).

The basis upon which these assertions are made is usually unjustified, misinformed and rooted in a material or political commitment to the status quo. These claims bear some scrutiny. What is 'practical'? What is 'feasible'? How do we measure these concepts, and who determines the measurements? Surely not those most negatively affected by current nuclear weapons development, testing, stockpiling and threatened use: women, indigenous peoples, the poor, inhabitants of the areas in which the weapons are stored.

When the French government says the 'step-by-step' approach to nuclear disarmament – meaning the currently stalemated process of banning nuclear testing, stopping the production of fissile material, reducing nuclear arsenals, and so on – is the 'only realistic one, and so the only one that will allow us to progress', upon what data or precedent is this based (United Nations General Assembly 2014a)? Where is it written that this is the only possible approach? Certainly it is not in any current multilateral or bilateral agreements. The nuclear Non-Proliferation Treaty (NPT), the so-called cornerstone of the existing nuclear governance regime, simply calls for 'effective measures' for nuclear disarmament. Certainly it is not in the NPT's outcome documents, which make it clear that any interim measures they specify are neither exhaustive nor sequential.

When France demands that states must implement the step-by-step road map 'without deviating from the chosen path', we could ask, where is this path leading? Forty-seven years after the entry into force of the NPT, multilateral negotiations for nuclear disarmament, which are mandated by Article VI of the treaty, have not yet commenced. It is the nuclear-armed states that have deviated from the implementation of Article VI, while the vast majority of other states parties have stayed true to their non-proliferation commitments. Do we really feel that we are on the right path to global peace and security?

When the US government encourages states to 'join with the United States to advance realistic and achievable objectives', which objectives is it speaking about (United Nations General Assembly 2014b)? Who decides what is realistic and what is achievable? The core objective of the NPT, as set out in its preamble, is the elimination of nuclear weapons and their delivery systems. Is this objective no longer deemed realistic or achievable? The Trump administration plans to revisit this very question (Herman 2017). Does this administration hold the standard of what is realistic or achievable? Should we allow it to? Should we allow any tiny group of powerful states to do so?

When the United States or other nuclear-armed countries claim that reduction of their nuclear arsenals since the end of the Cold War has 'served the world well', do those who have suffered from nuclear testing think that is true (United Nations General Assembly 2014b: 3)? What about those who struggle to find jobs or shelter or food while their governments squander vast resources on the maintenance and modernization of these weapons? Has the majority of the world deemed the 'progress' declared by the nuclear-armed states practical or realistic?

'Certain parties would like to push us into taking another path, an ideological approach which aims to stigmatize and not to seek solutions', claimed the French ambassador in 2014 (Acheson and Gandenberger 2014). Stigmatization is a straightforward, logical human response to unacceptable practices. It is explicitly aimed at seeking and leading to solutions. Human society has progressed by identifying and condemning bad behaviour, which informs the building of norms and legal and political responses. It will be no different for nuclear weapons. They will be eliminated when the rest of the world has made it clear that they reject the purported 'value' of nuclear weapons, undermining the attempts of the nuclear-armed states to justify the risks and consequences of nuclear violence. Stigmatization, through the treaty to prohibit nuclear weapons, will be part of this shift in calculations. Similar strategies have been invoked by women's rights advocates seeking to eliminate the patriarchal bullying of sexual harassment and abuse. Stigmatization is a practical response to abuse of power, be it through wielding weapons or exploiting unequal gender status.

The attempt by nuclear-armed and nuclear-reliant states to undermine ban treaty proponents by asserting a monopoly on reason and legitimacy is classic patriarchy. As Cohn's work asserts, social constructions of gender ascribe contrasting characteristics to masculinity and femininity that are seen as mutually exclusive and in which the 'masculine' attribution is valued more highly than the 'feminine'. Such descriptors as strong, rational, serious and truth tend to be associated with masculinity, while weak, irrational, emotional and fiction tend to be associated with femininity (Cohn, Hill and Ruddick 2017). Feminist scholarship has raised challenges to these essentialist perceptions, leading the fields of political science and international relations to bring into question patriarchal behaviours of states and persons.

In the last few years, some representatives of the nuclear-armed states have tried to argue that even talking about the humanitarian consequences of nuclear weapons or calling for abolition is 'emotional'. They refused to attend the humanitarian initiative conferences. The Russian delegation to the United Nations argued that 'even children' know what a nuclear weapon does and that we should not 'waste time on such useless topics' (Acheson 2013).

The nuclear-armed states resist the humanitarian discourse because it focuses on what nuclear weapons actually do to human bodies, to societies, to the planet. Such evidence undermines the abstraction of nuclear weapons as deterrents and refocuses our attention on the fact that they are tools of genocide, slaughter, extinction. The resistance to the humanitarian discourse is reminiscent of a story in Cohn's 1993 article, 'Wars, Wimps and Women (Cohn 1993). A white male physicist, working on modeling nuclear counterforce attacks, exclaims to a group of other white male physicist about the cavalier way they are talking about civilian casualties. '*Only* thirty million!' he bursts out. '*Only* thirty million human beings killed instantly?' The room went silent. He later confessed to Cohn, 'Nobody said a word. They didn't even look at me. It was awful. I felt like a woman'.

The association of caring about the murder of 30 million people with 'being a woman' is all about seeing that position – and that sex – as being weak, caring about wrong things; letting your 'emotions' get the better of you; focusing on human beings when you should be focused on 'strategy'. Caring about the humanitarian consequences of nuclear weapons is feminine, weak and not relevant to the job that 'real men' have to do to 'protect' their countries. It not only suggests that caring about the use of nuclear weapons is spineless and silly but also makes the pursuit of disarmament seem to be an unrealistic, irrational objective.

Within this patriarchal construct, disarmament seems impossible (Acheson 2016b) – like a utopian vision of a world that cannot exist because, the argument goes, there will always be those who want to retain or develop the capacity to wield massive, unfathomable levels of violence over others, and therefore the 'rational' actors need to retain the weapons for protection against the irrational others. The refusal to constructively engage with the humanitarian discourse represents social acceptance of human beings intentionally put in harm's way, objects, viewed within an abstract calculus of casualty figures. It stands in stark contrast to the concepts and laws of human rights and dignity and poses a serious challenge to global justice. It also insists upon the notion that states, as coherent units, must always be at odds with one another, seeking an 'accommodation' of their differences rather than collectively pursuing a world in which mutual interdependence and cooperation could guide behaviour through an integrated set of common interests, needs and obligations, considerations that characterize human security, distinguishing it from state-centred notions of security.

Nuclear deterrence discourse has made it more difficult for heads of state, diplomats and the military to envision or articulate different security structures – such as those proposed by peace researchers and activists – that do not rely extensively on weapons and military might to 'protect' the 'nation' or its people. The security framework surrounding nuclear weapons means that most arguments in favour of their elimination rely on demonstrating that a world free of nuclear weapons brings security. Although this argument may be valid within a 'realist' worldview, it can become problematic in a 'defense' or war-planning context, where arguments in favour of nuclear disarmament tend to rely on commitments to bolster other technologies of violence. Thus, the pursuit of disarmament in these contexts becomes tied to the search for reassurance of security through technical, strategic and political substitutes for nuclear weapons (Mian 2009). Policy decisions are still based on conceptions of power imbued with mistrust, threat, fear and violence. Such policies do not allow for other types of interstate engagement or relationship between citizens and states; they dismiss alternatives as utopian and unrealistic.

This dismissal is also highly gendered. When those flexing their 'masculinity' want to demonstrate or reinforce their power and dominance, they try to make others seem small and marginalized by accusing them of being emotional, overwrought, irrational or impractical. This technique of dismissal and denigration has been experienced by women and the powerless for as long as gender hierarchies have existed.

In the nuclear sphere, dismissal is applied not only against those who want to eliminate nuclear weapons but also against those perceived as wanting to acquire them. The dominant arms control and non-proliferation discourse characterizes the possession of nuclear weapons by the established nuclear weapon states as legitimate while problematizing the nuclear weapons that spread to other states.

This distinction between the *self*, which has a right to possess nuclear weapons, and the *other*, who is too unpredictable to possess them, is highly gendered. When nuclear-armed states work hard to ensure that other countries don't obtain nuclear weapons, they create a context in which they are perceived as keeping other countries down, subordinating and 'emasculating' them.

Distinction between legitimate and illegitimate nuclear weapons possessors does nothing to prevent proliferation and only makes it more difficult to reduce the perceived value of nuclear weapons as a source of power. When governments act as though their power and security can only be guaranteed by a nuclear arsenal, they create a context in which nuclear weapons become the ultimate necessity for, and symbol of, state security. Given the known human and environmental consequences of the use nuclear weapons, insistence of such necessity is a vivid case of human security versus state security.

The denial of reason in one's 'opponent' – whether it's someone wanting to prohibit nuclear weapons or to acquire them – is not only patriarchal but also destabilizing. It is an attempt to take away the ground on which the other stands, projecting illusions about what is real, what makes sense or what is rational. One actor proclaims, 'I am the only one who understands what the real situation is. Your understanding of is not only incorrect but also delusional – *it is based upon a reality that does not exist*'. It means putting self as subject and the other as object, eliminating their sense of and eventual capacity for agency.

This is more than just an argument or a difference in interpretation. This is an attempt to undermine, discredit and ultimately destroy the other's entire worldview in order to maintain power and privilege. Objectification of others and control of 'reality', known as 'gaslighting', is as integral to patriarchy as it is to nuclear deterrence as a mechanism to maintain the current global hierarchy.

When the majority of states, international and civil society organizations all say, 'Nuclear weapons threaten us all and must be eliminated', as is the case with the ban treaty, the nuclear-armed states say, 'Nuclear weapons – in our hands – keep us safe and we must maintain them indefinitely'. When it is pointed out that they haven't complied with their disarmament commitments, they claim that they have.

This situation is extremely destabilizing politically. The political ramifications are that the majority of states and the world's publics are held hostage to the whim of a handful of governments that claim to know best while playing Russian roulette with our lives and our planet.

Denial of lived experienced

It's not just the reason or rationality of those supporting the prohibition and elimination of nuclear weapons that is denied. It is also the lived experience of everyone who has ever suffered from a nuclear explosion, or mining of nuclear weapons, or burial of nuclear waste.

When Nikki Haley essentially said, 'I don't think nuclear weapons should be banned because I'm a mom and I care about my family', Fijian antinuclear activist Vanessa Griffen pointed out that her statement was a slap in the face to every woman who has given birth to 'jellyfish' babies as a result of US or French or British nuclear weapons testing in the Pacific Islands or Australia. 'Pacific women – mothers and non-mothers alike – have spoken out against nuclear weapons repeatedly and want them banned', she wrote. 'Anyone who knows the impact of nuclear weapons knows their effects on women, and on children'.[1]

Studies on women's health in the aftermath of the Hiroshima and Nagasaki bombings, nuclear testing in Marshall Islands and in Kazakhstan and the Chernobyl disaster provide useful but incomplete analysis of ways in which women are uniquely impacted by radioactive violence (Fihn 2013). In particular, high rates of stillbirths, miscarriages, congenital birth defects and reproductive problems (such as changes in menstrual cycles and the subsequent inability to conceive) have been recorded. A possible link between breast cancer in young women and women who were lactating at the time of exposure to nuclear radiation has also been found to exist.

In 2012, Calin Georgescu, the UN Special Rapporteur on the Implications for Human Rights of the Environmentally Sound Management and Disposal of Hazardous Substances and Wastes visited the Marshall Islands to assess the impact on human rights of the nuclear testing conducted by the United States from 1946 to 1958. He found that the full effects of radiation on Marshallese women might have been underestimated. Among other things, the bathing and eating habits of women potentially played a role in their higher rates of contamination. The Special Rapporteur found that women often bathed in contaminated water, which may have been overlooked as a possible means of exposure, as was the fact that women eat different parts of fish than men, such as bones and organ meat, in which certain radioactive isotopes tend to accumulate. The Special Rapporteur also notes,

> Apparently, women were more exposed to radiation levels in coconut and other foods owing to their role in processing foods and weaving fibre to make sitting and sleeping mats, and handling materials used in housing construction, water collection, hygiene and food preparation, as well as in handicrafts.
>
> (Georgescu 2012)

The claim that protection of womanhood or motherhood is a justification for the possession of genocidal weapons is absurd. Yet it is those calling for prohibition and elimination who are alleged to be irrational. This denial of lived experience in order to project the 'realism' of absurd arguments is patriarchal and abusive. It dismisses the very real pain and suffering – often intergenerational – of those who have experienced the consequences of use or testing of nuclear weapons. These experiences are viewed as not relevant to the policies and practices of governments charged with 'protecting' civilians. It overrides lived human reality, sweeping it under the carpet so that abstract theories about 'deterrence' and 'stability' can hold court in policy and even public circles.

What can gender analysis do for disarmament?

In the nuclear-armed states, there are still rooms mostly full of men, still talking about 'vertical erector launchers, thrust-to-weight ratios, soft lay downs, deep penetration' (Cohn 1987a, p. 693). The language that assesses the power of nuclear weapons has long been observed by feminists to illustrate how weaponry is symbolic of male sexual potency. The dominance of militarist masculinities persists through strategic discourse upholding nuclear and other arms as necessary to security. But there are other rooms now, rooms full of civil society activists of diverse genders and ethnicities, talking about the prohibition and elimination of nuclear weapons.

Taking a human-focused approach to disarmament, and thereby challenging the dominant state-centred approach to international peace and security, was instrumental in establishing negotiations on the nuclear ban treaty (Bolton and Minor 2016). The humanitarian initiative, with its purposeful deconstruction of nuclear weapons as weapons of terror and massive violence, has led to the majority of states being ready and willing to negotiate a legal prohibition. This initiative has regained ground in terms of how nuclear weapons are discussed and perceived internationally. The re-emergence of a focus on the physical effects of a nuclear weapon detonation has initiated a process of further stigmatizing these weapons through international law as it is in the UN Treaty on the Prohibitions of Nuclear Weapons. An understanding of the gendered meanings and characterizations embedded in the discourse and politics of nuclear weapons will support that process.

This process is not a theoretical exercise. It has practical implications for bringing into force this treaty for the prohibition and elimination of nuclear weapons. A gender perspective challenges governments and people to act on moral, ethical, humanitarian, environmental, legal, political and economic grounds without waiting for permission from those benefiting from the status quo – because that permission will never come.

Humanitarian discourse intended to relieve multiple human suffering requires the recognition that nuclear weapons represent a constant threat of terror and that they perpetuate inequity between countries, with broader implications for humanity (Acheson 2016b). Explorations of injustice help unmask their immorality. Within this more complex critique, gender analysis is crucial to illuminating and challenging the structures of power that impose injustice and deprivation and sustain nuclear weapons.

Just as the humanitarian discourse undermines the perceived legitimacy of nuclear weapons, a gender analysis of nuclear discourse helps to deconstruct nuclear weapons as symbols of power and tools of empire. It can show that the enshrinement of nuclear weapons as an emblem of power is not inevitable and unchangeable but a gendered social construction designed to maintain the patriarchal order (Cohn, Hill and Ruddick 2006).

As Cohn, Hill, and Ruddick wrote, a gender analysis that highlights the patriarchy and social constructions inherent in this valuation of nuclear weapons helps to 'multiply, amplify, and deepen' arguments for nuclear disarmament and question the role of a certain kind of masculinity of the dominant paradigm. Disarmament, sometimes cast by its detractors as a weak or passive approach to security, can instead be shown for what it is – rational, just, moral and necessary for our survival.

Gender analysis also highlights the ways in which the possession and proliferation of nuclear weapons are silently underwritten and supported by an image of hegemonic masculinity, demonstrating just how dangerous and illusory an image of security produces. Being aware of the gendered meanings and characterizations embedded throughout the discourse and politics of nuclear weapons helps to 'confront the traditionally constructed meanings and redefine terms such as "strength" and "security" so that they more appropriately reflect the needs of all people' (Cohn, Hill and Ruddick 2006, p. 8). This kind of awareness can help us to understand and improve how we think, talk and act about weapons, war and militarism in a broader sense.

The legal prohibition of nuclear weapons will not assure their speedy and lasting elimination. It does not solve the all the problems of global insecurity and injustice. But it is a catalyst for change – as was the process of starting and completing the negotiations. Nor will it assure the sustainable peace that depends on complete and general disarmament, the demilitarization of security for which this book argues. Understanding the gendered aspects of the nuclear weapons world and challenging the patriarchal norms behind it are part of this process. Exposing the gendered aspect of the work is important not only to achieving our objective of banning nuclear weapons but also to changing those norms of patriarchy working against nuclear abolition.

It took courage for states drafting and signing the ban treaty to stand up to the nuclear powers and their rich allies (Acheson 2017a). Most of us – whether diplomats, activists or academics – have had to live in the space created for us by the nuclear-armed states. They have decided that they alone have the power and authority to determine when and where they will eliminate nuclear weapons. So far their obligations and commitments have amounted to naught. Yet these states have controlled the narrative and even much of the scholarship for so long that most of the world believes they have the legitimate right to do so. But they don't. The adoption of the treaty prohibiting nuclear weapons makes this very clear. Global civil society and the majority of the world's states, following in the steps of feminist peace scholars and activists, rejected the dominant narrative 'to write a new history'.

As Ambassador Patricia O'Brien of Ireland said on the opening day of the treaty negotiations in March 2017, 'We are not just writing a new and complementary treaty here, we are taking the opportunity to write a new history, and in so doing to create a new, more stable, more secure and more equal future for all' (Permanent Mission of Ireland 2017).

This is the crux of the ban treaty. It was negotiated on the basis of courage and hope rather than on fear and inequality (Acheson 2017c). It was a case of states and civil society coming together to stand up to power and violence, to say to the nuclear powers, 'Enough, we are going to craft a different world, whether you like it or not'.

Change happens when the 'discomfort of doing something new becomes less than keeping things the same', said Ambassador O'Brien (Permanent Mission of Ireland 2017). This treaty is already making nuclear-armed and nuclear-reliant states increasingly uncomfortable. The process of developing this treaty, as well as its adoption and entry into force, will have a transformative effect on nuclear weapons policies and practices. It is already having a transformative impact on international relations and on the United Nations (Acheson 2017b). Understanding and paying attention to the gender dynamics involved in the pursuit of nuclear abolition could also contribute to transcending patriarchy and to moving toward a viable human security system. It is only a matter of the effort and care we put into it.

Note

1 Personal communication, 28 March 2017.

References

Acheson, R. 2017a, Simply Banning Nuclear Weapons, Nuclear Ban Daily, Reaching Critical Will, Women's International League for Peace and Freedom, July 7, Vol. 2, No. 14, pp. 1–4. www.reachingcriticalwill.org/images/documents/Disarmament-fora/nuclear-weapon-ban/reports/NBD2.14.pdf.

Acheson, R. 2017b, Courage is the Crux of the Ban Treaty, Nuclear Ban Daily, Reaching Critical Will, Women's International League for Peace and Freedom, Vol. 1, No. 2. http://reachingcriticalwill.org/images/documents/Disarmament-fora/nuclear-weapon-ban/reports/NBD1.2.pdf.

Acheson, R. 2017c, Courage and Collaboration, Nuclear Ban Daily, Reaching Critical Will, Women's International League for Peace and Freedom, Vol. 1, No. 6. p. 1. http://reachingcriticalwill.org/disarmament-fora/nuclear-weapon-ban/reports/11398-nuclear-ban-daily-vol-1-no-6.

Acheson, R. 2016a, First Committee Monitor, No. 3 NGO Reporting on the United Nations General Assembly First Committee on Disarmament and International Security 3 October–2 November 2016, Reaching Critical Will. http://reachingcriticalwill.org/disarmament-fora/unga/2016/fcm/11188-2016-no-3.

Acheson, R. 2016b, Foregrounding Justice in Nuclear Disarmament: A Practitioner Commentary, Global Policy, Issue 7, Issue 3, Nottingham Trent University, pp. 405–7. http://onlinelibrary.wiley.com/doi/10.1111/1758-5899.12338/abstract.

Acheson, R. 2015, First Committee Monitor, Reaching Critical Will, No. 2. NGO Reporting on the United Nations General Assembly First Committee on Disarmament and International Security 8 October–9 November 2015. http://reachingcriticalwill.org/images/documents/Disarmament-fora/1com/FCM15/FCM-2015-No2.pdf.

Acheson, R. 2013, Overcoming Obusfication First Committee Monitor, Reaching Critical Will, Women's International League for Peace and Freedom, October 28, No. 4. NGO Reporting on the United Nations General Assembly First Committee on Disarmament and International Security 7 October–5 November 2013, p. 3. www.reachingcriticalwill.org/images/documents/Disarmament-fora/1com/FCM13/FCM-2013-4.pdf.

Acheson, R. and Gandenberger, M. 2014, First Committee Monitor NGO Reporting on the United Nations General Assembly First Committee on Disarmament and International Security 7 October–5 November 2014, No. 2, 13 October, p. 3. http://reachingcriticalwill.org/images/documents/Disarmament-fora/1com/FCM14/FCM-2014-No2.pdf.

Barry, E. 2017, Sweden's Proponent of 'Feminist Foreign Policy,' Shaped By Abuse, *The New York Times*, November 17. https://www.nytimes.com/2017/11/17/world/europe/margot-wallstrom-sweden.html.

Bolton, T. and Minor, E. 2016, The Discursive Turn Arrives in Turtle Bay: The International Campaign to Abolish Nuclear Weapons' Operationalisation of Critical IR Theories, Global Policy, Vol. 7, No. 3, June 7, pp. 385–395. http://onlinelibrary.wiley.com/doi/10.1111/1758-5899.12343/full.

Cohn, C. 1993, Wars, Wimps and Women: Talking Gender and Thinking War, in M. Cooke and A. Woollacott (eds.) *Gender and War Talk*, Princeton University Press, Princeton, NJ, pp. 226–46.

Cohn, C. 1987a, Sex and Death in the Rational World of Defense Intellectuals, Within and Without: Women, Gender, and Theory, *Signs* (Summer), Vol. 12, No. 4, pp. 687–718.

Cohn, C. 1987b, Slick 'Ems, Glick 'Ems, Christmas Trees, and Cookie Cutters: Nuclear Language and How We Learned to Pat the Bomb, *Bulletin of the Atomic Scientists*, June, pp. 17–24.

Cohn, C., Hill, F. and Ruddick, S. 2006, The Relevance of Gender for Eliminating Weapons of Mass Destruction, The Weapons of Mass Destruction Commission, No. 38.

Democracy Now 2017, U.N. Considers a Historic Ban on Nuclear Weapons, But U.S. Leads Boycott of the Talks, Daily TV Show, Thursday, March 30. www.democracynow.org/2017/3/30/un_considers_a_historic_ban_on.

Egeland, K. 2016, UK Nukes: Why the World Is Asking Britain to Disarm, New Internalist (The World Unspun), October 26. https://newint.org/blog/2016/10/26/the-uk-and-nukes-why-the-global-south-is-asking-to-disarm.

Enloe, C. 2014, *Bananas, Beaches and Bases: Making Feminist Sense of International Politics*, University of California Press, Berkeley.

Fihn, B. ed., 2013, Unspeakable Suffering: The Humanitarian Impact of Nuclear Weapons, Report of Reaching Critical Will: A Programme of Women's International League for Peace and Freedom. Geneva. https://ext.d-nsbp-p.admin.ch/NSBExterneStudien/191/attachment/de/743.pdf.

Georgescu, C. 2012, Report of the Special Rapporteur on the Implications for Human Rights of the Environmentally Sound Management and Disposal of Hazardous Substances and Wastes, Human Rights Council, Twenty-First Session, Agenda Item 3, Promotion and Protection of all Human Rights, Civil, Political, Economic, Social and Cultural Rights, Including the Right to Development, pp. 1–19. www.un.org/en/ga/search/view_doc.asp?symbol=%20A/HRC/21/48/Add.1.

Graham, D.B., Cabasso, J., Robinson, N., Parrish, W. and Acheson, R. 2010, Rhetoric vs. Reality: The Political Economy of Nuclear Weapons and Their Elimination, in R. Acheson (ed.) *Beyond Arms Control: Challenges and Choices for Nuclear Disarmament*, Reaching Critical Will, a Project of the Women's International League for Peace and Freedom, Geneva, pp. 9–32. www.reachingcriticalwill.org/images/documents/Publications/BAC/chapter1.pdf.

Harries, M. 2017, The Real Problem with a Nuclear Ban Treaty, Carnegie Endowment for International Peace, March 15. http://carnegieendowment.org/2017/03/15/real-problem-with-nuclear-ban-treaty-pub-68286.

Herman, S. 2017, Trump Administration Reviewing What Role US Nuclear Weapons Should Play, VOA News, March. www.voanews.com/a/trump-administration-reviewing-role-us-nuclear-weapons/3781464.html.

International Campaign to abolish Nuclear Weapons (ICAN) 2017, Position of Treaty. www.icanw.org/why-a-ban/positions/.

Intondi, V.J. 2017, Standing with the Nonwhite World to Ban Nuclear Weapons, *HUFFPOST*, February 15. www.huffingtonpost.com/entry/standing-with-the-nonwhite-world-to-ban-nuclear-weapons_us_58a502a9e4b0fa149f9ac184.

Mason, R., Asthana, A. and Sayal, R. 2016, Theresa May would authorize nuclear strike causing mass loss of life, *The Guardian*, July 18. www.theguardian.com/uk-news/2016/jul/18/theresa-may-takes-aim-at-jeremy-corbyn-over-trident-renewal.

Mian, Z. 2009, Beyond the Security Debate: The Moral and Legal Dimensions of Abolition, in G. Perkovich and J. Acton (eds.) *Abolishing Nuclear Weapons: A Debate*, Carnegie Endowment for Peace, pp. 295–305. http://carnegieendowment.org/files/Mian.pdf.

Mian, Z. and Ramana, K.V. 2017, Ending Nuclear Lawlessness, *The Hindu*, April 13. www.thehindu.com/opinion/lead/ending-nuclear-lawlessness/article17960731.ece.

Morgan, D. 2007, Kissingers Joins Call for Global Nuke Ban, *CBS News*, January 4. www.cbsnews.com/news/kissinger-joins-call-for-global-nuke-ban/.

Obama, B. 2009, Remarks by President Barak Obama in Prague as Delivered. https://obamawhitehouse.archives.gov/the-press-office/remarks-president-barack-obama-prague-delivered.

Permanent Mission of Ireland 2017, Statement by Ambassador Patricia O'Brien Permanent Representative of Ireland to the United Nations and Other International Organisations at Geneva at the United Nations Conference to Negotiate a Legally Binding Instrument to Prohibit Nuclear Weapons, Leading toward Their Total Elimination, High Level Segment New York, March 27–31. April 5. http://reachingcriticalwill.org/images/documents/Disarmament-fora/nuclear-weapon-ban/statements/27March_Ireland.pdf.

United Nations General Assembly 2014a, First Committee "General Debate" New York, October 8. 69th session Statement by Mr Jean-Hugues Simon-Michel Ambassador, Permanent Representative of France to the Conference on Disarmament. http://reachingcriticalwill.org/images/documents/Disarmament-fora/1com/1com14/statements/8Oct_France.pdf.

United Nations General Assembly 2014b, 69th session First Committee General Debate Statement by Rose E. Gottemoeller Under Secretary of State for Arms Control and International Security, October 7, p. 2. http://reachingcriticalwill.org/images/documents/Disarmament-fora/1com/1com14/statements/7Oct_US.pdf.

Conclusion
Framing a gender and human security discourse: initiating the inquiry

Betty A. Reardon

The core purpose of *The Gender Imperative* is to bring a gender perspective to a deeper, more comprehensive discourse on human security. Toward that purpose we set forth the following inquiry based on the individual articles. Rather than suggesting questions on the text itself, the inquiry comprises queries to guide reflection on and discussion of the gender and human security implications of the text and to initiate serious consideration of alternatives to the militarized state security system.

The questions or queries posed for reflection on each chapter suggest some of the lines of inquiry that might nurture a more open and productive discussion of gender and human security and serve to integrate it into the general framework. Readers are encouraged to devise their own queries and to extend the inquiry so as to contribute to the broader security discourse we seek and to bring it into the public sphere of policy discussions.

Part 1: confronting the militarized state security paradigm: human security from a feminist perspective

The three articles in this first section serve as the conceptual core of the inquiry into human security that this book hopes to inspire. The authors write from a feminist perspective that challenges the prevailing militarized state security system. Feminism, as noted, has sought to analyze the system in terms that illuminate the causes of militarization as they are embedded in social, political and cultural practices and structures of patriarchy. It is important to recognize that this analysis derives from women's actual, widely documented experiences of militarized security as reported in Kozue Akibayashi and Suzuyo Takazato's article and subsequent articles in Section 2.

1. Women and human security: a feminist framework and critique of the prevailing patriarchal security system

Betty A. Reardon

In this article, Reardon asserts that in the absence of systemic critiques of the existing global security system, progress toward the reduction, of arms dependence and global violence and the achievement of authentic human security remain in the realm of a widely desired 'impossible dream'. In the hope of raising serious discussion of moving these dreams into the realm of politically practical goals, readers might reflect upon what actually would constitute authentic human security, as addressed in this introductory article. One of the central arguments is that the most potentially constructive approaches to illuminating human security possibilities is comprehensive, holistic and systemic. Reardon offers one example of this type of approach by proposing a feminist framework. This framework is intended as a basis to begin the requisite security discussion to be pursued by a wide-ranging inquiry. To begin the inquiry, the following queries are proposed for discussion of this article.

What challenges, additions and amendments might be made to the holistic and comprehensive feminist human security framework proposed here? What institutional changes might be necessary to achieve it? What social and educational developments might be needed to make it politically feasible to propose the holistic and systemic changes deemed necessary to overcoming patriarchy as a core obstacle to human security? What elements of a women's or feminist perspective are essential or irrelevant to devising practical, non-violent alternatives to present security policies? What elements might other holistic perspectives, such as an Earth-centred/ecological or a human rights perspective, bring to a consideration of alternative security systems? What ways of thinking about security are most in need of change so as to prioritize human security over state security?

2. Gendered insecurity under long-termmilitary presence: the case of Okinawa

Kozue Akibayashi and Suzuyo Takazato

In this article, Akibayashi and Takazato demonstrate that nothing so reveals the human security deficits resulting from dependence on armed forces for national security as long-term military presence. The stationing of military personnel and equipment in the thousands of military bases maintained by the great military powers has been costly to the powers and more so to the peoples of the foreign lands. The majority of these are American bases, several of which occupy a large percentage of the formerly agricultural lands of Okinawa. A worldwide anti-base movement has opened discussion on whose security is actually served by this global network of military bases, a question essential to any assessment of militarized state security.

Does the global network of US military bases actually contribute to the human security of ordinary American citizens? What effects do the bases have on the human security of the residents of these militarized communities, especially of women, children and other vulnerable groups? What are the current and potential long-range environmental consequences of constant and on going military activities? What can we learn about the qualities and requirements of authentic human security from cases of long-term military presence, such as Okinawa? How do such cases enable us to understand the significance of women's experience to the human security of a people? How does it exemplify the framework presented in Reardon's introductory article? Are there possibilities for the conversion of these bases to civilian uses to increase the human security of local residents? Who should be responsible for bearing the costs of such conversion? How might these costs compare to the costs of maintaining foreign bases?

3. Human security and intersectional oppressions: women in South Africa

Bernedette Muthien

For decades, peace research has inquired into causes and consequences of violence and obstacles to human well being. The analysis produced by this research has defined the concept of structural violence through which to assess the frustration of human needs fulfillment, generally deemed as basic to human security. Building on that theory with other concepts of violence described in this article, Muthien enables us to discern the gendered nature of both national/state security and human security. She introduces concepts essential to any discussion of human security within a systemic approach, recognizing the structural, political, economic and cultural aspects of security systems. This article provides some conceptual tools with which to assess state security systems and the human security possibilities of non-violence.

In what ways might multiple concepts of violence and principles of non-violence facilitate inquiry into human security? What possible applications of these concepts and principles a review of the national securityparadigm could reveal its effects on human security? What should be the function of the state in providing and assuring human security? How might states relate to one another in ways that might enhance the possibilities for the advancement of human security? What new approaches to the prevention and reduction of violence might lead to progress toward greater assurances of human security? In what ways might violence against women be accounted for within the concepts of violence outlined in this article? How could gender violence be situated in the larger system of global violence that manifests in war and global injustice? Are there possibilities and opportunities for states and other political actors to pursue policy goals through non-violent means? How might a politics of non-violence be used in political strategies for the pursuit of gender equality and human security? How might such a politics include the integral relationship between gender equality and human security?

Part 2: patriarchal conditioning to violence and human insecurity

This section offers examples of situations that derive from the dominant assumptions about the utility of violence as a means to achieve political goals and about the secondary to marginal significance given to the well being and security of women in the formation and pursuit of those purposes. The first three articles provide ample evidence that the political exclusion of women that permits their abuse in conflict and post-conflict situations is at the core of the larger system of violence and is perhaps the most significant of all obstacles to human security. The fourth article, using news reporting on security controversies, reveals the media as one of the most powerful tools for conditioning publics to the acceptance of patriarchal approaches to national security. The questions suggested for review of this section are designed to illuminate these circumstances and to pursue alternatives.

4. *Challenging the patriarchal national security paradigm: the role of Ethiopian women in peace and security*

Mesfin G. Ayele

Patriarchy, as we argue throughout this book, is at the core of the major dilemmas of human security. Ayele describes in detail how patriarchal cultural roots and political practices impede the potential contributions of women to the well being of the Ethiopian nation.

The failure to meet women's needs and their continued exclusion from power serve to illuminate how the priority given to national security as militarized state security obviates efforts to strengthen human security. Inquiring into the problematic of gender and human security posed by Ayele calls us to assess the political status and potential of women and the links between democracy and human security.

Should struggles for national independence and/or democracy put a priority on gender equality as essential to the realization of human rights as the foundation of democracy? In what ways might advances in broadening political participation move a society toward greater human security? What specific effects on possibilities for human security might be expected from the political empowerment of women? Might such effects also influence the human security of other vulnerable groups? What elements and components of comprehensive human security are most imperiled by patriarchal political orders? Are there any circumstances in which progress toward human security might be made within a patriarchal order? What might be some potential strategies to transform patriarchy and other forms of authoritarianism while striving toward comprehensive human security?

5. War and armed conflict: threat to African women's human security

Fatuma Ahmed Ali

For centuries, women have suffered immeasurable, devastating consequences of wars they had no hand in making. But even, as was exemplified in Ayele's article, when they have been participants, the gendered devastation of war has gone unmeasured, not because it was immeasurable but because it has been seen as an inevitable if regrettable harm integral to the armed conflicts conducted in the name of national security or national interest. Ahmed Ali presents evidence of how, over recent decades, Africa has suffered an inordinate degree of this devastation. Such waste of human lives and talents has led many to question the utility of armed conflict as well as the efficacy and morality of war itself. The dimensions of the African tragedies and their femicidal consequences highlight the urgency of devising and implementing analternative security system to assure the human security of women and the nations whose well being depends upon them. The contributors to this volume, inarguing for such a system change, for the elimination of armed conflicts and the weapons with which they are conducted, suggest the following inquiry toward the consideration of these goals.

How might we assess and analyze the multiple forms of violence suffered by women in armed conflict and war so as to diagnose the pervasive and long-lasting effects of wars on all affected societies? Might such an assessment provide us with insights into the ineffectiveness of war as a mechanism to protect the physical security of nations? Can a case be made that these are forms of the avoidable harm which a system designed to achieve human security might reduce and eliminate? How do the multiple roles of women in warfare belie the assumption that women's involvement is only secondary to men's in the pursuit of military goals? Are there ways in which the perpetrators of violence against women are themselves victimized by gender violence as a weapon of war? Can we make a case that war also imposes forms of gender-based violence against men? What relationship does sexual violence in armed conflict have to other forms of gender-based violence? What case can be made for the theory that violence against women is at the very core of the war system? How might this theory affect policies and strategies designed to achieve human security? Some argue that weaponry itself is a considerable factor in strategic sexual violence. Might we argue that disarmament may be essential to the reduction of such violence and the frequent incidence of armed conflict?

6. Sexual violence and genocide, the greatest violation of human security: responses to the case of Darfur

Lisa S. Price

Genocide is war in the extreme. All war aims to overcome the adversary. Genocide aims to destroy a designated enemy. It is total and complete denial of human security and all its essential elements that are always undermined in any armed conflict. Sexual violence against women increases with the severity of armed conflict. In genocide it is a strategy for the destruction of a people, and Price reminds us of what we have called the quotidian or every day conditions that actually comprise human security. Without day-by-day expectations of well being, there can be no human security. The gendered nature of daily security attests to the essentially gendered nature of human security and to the necessity to address it as such. So, too, remedies and strategies for prevention must be cast in a gender perspective by posing policy queries, such as the ones following.

What are the ways in which the every day human security of most people are impeded in war time and peace time by the priority the present system places on state security? In what ways are gender roles impediments to the protection of persons and communities in armed conflict? Are there any such impediments outside conditions of armed conflict? Might we discern in what Price refers to as 'cascading victimhood, a pattern of harm that demonstrates the centrality of sexual violence to the war system? How might this discernment serve to guide the proposal of strategies, policies and institutions for reduction and ultimate elimination of armed conflict? What can we learn about the political and institutional change required to free human security goals from the political realism that deters the United Nations and its Security Council from applying the legal measures for violence prevention now open to them? What campaigns and strategies might citizens and their organizations undertake to realize the potential of the UN Charter to serve as 'an instrument of human security'?

7. Security discourses: a gender perspective
Michele W. Milner

For centuries, the patriarchal paradigm has been the predominant model of human social organization and conceptualization of social relations and processes. Among the most significant obstacles to the achievement of human security are the ways in which we think about it. The ways of thinking, the rationalizations of the gendered power order and the very language and metaphors with which we communicate have been conditioned by patriarchy. How this conditioning affects contemporary security discourse as communicated through the information media is shown by Milner to be a significant obstacle to clarity of discourse about contemporary security challenges, such as the War on Terror. In this article, she reveals the gendered, militarized language that dominates security discourse and the contestations of the very meaning of security.

In what ways is the role of language important when discussing the concept of human security? How must the depiction of human security be changed to gain rhetorical force and to realize its transformative possibilities? How can we recognize the patriarchal and military markers in the language of the media? How might we devise and apply alternatives to the patriarchal language of the militarized state to articulate a gender-equal human security paradigm? How might controversies over dispatching troops to foreign wars be described so as to give serious thought to the changing of the security system? Might one alternative to avoid such problems and controversies as the dispatching of national forces to an international conflict be a global collective security system, supplemented by state-controlled rapid civil forces setup to meet disaster-related risk, providing assistance to civilians, being used sparingly and only when required? How might the media describe such suggestions for alternatives to the present security system? How might the media make them politically viable? How might the media serve to advance women's needs and gender justice in the present security system and/or in an alternative system designed to achieve human security? What guidelines and criteria for media coverage of security issues that would promote open and unbiased democratic public discussion to ward change could be put forward?

Part 3: militarization/demilitarization: eroding and promoting human security

In this section, we offer cases of women's responses to militarization and its violation of their human security. We have described gender violence as the hallmark of the larger system of patriarchal violence manifest in war and armed conflict. From the beginning of our inquiry, we have made reference to women's resistance. Here we focus on specific cases in which women have presaged human security through peacemaking and anti-militarist actions and campaigns, such as those of the Pacific Islands pushing peace negotiations, Afghan girls seeking education toward equality and human fulfillment and Russian mothers liberating their sons from militarist abuse in the armed forces.

8. *Seeking human security in a militarized Pacific: struggles for peace and security by Pacific Island Women*

Ronni Alexander

Colonialism has been a violent and gendered process through which Western patriarchal states have undermined the human security of the colonized while exploiting pre-colonial sociopolitical divisions and reinforcing existing oppressions. The history of Western colonization across the globe reveals that it established its own male-dominated structures, excluding women from political and economic activity. Alexander's article calls attention to the continued violence against women in postcolonial and post-conflict situations and recounts women's efforts to address the militarized security that exacerbates it, taking action to advance the cause of peace as exemplified in Guam and Okinawa. The gendered nature of colonialism can be discerned in similarities and differences evident in these two cases of militarized colonialism.

How might these similarities and differences be factored into a transition strategy intended to transform the present systems of neocolonialism, neoliberalism and militarism into one based on the pursuit of human security? What might be the significance of the similarities between these women's peace actions on these two colonized islands in each of which women have a somewhat different status? What factors embolden women to take actions for change? Even in the chaos of break down of social rules in situations of armed conflict and radical political change, might there be opportunities to advance gender equality and human security? What appear to be the human security consequences of the forces at play in modern neocolonialism, including globalization, militarized coerced prostitution, political repression of unarmed indigenous people and exploited environments? In what ways might we address each of these threats to human security in proposing steps toward demilitarization, authentic national independence and gender-equal democracy for postcolonial and neocolonial societies?

9. Education, violence and schools: the human security of girls in Afghanistan

Chloe Breyer

It is widely acknowledged within the human rights and peace movements that, in accordance with international standards, education is a fundamental human right and that educational opportunities equal to those of men are essential to women's realization of all other human rights. In that the human security framework proposed as the foundation of this volume asserts gender equality to be essential to its achievement, we hold that universal education is a basic component of the human needs that comprise the wellbeing integral to our concept of security. Denial or destruction of opportunities for education to women and girls is a denial of their human security and that of their communities and nations. Destruction of schools is a means to thwart democracy as well as to deny fundamental needs and therefore must be attended to as a threat to human security. Breyer demonstrates that such threats, when they derive from narrow, distorted, sexist interpretations of traditional religion that conflate masculinity with patriarchal power and control, manifest the hegemonic masculinity that we argue is at the core of the war system and human insecurity. Clearly the imperative of universal education and concepts of masculinity that oppose it form essential realms of inquiry into the nature of and possibilities for human security, leading us to raise the following questions.

What might be some human security-enhancing approaches to devising responses to such violations of the right to education as the burning of schools? If the responses are to be consistent with democratic principles and to contribute to human security, who should mount and pursue those responses? How might gender issues be integrated into such responses? Might non-governmental organizations (NGOs), especially international or foreign organizations, be able to provide aid in ways that respect social and cultural norms but that remain consistent with the fundamental human rights articulated by the United Nations and espoused by the international community? What might comprise some gender equality/human security guidelines for humanitarian aid projects intended to advance peace building in post-conflict societies? Might there be a need for institutions, such as the church, that espouses social justice and NGOs offering development aid to review their own structures and practices to assure that they are free of gender bias and/or patriarchal or militarist assumptions?

10. The soldiers' mothers, human security and the Russian-Chechen Wars

Valerie Zawilski

The national security paradigm, embedded as it is in patriarchy and dependence on armed force, has exploited an exclusive and gendered form of nationalism. In this paradigm, motherhood is a heroic service to the nation and a provider of personnel for the armed forces deployed in the name of defending the traditions and values of the nation. Exclusive cultural nationalism, like gender inequality, presents a significant obstacle to human security within a nation and with in the nations with which it may be in conflict. Such nationalisms tend also to stand against democratic practices that might threaten the authority of an unjust state. Zawilski presents a case in which Russian women under such conditions during the Russian-Chechen War turned this exploitation on its head as they struggled against the abuse of their sons in the Russian armed forces, a struggle that also enlisted fathers and Chechen parents in opposition to war and abusive military action. Their use of judicial procedures in seeking accountability for the crimes committed on both sides shows the potential of law as a replacement of force to resolve conflict in a non-violent security system designed to achieve and maintain human security. The Russian mothers' resistance to militarized state security exemplifies civil society actions of the sort that will be required to create public consciousness integral to support for significant changes in the war system revealed to abuse men as well as women. They demonstrated the complex roles of women in militarized societies that must be explored in a gender analysis of militarism as a basis for exploring possibilities for gender equality and authentic democracy. Such possibilities suggest the following questions.

What possibilities might we identify that women in other societies have or could turn the limits of traditional gender roles into opportunities to raise consciousness and to gain public support for resisting militarism and armed conflict and rejecting the war system? Are there other such cases to explore? In such a process, might it be possible to design the actions so as to contribute to the gender equality that is a fundamental principle of human security? Can we discern relationships among concepts of masculinity, state authority and the abuse of soldiers in the military? How might the illumination of these possible relationships serve to suggest arguments and strategies for the demilitarization of security? What useful lessons can be found in the anti-war struggles of generations of mothers from many countries of the world? How can we move beyond the contestation of motherhood as a restrictive role to use these lessons? Do the involvement of Russian soldiers' fathers and the more active and involved roles fathers are coming to play in family life offer any possibilities for understanding the possibilities for gender equality and human security?

Part 4: alternative and transitional approaches to human security

Throughout this volume, we have raised queries about change and considerations of alternatives to militarized state security so as to move the international system toward a comprehensive, gender-equal human security system. We have argued that such movement involves re-conceptualizing and thinking about security in distinctly different terms from those now commonly used. We have raised questions and posed queries to demonstrate to readers some possible approaches to new, gendered security thinking. The four articles in this section suggest several such approaches: an international standards approach as exemplified in Security Council Resolution 1325 taken by the United Nations; applying women's concepts of security revealed in a study conducted in Jordan; using health as the fundamental marker of human security as well being; and, instituting human security measures in a strategy to bring an active conflict to a close through providing to communities needs they have been denied during the conflict over the Kashmir border as contested between India and Pakistan. Finally, the one new article in this edition on the process of adoption of the UN treaty banning nuclear weapons brings to the discussion disarmament as a means to human security.

11. Security Council Resolution 1325: toward gender equality in peace and security policy making

Soumita Basu

Although still limited by the virtual sanctity of the cornerstone of the present international system, national sovereignty, international standards and goals set by the United Nations serve to demonstrate the potential of institutional and legal approaches to human security. An example most relevant to our inquiry is Security Council Resolution 1325 on women, peace and security. While recognized as an important tool to be used in the construction of a gender-equal human security system, this resolution is still, as Basu asserts, caught in the 'strong militarist and patriarchal embrace of the Security Council', a creature of the international state system. Of the three conceptual foundations of the resolution, participation, protection and prevention, protection of women in armed conflict, more readily acceptable to the patriarchal mindset, has received some of the council's attention, relegating the other two to the margins of consideration in the relatively few efforts to implement the resolution. This history serves to strengthen our argument that comprehensive human security can not be realized within the patriarchal structures of the state system. Yet this is the system in which we must launch transition strategies and actions toward the requisite system change. We must inquire into ways in which our efforts can contribute toward that change, the potential transformation which would provide the conditions for the realization of all the fundamental elements of comprehensive human security.

What criteria for monitoring Security Council Resolutions 1325 and 1820 and the multiple resolutions based on them might provide better assurance of protection while advancing the human security requisites of women's participation in security matters and the prevention of armed conflict? What relationship might we argue to exist between women's participation in security policy making and the prevention of armed conflict? Might there be ways in which the focus on protection could be used as the impetus toward exploration of the larger system of gender-based violence that feminists argue includes violence against women in armed conflict as one particularly egregious component? Would it be possible to build an enforcement strategy for Resolutions 1325 and 1820 and the subsequent resolutions that would integrate them with other UN policy statements, such as the Convention on the Elimination of All Forms of Discrimination against Women and the Beijing Platform for Action, into a comprehensive framework for a gendered legal/institutional approach to achieving human security?

12. Jordanian women define security: a feminist approach to an age-old problem
Norma Nemeh

One of the most promising sources for re-conceptualizing security to replace the present state-centred militarized security with a person-based human security system is in women's perceptions and experience of what makes them, their families and societies secure. The concepts of security that Nemeh identified in her research with Jordanian women reflect the fundamental components of a comprehensive human security framework and resonate with security perspectives of other women, such as the South African women cited in Muthien's article. In both cases, we see women's perspectives pointing toward human and social well being as the essence of human security. Jordanian women, in placing the highest priority on economic security, indicate that without the fulfillment of basic human needs, there can be no human security. The perspectives of Jordanian women provide an instructive example of transition to new ways of thinking about security. Especially significant to the assertion that education is a basic need is their linking of economic security to education, as we would link the education of women to changes in their subservient status and to the development of the authentic democracy integral to human security. This article illuminates the critical interrelationship between militarized state security and women's subservience that attests to the need to confront the 'militarism/sexism symbiosis' in strategizing further transition to human security. Toward that end, we suggest consideration of the following queries.

Why and in what ways is culture a significant factor in understanding the obstacles to and possibilities for the achievement of human security? What might be potential approaches to a strategy directed toward simultaneously overcoming both sexism and militarism? How might women silenced by militarized society gain a voice in the planning and implementing of policies designed to meet their security needs? What other voices have been silenced in the security discourse in militarized society, and are the needs of groups other than women also subservient to 'sovereign' state authority? Might all the excluded form human security partnerships? What actions and conditions might make such partnerships possible, even in ethnically diverse and/or tribal societies? What might be the common ground upon which diverse groups could build such collaborative partnerships? Are there any examples of such collaboration in women's movements and peace movements mentioned in this volume or described elsewhere?

13. Public health and patriarchy: militarism and gender as determinants of health insecurity

Albie Sharpe

Within a concept of human security defined as human well being, there are no more cogent or comprehensive indicators of the security of a society than health and healthcare. Peace researchers have often used medicine and illness as metaphors in the study of war and armed conflict. Sharpe, however, in bringing the issue of health itself into the very centre of the human security discourse, makes a transformative conceptual shift that brilliantly illuminates the argument that human security is incompatible with and cannot be achieved within a system of militarized state security, which is obscured by the conceptual cloak of 'national security'. Health, as he demonstrates, shows more clearly than any other single example the links between gender as a power determinant, militarism as patriarchal power maintenance and human insecurity as the fundamental condition of deprivation – like sexual violence – inevitably worsened by war and armed conflict.

As health and health care constitute barometers of human security, how might they be factored into assessing the costs of conflict and providing for post-conflict daily security needs? What arguments can we make that, in addition to the physical and psychological health damages of armed conflict, the reproductive needs of women should be included in health care plans in conflict and post-conflict situations? How might these needs, rarely fulfilled in militarized states, casualties of war and entrenched patriarchal principles, become part of international dialogues on trade, climate change and the financial crisis? How might we advance the issues beyond the World Health Organization to a place on the agenda of all agencies dealing with human security, conflict resolution, post-conflict service and peace building? How effective in serving the well being of a nation is a national security system that undervalues national health and ignores women's right to sex-specific health care? Were gendered health security to emerge as an important issue, how might concepts of and approaches to national security change? How might any resulting positive changes be sustained? Do we see a need for new international institutions to regularly and systematically address health as fundamental to human security? What health questions might we pose to existing agencies that deal with security and conflict issues? What might we propose as health criteria for assessment of national security and progress toward human security? What other constructive possibilities do we see in health as a tool of analysis for seekers of human security?

14. Human security: the militarized perception and space for gender

Asha Hans

Hans focuses on an element largely ignored in the human security discourse, the tensions that a feminist perspective reveals to be inevitable in the attempt to reconcile human security and militarized state security. *Human Security Now* (Ogata and Sen 2003) suggests a complementary relationship between the two concepts of security, a kind of 'both/and' approach. A feminist perspective, on the other hand, sees 'either/or', arguing that the two approaches are incompatible and mutually exclusive. Yet the problem of how we might move from militarism to human security is one that all who advocate for system change will have to address. Proposals, processes and experiments in transition, such as those referenced in this inquiry, should be advanced and explored. Operation Good Will described in this article is one such experiment. It is not uncommon to use service to civilians and quality of life strategies to reinforce or gain acceptance for military initiatives, as in the Vietnam, Afghanistan and Iraq wars. Yet these experiments may also provide opportunities to learn about their potential effectiveness intransition to human security. Clearly one significant area calling for change as we strive to assure human security is the militarized nationalism that states cultivate to gain and maintain support for military undertakings, as noted also by Ayele. Changing minds and ways of thinking about security will be essential to gaining support for transition strategies and policies. No agent can be more effective in this than the voices of women heard in this article.

What is to be learned from women's experiences and the human security experiment in the India-Pakistan border area that may help in planning transition toward a more human security-oriented system? What other similar efforts might we find to study in our quest to identify and refine strategies for transition to a transformed security system? What attributes would characterize such a system? What do the experiences and perspectives of women on borders teach us in our quest to conceptualize and achieve human security? How does military violence against women reveal the incompatibility of militarized security and human security? What attitudes toward and perceptions of militarized sexual violence contribute to the toleration of these crimes? What perceptions and attitudes could we substitute? How might law and international standards be used more effectively to abolish military sexual violence? How might we imbed the abolition of sexual violence in a generalized strategy for the abolition of war?

15. Patriarchy and the bomb: banning nuclear weapons against the opposition of militarized maculinities

Ray Acheson

In this article, Acheson illuminates the fierce struggle waged by those at the top of the global patriarchy, the nuclear powers, to prevent the banning of nuclear weapons. A fundamental assumption of the authors of this collection is that armed force is a major mechanism for maintaining the global gender order both among and within states. The enforcement of the patriarchal hierarchy with weaponry culminates with the most powerful states tenaciously holdingon to the most powerful, destructive weaponry ever devised – nuclear bombs. So fearful are they of falling from the top that they defy democratic principles and risk the survival of their own and all other nations. So, too, they fear that abolishing nuclear weapons could well lead to the abolition of all offensive weapons and ultimately to the general and complete disarmament that would be the foundation of a true human security system with an unprecedented degree of global democracy.

The goal of peace through general and complete disarmament has long been espoused by the Women's International League for Peace and Freedom (WILPF). Ray Acheson represented WILPF among the civil society groups who worked with UN member states to draft and adopt the Treaty on the Prohibition of Nuclear Weapons. Women of many organizations played a crucial role in the process led by the International Campaign to Abolish Nuclear Weapons (ICAN), the 2017 Nobel Peace Prize laureate. It is significant that the major speeches at the prize ceremony were given by women. It is fitting that we close our inquiry into the possibilities for achieving human security with queries about the twin imperatives of gender equality and disarmament.

Acheson focuses on the 'gendered' nuclear discourse. As feminists have sensitized many to sexist language, how might we do the same with militarist language and the sexist-militarist language that conditions discussion of arms and security policy? 'Realist' thinking was much at play in the opposition to the treaty. In what ways can feminist human security activists engage with realists? Why are the nuclear powers so resistant to the 'humanitarian' discourse that won over the 130 member states that supported the treaty? How might we apply an understanding of that resistance to dialogue with the nuclear powers? How might the partnership between member states and civil society continue in efforts to bring the treaty 'into force'? What similarities might be discerned between deterrence policy and gender violence as a means of maintaining militarized patriarchy? What arguments and considerations uphold Acheson's claim that the treaty is transformative? How can recognizing women's lived experiences and men's identity stake in coercive power contribute to a transition to alternative thinking about security? Coming full circle to Weiss's assertion that The Hague Agenda for Peace provides practical steps toward the abolition of war and Reardon's noting of various proposals for sustainable peace and authentic human security put forth at the beginning of our considerations of gender and human security, how might we use such proposals toward education for a global system transformed by gender equality and non-violence?

Annexure
Security Council Resolutions 1325 and 1820

United Nations
Security Council

00–72018(E)

S/RES/1325 (2000)
Distr.:General
31 October 2000

Resolution 1325 (2000)
Adopted by the Security Council at its 4213th meeting, on
31 October 2000
(Accessed 12 March 2010.)

The Security Council,

Recalling its resolutions 1261 (1999) of 25 August 1999, 1265(1999) of 17 September 1999, 1296 (2000) of 19 April 2000 and 1314 (2000) of 11 August 2000, as well as relevant statements of its President, and *recalling also* the statement of its President to the press on the occasion of the United Nations Day for Women's Rights and International Peace (International Women's Day) of 8 March 2000 (SC/6816),

Recalling also the commitments of the Beijing Declaration and Platform for Action (A/52/231) as well as those contained in the outcome document of the twenty-third Special Session of the United Nations General Assembly entitled 'Women 2000: Gender Equality, Development and Peace for the Twenty-First Century'(A/S-23/10/Rev.1),in particular those concerning women and armed conflict,

Bearing in mind the purposes and principles of the Charter of the United Nations and the primary responsibility of the Security Council under the Charter for the maintenance of international peace and security,

Expressing concern that civilians, particularly women and children, account for the vast majority of those adversely affected by armed conflict, including as refugees and internally displaced persons, and increasingly are targeted by combatants and armed elements, and *recognizing* the consequent impact this has on durable peace and reconciliation,

Reaffirming the important role of women in the prevention and resolution of conflicts and in peace building, and *stressing* the importance of their equal participation and full involvement in all efforts forth maintenance and promotion of peace and security, and the need to increase their role in decision-making with regard to conflict prevention and resolution,

Reaffirming also the need to implement fully international humanitarian and human rights law that protects the rights of women and girls during and after conflicts,

Emphasizing the need for all parties to ensure that mine clearance and mine awareness programmes take into account the special needs of women and girls,

Recognizing the urgent need to mainstream a gender perspective into peacekeeping operations, and in this regard *noting* the Windhoek Declaration and the Namibia Plan of Action on Mainstreaming a Gender Perspective in Multidimensional Peace Support Operations (S/2000/693),

Recognizing also the importance of the recommendation contained in the statement of its President to the press of 8 March 2000 for specialized training for all peace keeping personnel on the protection, special needs and human rights of women and children in conflict situations,

Recognizing that an understanding of the impact of armed conflict on women and girls, effective institutional arrangements to guarantee their protection and full participation in the peace process can significantly contribute to the maintenance and promotion of international peace and security,

Noting the need to consolidate data on the impact of armed conflict on women and girls,

1. *Urges* Member States to ensure increased representation of women at all decision-making levels in national, regional and international institutions and mechanisms for the prevention, management, and resolution of conflict;
2. *Encourages* the Secretary-General to implement his strategic plan of action (A/49/587) calling for an increase in the participation of women at decision-making levels in conflict resolution and peace processes;
3. *Urges* the Secretary-General to appoint more women as special representatives and envoys to pursue good offices on his behalf,

and in this regard *calls on* Member States to provide candidates to the Secretary-General, for inclusion in a regularly updated centralized roster;

4 *Further urges* the Secretary-General to seek to expand the role and contribution of women in United Nations field-based operations, and especially among military observers, civilian police, human rights and humanitarian personnel;

5 *Expresses* its willingness to incorporate a gender perspective into peace keeping operations, and *urges* the Secretary-General to ensure that, where appropriate, field operations include a gender component;

6 *Requests* the Secretary-General to provide to Member States training guidelines and materials on the protection, rights and the particular needs of women, as well as on the importance of involving women in all peace keeping and peace building measures, *invites* Member States to incorporate these elements as well as HIV/AIDS awareness training into their national training programmes for military and civilian police personnel in preparation for deployment, and *further requests* the Secretary-General to ensure that civilian personnel of peace keeping operations receive similar training;

7 *Urges* Member States to increase their voluntary financial, technical and logistical support for gender-sensitive training efforts, including those undertaken by relevant funds and programmes, interalia, the United Nations Fund for Women and United Nations Children's Fund, and by the Office of the United Nations High Commissioner for Refugees and other relevant bodies;

8 *Calls on* all actors involved, when negotiating and implementing peace agreements, to adopt a gender perspective, including, interalia:

(a) The special needs of women and girls during repatriation and resettlement and for rehabilitation, reintegration and post-conflict reconstruction;

(b) Measures that support local women's peace initiatives and indigenous processes for conflict resolution, and that involve women in all of the implementation mechanisms of the peace agreements;

(c) Measures that ensure the protection of and respect for human rights of women and girls, particularly as they relate to the constitution, the electoral system, the police and the judiciary;

9 *Calls upon* all parties to armed conflict to respect fully international law applicable to the rights and protection of women and girls, especially as civilians, in particular the obligations applicable to them under the Geneva Conventions of 1949 and the Additional Protocols thereto of 1977, the Refugee Convention of 1951 and the Protocol thereto of 1967, the Convention on the Elimination of All Forms of Discrimination against Women of 1979 and the Optional Protocol thereto of 1999 and the United Nations Convention on the Rights of the Child of 1989 and the two Optional Protocols there to of 25 May 2000, and to bear in mind the relevant provisions of the Rome Statute of the International Criminal Court;

10 *Calls on* all parties to armed conflict to take special measures to protect women and girls from gender-based violence, particularly rape and other forms of sexual abuse, and all other forms of violence in situations of armed conflict;

11 *Emphasizes* the responsibility of all States to put an end to impunity and to prosecute those responsible for genocide, crimes against humanity, and war crimes including those relating to sexual and other violence against women and girls, and in this regard *stresses* the need to exclude these crimes, where feasible from amnesty provisions;

12 *Calls upon* all parties to armed conflict to respect the civilian and humanitarian character of refugee camps and settlements, and to take into account the particular needs of women and girls, including in their design, and recalls its resolutions 1208(1998) of 19 November 1998 and 1296(2000) of 19 April 2000;

13 *Encourages* all those involved in the planning for disarmament, demobilization and reintegration to consider the different needs of female and male ex-combatants and to take into account the needs of their dependants;

14 *Reaffirms* its readiness, whenever measures are adopted under Article 41 of the Charter of the United Nations, to give consideration to their potential impact on the civilian population, bearing in mind the special needs of women and girls, in order to consider appropriate humanitarian exemptions;

15 *Expresses* its willingness to ensure that Security Council missions take into account gender considerations and the rights of women, including through consultation with local and international women's groups;

16 *Invites* the Secretary-General to carry out a study on the impact of armed conflict on women and girls, the role of women in peace building and the gender dimensions of peace processes and

conflict resolution, and *further invites* him to submit a report to the Security Council on the results of this study and to make this available to all Member States of the United Nations;

17 *Requests* the Secretary-General, where appropriate, to include in his reporting to the Security Council progress on gender mainstreaming throughout peace keeping missions and all other aspects relating to women and girls;

18 *Decides* to remain actively seized of the matter.

United Nations
Security Council

S/RES/1820 (2008)
Distr.: General
19 June 2008

08-39144 3

**Resolution 1820 (2008) Adopted by the
Security Council at its
5916th meeting, on 19 June 2008**
(Obtained from htpp://dacess_dds_ny.un.org/doc/UNDOC/GEN/
N08/391/44/PDF/No839144.pdf?Open Element. Accessed 20
April 2010.)

The Security Council,

Reaffirming its commitment to the continuing and full implementation of resolution 1325 (2000), 1612 (2005) and 1674 (2006) and recalling the Statements of its president of 31 October 2001 (Security Council/PRST/2001/31), 31 October 2002 (Security Council/PRST/2002/32), 28 October 2004 (Security Council/PRST/2004/40), 27 October 2005 (Security Council/PRST/2005/52), 8 November 2006 (Security Council/PRST/2006/42), 7 March 2007 (Security Council/PRST/2007/5), and 24 October 2007(SecurityCouncil/PRST/2007/40);

Guided by the purposes and principles of the Charter of the United Nations,

Reaffirming also the resolve expressed in the 2005 World Summit Outcome Document to eliminate all forms of violence against women and girls, including by ending impunity and by ensuring the protection of civilians, in particular women and girls, during and after armed conflicts, in accordance with the obligations States have undertaken under international humanitarian law and international human rights law;

Recalling the commitments of the Beijing Declaration and Platform for Action (A/52/231) as well as those contained in the outcome document of the twenty-third Special Session of the United Nations General Assembly entitled 'Women 2000: Gender Equality, Development and Peace for the Twenty-first Century' (A/S-23/10/Rev.1), in particular those concerning sexual violence and women in situation so farmed conflict;

Reaffirming also the obligations of States Parties to the Convention on the Elimination of All Forms of Discrimination against Women, the Optional Protocol thereto, the Convention on the Rights of the Child and the Optional Protocols thereto, and *urging* states that have not yet done so to consider ratifying or acceding to them,

Noting that civilians account for the vast majority of those adversely affected by armed conflict; that women and girls are particularly targeted by the use of sexual violence, including as a tactic of war to humiliate, dominate, instilfearin, disperse and/or forcibly relocate civilian members of a community or ethnic group; and that sexual violence perpetrated in this manner may in some instances persist after the cessation of hostilities;

Recalling its condemnation in the strongest terms of all sexual and other forms of violence committed against civilians in armed conflict, in particular women and children;

Reiterating deep concern that, despite its repeated condemnation of violence against women and children in situations of armed conflict, including sexual violence in situations of armed conflict, and despite its calls addressed to all parties to armed conflict for the cessation of such acts with immediate effect, such acts continue to occur, and in some situations have become systematic and widespread, reaching appalling levels of brutality,

Recalling the inclusion of a range of sexual violence offences in the Rome Statute of the International Criminal Court and the statutes of the adhoc international criminal tribunals,

Reaffirming the important role of women in the prevention and resolution of conflicts and in peace building, and *stressing* the importance of their equal participation and full involvement in all efforts for the maintenance and promotion of peace and security, and the need to increase their role in decision-making with regard to conflict prevention and resolution,

Deeply concerned also about the persistent obstacles and challenges to women's participation and full involvement in the prevention and resolution of conflicts as a result of violence, intimidation and discrimination, which erode women's capacity and legitimacy to participate in post-conflict public life, and acknowledging the negative impact this has on durable peace, security and reconciliation, including post-conflict peace building,

Recognizing that States bear primary responsibility to respect and ensure the human rights of their citizens, as well as all individuals within their territory as provided for by relevant international law,

Reaffirming that parties to armed conflict bear the primary responsibility to take all feasible steps to ensure the protection of affected civilians,

Welcoming the ongoing coordination of efforts within the United Nations system, marked by the interagency initiative 'United Nations Action against Sexual Violence in Conflict', to create awareness about sexual violence in armed conflicts and post-conflict situations and, ultimately, to put an end to it,

1. *Stresses* that sexual violence, when used or commissioned as a tactic of war in order to deliberately target civilians or as a part of a widespread or systematic attack against civilian populations, can significantly exacerbate situations of armed conflict and may impede the restoration of international peace and security, *affirms* in this regard that effective steps to prevent and respond to such acts of sexual violence can significantly contribute to the maintenance of international peace and security, and *expresses its readiness*, when considering situations on the agenda of the Council, to, where necessary, adopt appropriate steps to address wide spread or systematic sexual violence;
2. *Demands* the immediate and complete cessation by all parties to armed conflict of all acts of sexual violence against civilians with immediate effect;
3. *Demands* that all parties to armed conflict immediately take appropriate measures to protect civilians, including women and girls, from all forms of sexual violence, which could include, interalia, enforcing appropriate military disciplinary measures and upholding the principle of command responsibility, training troops on the categorical prohibition of all forms of sexual violence against civilians, debunking myths that fuel sexual violence, vetting armed and security forces to take into account past actions of rape and other forms of sexual violence, and evacuation of women and children under imminent threat of sexual violence to safety; and *requests* the Secretary-General, where appropriate, to encourage dialogue to address this issue in the context of broader discussions of conflict resolution between appropriate UN officials and the parties to the conflict, taking into account, interalia, the views expressed by women of affected local communities;
4. *Notes* that rape and other forms of sexual violence can constitute a war crime, a crime against humanity, or a constitutive act with respect to genocide, *stresses the need for* the exclusion of sexual violence crimes from amnesty provisions in the context of conflict resolution processes, and *calls upon* Member States to comply with their obligations for prosecuting persons responsible for such acts, to ensure that all victims of sexual violence, particularly women and girls, have equal protection under the law and equal access to justice, and *stresses* the importance of ending impunity for such acts as part of a

comprehensive approach to seeking sustainable peace, justice, truth, and national reconciliation;

5 *Affirms its intention,* when establishing and renewing state-specific sanctions regimes, to take into consideration the appropriateness of targeted and graduated measures against parties to situations of armed conflict who commit rape and other forms of sexual violence against women and girls in situations of armed conflict;

6 *Requests* the Secretary-General, in consultation with the Security Council, the Special Committee on Peacekeeping Operations and its Working Group and relevant States, as appropriate, to develop and implement appropriate training programmes for all peace keeping and humanitarian personnel deployed by the United Nations in the context of missions as mandated by the Council to help them better prevent, recognize and respond to sexual violence and other forms of violence against civilians;

7 *Requests* the Secretary-General to continue and strengthen efforts to implement the policy of zero tolerance of sexual exploitation and abuse in United Nations peacekeeping operations; and *urges* troop and police contributing countries to take appropriate preventative action, including pre-deployment and in-theater awareness training, and other action to ensure full accountability in cases of such conduct involving their personnel;

8 *Encourages* troop and police contributing countries, in consultation with the Secretary-General, to consider steps they could take to heighten awareness and the responsiveness of their personnel participating in UN peace keeping operations to protect civilians, including women and children, and prevent sexual violence against women and girls in conflict and post-conflict situations, including wherever possible the deployment of a higher percentage of women peace keepers or police;

9 *Requests* the Secretary-General to develop effective guidelines and strategies to enhance the ability of relevant UN peace keeping operations, consistent with their mandates, to protect civilians, including women and girls, from all forms of sexual violence and to systematically include in his written reports to the Council on conflict situations his observations concerning the protection of women and girls and recommendations in this regard;

10 *Requests* the Secretary-General and relevant United Nations agencies, interalia, through consultation with women and women led organizations as appropriate, to develop effective mechanisms for providing protection from violence, including in particular sexual violence, to women and girls in and around UN managed refugee

and internally displaced persons camps, as well as in all disarmament, demobilization, and reintegration processes, and injustice and security sector reform efforts assisted by the United Nations;

11 *Stresses* the important role the Peace building Commission can play by including in its advice and recommendations for post-conflict peace building strategies, where appropriate, ways to address sexual violence committed during and in the aftermath of armed conflict, and in ensuring consultation and effective representation of women's civil society in its country-specific configurations, as part of its wider approach to gender issues;

12 *Urges* the Secretary-General and his Special Envoys to invite women to participate in discussions pertinent to the prevention and resolution of conflict, the maintenance of peace and security, and post-conflict peace building, and encourages all parties to such talks to facilitate the equal and full participation of women at decision-making levels;

13 *Urges* all parties concerned, including Member States, United Nations entities and financial institutions, to support the development and strengthening of the capacities of national institutions, in particular of judicial and health systems, and of local civil society networks in order to provide sustainable assistance to victims of sexual violence in armed conflict and post-conflict situations;

14 *Urges* appropriate regional and sub-regional bodies in particular to consider developing and implementing policies, activities, and advocacy for the benefit of women and girls affected by sexual violence in armed conflict;

15 *Also requests* the Secretary-General to submit a report to the Council by 30 June 2009 on the implementation of this resolution in the context of situations which are on the agenda of the Council, utilizing information from available United Nations sources, including country teams, peace keeping operations, and other United Nations personnel, which would include, interalia, information on situations of armed conflict in which sexual violence has been widely or systematically employed against civilians; analysis of the prevalence and trends of sexual violence in situations of armed conflict; proposals for strategies to minimize the susceptibility of women and girls to such violence; benchmarks for measuring progress in preventing and addressing sexual violence; appropriate input from United Nations implementing partners in the field; information on his plans for facilitating the collection of timely, objective, accurate, and reliable information on the use of sexual violence in situations of armed conflict, including through

improved coordination of UN activities on the ground and at Headquarters; and information on actions taken by parties to armed conflict to implement their responsibilities as described in this resolution, in particular by immediately and completely ceasing all acts of sexual violence and in taking appropriate measures to protect women and girls from all forms of sexual violence;

16 *Decides* to remain actively seized of the matter.

Index

Abdurakhmanov, Dukuvakha 266
Acheson, Ray 19, 32, 425–6
adaptive patriarchy 396–7
Adrian-Paul, Ancil 154
advancement of women 14
Afghanistan: girls, human security of 222–43, 418–19; militarization of 226; school attacks in 227; security assistance to 228; Soviet occupation of 226
Afghan National Army 222
Afghans4Tomorrow 234, 235, 238, 239, 242
Afghan women 170, 226
African women 78, 142, 410; armed conflict on 108–11; in Darfur 134; human security 108–31, 414–15
Ahmed Ali, Fatuma 20
Akibayashi, Kozue 18, 168
Al Baq'aa refugee camp 307, 320, 323, 324
Al-Bashir, Omar Hassan Ahmad 158
Alexander, Ronni 18
Al Karak 306, 321, 324
Al-Qaeda 169, 170, 179, 229
Al Safa'wy 306, 323, 324
Amerasian children 48
American Declaration of Independence 27
Amman, Jordan 306
Amnesty International 70, 122, 156
Anderlini, Sanam Naraaghi 154
Animal Farm 397
Annan, Kofi 168, 246
anti-nuclear imperialism 396
Arab Human Development Report 309

armed conflict 31, 108–31, 277, 289, 414–15; on African women 108–11; gender-based violence and 120–5; gender relations in 125–30; on women 111–20
Army Development Group (ADG) 378
Ashe, Geoffrey 76
Ashford, M. 342–3
Association of war-affected women 155
Australia 69
avoidable harm, protection 21–2
Ayele, Mesfin G. 19

Bamiyan 225
Bananas, Beaches, and Bases: Making Feminist Sense of International Politics 238
Bano, Zubeda 375
barbarity-civilization 72
'bargain basement' model 228
Barnett, Michael 149
Bart camp 263
Bashir, Halima 142
basic human needs 19
Basu, Soumita 29
Battle of Adwa Victory 87
Beijing Platform of Action 41
Belenky, Mary 11
Bellamy, Alex J. 146
Bennett, Jane 74
Betts, Richard 231
Biketawa Declaration 200
binary oppositions 71
Bogaletch Gebre 98
Bougainville Crisis 192, 199, 214, 215

Bouta, T. 125
Boutros-Ghali, Boutros 281
Boyd, Rosalind 152
Breins, Ingeborg 232
Breyer, Chloe 24, 128
British 87
Brittain, Vera 59
Brownmiller, Susan 20, 41
Brundtland, G. H. 351
Bull, Hedley 61
Burns, Robin 229
Buzan, Barry 60, 61, 316

Caballero-Anthony, M. 360
Canada 69
Canadian troops, Afghanistan 169–71
Carr, E. H. 61
Caucasic languages 250
Charteris-Black, J. 173
Chayes, Sarah 177
Chechen-Ichkeria 249
Chechen immigrants 251
Chechen nationalism Islamization 260–5
Chechens 246
Chechen war 28
Chechnya: military invasion of 252, 253; price of peace in 265; Russian Federal Security Forces in 252, 253
Chechnya-Ingush 249
Chen, L. 338
children 11, 12, 15, 18, 25, 30, 44, 45, 68, 70, 74, 289, 309, 313, 318; Amerasian 48; security in Okinawa 46–8
Chilton, P. A. 173, 174, 178
China 280
Chowdhury, Anwarul K. 293
Christian Arabs 320
civilization 87
civil society organizations 201
civil war 226, 257
climate science deniers 19
Cockburn, Cynthia 155, 295
Cock, Jacklyn 91
cognitive heuristic 173
Cohn, Carol 170, 172, 294, 392, 394, 399, 405
collateral damage 23

Collins, James 253
colonialism 63, 151, 198, 417–18
colonization 197
Commission on Human Security (CHS) 39, 336, 346, 351, 355, 356
Committee of Soldiers' Mothers (CSM) 248, 256, 257
community activists 63
community bonds 138
comprehensive approach, human security 22–6
comprehensive security system 25
conflict resolution 231
conflict situations: human needs issues in 371–6; masculinity in 371; violence in 371; women in 371–6
Connell, R. W. 13
Conquest of War, The (1986) 26
contemporary conflicts 111
contemporary patriarchs 14
Convention on the Elimination of All Forms of Discrimination against Women (CEDAW) 200, 294
Cook, R. 345
critical discourse analysis (CDA) 171
Cuellar, Pérez de 281
cultural governance 194, 195, 197
cultural legitimization 65
cultural violence 65
culture of shame 316–24
cyber space war 24

Dalai Lama 78
Dallaire, Roméo 163
Darfur 134–64; genocidal rape in 135–43
Darfuri women 135, 153, 161–3
decision-making process 86, 98, 129
Declaration on the Elimination of Violence against Women (DEVAW) 73, 117
Deir All'aa 306, 324
deMause, Lloyd 70
demilitarization 2, 26–32, 215, 417–20
democracy 101
Democratic Republic of Congo (DRC) 110
democratization 104

Derg regime 92
Derlugian, Georgi 261
De Watteville 94
dignity and identity 19–20
displacement 115, 116
divine creator 12
domestic violence 112, 113, 121, 370
dominant media discourses 174–5
dominant security paradigm 25
Dudayev, Dzhokhor 252, 254
Dugong v. Rumsfeld 51

Ebadi, Shirin 59
economic depression 251
economic downturn 8
economic security 51
education: hallmark of human security 222–4
Egyptians 87
Eisler, Riane 71
El Jack, A. 115, 125, 128, 129
Elkner, Julie 255
embedded feminism 249
Emebet, Mulugeta Tefera 93
empowerment 336, 374
Enloe, Cynthia 170, 172, 195, 226, 231, 238, 396
environmental degradation 105
environmental destruction 48–51
environmental security 322–4
EPRDF 91, 93, 94
Epstein, H. 357
Eritrean struggle 127
Ethiopia 85–105; democratic principles 89; human security in 87–90
Ethiopian foreign affairs 100
Ethiopian Foreign Affairs and National Security Policy and Strategy (EFANPS) 102
Ethiopian national security policy 98–104
Ethiopian women: human security problems of 95–8, 105; in peace and security 85–105, 413–14; problems 98; traditional security paradigm 90–5
ethnic discrimination 197
ethnic tensions 251
European Refugee Fund (ERF) 264

fear 370
FeDem 53, 184
Felice, W. 353
female vulnerability 141
feminism 11, 306
feminist comprehensive framework 8
feminist foreign policy 397
feminist framework: human security 15–18
feminist human security framework 169
feminist international relations scholars 39
feminists 11, 104
feminization of poverty 92
First Chechen War, sociopolitical origins of 249–54
First Russian-Chechen War 258; Committee of Soldiers' Mothers and 254–60
forced displacement 116
France 280
Freedman, L. 351
From Dictatorship to Democracy 28
Furlong, K. 351

Galtung, Johan 59, 64, 229
Gandhi, Ela 59
Gandhi, Mohandas 59, 76, 77, 389
Gateva, Khadijad 259
Geiger, H. J. 342
gender 12; as determinant 335–61, 423–4; epidemiology of 341–6; social construct 288; space for 366–90, 424–5
gender analysis, disarmament 404–7
gender-based violence (GBV) 59, 68, 71–4, 76, 117, 120, 123, 150; during armed conflict 120–5
gender, concept 279–80
gender discrimination 116, 242
gendered discourse 393–7
gendered identities 194
gendered insecurity: long-term military presence 37–56; in Okinawa 411–12
gendered peace activism 201–14; Bougainville Crisis 201–6; Guam, Mariana Islands 207–10; Okinawa, Japan 210–14

gendered weapons 393–7
gender equality 7, 26–32, 199; in peace 277–97, 421–2; in security policymaking 277–97, 421–2
Gender in International Relations 230
gender justice 30
Gender Justice Caucus 31
gender relations: in war 125–30
gender roles 130–1
gender specificity 163
gender violence 3, 68–76, 112, 196, 200
genealogical rape 140
Geneva Conventions for prisoners of wars 118
genocidal levels 68–76
genocide 64, 162, 415–16
Genocide Convention 147–8
Georgescu, Calin 403
Ghazni 225
Gilligan, Carol 11
Gimbutas, Marija 71
Ginerich, Tara 136
Ginwala, Frene 151
global patriarchal hierarchy 3
good Muslims 226
Goodwill Schools 379, 380
Griffen, Vanessa 403
Guenther, Lora 264
guerilla insurgencies 254

Hagan, John 143
Hague Agenda for Peace and Justice in the 21st Century, The (1999) 26, 31, 32
The Hague Appeal for Peace Civil Society Conference 17, 169
Haley, Nikki 392, 403
Hall, S. 174
Hammami, Rena 258
Hans, Asha 31, 59, 279, 295, 424–5
Haqqani, Jalaludin 228
Harding, Luke 266
Hazara women 225
health: democratization 354–7; determinants' approach 337–8; empowerment 354–7; human rights issue 351–4
Hekmatyar, Gulbuddin 227, 228
hetero-patriarchy 70

Heymann, D. 346
Hill, Felicity 295, 394, 405
Hillier, Rick 176
HIV/AIDS 86, 95, 97, 105, 114, 120
Hobbes, Thomas 61
Hojer, Maja 255
homeland security discourse 10
hooks, bell 306
Hudson, Heidi 75, 93
Huet-Vaughn, Y. 342, 343
Human Development Report 37, 52, 336
human dignity 169; violations 341
human insecurities 19
humanitarian discourse 405
human rights 161–3
Human Rights Watch report 222, 223, 227–9, 233, 262
human security deficits 1, 10
Human Security Now report 66, 149, 340, 350
human wellbeing 2, 4, 18, 24, 33, 79
Hurricane Katrina 10

India 9, 28, 66, 197, 367
Indian Army 9, 368
Indo-Pakistan border 376–7
Indo-Pakistani War 369
inhuman security 215
institutionalized gender hierarchies 191
Institutional religion 13
insurgency wars 180
integrated approach, human security 22–6
internally displaced persons (IDPs) 115, 117
International Court of Justice (ICJ) 27
International Criminal Court (ICC) 30, 158–61
International Criminal Tribunal for Rwanda (ICTR) 145, 160
International Criminal Tribunal for the former Yugoslavia (ICTY) 145, 160
International Peace Bureau (IPB) 27, 258
International Women's Summit 2000 52, 53
intersectional oppressions 59–80, 412–13

Index

Islamic Khomeini Memorial Trust 381
Ismael Mayar Primary School, Wardak Province 224, 233–42
Israel 69
Italians 87

Jack, Andrew 260
Janjaweed 135, 137
Jansen, G. G. 125
Japan 43
jihad 225, 261
Johansen, Robert C. 38, 64
Johnson, M. 172
Johnson-Sirleaf, Ellen 119
Jordanian society, militarization of 305
Jordanian women: culture of shame 316–24; economic security 308–13; environmental security 322–31; feminist approach, age-old problem 303–34, 422–3; feminist framework 307–16; militarism and sexism 304–6; national security 328–31; security and 303–34, 422–3; social and cultural security 313–16

Kandahar 232
Kaplan, Laura 195
Kelkay, Berhane 97
Khan, Shahnaz 329
Khassaviurt Agreement 259
Khong, Yuen Foong 294
King, Martin Luther Jr. 59
Kissinger, Henry 395
Klot, Jennifer 283
Krasner, Stephen D. 247
Kreager, Philip 77
Kristof, Nicholas 143

Lakoff, G. 172
language 186
Laverack, G. 354
Leaning, Jennifer 136
Lederach, John Paul 242
Lee, K. 360
Leitana Nehan Women's Development Agency (LNDA) 205
liberation movement 104
Liberia 127
life-sustaining environment 2

line of control (LOC) 367–70
local violence 197
Lorde, Audre 152
Lord's Resistance Army (LRA) 118
Luarca Declaration of the Human Right to Peace 28

Maathai, Wangari 59, 119
MacFarlane, S. Neil 294
Mack, A. 351
Macke, Richard C. 47
MacKinnon, Catharine 141
Macleans (newsmagazine) 175
male-dominated public realm 63
male élites 16, 143
Malikyar, Helena 224
malnutrition 373
Mandela, Nelson 59, 77
Mann, J. M. 340, 341, 361
Man, the State, and War 230
marginalization 192
masculinist 11
Maskadov, Aslan 254–60
Maskhadov, Aslan 260, 266
Maslow, Abraham 310
mass killing 254
maternal illness 337
Mayar, Ehsan 235, 237
Mayar, Masude 235
McInnes, C. 360
Melinkova, Valentina 256
mental health 114
mental illness 22
militarism 10, 304–6; as determinant 335–61, 423–4; epidemiology of 341–6
militarization 192, 193, 195, 196, 206, 216, 305, 367, 382, 387, 417–20; global system 2
militarized interstate system 277
militarized masculinities 392–407, 425–6
militarized Pacific: human security in 191–219, 417–18
militarized patriarchy 7
militarized perception 366–90, 424–5
militarized security 4, 11, 223
militarized state security 15–18, 22, 24, 410–13
militarized world, human security problem 8–12

Index 443

military coercion 194
military occupation of the womb 139
military training 20
Millennium Development Goals (MDGs) 350
Milliken, J. 172
Milner, Michele W. 9, 25, 416–17
Minale, A. 90
Mitchell, Andrew 146
modern representative democracy 13
Morgenthau, Hans 61, 231
mortality 337
'Mountain Thrust' 182
Mrscevic, Zorica 370
Muthien, Bernedette 8

Nangarhar 225
narrow state-centrism 62
national action plans (NAPs) 293
national security 8, 59, 67, 246, 366, 374, 385–6
negative peace 63
Nemeh, Norma 10, 422–3
neocolonialism 151
neo-liberal economic model 103
New York Times 8, 227
9/11 attacks 167, 169, 236
Non-Proliferation Treaty (NPT) 398
non-violent movement 28
nuclear deterrence 395, 401
nuclear weapons, banning 392–407, 425–6
Nunn, Sam 395

O'Brien, Patricia 406
obstacles, confronting 26–32
O'Connor, Gordon 179
Ogata, Sadako 66, 149
Ogata-Sen model 153
Ogata-Sen report 23, 66
Okinawa: children security in 46–8; gendered insecurity in 411–12; militarization of 43; women security in 46–8; Women's peace movement in 42–6
Okinawa Women Act Against Military Violence (OWAAMV) 37, 41, 45, 47, 48, 52, 53, 55, 56
Omar, Mullah 228
Omar, Wahid 233, 235, 237
Oosterveld, Valerie 288

Operation Goodwill 367, 376–80, 382, 384, 386–8; limitation of 383–5
Operation Sadbhavana 376
organized violence 129
Orwell, George 397
Orwellian 'war is peace' 147
othering process 71
Otto, Dianne 289
Ottomans 87
Oxford English Reference Dictionary (1996) 69

Pacific Islands region: peace in 199–201
Pacific Island women: peace and security by 191–219, 417–18; views of militarized Pacific 193–8
Pacific Women's Bureau (PWB) 199
Pakistan 367
Paris Accords 30
Paris Climate Accords 32
Parker, Patricia 143
patriarchal militarism 195, 196
patriarchal national security paradigm 85–105, 413–14; national security 87–90
patriarchal paradigm 19
patriarchal power paradigm 13
patriarchal security system 7–34, 411
patriarchal thinking 13
patriarchal violence 279; challenging 1–4
patriarchal war system 411
patriarchs. 25
patriarchy 12, 17, 63, 71, 305, 335–61, 423–4; bomb and 392–407, 425–6; denial of lived experience 402–4; epistemology of 24; gender analysis, disarmament 404–7; gendered discourse 393–7; gendered weapons 393–7; gender injustice source 12–15; human insecurity framework 12–15; realism, monopoly on 397–402; sociopolitical structure 25
peace 65, 116
peacebuilding 233, 246
Peace Building Fund 247
peace dividend 55
peacemaking 233
Peace Plan 263

Peacock, D. 339
people-centred security 96
perpetrators 73, 74
Perry, William 395
Petchesky, R. P. 351, 353
Peterson, V. Spike 40
phallogocentrism 66, 67
physical assault 65
Pietilä, Hilkka 157
political activism 17
political realism 1
poverty 66, 105
power 71
Price, Lisa S. 20, 21, 113, 121
Price-Smith, A. 346
protection from threats 346–7
protest movement 45
psychological scars 22
public health 335–61, 423–4
public security discourse 25
Purple Primer: The Psychology of Militancy (1997) 383
Putin, Vladimir 260, 262, 266

Quito conference 54
Qu'ran 236

racial minorities 20
Rahnema, Majid 304
Rajoo, K. 112
Randall, Vicky 74
rape 114, 123, 137, 139, 141, 142, 148, 159, 344, 368, 369
Ray, Arjun 368, 376, 379, 382
realism, monopoly on 397–402
realists 40
Reardon, Betty A. 53, 59, 64, 66, 100, 168, 193, 240, 279, 295, 339
redistributive justice 78
'Red Terror' campaign 92
Reed, L. 110
Refugee International's 2007 report 138
Rehn, E. 125
reproductive health problems 50
resources, redistribution 348–51
responsibility to protect doctrine 145–7
'Responsibility to Protect' (R2P) 21
rights of man 13
rights of women 13
Rohingya people 78

Rotary Club of Afghanistan 234
Rousseau, Jean-Jacques 230
Rubin, Elizabeth 227
Ruddick, Sara 394, 405
Russia 280
Russian-Chechen relations 252
Russian-Chechen Wars 246–70, 419–20
Russian Soldiers' Mothers: agnatic capacity 249
Russophobia 251
Rwandan genocide 119, 145
Rymond-Richmond, Wenona 143
Ryukyu Shimpo (newspaper) 44

Saharawi women 116
Saliah Mahmoud Osman 159
satyagraha 76
Schoeman, Maxi 61
schools: Afghan girls 230–3; repression targets in Afghanistan 224
Schreiner, Olive 59
SCR 1820 291–4, 427–37; actors and interpretations 293–4; two resolutions 292–3
Second Russian-Chechen War 260–5
Security Council Resolution 1325 29, 153–6
Security Council Resolutions (2001–2008): gender use, implications 288–91; patterns and rhetoric 285–8; women and gender in 284–91
Security Council Resolutions (SCR) 1325 110, 277–97, 421–2, 427–37; gender concept and 279–80; human security concept and 279–80; potential of 280–4
security, determinants' approach 337–8
security discourses 167–87, 416–17; Canadian troops, Afghanistan 169–71; dominant media discourses 174–5; language and power 171–2; metaphoric schema 175–87; metaphors and security 172–4
security policy implications 12
Seifert, T. 344
Self-Defense Forces 28, 55
Self Help group (SHG) 374
Sen, Amartya 39, 149

sexism 304–6
Sexism and the War System 240
sexual abuse 141, 369
sexual assaults 68, 137
sexual humiliation 148
sexual offences 68
sexual slavery 161, 162
sexual violence 17, 134–64, 344, 415–16; international mechanisms, response 144–7
Sharia laws 317
Sharpe, Albie 25, 423–4
Sheik Yassine village 235
Shepherd, Laura J. 295
Shia community 379
Shultz, George 395
Siberia of Utopianism 4
siege mentality 100
Sirleaf, E. J. 125
Sirleaf, Johnson 127
social activism 76
social destabilization 116
social functions 12
social illnesses 326
social movement 261
social support 128
soldiers' mothers 246–70, 419–20
Soldiers' Mothers Organization (SMO) 255
Somalia 114
Somalis 87
South Africa 59–80, 412–13
South African Domestic Violence Act 73
South African National Defence Force (SANDF) 66
South African Police Services (SAPS) 68
sovereignty 89
Soviet-Afghanistan War 248, 255
Soviet Union 27
space war 24
Sri Lanka 257
State-centred security concerns 60
state power 25
state-sanctioned violence 1
state security framework 2
state-sponsored human security 382–3
Status of United States Armed Forces in Japan (SOFA) 43
Stiehm, Judith 232
stigmatization 399

St. Petersburg Press 256, 257
structural sexism 64
structural violence 65
submissiveness 20
Sudanese Armed Forces (SAF) 135
Sudanese women 113
suicides 22
survival needs, fulfillment 19
Sustainable Development Goals 32
sustainable environment 18–19
Suttner, Bertha von 26, 29
Suu Kyi, Aung San 77–9
Sylvan, D. 172
system-shaking retaliation 20

Takazato, Suzuyo 18, 53, 168
Taliban identity 225
Taliban movement 227
Taliban's neofundamentalist movement 261
Taraki, Noor Mohammad 234
Taylor, Diana 256
Teaching to Transgress: Education as the Practice of Freedom (1994) 306
Tehranian, M. 110
terrorists 16
Tickner, Ann 230–2
Tickner, J. A. 39, 43, 167
Tigrean Peoples Liberation Front (TPLF) 90, 91
Time (newsmagazine) 175
'Toward Human Security: A Feminist Framework for Demilitarization' 7
traditional gender roles 12
traditional national security 63
traditional Pashtun society 223
transformation, rethinking 76–8
transitional approaches 420–6
transitional government (TGE) 94
transnational corporations 14
transnational networks 52–5
Treaty of Mutual Cooperation and Security 43
Treaty of Westphalia 247
Treaty on the Prohibition of Nuclear Weapons 32
*Tretii Sektor (*journal) 255
tribal affiliation 320
Tsegay 92
Tutsi women 148

Uganda 120
ultranationalist xenophobia 13
UNAIDS 343
UN Assistance Mission in Afghanistan (UNAMA) 289
UN Charter 144–5, 227, 281
UN Declaration on the Elimination of Violence against Women (DEVAW) 156–8
UN Development Programme (UNDP) 37
unemployment rate 51
UN High Commission for Refugees (UNHCR) 115, 222
UN Human Rights Commission 253
United Kingdom 280
United Nations 14, 21, 27, 32, 41, 154, 246, 247, 281, 294, 393
United States 9, 10, 27, 43, 69, 226, 280
UN Refugee Convention 115
UN Trust Fund for Human Security 354
Uruzgan 225
Ury, William 233
US Forces Agreement 43
US National Historic Preservation Act 51
Uwilingiyimana, Agathe 118

Vatchagaev, Maribek 267
Veale, Angela 91, 93, 94
Velvet Revolution 28
Vickers, Jeanne 157
victimhood/survivorship 74
violation of human security 134–64
violence 222–43; public health issue 340–1

WABEKBON 96, 97
Wagner, Justin 137
Wahhabism 224, 261
Wallerstein, Immanuel 61
Wallström, Margot 397
Waltz, Kenneth 61, 230
war 7, 108–31, 414–15; gendered impacts of 111–20; gender relations in 125–30
Wardak Province 223
Wardak, Roshanak 235
war of choice 22
War on Terror 10, 123
'Wars, Wimps and Women' 400
well-behaved child 20

Weston, M. 339
Whitworth, Sandra 294
Williams, Jody 59
Williams, Paul D. 146
wise men 25
women 31; abuse and assaults 20; armed conflict on 111–20; in civil war 93; combatants 118; in conflict situations 371–6; employment 96; empowerment 104; human security and 7–34; human superiority 11; legal protection of 48; on line of control 367–70; politicians 118–19; in power structures 102; productive powers 74; repression targets in Afghanistan 224; reproductive power 74; security for 60; security in Okinawa 46–8; in South Africa 59–80, 412–13; status 96; traditional roles, changes 126–31; violence against 60, 64, 110, 112; war and violence against 14
Women and Peace of the International Peace Research Association 14
'women, peace and security' (WPS) 153–6, 278, 283, 284, 286, 293, 294
Women's Asia 7
Women's International League for Peace and Freedom (WILPF) 59
Women's International Network on Gender and Human Security (WINGHS) 17, 53, 307–16
women's peace movement: in Okinawa 42–6
World Health Organization (WHO) 68, 69, 340, 354
World Peace Through World Law (1966) 26
World Report on Health and Violence 340
World Trade Towers 10
worldwide movement 28
Wright, Ann 54

Yewubmar, Assefaw 91–3

Zabul 225
Zawilski, Valerie 28
Zeijl, Femke van 143
zones of conflict 111